# Writers and their Background

## ROBERT BROWNING

*Also in the same series*

MATTHEW ARNOLD    edited by Kenneth Allott
GEOFFREY CHAUCER    edited by D. S. Brewer
S. T. COLERIDGE    edited by R. L. Brett
JOHN DRYDEN    edited by Earl Miner
ALEXANDER POPE    edited by Peter Dixon
TENNYSON    edited by D. J. Palmer

*Robert Browning: Portrait by Feld Talford*
*(National Portrait Gallery)*

*Writers and their Background*

# ROBERT BROWNING

## EDITED BY ISOBEL ARMSTRONG

OHIO UNIVERSITY PRESS • 1975

© G. BELL & SONS LTD. 1974
PRINTED BY OFFSET AND BOUND IN THE
UNITED STATES OF AMERICA
FOR OHIO UNIVERSITY PRESS, ATHENS, OHIO
BY EDWARDS BROTHERS, INC., ANN ARBOR, MICHIGAN


LC 72-96846

ISBN 8214-0131-9

# Contents

# LIST OF ILLUSTRATIONS

*Frontispiece*

ROBERT BROWNING

(*National Portrait Gallery*)

*Between pages 190 and 191*

1. THE GUARDIAN ANGEL, BY GUERCINO

(*Museo Civico Malatestiano. Fano*)

2. ANDREA DEL SARTO AND HIS WIFE

(*Pitti Palace, Florence*)

*Between pages 206 and 207*

3. THE SALONE AT CASA GUIDI, BY GEORGE MIGNATY

4. CHRIST AT THE COLUMN, BY POLLAIUOLO

5. VIRGIN AND CHILD AND ST. HILARION, BY FILIPPO LIPPI

(*Uffizi Gallery, Florence*)

6. THE CORONATION OF THE VIRGIN, BY FILIPPO LIPPI

(*Uffizi Gallery, Florence*)

# The Contributors

DR. ISOBEL ARMSTRONG
*Lecturer in English, University of Leicester*

PHILIP DREW
*Reader in English, University of Glasgow*

PENELOPE GAY
*Lecturer in English, University of Sydney*

DR. PETER KEATING
*Lecturer in English Literature, University of Edinburgh*

PROFESSOR TREVOR LLOYD
*Professor of History, University of Toronto, Canada*

MICHAEL MASON
*Lecturer in English, University College, University of London*

BARBARA MELCHIORI
*Acting Professor of English, University of Rome, Italy*

LEONEE ORMOND
*Lecturer in English, King's College, University of London*

PROFESSOR MORSE PECKHAM
*Distinguished Professor of English and Comparative Literature, University of South Carolina, U.S.A.*

PROFESSOR ROGER SHARROCK
*Professor of English Language and Literature, King's College, University of London*

JOHN WOOLFORD
*King's College, Cambridge University*

# Abbreviations

*Centenary Edition: The Works of Robert Browning*, with introductions by F. G. Kenyon, 10 vol (1912).

*Dearest Isa: Dearest Isa. Robert Browning's Letters to Isabella Blagden*, ed C. C. McAleer, Austin, Texas & Edinburgh (1951), Cambridge, Mass (1966).

*Domett Letters: Robert Browning and Alfred Domett*, ed F. G. Kenyon (1906).

*Letters: The Letters of Robert Browning and Elizabeth Barrett Barrett 1845–1846*, ed R. W. Barrett Browning, 2 vol (1899).

*Letters, Kintner: The Letters of Robert Browning and Elizabeth Barrett 1845–1886*, ed Elvan Kintner, 2 vol, Cambridge, Mass (1969).

*New Letters: New Letters of Robert Browning*, ed William C. DeVane and K.L. Knickerbocker, New Haven (1950), London (1951).

*Wedgwood Letters: Robert Browning and Julia Wedgwood: a broken friendship as revealed in their letters*, ed Richard Curle (1937).

*Wise Letters: Letters of Robert Browning, collected by Thomas J. Wise*, ed Thurman L. Hood, New Haven (1933).

Griffin and Minchin: *The Life of Robert Browning* (1910, reissued 1938).

Unless otherwise stated, all quotations and line numbers from Browning's works are taken from the Centenary Edition.

# General Editor's Preface

THE STUDY OF literature is not a 'pure' discipline since works of literature are affected by the climate of opinion in which they are produced. Writers, like other men, are concerned with the politics, the philosophy, the religion, the arts, and the general thought of their own times. Some literary figures, indeed, have made their own distinguished contributions to these areas of human interest, while the achievement of others can be fully appreciated only by a knowledge of them.

The volumes in this series have been planned with the purpose of presenting major authors in their intellectual, social, and artistic contexts, and with the conviction that this will make their work more easily understood and enjoyed. Each volume contains a chapter which provides a reader's guide to the writings of the author concerned, a Bibliography, and Chronological Tables setting out the main dates of the author's life and publications alongside the chief events of contemporary importance.

Browning was a puzzling figure to his contemporaries and has remained so ever since. Literary historians find it difficult to 'place' him in reference to his contemporaries and successors. Biographers are baffled by the gap that separates his public life and the private life that one senses in his poetry. Critics are confused and even contradictory in their judgements about the value of the poetry. It is difficult to avoid the feeling that no light has fallen on our darkness since Henry James, writing of the authors who have been buried at Westminster Abbey, declared of Browning that '. . . none of the odd ones have been so great and none of the great ones so odd'. But further reflection suggests that this is too pessimistic a conclusion. The present volume which draws on the wealth of scholarship and criticism that has accumulated in recent years and which also provides a guide to this work, brings before us a man with manifold gifts and interests, but above all a writer who made these the servants of his genius as a poet. None of the contributors brought together by Mrs. Armstrong would wish to maintain, I imagine, that what they have written is a final assessment of Browning's achievement, but this volume will make the issues clearer and will provide the reader with the means for making his own assessment.

R.L. BRETT

# Editor's Preface

THE VARIETY OF topics in this book expresses the extraordinarily wide-ranging interests of Browning's poetry. It can be seen in the context of contemporary politics, particularly in the early years of his *avant garde* preoccupation with radical and utilitarian ideas, or it can be seen in the context of the philosophical debate between intuitionists and utilitarians. Browning's knowledge of painting and of music can be related to Victorian taste and to changes in taste. Several writers in this volume have remarked on his interest in portraying states of mania and morbid emotional states, and Michael Mason has shown how closely he followed developments in contemporary psychological theory. Other writers have looked at his connections with history and the philosophy of history and with other great nineteenth-century forms such as the novel. In fact, Browning's poetry could be said to have many different backgrounds or contexts: philosophical, aesthetic, contemporary and historical, English and Italian.

It is also true that both as a man and a writer Browning is closely bound to two contexts—the Victorian and the Romantic, even though the eighteenth century presses against Browning's Romantic values. I have looked at this doubleness, this duality, in my essay, and Roger Sharrock also demonstrates that Browning, of all the Victorian poets, was most a Romantic. Morse Peckham explores the possibilities that the Romantic experience held out for Browning, and the dilemmas it created for him. Penelope Gay stresses the essentially Romantic nature of Browning's ideas on music, even though paradoxically, they derive from late eighteenth-century, non-Romantic sources. In his essay on Browning's reading, John Woolford shows how pre-Romantic sources formed Browning's response to Romantic values.

What did this double context mean for Browning's poetry? In the first place, I think that it explains the curious mixture in his work of boldness and pedantry, originality—even eccentricity—and conventionality, slapdashness and a care for minutiae, ambitiousness and conservatism. It also explains, I think, another quality of his poetry, and that is its often twisting, restive, self-undermining choppiness and tortuousness, swerving as it does between conflicting modes and stances.

Most of the contributors to this volume notice how strangely a mixture of boldness and conventionality is at work in the poetry. Mrs. Melchiori notes an oddly conventional response to Italy. Leonee Ormond points to the amateurishness of Browning's knowledge of painting, his wild attributions to unknown primitives, the way he keeps only a step in front of contemporary taste, if that. Penelope Gay's verdict on Browning's musical thinking is much the same: in spite of immense knowledge he was thought of as being, and often was, amateurish, and even behind contemporary thinking about music. Trevor Lloyd traces Browning's political ideas and shows how, throughout his life, all Browning's most progressive ideas were 'steadily turned into law' while his thinking failed to evolve further. But this information by itself would make Browning shrink from his huge stature; it tells only half the story. The writers of these essays also recognize Browning's daring, intuitively imaginative way of seizing upon the large issue, the crucial question.

Time and again this is the result of articulating concepts and situations as Romantic ones, even when he is most critical of Romantic values. Upon his musical and aesthetic knowledge are imposed huge Romantic questions: he grasped the nature of the historical epoch and historical change as a romantic would have done; above all his understanding of Romantic epistemology enabled him to make, *sui generis* almost, an astounding exploration of the difficulties of the Romantic position for the young poet. But perhaps the strangest fact about Browning's grasp of such large issues is that there *are* no facts about them. Browning seems to have understood these ideas without going directly to their sources. Penelope Gay shows that there is no direct evidence for Browning's knowledge of German writing on music. Philip Drew thinks that Browning and Kierkegaard, whose ideas Browning's religious position so curiously echoes, probably never knew of one another's existence. Morse Peckham shows how scanty were the models of Romantic experience directly available to Browning. John Woolford demonstrates how deeply Browning read in seventeenth- and eighteenth-century literature. One can only suppose that he picked up such ideas, much as he picked up unsystematically his more trivial and recondite knowledge. This makes the work of source-tracing and influence-hunting quite a

different procedure from what it becomes in, say, the poetry of Coleridge or of Blake, or in the novels of George Eliot.

Another consequence of this double context of Victorianism and Romanticism for Browning's poetry was that he did not feel comfortable
with either; each interfered with the other. A more sober Victorian position is called in to modify Romantic largeness, extravagance and optimism. Romantic concepts constantly push against and dislodge a more
restricted Victorian view. This, I think, is not an unconscious process. It
is this double awareness which gives Browning's explorations of almost
any topic a shifting, unpredictable nature. Poems double back on themselves, fragment, fracture the conclusions to which they seem to be leading. Or even where a conclusion is predictable, it is arrived at by a
swerving and disorientating method. Philip Drew notices Browning's
delight in following a narrow line between two perils, or taking a sceptical premise to an optimistic conclusion. He might have added with equal
justice that Browning also rejoices in drawing a pessimistic conclusion
from optimistic premises. I have tried to show how Browning's love
poems are shot through with a sceptical, restive, complicated undermining of free and spontaneous feeling. Peter Keating uses James's 'double
Browning'—the Browning who is conventional externally but who is
also a great and original creative artist—as a way of confronting
Browning's work. The chapters in this book do not solve the Browning
puzzle, but they do colour some of its pieces.

ISOBEL ARMSTRONG

| | The main events of Browning's life | The main events of literary and intellectual importance in Browning's lifetime | The main events of historical importance in Browning's lifetime |
|---|---|---|---|
| 1812 | Browning born (1 May) in Camberwell | Byron, *Child Harold's Pilgrimage* (completed 1818) | U.S.A. declares war on Britain |
| 1813 | | Shelley, *Queen Mab* Jane Austen, *Pride and Prejudice* | |
| 1814 | Browning's sister, Sariana, born | Scott, *Waverley* Dulwich Gallery opened. First collection accessible to public | |
| 1815 | | Wordsworth, *White Doe of Rylstone*, *Loadamia* | Wellington and Blucher defeat Napoleon at Waterloo Congress of Vienna ends Napoleon abdicates Corn Law passed in England |
| 1816 | | Shelley, *Alastor* Goethe, *Journey to Italy* | |
| 1817 | | Ricardo, *Principles of Political Economy* Hegel, *Encyclopaedia of Philosophy* | |
| 1818 | | Keats, *Endymion* Hazlitt, *Lectures on the English Poets* | |
| 1819 | | Wordsworth, *Peter Bell* Keats, *Eve of St. Agnes* Byron, *Don Juan* Victor Hugo, *Odes* | Queen Victoria born 'Peterloo' riots First Factory Act passed |
| 1820 | Becomes a weekly boarder at the school of Rev. Thomas Read, Peckham (until 1826) | Malthus, *Principles of Political Economy* Keats, *Hyperion and Odes* Shelley, *Prometheus Unbound* | Accession of George IV |

| | | | |
|---|---|---|---|
| 1821 | | De Quincey, *Confessions of an Opium Eater* Shelley, *Adonais and Epipsychidion* Hegel, *Philosophy of Right* | Austrians repress revolutions in Naples and Piedmont Death of Napoleon |
| 1822 | | Beethoven, *Missa Solemnis* *Biographie Universelle*, 50 vols., published (purchased by Browning's father) Death of Shelley | Death of Castlereagh by suicide |
| 1823 | | | |
| 1824 | Association with W. J. Fox and his circle begins when *Incondita*, Browning's first (but never published) volume of poems sent to Benjamin Flower, editor of *Cambridge Intelligencer* | Death of Byron | Repeal of Combination Laws |
| 1825 | | Coleridge, *Aids to Reflection* Hazlitt, *Spirit of the Age* | Stockton and Darlington Railway opened Trade Unions made legal in Britain |
| 1826 | Reads Shelley's poems and becomes an atheist and vegetarian | | |
| 1827 | | Keble, *Christian Year* Tennyson, *Poems by Two Brothers* Blake dies | |
| 1828 | Began to attend classes at London University but did not complete the session | Thomas Arnold becomes Headmaster of Rugby | Wellington Prime Minister |
| 1829 | Friendship with Alfred Domett | | |
| 1830 | | Cobbett, *Rural Rides* Tennyson, *Poems, chiefly Lyrical* Charles Lyell, *Principles of Geology* | July Revolution in France, Louis Philippe elected king Grey Prime Minister Liverpool-Manchester Railway |
| 1831 | | | |

| 1832 | Sees Edmund Kean in Shakespeare's Richard II | Death of Goethe and publication of *Faust II* | Mazzini founds 'Young Italy' Reform Bill passed in England |
| 1833 | *Pauline* | Carlyle, *Sartor Resartus* Newman initiates *Tracts for the Times* | Factory Act passed Abolition of Slavery in British Colonies Oxford Movement under way |
| 1834 | Travels to St. Petersburg with Russian Consul-General (March, April) and considers a career as diplomat *Porphyrio's Lover* and *Johannes Agricola* written in Russia | Death of Coleridge | Poor Law Amendment Act |
| 1835 | *Paracelsus* Meets Macready and John Forster and makes acquaintance of Carlyle, 'Barry Cornwall', R. H. Horne, Monkton Milnes, Leigh Hunt | Dickens, *Sketches by Boz* Strauss, *Life of Jesus* | Melbourne Prime Minister Municipal Corporation Act |
| 1836 | Toasted at Sergeant Talfourd's dinner as among the 'Poets of England' in presence of Wordsworth | Dickens, *Pickwick Papers* Ranke, *History of the Popes* | Louis Napoleon exiled to America Chartist Movement under way in England |
| 1837 | *Strafford* produced by W. C. Macready at Covent Garden | Carlyle, *French Revolution* Dickens, *Oliver Twist* Death of Constable | Accession of Queen Victoria |
| 1838 | Browning visits Italy for the first time | Dickens, *Nicholas Nickleby* Tupper, *Proverbial Philosophy* | Austrians evacuate Papal States except Ferrara Chartists issue 'People's Charter' Anti-Corn Law League founded |
| 1839 | | Invention of photography by Daguerre Stendhal, *La Chartreuse de Parme* George Sand, *Spiridion* Turner exhibits *The Téméraire* | |

| | | | |
|---|---|---|---|
| 1840 | *Sordello*, Browning's literary reputation damaged The Browning's move to Hatcham, Surrey | Dickens, *Old Curiosity Shop* | Attempted coup by Louis Napoleon Penny postage introduced Marriage of Queen Victoria and Prince Albert of Saxe-Coburg-Gotha |
| 1841 | *Pippa Passes*, first poem in *Bells and Pomegranates*, 1841–6 | Carlyle, *Heroes and Hero-worship* Feuerbach, *Essence of Christianity* *Punch* begins publication | Peel Prime Minister |
| 1842 | *Dramatic Lyrics, Bells and Pomegranates*, No. III Alfred Domett, closest of Browning's Camberwell friends, emigrates to New Zealand | Tennyson, *Poems*, 1842 Macaulay, *Lays of Ancient Rome* Auguste Comte, *Cours de Philosophie positive* | Chartist riots Ashley's act makes child and female labour underground illegal |
| 1843 | *A Blot in the 'Scutcheon* | J. S. Mill, *System of Logic* Macaulay, *Critical and Historical Essays* Dickens, *Christmas Carol* R. H. Horne, *Orion* | Rochdale Co-operative Societies established |
| 1844 | Second visit to Italy (Naples, Rome) | R. H. Horne, *A New Spirit of the Age* Elizabeth Barrett, *Poems* Disraeli, *Coningsby* J. von Liebig, *Letters on Chemistry* | Factory Act regulates working hours of women and children |
| 1845 | Meets Elizabeth Barrett (20 May). They have common friends— John Kenyon, Richard Hengist Horne *Dramatic Romances and Lyrics, Bells and Pomegranates*, No. VII (November) | Disraeli, *Sybil* Poe, *Tales of Mystery* Carlyle, *Cromwell* F. Engels, *Situation of the Working Classes in England* Wagner, *Tanhäuser* | |

| 1846 | Marries Elizabeth Barrett secretly (12 September) and travels to Italy Elizabeth Barrett Browning writes *Sonnets from the Portuguese* | Grote, *History of Greece* begins publication Lear, *Book of Nonsense* | Repeal of Corn Laws (May) Lord John Russell Prime Minister (June) |
|---|---|---|---|
| 1847 | Settles in Casa Guidi Florence, where the Brownings live until 1861 | Tennyson, *The Princess* Charlotte Brontë, *Jane Eyre* Emily Brontë, *Wuthering Heights* | |
| 1848 | Elizabeth Barrett Browning a partisan of the Italian Risorgimento | Clough, *Bothie of Tober-Na-Vuolich* Thackeray, *Vanity Fair* Pre-Raphaelite Brotherhood formed Balzac, *Comedie Humaine* completed, Marx, Engels, *Communist Manifesto* | Chartist Petition Ten hour Factory Act Public Health Act in England Beginning of Christian Socialism Revolutions of 1848 In France Louis Philippe abdicates and a Republic proclaimed (Feb.), Louis Napoleon elected President (Dec.) |
| 1849 | First collected edition of Browning's works, 2 vols. Birth of son, Robert Wiedmann Barrett in March Death of Browning's mother in the same month | Macaulay begins publication of his *History of England* A. de Lamartine *Histoire de la révolution de* 1848 P. J. Proudhon, *Confessions d'un révolutionnaire* Death of Chopin | In Italy the movement for unification and liberation was hampered by internal strife and the intervention of Austria and France. Naples recovered Sicily after a revolt in Jan. 1848. Revolution in Lombardy and Venice, supported by the king of Sardinia (Charles Albert, father of Victor Emmanuel) was suppressed by Austria in 1849, when the Austrians also restored the Grand Duke of Tuscany. Though Mazzini declared Rome a Republic in Feb. 1849 and resisted (with |

| 1849 | | | Garibaldi in May) the attacks of the French, Rome was finally taken by the French in July. |
|------|--|--|------|
| 1850 | *Christmas-Eve and Easter-Day* The Brownings' social life becomes fuller. They meet Isa Blagden, Margaret Fuller, Greenough | Dickens, *David Copperfield* Tennyson, *In Memoriam* Wagner, *Lohengrin* produced by Liszt Deaths of Balzac, Wordsworth Tennyson Poet Laureate | Pius IX re-enters Rome Cavour appointed Minister in Piedmont |
| 1851 | Browning's poetry favourably reviewed by Milsand in Aug. First visit to England since his marriage Visited by Carlyle, Forster, Fanny Kemble, Barry Cornwall Visit to Paris | Great Exhibition in England Ruskin, *Stones of Venice* Melville, *Moby Dick* Verdi, *Rigoletto* Death of Turner | Louis Napoleon's *coup d'état* in France |
| 1852 | Meets George Sand Writes introduction to letters of Shelley later found to be spurious Visit to London in June Meets Landor, Ruskin, Patmore, Rossetti, Kingsley, Tennyson | Matthew Arnold, *Empedocles on Etna* Dickens, *Bleak House* Thackeray, *Henry Esmond* Harriet Beecher Stowe, *Uncle Tom's Cabin* Dumas, *La Dame aux Camélias* Death of Wellington | Louis Napoleon proclaimed Napoleon III Cavour Prime Minister of Piedmont Constitution of Tuscany abolished |
| 1853 | Bagni di Lucca (July–October) Visits Rome (November) Brownings meet Thackeray, Aubrey de Vere, Lockhart, Leighton | Matthew Arnold, *Poems* Kingsley, *Hypatia* Mrs. Gaskell, *Cranford* Wagner, *Ring* cycle | |
| 1854 | Return to Florence (May) | Patmore, *The Betrothal* (first vol. of *Angel in the House*) Tennyson, *Charge of the Light Brigade* Comte, *Système de* | Crimean War End of Chartist Movement |

| | | | |
|---|---|---|---|
| 1854 | | *politique positive* completed Working Men's College founded in London | |
| 1855 | *Men and Women* Visit to London Browning reads *Fra Lippo Lippi* before Tennyson, Rossetti Visit to Paris (October) | Matthew Arnold, *Poems*, second series Kingsley, *Westward Ho!* Trollope, *The Warden* Tennyson, *Maud* Longfellow, *Hiawatha* Whitman, *Leaves of Grass* | Piedmont joins in Crimean War |
| 1856 | Elizabeth Barrett Browning, *Aurora Leigh* Return to England (June) John Kenyon's will leaves the Brownings legacies amounting to £11,000 | Froude, *History of England* begins publication Pasteur made Professor in University of Paris Birth of Sigmund Freud | Paris Peace Congress settles Territory after Crimean War |
| 1857 | Death of Elizabeth's father, Edward Moulton-Barrett Return to Italy (January) Bagni di Lucca (July–October) | Dickens, *Little Dorrit* Flaubert, *Madame Bovary* Buckle, *History of Civilisation* | Italian National Association founded |
| 1858 | July–October Paris and holiday with Browning's sister and father at Havre | Matthew Arnold, *Merope* Tennyson, *Idylls of the King* Carlyle, *Frederick the Great* | Cavour enters into alliance with Napoleon III in order to secure unification of Italy Alexander II begins emancipation of the serfs in Russia |
| 1859 | Return to Florence (May) Siena (July–September) Friendship with Walter Savage Landor, Edward Burne-Jones Winter in Rome | Darwin, *Origin of Species* J. S. Mill, *On Liberty* Meredith, *Ordeal of Richard Feverel* | France in alliance with Piedmont defeats Austria at Magenta and Solferino Cavour resigns when Piedmont obtains only Lombardy and Parma De Lesseps works on Suez Canal |
| 1860 | Mrs. Browning, *Poems Before Congress* Leave Rome (June) Return to Florence in Sept. | *Essays and Reviews*, broad church essays on religion George Eliot, *The Mill* | Cavour annexes Tuscany Garibaldi takes Naples Victor Emanuel invades |

| | | | |
|---|---|---|---|
| 1860 | after period at Siena<br>Winter in Rome | *on the Floss*<br>Ruskin, *Unto this Last*<br>J. S. Mill, *Treatise on Government* | papal state<br>Plebiscites bring southern Italy into union with north |
| 1861 | Return to Florence (May)<br>Death of Elizabeth Barrett Browning (June)<br>Browning assisted to Paris by Isa Blagden<br>Browning moves to London (November) after holiday in France with father and sister | George Eliot, *Silas Marner*<br>Hans Anderson, *Fairy Tales* completed | Victor Emanuel proclaimed king of Italy<br>Death of Prince Albert |
| 1862 | Browning takes 19 Warwick Crescent as his permanent London home<br>Pyrenees (August)<br>Biarritz (September)<br>*The Ring and the Book* takes shape | Clough, *Poems* (with a memoir by F. T. Palgrave)<br>Meredith, *Modern Love*<br>Victor Hugo, *Les Misérables*<br>Turgeneff, *Fathers and Sons* | Bismark made Prussian Prime Minister |
| 1863 | Begins to take part in London life<br>Collected edition of his poems published in three volumes | J. S. Mill, *Utilitarianism*<br>Renan, *Vie de Jesus*<br>Whistler, *Symphony in White*<br>Death of Thackeray | |
| 1864 | *Dramatis Personae* | Newman, *Apologia pro vita sua*<br>International Workers' Association founded in London<br>Anti-slum campaign of Octavia Hill begins | Florence made capital of Italy, which renounces claim on Rome |
| 1865 | | Swinburne, *Atalanta in Calydon*<br>Lewis Carroll, *Alice in Wonderland*<br>Tolstoy, *War and Peace*<br>General Booth founds Salvation Army<br>Wagner, *Tristran and Isolde* | Death of Palmerston<br>Russell Prime Minister with Gladstone as Leader of the House<br>Napoleon acknowledges a united Italy |
| 1866 | Death of Browning's father, sister joins him and they holiday at Le Croisic | Swinburne, *Poems and Ballads* first series<br>Huxley, *Elementary Philosophy* | Defeat of Italy by Austria |

| | | | |
|---|---|---|---|
| 1866 | | Dostoievsky, *Crime and Punishment* | |
| 1867 | Honorary M.A. of Oxford and honorary Fellow of Balliol<br>Holiday at Le Croisic | Matthew Arnold, *New Poems*<br>Les Parnassiens (Gautier, Verlaine, Baudelaire) formed<br>Ibsen, *Peer Gynt*<br>Marx, *Capital*, part I<br>First University Extension courses | Second Reform Bill<br>Factory inspection Act<br>Garibaldi marches unsuccessfully on Rome |
| 1868 | Smith, Elder, become Browning's publishers<br>*The Ring and the Book* (published between November 1868 and February 1869)<br>Death of Arabel Barrett, wife's favourite sister | William Morris, *Earthly Paradise* | Disraeli Prime Minister (February) but defeated in December election and succeeded by Gladstone |
| 1869 | Proposes to Lady Ashburton and is rejected | Clough, *Poems and, Prose Remains*<br>Matthew Arnold, *Culture and Anarchy*<br>Mill, *Subjection of Women*<br>Girton College founded in Cambridge | Disestablishment of the Irish Church |
| 1870 | Holiday with Milsand near Havre | D. G. Rossetti, *Poems*<br>Death of Dickens | Forster's Education Act makes education compulsory in England<br>Irish Land Bill<br>Franco-Prussian War (–1871) |
| 1871 | *Balaustion's Adventure*<br>*Prince Hohenstiel-Schwangau*<br>Elected life-governor of University College, London | Satire of Alfred Austen (future poet laureate (1896) and poet of imperialism) *The Golden Age*<br>Swinburne, *Songs Before Sun-rise*<br>Darwin, *Descent of Man*<br>First Impressionist Exhibition (Paris)<br>Zola, *Les Rougon-Macquart* begins publication | Trade Unions legalised in England<br>Thiers head of French executive<br>Rome made capital of Italy |

| 1872 | *Fifine at the Fair*<br>Alfred Domett returns<br>Friendship with Miss<br>Thackeray during summer at<br>St. Aubin | Herbert Spencer,<br>*Study of Sociology* | Anglo-French Com-<br>mercial Treaty |
|---|---|---|---|
| 1873 | *Red Cotton Night-Cap<br>Country*<br>Establishes pattern of<br>summers in France and<br>Scotland to be continued<br>over the next few years,<br>and when his poetry was<br>mainly written | Pater, *Essays on the<br>Renaissance*<br>Brahms, *German<br>Requiem* | Death of Napoleon III<br>Gladstone defeated on<br>Irish University Bill |
| 1874 | | Stubbs, *Constitutional<br>History of England*<br>J. Strauss, *Die<br>Fledermaus* | Disraeli forms<br>conservative ministry<br>Factory Act regulates<br>working hours |
| 1875 | *Aristophanes' Apology*<br>*The Inn Album* | H. Taine, *Origines de<br>la France Contemporaine*<br>Mark Twain, *Adventures<br>of Tom Sawyer*<br>Bizet, *Carmen* | Disraeli buys control<br>of Suez Canal |
| 1876 | *Pacchiarotto*<br>Slight signs of ill health | Wagner, *Ring*<br>performed at first<br>Bayreuth Festival | Turkish massacres in<br>Bulgaria provoke<br>controversy in England<br>(Gladstone, *Bulgarian<br>Horrors*)<br>First Socialist Inter-<br>national dissolved |
| 1877 | *The Agamemnon of Aeschylus*<br>Death of close friend, Miss<br>Egerton-Smith, prompts<br>Browning to begin *La<br>Saisiaz* | Ibsen, *Pillars of Society*<br>Tolstoy, *Anna Karenina*<br>Brahms first and<br>second symphonies | Queen Victoria made<br>Empress of India |
| 1878 | *La Saisiaz*<br>*The Two Poets of Croisic*<br>First visit to Italy since<br>death of his wife<br>Establishes annual visits to<br>Venice except for the years<br>1882, 1884 and 1886 | Swinburne, *Poems<br>and Ballads* second<br>series | Death of Victor<br>Emanuel of Italy |
| 1879 | *Dramatic Idyls* | Meredith, *The Egoist*<br>Zola, *L'Assommoir*<br>Strindberg, *The Red<br>Room*<br>Ibsen, *Doll's House* | |

| | | |
|---|---|---|
| 1880 | *Dramatic Idyls* second series | Dostoievsky, *Brothers Karamazov* | Gladstone forms Liberal ministry |
| | | | Relief Act for Ireland |
| 1881 | Foundation of Browning Society by Furnivall | D. G. Rossetti, *Ballads and Sonnets* | Death of Disraeli |
| | | Henry James, *Portrait of a Lady* | |
| | | Verlaine, *Sagesse* | |
| | | Ibsen, *Ghosts* | |
| | | Revised Version of New Testament | |
| 1882 | | Mark Twain, *Adventures of Huckleberry Finn* | Municipal Corporations Act |
| | | Mallarmé, *L'Aprés-Midi d'un Faun* | Phoenix Park murders in Ireland |
| | | Wagner, *Parsifal* | |
| | | Nietzsche, *Joyful Wisdom* | |
| 1883 | *Jocoseria* | R. L. Stevenson, *Treasure Island* | |
| | | Nietzsche, *Zarathustra* | |
| 1884 | *Ferishtah's Fancies* | Fabian Society founded | Third Reform Bill |
| | Made L.L.D. of University of Edinburgh | Oxford English Dictionary | British expansion in Africa (Basutoland, Somali Coast, Nigeria and New Guinea made British Protectorates) |
| | | E. Burne Jones exhibits *King Cophetua and the Beggar Maid* | |
| 1885 | | Pater, *Marius the Epicurean* | Conservative Ministry under Salisbury |
| | | Maupassant, *Bel Ami* | Irish Land Bill |
| | | Zola, *Germinal* | |
| 1886 | Death of Milsand | Ibsen, *Rosmersholm* | Brief Liberal Ministry under Gladstone defeated on Irish Home Rule Bill |
| | | Nietzsche, *Beyond Good and Evil* | Anglo-German agreement on E. African territory |
| 1887 | *Parleyings with Certain People of Importance* | Tolstoy, *Powers of Darkness* | Queen Victoria's *Golden Jubilee* |
| | Moves to 29 de Vere Gardens, Kensington | Strindberg, *Son of a Servant* | Independent Labour Party formed |
| | | Chekhov's first play *Ivanov* | |

| 1888 | *The Poetical Works* (–89) Last collected edition revised and supervised by Browning | Rudyard Kipling, *Plain Tales from the Hills* First English translation of Henri Bergson's work, *Time and Free Will* | County Councils established by Local Government Act |
|------|------|------|------|
| 1889 | *Asolando* Browning's death, 12 Dec., in Venice | Bernard Shaw, *Fabian Essays* William James, *Principles of Psychology* | Suez Canal internationalised |
| 1890 | | First vol. of Frazer, *The Golden Bough* Oscar Wilde, *Dorian Gray* Tolstoy, *Kreutzer Sonata* Death of Van Gogh | Bismarck dismissed |

# 1: *Sources and Resources in Browning's Early Reading*

## JOHN WOOLFORD

'And how I should like to know what poets have been your sponsors, "to promise and vow" for you,—and whether you have held true to early tastes, or leapt violently from them, and what books you read . . .'

Elizabeth Barrett Browning, *Letters*, 3 February, 1845

### I   *Romantic Infatuation*

#### I

*Sun-treader, life and light be thine forever!*
*Thou art gone from us; years go by and spring*
*Gladdens and the young earth is beautiful,*
*But thy songs come not, other bards arise,*
*But none like thee . . .*

(*Pauline*, 151–5)

SHELLEY, WE LEARN from Browning's precocious autobiography, had inaugurated a melodious apocalypse in which

*Men were to be as gods and earth as heaven,*
*And mine—ah, what a life was mine to prove!*

(426–7)

The very next words, however, discover a flaw in this millennial vision:

*My whole soul rose to meet it. Now Pauline,*
*I shall go mad if I recall that time!*

(428–9)

and the cause of this ominous retraction, always obscure in *Pauline* itself, receives illumination from the counterpointing 'true facts' of this first encounter with the heady stuff of Romantic Utopianism. At age fourteen, the story goes, Browning saw a volume of Shelley's poems advertised on a bookstall, and his curiosity aroused, sent his· mother to purchase this. Mrs Browning complied, and 'brought also three volumes of the still lesser known John Keats, on being assured that one who liked Shelley's works would like these also.'[1] The comedy lies in the employment of his mother, a devout Nonconformist, as the innocent instrument of his own exposure to free-thinking, for it was 'Mr Shelley's Atheistical Poem' *Queen Mab* that Browning had seen, and in the first overwhelming surrender to its 'delirious notes' he was to follow this new prophet into a Disbelief which sundered him, temporarily, from the woman he thought of as 'divine'. His new enthusiasm was, for a while, intoxicating and contagious: we read of his inducing tremors in the hitherto steadfast faith of his first love, Sarah Flower[2] She, however, lived to write 'Nearer My God to Thee'; and Browning too was not long in experiencing his own de-conversion, for *Pauline*, written at the age of twenty, proclaims 'A need, a trust, a yearning after God' 'always' to have been his 'lode-star',—a claim rendered slightly uncomfortable by its persistent adjacency to worship of the scoffer:

> *Sun-treader, I believe in God and truth*
> *And love; and as one just escaped from death*
> *Would bind himself in bands of friends to feel*
> *He lives indeed, so would I lean on thee!*

(1020—24)

This episode typifies Browning's relations with the Romantic poets. For the entire movement, as for individual poets within it, he experienced a passionate predilection, followed by a reaction; and the remainder of his life was characterized by an uneasy oscillation derived from this initial module. The year 1840 found him, in *Sordello*, still in a Shelleyan muse; but the *Essay on Shelley* of 1852 becomes embarrassed by its 'apology' for its subject's atheism; while tales of his hero's infidelity to his wife, reaching Browning at about the same time, left his reverence

[1] Mrs Sutherland Orr, *Life*, 1908, 38.
[2] See Betty Miller, *Robert Browning: A Portrait*, 1952, 32.

permanently impaired. True, he describes *The Cenci*, in *Cenciaja* (1876) as 'your superb/Achievement'; but in a letter to Furnivall of 1885 we find him admitting that 'For myself I painfully contrast my notions of Shelley the *man* and Shelley, well, even the *poet* with what they were sixty years ago.' And in *Parleyings* (1887), a last autobiography to match *Pauline*, Shelley is not even mentioned.

Byron too: who having (allegedly) inspired Browning's lost first collection of verse *Incondita*, went underground for many years, to re-emerge, in 'Dis aliter visum' and *The Inn Album* as the cynical rake, and in *Prince Hohenstiel-Schwangau* and *La Saisiaz* as the proponent of overweening Romantic arrogance. Not Keats, however, who almost breaks the pattern, having afforded no early rapture/rupture, and earning, over the years, Browning's growing regard until, in *Parleyings*, he alone is mentioned of those early stars. But only mentioned. The pattern persists.

2

I have no wish to suggest that Browning's early reading of the Romantic poets did not influence his own works. This claim would be absurd in face of the manifold indebtedness of—to begin with—*Pauline* to Shelley, and *Paracelsus* (in the poet Aprile) to Keats; both his satirical bias and its characteristic exposure in bathetic doggerel are clearly in part Byronic; and all these poets practised prototypes of his own dramatic monologue form. Yet these were influences he later became anxious to disavow, or at least to qualify, and I would like to consider the reasons for this.

The first reason is that in 1840 he more or less rejected Romanticism as a credo, and could scarcely have been expected to feel the same about its proponents. Intoxicated by visionary rapture, Paracelsus had declared

> 'Tis time
> *New hope should animate the world, new light*
> *Should grow from new revealings to a race*
> *Weighed down so long, forgotten so long; thus shall*
> *The heaven reserved for us at last receive*
> *Creatures whom no unwonted splendours blind . . .*
>
> (*Paracelsus*, 372–7)

the standard Romantic apotheosis; but even then, it was shown to exact a heavy price. Inspired indeed by the human spectacle, the hero repudiates

> *A station with the brightest of the crowd,*
> *A portion with the proudest of them all,*
>
> (455–6)

for *he* must

> *elevate myself far, far above*
> *The gorgeous spectacle*
>
> (459–60)

of human life, in order

> *At once to trample on, yet save mankind,*
> *To make some unexampled sacrifice*
> *In their behalf, to wring some wondrous good*
> *From heaven or earth for them, to perish, winning*
> *Eternal weal in the act,*
>
> (461–5)

inviting, as Paracelsus explicitly does, comparison with the customary Romantic archetype, Prometheus. His subsequent career indicates, by accumulating nemesis, the hubris involved; but it is in *Sordello* that Browning's disillusion reaches its first full articulation, when, admonished by the 'warped souls and bodies' in the Venetian scene, he humbles himself to

> *ask youth and strength*
> *And health for each of you, not more—at length*
> *Grown wise, who asked at home that the whole race*
> *Might add the spirit's to the body's grace,*
> *And all be dizened out as chiefs and bards.*
>
> (*Sordello*, III, 717–22)

And when, much later, he returned to Paracelsus's 'gorgeous spectacle', it was in a far different posture. Juan's portentous dream in *Fifine* (1872) figures mankind as a 'Carnival', first seen from 'far, far above' in Lilliputian littleness and silliness; but then 'plumb I pitched into the square', where

> *I found brutality encroach*
> *Less on the human, lie the lightlier as I looked*
> *The nearlier on those faces . . .*
>
> (*Fifine*, 1742–44)

the lesson being

> *one must abate*
> *One's scorn of the soul's casing, distinct from the soul's self*

> (1788–89)

which Paracelsus certainly did not do. It is Hohenstiel-Schwangau who
deflects this personal conversion into a critique of the Romantic poets,
ventriloquizing a certain 'Bard'—clearly Byron—who is represented in
a little pet of self-conceit and world-contempt, condemned, and recommended to learn

> *There are two things in the world still wiser folk*
> *Accept—intelligence and sympathy.*

> (556–7)

especially sympathy, for

> *Once pedestalled on earth,*
> *To act not speak, I found earth was not air.*
> *I saw that multitude of mine, and not*
> *The nakedness and nullity of air*
> *Fit only for a voice to float in free.*
> *Such eyes I saw that craved the light alone,*
> *Such mouths that wanted bread and nothing else,*
> *Such hands that supplicated handiwork . . .*

> (902–9)

a preference upheld by Browning's earlier claim that 'I don't go about
now wanting the fixed stars before my time; this world has not escaped
me, thank God . . .'[1] Not that the Romantic ignores the world: on the
contrary, his first endeavour, in such enterprises as Shelley's attempted
social reforms, is to transform it to accord with the transcendent design
of 'Time's completed plan' as he conceives this; but, baulked as he must
be by the nonconformity of things to his impetuous reformation, he
withdraws into a petulant self-absorption. It is this that Browning
rejects; and progressively he came, like his speakers, to abandon too the

[1] *Letters*, 3 May 1845.

'fixed stars' of Romantic vision in favour of a diurnal humanism of 'this world' until by 1887 he had become one of those who

> *contentedly abide*
> *Awake, nor want the wings of dream,—who tramp*
> *Earth's common surface, rough, smooth, dry or damp . . .*
>
> (*Lairesse*, 111–13)

Like many other Victorians, he had come to mistrust the poet as protagonist of eternity and millennial pretender.

The second reason for Browning's disavowal of Romantic influence is suggested in *Pauline*:

> *How my heart leapt as still I sought and found*
> *Much there, I felt my own heart had conceived,*
> *But there living and burning!*
>
> (417–19)

Note that Browning is saying not that Shelley *changed* his ideas, rather that he *confirmed* things already conceived. By the age of fourteen, one might add, the mind is usually formed; and if the antecedent childhood has been especially literate, the eventual poet may well exist in miniature. Browning's was such a childhood. Indeed I suspect that only John Stuart Mill was more comprehensively drenched with culture at a tender age, and Browning's case was far different: not moulded as a Steam Intellect, but permitted to browse 'omnivously, though certainly not without guidance' through a house 'literally crammed with books.'[1] It is surely with his early reading that we must begin the Identikit of Browning's mind.


## II   *Textual Inspection*

The task of reconstructing Browning's childhood reading is rendered difficult, though not impossible, by the disappearance of much of the evidence. Of his father's library only fragments survive, and those, mingled as they are in the 1913 catalogue of the sale of Browning's own

[1] Orr, *Life*, 29–30.

library[1] with later purchases of Browning's and the entire library of his wife, can only tentatively be identified. One is obliged to place along-side that catalogue tools which help to process it: hints in biographies, casual reminiscences in letters, of the works which possibly shaped Browning's mind, must be marshalled and deployed. If only he had responded to EBB's request for a record of his 'early tastes'! Then we would have had what we lack: an authoritative index to the volumes of his father's library, arranged according to their relative importance to the poet, permitting and enabling us to dissolve the surface of his poems and explore the exposed layers of chiaroscuro.

Well, there *is* one. Though he never answered his future wife's ques-tion, he did, in *Parleyings*, set out to rectify the omission by providing the world with an autobiography. That the work, when it appeared, turned out to consist of an *intellectual* autobiography comprising writers who had influenced his work suggests how important reading had in fact been to Browning; that this intellectual autobiography should never, then or since, have been properly deciphered, invites a further exegesis.

I

It seems that Browning's 'sponsors' and 'early tastes' were 'certain people of importance in their day: to wit: Bernard de Mandeville, Daniel Bar-toli, Christopher Smart, George Bubb Dodington, Francis Furini, Gerard de Lairesse, and Charles Avison.' Well might Mrs Orr remark that however 'important in their day,' these worthies were 'almost un-known in ours'![2] They remain so, and while not dismissing this as a joke, we may at least detect a hint of Browning's habitual grotesquerie, especi-ally since both poetry and letters amply testify to his having traversed the usual terrain—classics, Shakespeare, Milton and so on—of a literary education: other, more eminent writers had been 'his old familiar friends' with equal claim to 'connect themselves with the imaginative pleasures of his very earliest youth.'[3] What was Browning up to?

DeVane, in his excellent book *Browning's Parleyings: the Autobiography of a Mind* (1927), has isolated two purposes. Firstly, he suggests, Brown-ing wished to indicate some of the major sources of his material; second-

---

[1] This can be consulted in vol VI of 'Sale Catalogues of the Libraries of Eminent Persons', gen ed A. N. L. Munby, 1972.

[2] Orr, *Handbook*, 1896, 339.          [3] Ibid.

ly, he was concerned to activate a final expression of his own philosophy. This scheme tends to split the *Parleyings* into two groups: 'Lairesse', for instance, indicating a genuine and significant source, 'Furini', on the other hand, revealing only intellectual opportunism, as Browning annexes, for polemical purposes, the life-style of an unimportant painter. The objection to it is not only that its parts are contradictory, but that they do not even function efficiently in their own terms. If Browning wished to indicate sources, why omit classical writers, Wanley, Vasari . . . let alone the Romantics? And if his aim was to express his own views, why did he not do so as directly—or near-directly—as he had in *Ferishtah's Fancies?* One learns from DeVane that the *raison d'être* of 'Furini' is its attack upon John Caldecott Horsley, whose witch-hunt against painters from the nude had victimized Browning's son Pen. Well, even at the time only one reviewer noticed this. Is *Parleyings* a failure?

   To vindicate the collection, I must seem for a while to divagate from my central topic, and look at the poems in purely critical terms. Doing this, we soon become conscious of a thematic and imagistic unity which militates against DeVane's dualistic interpretation: each parleying contains, at some point and in some form, a passage from illusion to reality, from deceitful and petulant ideality to a reconciling pragmatism. 'Mandeville' sets out to refute the claim—Carlyle's—that God really ought to give his afflicted people some sign of being alive and well; and Browning's method is to call up the eighteenth-century Dutch philosopher/polemicist Bernard de Mandeville to expound *his* doctrine of the necessity and utility of evil, and the futility of all idealisms:

> *T'enjoy the World's Conveniencies,*
> *Be fam'd for War yet live in Ease,*
> *Without great Vices, is a vain*
> *EUTOPIA seated in the Brain.*

*(Fable of the Bees)*

'Bartoli' opens with a genial disputation between Bartoli—whose *Dei' simboli transportati al morale* loved to turn 'the ordinary events of history to some moral end'[1]—and Browning, who prefers undoctored truth; and proceeds to vindicate the superiority of 'chronicle' to 'legendary' with a plain unvarnished tale contrasted to one of the Don's dubious *récits*. 'Dodington'—with an irony that cuts many ways—takes as its premise a

[1] W. C. DeVane, *Browning's Parleyings*, 1927.

world denuded of any ideal and shows how a Disraeli's pretence of one is
sheer animal cunning; 'Furini', more earnestly, exalts perfection in 'the
naked female form' above the fake idealism of Victorian prudery. 'Lairesse', great poem that it is, is far subtler: Lairesse himself, the blind painter composing verbal pictures in 'that prodigious book he write', serves
Browning for a paradigm of purely mental vision, unilluminated by any
external apparition. This enables him to look 'Beyond the ugly actual' to
'Imagination's limitless domain,' ignoring (he cannot see them) 'trifles
mean and base/Which vex the sight that cannot say them nay', and pro-
ducing, in 'Fancy's rainbow-birth', 'Joves and Junos, nymphs and satyrs'
with all the elaboration of the classical ideal. This Browning contrasts to
his own

> *hard fast wideawake*
> *Having and holding nature for the sake*
> *Of nature only . . .*

(Lairesse, 122–4)

Conceding that there *may* have been a

> *chain which used to bind*
> *Our earth to heaven, and yet for you, since blind*
> *Subsisted still efficient and intact*

(146–8)

he goes so far as to imitate Lairesse's legendary 'Walk' with his own
pageant of mythic tableaux: only to conclude 'Enough! stop further
fooling, De Lairesse!', we must shake off this tainting nostalgia and work
in the world. Again there is a contemporary reference, this time to
Matthew Arnold, whose 1853 *Preface* had indeed claimed that we
should 'Dream afresh old godlike shapes' and 'recognize no worth/In
fact newborn unless 'tis rendered back/Pallid with fancy . . .'

  The pattern is, I think, clear; and I hope that my description has demonstrated its relation to that other progression from Romantic Infatuation
to diurnal humanism. The *Parleyings*, I would claim, propound the same
module; and the parleying I have omitted, with Christopher Smart,
shows this most clearly. Here we begin with an extended metaphor expressing the effect upon Browning of the 'Song to David', Smart's most
famous poem, and his only great one: this is like a radiant chapel in an
otherwise dull country-house, inexplicable illumination after which the

poetaster 'resumed sobriety'—i.e. mediocrity. Browning's point is that
the transience of this experience is a merciful dispensation, because it obscured, in its obliterating unanimity, the linear continuum of life, to prolong it would prolong only madness: as Shelley, in the fierce grip of
continual exposure to Divine truth, 'was liable to remarkable delusions
and hallucinations'; and as Browning himself would 'go mad' if he were
to recall 'that time' when he too, intoxicated with the 'delirious notes' to
*Queen Mab*, shared the visionary rapture. Now he can present an opponent ethic, exalting a mundane scientism which will 'scrutinize the
rose', overstepping 'no least one of the rows' (Browning's assonance, not
mine!) 'That lead man from the bottom where he plants/First foot of all,
to life's last ladder-top.' Now he actually satirizes the poetics of vision:

> *The other method's favoured in our day!*
> *The end ere the beginning: as you may,*
> *Master the heavens before you study earth . . .*

                                                              (Smart, 240–2)

an attack which, unspecific as it is, both matches those in the other
parleyings and connects these to the remarkably similar attack of
Hohenstiel-Schwangau on Byron, who likewise refused 'to walk upon
the common earth or to breathe the common air,' as Henry Taylor[1] put
it.

The Romantics are not missing from *Parleyings*, then. They are invisible protagonists, smuggled in via Browning's reiteration of a formula of
which they had been the most conspicuous, though not the original, constituents. The entire method of the collection, with its system of three-
way debates—Browning, his 'person of importance', and some contemporary—proposes the atemporal equivalence of all mind-styles, allowing not only the explicit anachronism of Furini's sermon to Victorian
London, but the implicit fostering of Romantic ideas and values on Bartoli, Smart and Lairesse. It is worth remembering that Browning's Romantic phase commenced when he 'lived/With Plato and had the key to
life' and that Hohenstiel-Schwangau turns to Kant when he has finished
with Byron: to Browning, baptized as he was in a Romantic *Weltans-
chauung*, Romantic concepts of Imagination and Inspiration represented
an indwelling spiritual verity, not a historical contingency, and were to
be intercepted at any time in any age. Shelley had similarly claimed,

[1] Preface to *Philip van Artevelde*, 1834.

explicitly in *Defence of Poetry*, implicitly in *Prometheus Unbound*, that the West Wind that blew through him was omniprevalent in space and time; and the Romantic habit of constructing its theories around artists of an earlier epoch—Dante, Shakespeare, Michelangelo—was a mute affirmation of the same credo. This it was that permitted Browning, in reviewing Wilde's *Life of Tasso*, to be reminded of the life-style of Chatterton, and discuss that instead. Or to project; in the figure of Greek Thamuris, a perfect likeness of the Romantic Bard. Or to associate Milton, Smart, Keats, Lairesse and Bartoli as equivalent proponents of creative inspiration. What we call Romanticism was for him the poetic spirit itself.

2

Thus *Parleyings* is polemical reminiscence, designed to reassert the rejection of Romanticism both explicitly, in the reiterated idea-pattern, and implicitly in the expulsion of the Romantic poets from direct participation. But in that case we have got no nearer Browning's childhood reading, or but little; DeVane's accusation of opportunism has recurred in another form. Disappointed, let us retrace our steps to the library itself, resigned to being unhelped, and attempt to analyze it *ab initio*.

We are not as helpless as might appear. His wife was fortunately an assiduous inscriber of *her* books, and we can for certain eliminate all that bear the words 'E. B. Barrett', and almost for certain those containing 'E. B. Browning'. I exclude too all books inscribed 'R. and E. B. Browning' in her handwriting. We can also ignore books whose inscriptions show them to have been presentation-copies from contemporary authors (except perhaps in the case of the Landor bequests);[1] and I also propose to ignore any with publication-dates after 1830, except where evidence suggests they formed replacements for older volumes. This leaves two categories: (1) books which are known to have been read by Browning in youth (either on the evidence of their inscriptions or from other information) and (2) books which, having eluded all these nets, achieve a substantial credibility as left-overs from his father's library. One problem is that Browning's inscriptions are both irregular and erratic: his habit of inscribing his books, not according to the year of purchase, but purely with reference to the quite arbitrary day of the inscription

[1] See Sale Catalogue (see p. 7, n. 1), lots 232–45, 814–55, and many others.

itself, is especially misleading. For the following analysis, I have simply amassed all the books which on positive or negative evidence would seem to belong to his father's library, ignoring his inscription except where this provides a definite record.

We are left with some two hundred books, and the difficulties involved in validating the presence of many oblige us to search for groups and patterns rather than to make specific attributions of influence. Unable to quantify whether or how often any particular work might have been read, we can at least look around for others of the same genre, and, if sufficient are found to propose and second, elect it. Having by this circular process defined groups rather than singulars, the next step is to graduate their relative importance by dividing them into the total and deriving a numerical ratio (this is crude, since the true ratio would involve number of readings rather than number of books: without external evidence we would never spot, under this scheme, the importance of Avison's *Essay on Musical Expression*, unsupported as this is by any substantial music section; but there is no choice).

After these multiplied reservations, it is a relief to find that 'Browning's books' do obediently cluster into well-defined groups, and that these do not outrage our previous sense of his concerns: with a pretty docility they arrange a coherent sequence of topics which we can then juxtapose with Browning's works in order to study the issue of the subsequent marriage. Rather than tabulating these, I propose to illustrate, first how a typical group may be built up, and second how this may indeed reflect and illuminate the inner structure of a known Browning concern. Take history. 'His wonderful store of information might really be compared to an inexhaustible mine. It comprised not merely a thoroughly scholastic outline of the world, but the critical points of ancient and modern history, the lore of the middle ages, all political combinations of parties, their description and consequences; and especially the lives of poets and painters, concerning whom he ever had to communicate some interesting anecdote not generally known.'[1] This description—no, it's not Browning—suggests, in its minute congruence with accounts of Browning's tastes and conversation, how truly that extraordinary bibliophile his father had been 'the source from which the Poet derived some of his most remarkable characteristics', for it depicts in fact the elder Mr Browning. And how was a taste so eloquently mutual dupli-

[1] Reuben Browning, quoted Griffin and Minchin, *Life*, 1910, 8.

cated in the library? Visibly enough: each of the categories listed above is prominently displayed there, as 'the critical points of ancient and modern history' in thirteen books of general history, 'all political combinations of parties' in four specifically political works, 'the lives of poets and painters' explicitly only in Vasari's *Lives*—but this supported on the one hand by six other books on painting, and on the other by eleven other biographical works, attesting a more diffused interest in biography which subsumes this particular facet. 'In short, he was a living encyclopaedia', Browning I mean, before he even began to write.[1]

If we call this aggregate 'history' we soon find, on looking at Browning's work, how powerfully this specimen of early reading had stamped his mind. For after Mill's critique of *Pauline* for its 'morbid self-consciousness',[2] the next work, *Paracelsus*, is embellished with learned historical notes (was Browning influenced by his father's habit of pasting extra pages into his books for notes and queries?) which go to the length of declaring 'the liberties I have taken with my subject' to be 'very slight'(!)—a scholarly objectivity that was to be sustained right up to *The Ring and the Book* in, most explicitly, *Strafford* (Browning is even rumoured to have helped Forster with his prose history on the same subject), and *King Victor and King Charles*, with its elaborate historical preface. *Sordello* seems to ratify this cultivation of the historian's territory; but a change of emphasis is signalled by Browning's warning of 1862 that 'the historical decoration was purposely of no more importance than a background requires; and my stress lay on the incidents in the development of a soul: little else is worth study.' DeVane rightly points out that at one stage at least, 'the wars of the Guelfs and Ghibellins about Ferrara . . . were of immense interest to Browning and almost bury Sordello from our sight,'[3] but Browning's comment, retrospective though it is, finds support from the very first lines of the poem:

> *Who will may hear Sordello's story told.*
> *His* story? *Who believes me shall behold*
> *The* man . . .

> (*Sordello*, I, 1–3)

[1] Sale Catalogue (see p. 7, n 1), 9.
[2] In an unpublished review, quoted DeVane, *Handbook*.
[3] DeVane, *Handbook*.

Biography, so prominent in the library, is asserting itself; and we know
that the ensuing tension was resolved, in the dramatic monologue,
towards what was indeed a biographical genre, history intercepted in the
souls of its protagonists. An 1855 reviewer, pointing out how advant-
ageously in the dramatic monologue 'a single object is exhibited, disen-
tangled from all others, concentrated in time, and painted on a plain
surface, instead of puzzling the eye with perspective illusions of solid
bodies,'[1] and Ruskin, saying of 'The Bishop Orders his Tomb', 'I know of
no other piece of modern English, prose or poetry, in which there is so
much told, as in these lines, of the Renaissance spirit,'[2] were simply con-
curring, as Browning had, in the thinking represented in Dr Johnson's
insistence that 'no species of writing seems more worthy of cultivation
than biography' because 'the general and rapid narratives of history,
which involve a thousand fortunes in the business of a day, and compli-
cate innumerable incidents in one transaction, afford few lessons applicable to private life' while biography 'is, of the various kinds of narrative
writing, that which is most eagerly read, and most easily applied to the
purposes of life.'[3] Hohenstiel-Schwangau contrasts 'history and falsehood' with the 'ineffective truth' of his own 'autobiography': history is a
record of doings, the 'outside-frame' where actions speak louder than
words or thoughts; the 'inside-archway', Hohenstiel-Schwangau's
'ghostly dialogue within the soul, is Browning's arena where, as he said
of *Luria*, 'all the events (and interest) take place in the *minds* of the
actors.'[4] The thrust, for Johnson, is a humanistic one: 'I have often
thought that there has scarce passed a life of which a judicious and faithful narrative would not be useful . . .' For Browning, musing on the
palace-steps in Venice, this became an urgent requisition of the
poet-historian's faculty as recording-instrument for the small life, the
long-forgotten person.

But haven't we been here before? This looks very like a repetition of
the old module, with history providing, this time, a *positive* alternative to
the 'morbid self-consciousness' of the Romantic. Yes, I think Browning
saw history in these terms: as a field for the anti-Romantic enterprise, a
methodology for the humbled genius, and I would emphasize that word

[1] R. Simpson, *The Rambler*, January 1856, V, 54–71.
[2] John Ruskin, *Modern Painters*, 1856, IV, 380.
[3] Samuel Johnson, *Rambler*, 60.
[4] *Letters*, I 395.

'methodology', for I believe that the library worked for Browning not by providing material so much as techniques, structures, genres, having in common this quality of factuality/human involvement. There is a corresponding dearth of purely imaginative literature: instead we find history, and satire, and encyclopaedias, and books of anecdote: all of which, I hope to show, promote methodological variants in Browning's formal strategy, and all of which affiliate those variants to fact rather than fancy, the humanistic student of life rather than the febrile Poet.

But if the library propounds the same module as the *Parleyings*, can we not, now, begin to see how the two connect up, how, perhaps, the poem can indeed operate as an index for the books? We can. We can see how Bartoli, however insignificant as a direct agent in Browning's development, acts as a *headline* for Browning's life-long article on history; and how each of the other parleyings similarly singles out some methodological opponent to the Romantic afflatus. Mandeville, I think, stands for satire (Guido's tremendous social satire in his second monologue employs the idea and method of *Fable of the Bees*). He also—an odd but significant relation—stands for *casuistry*: Griffin and Minchin surmised that Mandeville's *Vindications* of his position 'were not without influence upon the evolution of his own later defences of a Blougram or a Sludge . . .'[1] More explicitly representative of this category is Dodington, the eighteenth-century political trickster, contemplation of whose *Diary* affords some interesting insights into Browning's techniques. The editor's introduction to the diary, like the openings of *Sludge* and *Hohenstiel-Schwangau*, discover the protagonist in a compromised posture; and thereafter we are invited to inspect the pressure of his villainy on the subsequent discourse, constant in its practice of equivalent verbal fraud. Typical in the diary is a rhetorical manipulation designed to elicit some precalculated response: 'This, as I knew it would, fired him . . .' (*Diary* p. 45), 'Having extorted this confession, as a mark to remember this part of the conversation by, I left it there' (p. 26), reminiscent of revealing asides in *The Ring and the Book*: '(The right man, and I hold him!)' (Half-Rome, 16), '(That's for the Cardinal, and told, I think!)', and, worst of all, '(You'll see I have not so advanced myself/After my teaching the two idiots here!)' (Tertium Quid 1414, 1638–40). This impinges also on the characteristic manoeuvres of Browning's subtler casuists, comparably preoccupied with effect rather than truth (*cf.* Blougram's reflecting 'On

[1] *Life*, 19.

the whole I justify myself, rather than 'On the whole *I am right*')—and the slant of the monologue towards a localized auditor encourages this sense of an underlying—and undercutting—calculation: which, like Dodington's disingenuousness, we can judge, being at right angles to the rhetorical thrust, unpressured and unimpressed. The ironic purpose with which Dodington's editor published Dodington's diary is transacted, less openly but no less insistently, by Browning's brutal liberality with his speakers' self-hoisting petard.

I could go on, but I hope that the main point is now sufficiently clear: that Browning elicited from his early reading priorities and techniques for his post-Romantic works, which he eventually recorded in *Parleyings*. The dominant feature of all these was their obstinate refusal of imaginative transformation of 'things as they are'; each tackled, and helped to solve, the problem of constructing a non-imaginative aesthetic, a poetry of statement and fact. And all are found freely at work in the epic of that aesthetic, *The Ring and the Book*, where the imagination is seen as no more than a catalyst, the alloy which 'flies off in fume' after processing 'pure crude fact' into a manageable ring—history everywhere (and its importance is signalled by the opening of the Pope's monologue); satire in Tertium Quid, casuistry in the lawyers and Guido—oh, and everywhere, all these, intricately deployed to consummate Browning's self-denying ethic.

3

It seems odd that after such a triumph Browning should have expressed the reservations he did in a letter to Julia Wedgwood: 'The business has been to explain *fact*—and fact is what you see . . . *Before I die, I hope to purely invent something*,—here my pride was concerned to invent nothing . . .'[1] (my italics).

And when a later friend, Mrs Fitzgerald, taking, as it were, the permission to 'slip the foregoing scenes between the leaves of any memoir of Paracelsus' as a general licence to check the facts of later poems, asked him for a few notes on *Jochanan Hakkadosh*, he was strangely incensed: 'the poem *tells* you *who* he was, what he was, when he lived, and why he was about to die: what more do you want . . . all the other stories are told at just enough length as is requisite for the purpose, and years of

---

[1] *Wedgwood Letters*, letter of 19 November 1868.

study of dictionaries and the like would make the student learned enough in another direction but not one bit more in the limited direction of the poem itself. I say all this because you imagine that with more learning you would "understand" more about my poetry—as if you would somewhere find it already written—only waiting to be translated into English and my verses: whereas I should consider such an use of learning to be absolutely contemptible: for poetry, if it is to deserve the name, ought to create—or re-animate something,—not merely reproduce *now* fact taken from somebody else's book.' (17 March, 1883) Why this volte-face?

'All genius,' Browning remarked apropos Chatterton's forgeries, 'almost invariably begins to develop itself by imitation. It has, in the short-sightedness of infancy, faith in the world: and its object is to compete with, or prove superior to, the world's already-recognized idols, at their own performances and by their own methods.'[1] Sordello's first triumph was of this kind:

> *A man*
> *Recounted an adventure, but began*
> *Imperfectly; his own task was to fill*
> *The frame-work up, sing well what he sung ill*
>
> (*Sordello*, 129–32)

by

> *Taking the other's names and time and place*
> *For his . . .*
>
> (83–4)

*Pauline* shows this to be autobiographical: as a poetic novice, Browning

> *rather sought*
> *To rival what I wondered at than form*
> *Creations of my own*
>
> (*Pauline*, 390–2)

so he

[1] Donald Smalley, *Browning's Essay on Chatterton*, 1948.

> *turned to those old times and scenes where all*
> *That's beautiful had birth for me, and made*
> *Rude verses on them all . . .*
> (380–2)

But, the *Essay on Chatterton* goes on, Genius proceeds to develop 'faith in itself; and, no longer taking the performance and method of another for granted, it supersedes them by processes of its own. It creates, and imitates no longer.' This is, of course, something of a critical commonplace: Dr Johnson, remarking 'no man ever became great by imitation,' everywhere extols the merits of invention; EBB agrees:

> *And so, like most young poets, in a flush*
> *Of individual life I poured myself*
> *Along the veins of others, and achieved*
> *Mere lifeless imitations of live verse . . .*      (*Aurora Leigh*, II)

and it achieves its most intransigent form in another letter to Mrs Fitzgerald: 'Does not all mediocrity (educated mediocrity) come of a beginner's determining to look at the world through the eyes of his predecessors who assuredly began by looking for themselves?' (9 September, 1880) '. . . as a poet,' he repeated on 24 March, 1883, 'I do not let my imagination lie so idle as to versify what others have already invented', i.e. 'poetry, if it is to deserve the name, ought to create—or reanimate something—not merely reproduce *now* fact taken from someone else's book.'

What is odd is Browning's employing an argument based on purely formal and stylistic criteria—imitation in this phase being, like Chatterton's, literary—in the context of his *historicism*. It rather looks as though imitation means rather more to him than it did to Dr Johnson; and indeed, looking back to Sordello's imitation, we observe that the imitative act involved appropriating not only Eglamor's *techniques*, but also his 'names and times and place', i.e. the historical/biographical locus of his poem. Similarly, when Browning 'sought/To rival what I wondered at,' he 'turned *to those old times and scenes*'—a proceeding which requires only minor extension to implicate *history itself* as a 'frame-work' to be filled up in the same way. And in *The Ring and the Book*, Man

> *May so project his surplusage of soul*
> *In search of body, so add self to self*
> *By owning what lay ownerless before,—*

> *So find, so fill full, so appropriate forms—*
> *That, although nothing which had never life*
> *Shall get life from him, be, not having been,*
> *Yet something dead may get to live again,*
> *Something with too much life, or not enough,*
> *Which, either way imperfect, ended once:*
> *An end whereat man's impulse intervenes,*
> *Makes new beginning, starts the dead alive,*
> *Completes the incomplete and saves the thing.*
>
> (I, 723–34)

'I poured myself/Along the veins of others', in other words: history is imitation.

Satire, too, is imitation, as emerges very clearly from 'The Glove', where Browning appropriates 'names and time and place' in order to ridicule and rectify Leigh Hunt's morality in 'The Glove and the Lions'. Parodic technique—the 'imitation' of a verbal texture—is in order, for where Hunt wrote 'No love, quoth he, but vanity, set love a task like that,' Browning sarcastically substitutes, '"twas mere vanity,/Not love, set that task to humanity!' debagging King Francis's pontification in accordance with his own interpretation. This is a common device in his work. 'Rabbi ben Ezra', for instance, has been shown to be an exact inverse parallel of Fitzgerald's 'Rubaiyat':[1] *Fifine* is made out, by different critics, to be based on Shelley's *Epipsychidion* and Rossetti's *Jenny*[2] (it also 'corrects' Molière): Browning seems to have found the disposal of his own ideas easiest in someone else's mould, with, in these cases, the satirist's negative charge. It seems probable that he learned this skill from his father's favourite, Pope, who similarly relies on a deadly mimetic aptitude as his principal satiric weapon (and was cited by Johnson as the principal exponent of 'imitation').

The next step, seen in poems like 'Waring', 'Bishop Blougram', 'Sludge', 'Prince Hohenstiel-Schwangau' and may others, is the adoption of some contemporary's mind/life-style as the satiric object, making casuistry in turn a form of imitation, as we have seen it to be a form of satire. In brief, *all* of Browning's post-Romantic strategies are imitation, with the term redefined to incorporate *any* dealings of the part

[1] E. L. Cary, *Browning*, 1889, 129.

[2] See DeVane, *Handbook*.

of the poem with antecedent or current reality. Now we can understand his dissatisfaction with the *Ring and the Book*. This work, which I have shown to 'consummate Browning's self-denying ethic', conforms to a model which, being imitation, had to be superseded by invention: his annoyance with Mrs Fitzgerald arose from her tying him to the role of 'biographer or historian' when he wanted to *create*.

But this is precisely the reverse of the normal module! Hitherto, we have always seen invention—the Romantic 'self-sufficing central light'—superseded by imitation,—the poet 'pouring himself along the veins of others' in the redemptive act of sympathetic self-extension. The simplest way to explain this is by saying that imitation, in Browning's vocabulary, represents the activity of the 'objective poet', 'whose endeavour has been to *reproduce things external*' (my italics) '(whether the phenomena of the scenic universe, or the manifested action of the human heart and brain)' and who 'chooses to deal with the doings of men'—while invention is the mark of the 'subjective poet' who, 'impelled to embody the thing he perceives, not so much with reference to the many below as to the one above him,' 'digs where he stands' in search of 'not what man sees, but what God sees.'[1] And these in turn stand for his own Romantic and anti-Romantic phases, syllogistically making invention Romantic and imitation post-Romantic; the point being that the objective poet's imitation is, at certain stages of Browning's career, subordinated to the subjective poet who *as a Romantic* had already been discarded. True, he had, after *Sordello*, depicted 'the manifested action of the human heart and brain' first—crudely—in drama, then in refined transposition to the inner stage of the dramatic monologue; but in 1845 we find him remarking apropos these very works, 'You speak out, *you*,—I make men and women speak, give you truth broken into prismatic hues, and fear the pure white light, even if it is in me'[2] and proposing the exposure of his own 'pure white light' in a project which was to become *Christmas Eve and Easter Day* (1850). This preference is echoed in the *Essay on Shelley*'s (1852) insistence that the subjective 'must seem the ultimate requirement of every age.' Browning still believed that 'Time's completed plan' was 'nobler prize' than the 'many secrets' of a limited world.

But 'when you have your men and women aforesaid, you are busied

[1] *Essay on Shelley*, 1852.

[2] *Love-Letters*, 6.

with them, whereas it seems bleak melancholy work, this talking to the wind.'[1] Browning had a chronic difficulty in envisaging what the subjective poet could write *about* (apart from himself, which, as we have seen, he must not): it looks perilously like 'the nakedness and nullity of air' when compared to Aprile's glowing programme:

> common life, its wants
> *And ways would I set forth in beauteous hues:*
> *The lowest kind should not possess a hope,*
> *A fear, but I'd be by him, saying better*
> *Than he his own heart's language. I would live*
> *Forever in the thoughts I thus explored . . .*
>
> (*Paracelsus*, II, 556–61)

and Juan, like Hohenstiel-Schwangau, annexes this humanism to renewed anti-Romantic polemic:

> to get
> *Acquaintance with the way o' the world, we must nor fret*
> *Nor fume, on altitudes of self-sufficiency,*
> *But bid a frank farewell to what—we think—should be,*
> *And, with as good a grace, welcome what is—we find.*
>
> (*Fifine*, 1880–4)

echoing EBB's distinction

> he overfull
> *Of what is, and I, haply, overbold*
> *For what might be . . .*
>
> (*Aurora Leigh*, II)

but reversing her attitude and his own earlier acceptance of it.

There can be no doubt that his wife represented for Browning a renewed and urgent version of Romantic subjectivity; and the result, in works written after her death, was that this can assume a female form, notably in the figure of Balaustion: to whom Browning opposes Aristophanes, who, in a remarkable conflation of history, humanism and satire recapitulating the modes of imitation, demolishes the subjective poet's enterprise.[2] As Browning does: in a letter of 1845, EBB had asked him if he could not see that she, in 'this seclusion' was 'in a manner, as a Blind

---

[1] *Ibid.* 24.
[2] See *Aristophanes Apology*, 1875.

poet?'[1]—the shortcomings of Lairesse, Thamuris, and Homer, all blind, perhaps extend this implicit critique.

Rather than ramifying an already intricate dialectic, I would like to show its bearing on my argument. The point is that whereas to Dr Johnson, propounding an ultimately harmonious aesthetic, imitation and invention are simple and potentially fusible constituents of the poet's make-up, for Browning they are components of a fatal dualism and irrevocably forked apart. When Paracelsus declares

> *I saw no use in the past: only a scene*
> *Of degradation, ugliness and tears,*
> *The record of disgraces best forgotten,*
> *A sullen page in human chronicles*
> *Fit to erase,*

(V, 812–16)

he is both echoing a commonplace Romantic self-sufficiency and opposing this to *all* past informations, to history in fact, and not just history but the 'barren leaves' of all existing literature. Festus makes the mistake of believing that his 'truth' can notwithstanding be devoted to an anterior object:

> *Call this, truth—*
> *Why not pursue it in a fast retreat,*
> *Some one of learning's many palaces,*
> *After approved example?—seeking there*
> *Calm converse with the great dead, soul to soul,*
> *Who laid up treasure with the like intent*
> *—So lift yourself into their airy place,*
> *So fill out full their unfulfilled careers . . .*

(I, 382–9)

and to note how accurately this corresponds to Browning's own aims in *The Ring and the Book* is to see the divisiveness busy, for in 'Cleon', 'The Last Ride Together', 'Sibrandus Schafnaburgensis' and perhaps 'The Grammarian's Funeral' he was to ridicule these. The very act of seeking, in history, the extant world, or in books, formal, stylistic, or life-stylistic models, was a fundamental betrayal of the exclusivist Romantic mission.

---

[1] *Letters*, 20 March 1845.

> *To need become all natures, yet retain*
> *The law of my own nature, to remain*
> *Myself, yet yearn . . .*
>
> (*Sordello*, III, 39–41)

It is obviously desirable that subjective and objective, imitation and invention, Romantic and Victorian, should somehow be combined. But Browning had no idea how to set about this. He could only insist, in the *Essay on Shelley*, that they will forever succeed each other in endless antithetical oscillation: the best we can hope for is that 'these two modes of poetic faculty' may 'issue hereafter from the same poet in successive perfect works', as its title declared to be the aim of *Bells and Pomegranates*.

Yet 'You have in your vision two worlds, or to use the language of the schools of the day, you are both subjective and objective in the habits of your mind. You can deal with both abstract thought and human passion in the most passionate sense,'[1] EBB told him. And 'in one sense the most subjective of poets, in another he ranks among the most objective, he identifies himself with those he portrays; hidden behind these, we can scarcely catch a glimpse of him. But it is not their outward bearing that he chiefly reveals; he rather unveils the hidden centres from which all action must spring.'[2] That is by rendering the *subjectivity* of *someone else* the dramatic monologue implicitly blend the two genres. In his second essay on biography, Johnson finds its apotheosis in *autobiography* because 'The writer of his own life has at least the first qualification of a historian, the knowledge of the truth . . .'[3] and in the dramatic monologue we confront the defiant irony that the pursuit of an ultimate historical veracity, a perfect objectivity, lands us squarely in the chamber of the consciousness! It is not perhaps surprising that so large a part of Browning's library consists of autobiography, memoir and epistle,—all forms which promote this subjective/objective conflation.

Browning perhaps perceived the possibility of this synthesis: Aprile, after a salute to the 'first' place of the subjective poet, delineates his own humbler enterprise, but adds

> *Nor this*
> *Would need a meaner spirit than the first:*

[1] *Letters*, 15 January 1845.
[2] *London Quarterly Review*, 1864.
[3] Johnson, 'On Biography', *Idler*.

> *Nay, 'twould be but the self-same spirit, clothed*
> *In humbler guise, but still the self-same spirit . . .*
>
> (*Paracelsus*, II, 566–9)

and in *The Ring and the Book* we see how. 'In the beginning God made
heaven and earth', so Man, repeating God's process in man's due degree,
'Creates, no, but resuscitates, perhaps . . .'—an operation premising the
prior and current entity of the external world—and projects his surplus-
age of soul 'in search of body' to imitate 'by owning what lay ownerless
before' 'something dead' which thus 'may get to live again.' He may

> *So find, so fill full, so appropriate forms . . .*

but note, in the midst of this apparent objectivity, an ingenious transition: through history, yes, the poet can 'find' an external referent, and in
biography 'fill full' what he finds; but the last act, to 'appropriate' it, cuts
it away from its objective source and invests it with an inviolable subjectivity. This would account for his coyness to Mrs Fitzgerald about the
'source' of his poem: the process of edging along the axis from objective
to subjective finishes up with a special creation, derived from the world
but no longer of it. 'I undoubtedly had Wordsworth in my mind,'
Browning relevantly remarked of 'The Lost Leader', 'but simply as a
"model"; you know an artist takes one or two striking traits in the features of his "model", and uses them to start his fancy on a flight which
may end far enough from the good man or woman who happened to be
"sitting" for nose and eye . . . once call my fancy-portrait *Wordsworth*
—and how much more ought one to say,—how much more would I not
have attempted to say.'[1] 'A miracle happens: from the lucky conjunction
of a Persian astronomer who ventures into poetry and an English eccentric who explores Spanish and Oriental texts without understanding
them entirely, emerges an extraordinary poet who resembles neither of
them.' These words, used by Borges to illuminate 'The Enigma of
Edward Fitzgerald', illustrate a parallel reciprocity. We know of course
that *The Rubaiyat* is a translation; but we are not to question its accuracy
as such, since to do so will fracture the fragile oneness of the product.
'Sordello's story' participates in the dead text of history: 'the man' is the
'extraordinary poet' precipitated from the encounter between this and
Browning.

[1] Letter to Miss Lee, 1875.

But the mutual hostility of the components is not so easily fooled. At the beginning of *Sordello* we read this:

> *Then, appear,*
> *Verona! stay—thou, spirit, come not near*
> *Now—not this time desert thy cloudy place*
> *To scare me, thus employed, with that pure face!*
>
> (I, 59–62)

The 'spirit' is Shelley: reading this, we realize that the subjective poet can never condone any adulteration of his song. It is he who dubs this 'imitation'. It is he who, comprehending (as Browning does), history, satire, science and the rest in that word, damns its practitioner's dereliction of duty. Yet the objective poet has a comeback:

> *so, Sludge lies!*
> *Why, he's at worst your poet who sings how Greeks*
> *That never were, in Troy that never was,*
> *Did this or the other impossible great thing!*
>
> (*Mr Sludge*, 1435–38)

to the true objectivist, poetry is 'make-believe', 'white lies', and poets are 'impostors, drivellers, dotards' as Wordsworth imagines 'the ape Philosophy' calling them.

Neither side is content, then: and the double failure of this synthesis spawns its own black synthesis in what I call the 'debased occult', the figure of the compromised fraud who either practises impure magic or pretends to non-existent magical powers or both.

I find no fewer than five books dealing with the occult in Browning's library, and it figures largely in the books of anecdote. In Wanley's *Wonders of the Little World*, for instance, Browning came across Cornelius Aggrippa, from whose works he gleaned the portentous preface to *Pauline*. Paracelsus, Aggrippa's friend and brother sorcerer, was Browning's second hero, who likewise claimed to raise the dead; and the opening of the third poem, *Sordello* portrays—betrays?—*Browning* in the same posture—or imposture?—of resurrection:

> *Confess now, poets know the dragnet's trick,*
> *Catching the dead, if fate deny the quick . . .*
>
> (I, 35–6)

The persistence of this personification, and a persistent guilt attaching to it, are both glimpsed in *The Ring and the Book* when Browning, after the passage I have already quoted, goes on to compare his 'resuscitation' to the activities of a certain 'Mage', who 'by a special gift, an art of arts' can send 'half of my soul' 'O'er old unwandered waste ways of the world', where it

> '*May chance upon some fragment of a whole,*
> '*Rag of flesh, scrap of bone in dim disuse,*'
>
> (*The Ring and the Book*, I, 752–3)

which it enters, 'spark-like', and, by the practice of dire powers, leads out

> '*(By a moonrise through a ruin of a crypt)*
> '*What shall be mistily seen, murmuringly heard,*
> '*Mistakenly felt: then write my name with Faust's!*'
>
> (757–9)

'Mage' was Browning's word for the *poet* John in 'Transcendentalism'; and the source for this Sorcery is to be found in Wanley's account of the activities of—Aggrippa. Poetry ('which ought to create—or *re-animate* something') is the debased occult.

Or alternatively, a pack of lies. Sludge likewise professes to call up the dead, and, admitting that this is an imposture, compares and confounds all the claims of poetic language. The pattern here is of a protagonist who pretends to a God-given insight, and it runs from Djabal—who in *The Return of the Druses* pretends to be 'God Hakeem'—through Sludge to Disraeli, who in the parleying with Dodington is represented as a dark charlatan exploiting 'Man's despot, the supernatural' by an adroit adjustment of words and actions to imply occult powers. Even Blougram cannot wholly refute the accusation of having manipulated a supernatural sanction in which he does not wholly believe.

This uneasy sense of a fraud in the fiction-making process, a black magic of the imagination itself, must account for Browning's preoccupation with *forgery*. 'The first book I ever bought in my life was Ossian, . . .'[1] he wrote to EBB; and the first prose work you wrote, she might have replied, was an essay on Chatterton. And this, significantly parallel to the *Essay on Shelley*, makes it clear that the 'marvellous boy' was for Brown-

[1] *Letters*, 25 August 1846.

ing a 'subjective' poet who from modesty or shame or deceitfulness chose an artifice to ingratiate his muse: 'The first communication, . . . is sure to be "the work of a friend", if not "something extracted from a magazine", or "Englished from the German". So is the way gracefully facilitated for Reader and Hearer finding themselves in a new position with respect to each other.' In Chatterton's case, it was 'an old manuscript I found', and Rowley the medieval monk was born, and with him, seductively, an entire idiom and technique and best of all an *authority*: 'If only a foreign word clung to his vocabulary, he is sure to reproduce it as if a whole language lay behind, setting to work sometimes with the poorest materials . . .' Browning affirms that 'what *is* poetry, whether old or new, will have its full flow in such a scheme; and any difficulty or uncouthness of phrase which elsewhere would stop its course at once, here not only passes with it, but confers the advantage of *authenticity* on what, in other circumstances, it deforms: the uncouthness will be set down to our time, and whatever significancy may lurk in it will expand to an original meaning of unlimited magnitude.'

Browning's quest for objective authority, as his praise implies, took a similar form. He too put 'my whole pride, if that is the proper name, in the being able to work with the poorest possible materials'[1], he too erected *personae* to mouth his message, and he too is 'sure to reproduce' a foreign or antique word 'as if a whole language lay behind.' It is almost comic to see him, in 'Childe Roland', uncritically adopting Chatterton's 'slug-horn' as the instrument of Roland's challenge—Chatterton in turn had misunderstood a word which in fact means 'slogan'. Browning loved to snatch words out of dictionaries in this impetuous manner to encrust his utterance with archaic dignities: notoriously in the use of the word 'twat', an obscenity he innocently supposed to signify a nun's wimple! Seriously though, he did in fact follow Chatterton's example in creating a special idiom, a 'no language' promiscuously culled from Shakespeare, Spenser and Chaucer. When Blougram says, 'Another glass for me, though; cool, i' faith!' we cannot hear a real voice: it is 'a composition of the mixed sort . . . which, retaining what he supposed the ancient garb should also include every modern refinement.'[2] As a result, 'There is such a thing as an efficacious knowledge of and belief in the politics of Junius or the poetry of Rowley, though a man should at the same time

[1] *Letters.*
[2] *Essay on Chatterton* (see p. 17, n 1).

dispute the title of Chatterton to one, and consider the other, as Byron wittily did, "really, truly, nobody at all" '[1] The text is its own truth, independent of either the world or the personality of the writer.

But it is a fraud. 'I found a vile dissertation of Laing . . . all to prove Ossian was not Ossian . . . I would not read it, but could not help knowing the purpose of it, and the pith of the hatefully-irresistible arguments. [2] The glowing vision of a textual reality, freely inventing itself as it goes, is subject, like other Romantic visions, to experiential questioning. Even the Homeric text, cherished by the young Browning as a Bible, crumbles: there was

> *No actual Homer, no authentic text,*
> *No warrant for the fiction I, as fact,*
> *Had treasured in my heart and soul so long . . .*
>
> ('Development' (*Asolando*), 71–3)

and Browning correspondingly questions his own fiction in the anxious reiteration, at the beginning of *Sordello*—'Only believe me; ye believe? . . .' No: the ending of *Sordello* is pure invention and Jochanan Hakkadosh, like Junius, is—'why, *nobody*'. There was, perhaps, something prophetic about Browning's 'first composition' of 'something in *imitation* of Ossian, whom I had not read, but *conceived*, through two or three scraps in other books.'[3] The Romantic assumption was ultimately that language can propose its own truth: the very assumption of the forger premises its vacuity.

And it doesn't work. '. . . it is part of our proof to show that his'—Chatterton's—'distress arose out of the impossibility of saying anything to the real purpose.' Rowley being a fiction, Chatterton's poems labour under the double handicap of being, like Browning's Ossianaic imitations, the fiction of a fiction, penumbra of a fraudulent text, emanation of nothing but itself, written by 'really, truly, nobody at all.' 'There was the sense of his being the author of the transcendent chorus to freedom, or the delicious roundelay in Ella; ever at fierce variance with the pitiful claim he was entitled to make in the character of their mere transcriber.' This is the *cri de coeur* of the subjective/objective synthesis, for 'in our approach to the poetry' of the true, pure subjective

[1] *Essay on Shelley* (see p. 20, n 1).

[2] *Ibid.*

[3] *Ibid.*

poet, 'we necessarily approach the personality of the poet,'[1] as now we cannot.

> *Sludge acts Macbeth, obliged to be Macbeth,*
> *Or you'll not hear his first word!*

(651–2)

'Why haven't I leave to play tricks, Sludge as Sludge?'—or Chatterton as Chatterton: but no, they must be Lippi, Rowley, Macbeth, ventriloquizing something that could only have its full meaning in their own mouths through a puppet outraged by the appropriation. So again

> *Sordello vanished utterly,*
> *Sundered in twain . . .*

(II, 656–7)

The oddest twist of all to this sad story is that the only way the poet can claim his poem is by *admitting* the forgery, giving bystanders a 'subintelligential nod and wink,' to tell them it's all baloney and therefore his own:

> *It's a history of the World, the Lizard Age,*
> *The Early Indians, the Old Country War,*
> *Jerome Napoleon, whatsoever you please,*
> *All as the author wants it. Such a scribe*
> *You pay and praise for putting life in stones,*
> *Fire into fog, making the past your world.*
> *There's plenty of 'How did you contrive to grasp*
> *'The thread which led you through this labyrinth?*
> *'How on so slight foundation found this tale,*
> *'Biography, narrative?' or, in other words,*
> *'How many lies did it require to make*
> *'This portly truth you here present us with?'*
> *'Oh,' quoth the penman, purring at your praise,*
> *' 'tis fancy all; no particle of fact:*
> *'I was poor and threadbare when I wrote that book*
> *' "Bliss in the Golden City." I at Thebes?*
> *'We writers paint out of our heads, you see!'*

(*Mr Sludge*, 1450–67)

---

[1] *Essay on Shelley.*

Or 'I sensed that Averroes, striving to imagine a drama without ever having suspected what a theatre was, was no more absurd than I, who strive to imagine Averroes with no other material than some fragments from Renan, Lane and Asin Palacios. I sensed, on the last page, that my narrative was a symbol of the man I was while I wrote it, and to write that story I had to be that man, and to be that man I had to write that story, and so to infinity (The instant I stop believing in him, 'Averroes' disappears)'

> Borges: *Averroes Search ( A Personal Anthology)*

### 4

After deprecating his Mage's practice of the debased occult, Browning goes on:

> *Oh Faust, why Faust? Was not Elisha once?*

and proceeds to authorize his own 'resuscitation' by citing the devout resurrection of a dead man by the prophet. In exploring the more positive ways in which Browning sought to establish an objective/subjective synthesis, let us first examine 'the Way, the Truth and the Life'.

This involves crossing, so to speak, from his father's shelf in the library to his mother's. Mrs Browning was deeply pious: I have hypothesized her instrumentality in Browning's initial revulsion from Romantic atheism; the intellectual format of her piety is contained in no less than eighteen seventeenth-century Puritan pamphlets, plus Bibles, works of Bible criticism, and much devotional poetry. By this means, she came to pervade her son's post-Romantic strategy: the 'selfishness' in *Pauline* is continually mitigated by

> *A need, a trust, a yearning after God . . .*

> (*Pauline*, 295)

his past self-worship being Satanic:

> > *as some temple seemed*
> *My soul, where nought is changed and incense rolls*
> *Around the altar, only God is gone,*
> *And some dark spirit sitteth in his seat.*

> (469–72)

By asking 'should my heart not worship too?' he shows he 'is evidently *dissatisfied.*' as Mill observed;[1] subsequently he explores—tentatively —various possible objects for this 'worship': Humanity, Andromeda, England are all passed in review, uselessly, for 'what is it that I hunger for but God?'

> *Why have I girt myself with this hell-dress?*
> *Why have I laboured to put out my life?*
> *Is it not in my nature to adore,*
> *And e'en for all my reason do I not*
> *Feel him, and thank him, and pray to him—now?*

(831–5)

In Christ he finds an imitable life-style:

> *oft have I stood by thee,*
> *Have I been keeping lonely watch with thee*
> *In the damp night by weeping Olivet,*
> *Or leaning on thy bosom, proudly less,*
> *Or dying with thee on the lonely cross,*
> *Or witnessing thine outburst from the tomb.*

(849–54)

'proudly less': in these words Browning expresses and resolves his need for an exterior object: in 'Saul', 'Cleon', 'Karshish' and other middle-period works he was to package religion into the single fact of the Incarnation, and employ this as the final cadence, transcendent apparition from without dissipating the defeats of self-worship.

In this sense, religion is 'objective', a matter of historical fact. But how can the individual spirit occupy that fact? Clearly Christ's birth, our fact, *was* revelation, and therefore vision and subjective truth; but to be that *now* it has to be acted out in the chamber of the individual consciousness. How?

'Johannes Agricola in Meditation', another early Browning poem, consists of the monologue of an 'antinomian', professor of the faith that to him to whom the identity of God's will has been disclosed, human laws are inapplicable: assured of his heavenly destination, he can afford to live it up on earth. One source for this figure was

---

[1] Unpublished review of *Pauline*: see Griffin and Minchin, 59–60.

probably the Ranters, the seventeenth-century sect Bunyan attacks in *Grace Abounding*, and let us note how abundantly Puritan Browning's religious background was: ten works of seventeenth-century poetry, chiefly Milton, appear in the library, alongside all those Puritan pamphlets with titles like 'A practical discourse of effective calling and perseverance', dogmatizing that 'inner light' and 'private reason' which so blatantly portend the Romantic 'self-sufficing central light'. In the Puritan mind-style—and indeed all extreme Protestant sects—Browning, like other Victorians, saw a version of Romantic vision which, being of and under God, avoided 'self-worship' with no sacrifice of intensity.

But 'Johannes' is a satire. Even at this early stage, religious ecstasy is comprehended in the mistrust of subjectivity, and looking ahead through the remainder of Browning's career, we see a sad dismantling of, in turn, religious vision. Smart's madness merely summarizes Browning's cumulative alarm: what this poet experienced may well have been the 'impingment' of the 'all-unapproachable' God, but this burned with a self-dissipating fierceness, and left the recipient a burnt-out case. 'I can see nothing that comes from absolute contact, so to speak, between God and man',[1] Browning had written to Julia Wedgwood: Smart closes the chapter of religious vision.

And unsustained by experience, religion shrinks into history, becoming, in the process, subject to historical/textual criticism. The Higher Criticism touched Browning on the raw precisely because it confirmed an existing dubiety: he had assembled a massive collection of different Bibles, learned Hebrew, gathered thirteen works of Bible criticism; all, one suspects, to try to filter out the pure white truth from these prismatic textual variant; a procedure very like that of the other great textual exploration, *The Ring and the Book*; and Browning may have gone into it with a similar confidence that

> *Truth, nowhere, lies yet everywhere in these—*
> *Not absolutely in a portion, yet*
> *Evolvible from the whole,*
>
> (*The Ring and the Book*, X, 228–30)

only similarly to learn

[1] *Ibid.* (see p. 16, n 1, letter of 2 September 1864).

> *This lesson, that our human speech is naught,*
> *Our human testimony false, our frame*
> *And human estimation words and wind.*

(XII, 834–6)

The dialectic implodes once more.

5

And so to music. This, Mrs Browning's other bequest to her son, is represented in the library almost solely by Charles Avison's *Essay on Musical Expression* (1752), yet this seems appropriate in a way, seeing that its author is given the climactic Parleying, and seeing, too, that it fulfilled, in my view, a vital role in Browning's development.

I believe that Avison's little monograph might have been Browning's first introduction to a Romantic interpretation of art. Indeed, the organist of Newcastle anticipates some of the major ideas of Johnson, Burke and Wordsworth: like Johnson he has perceived that aesthetic experience is 'a peculiar and internal sense; but of a more refined nature than the external senses . . .'[1] like Burke, he understands that 'the *terror* raised by *musical expression* is always of that grateful kind which arises from an impression of something terrible to the imagination, but which is immediately dissipated by a subsequent conviction that the danger is entirely imaginary',[2] and like Wordsworth he perceives that the basis of all art is *pleasure*, saying of 'Grief' that 'as it always has somthing of the social kind for its foundation, so is it often attended with a kind of sensation, which may with truth be called *pleasing*.' 'We have no sympathy,' claimed Wordsworth, 'but what is propagated by pleasure . . . wherever we sympathize with pain, it will be found that the sympathy is produced and carried on by subtle combinations with pleasure.'[3] Avison's attack on the frigid decorations of Italian neo-classicism, calling for 'an unaffected strain of nature and simplicity' as a purificatory programme, continue to remind us of Wordsworth.

The *Essay* could have been Browning's private 'Preface to the Lyrical Ballads'; and Avison's constant comparing of music to painting must have quickened Browning's sense that music could promote vision. For

[1] Cf. Johnson's discussion of the classical unities in *Preface to Shakespeare*.

[2] Cf. Edmund Burke's account of the 'sublime' in *Origin of our Ideas of the Sublime and Beautiful*, 1757.

[3] William Wordsworth, Preface to *Lyrical Ballads*, 1802.

this is what, stimulated by Avison's account, he sees it as doing: providing an external agency capable of promoting an internal ecstasy; and he makes, in the parleying, a consequent emphasis, not on Avison's 'March' (which he admits is 'thinnish') but on the pictures it gives rise to in his mind—the vision, if you like, it creates.

Avison's analysis transfers the artifact from cause to effect, from instrument to hearer, where it floats, as it were, within his tranforming apprehension. He even seems to have sensed that this was a generalizable speculation in adding 'how commanding the power of expression may be found, from a different manner of reading the same author; especially in poetry, where a just and spirited emphasis is so highly essential to point out those interesting strokes, which are peculiarly designed to delight the imagination and affect the heart.' As early as *Paracelsus*, Browning shows an awareness that the text can be *fact* to the reader's *fancy*: 'A work like mine,' he wrote in the Preface, 'depends upon the intelligence and sympathy of the reader for its success—indeed, were my scenes stars, it must be his co-operating fancy which, supplying all the chasms, shall collect the scattered lights into one constellation . . .' Note that 'intelligence and sympathy' were the virtues commended by Hohenstiel-Schwangau against the Romantic 'Bard': the 'stars' of subjective ecstasy must be so arranged as to admit the 'co-operating fancy' of the reader, whose facts they thus become. In *Fifine* this is said directly:

> Art is my evidence
> That something was, is, might be; but no more thing itself,
> Than flame is fuel. Once the verse-book laid on shelf,
> The picture turned to wall, the music fled from ear,—
> Each beauty, born of each, grows clearer and more clear,
> Mine henceforth, ever mine!
>
> (628–33)

and that music promoted this insight is attested by its efficacy as the agent of Juan's later dream: after playing 'Schumann's *Carnaval*' he dozes into a vision of the Carnival of this life; and as though to demonstrate that all had been put right by this synthesis, the vision is no Shelleyan 'vain /EUTOPIA seated in the brain', but a simply humanist paeon, 'a tune upon the blue guitar/Of things exactly as they are.' Similarly the shift in 'Avison' from 'March'—the season—to Avison's 'March' duplicates linguistically the musical fluidity in a sort of enharmonic modulation and induces an equivalent historic versatility, as Browning shoots through time back to the seventeenth century where Avison, rhymed to the physical Marching of Puritan feet, harmonizes music, religion, poetry and social reform into a tonic chord. Now, let the vision flow as it never had before:

> Sharps and flats
> Lavish at need, shall dance athwart thy score
> When ophicleide and bombardon's uproar
> Mate the approaching trample, even now
> Big in the distance—or my ears deceive—
> Of federated England, fitly weave
> March-music for the future!

(Avison, 383–9)

As nowhere else, the vision dares to claim its *social* extension, vindicated by the 'flat forthright persisting melody' its factual premise, celebrating the unique relation of performer to the tune he transforms.

A poem which attempts an even closer synthesis is 'Abt Vogler'. There, by extemporizing on 'the musical instrument of his invention', the protagonist is actually *creating what he hears*, his vision induced *by himself* via the external agency of the organ. This restoration of creative subjectivity is greeted by even wilder, more intransigent illuminations: Romantic, religious and musical visions are vibrantly fused in the Apocalypse, the New Jerusalem:

> But here is the finger of God, a flash of the will that can,
> Existent behind all laws, that made them and, lo, they are!
> And I know not, if, save in this, such gift be allowed to man,
> That out of three sounds he frames, not a fourth sound, but a star.

True, the ecstasy must be quitted:

> Well, it is gone at last, the palace of music I reared;

a due sobriety must be recovered;

> Well, it is earth with me . . .

But as in no other Browning version of Romantic vision, the visionary retains a fertile and stable relation with its fading anthem,

> *Surveying awhile the heights I rolled from to the deep*

conferring an unprecedented *confidence*:

> *The rest may reason and welcome: 'tis we musicians know.*

Of course, both Browning and Avison are deeply indebted to classical and Renaissance theories of the sublimity of music. In *The Merchant of Venice*, Shakespeare too is simply echoing a traditional sense of music as reflector of divine harmony:

> *Here will we sit, and let the sounds of music*
> *Creep in our ears . . .*
> *            . . . look how the floor of heaven*
> *Is thick inlaid with patines of bright gold:*
> *There's not the smallest orb that thou behold'st*
> *But in his motion like an angel sings*
> *Still quiring to the young-eyed cherubins,*
> *Such harmony is in immortal souls,*

Avison's view of the active as well as this descriptive power of music is comprised:

> *            . . . therefore the poet*
> *Did feign that Orpheus drew trees, stones and floods;*
> *Since naught so stockish, hard and full of rage,*
> *But music for the time doth change his nature.*

Clearly, Shakespeare exalts his own art in this description, and the Orphic poet was to become a commonplace of Romantic theory: 'If your delineation be authentically *musical*, musical not in word only, but in heart and substance, in all the thoughts and utterances of it, in the whole conception of it, then it will be poetical; if not, not . . .' Carlyle goes on, 'A *musical* thought is one spoken by a mind that has penetrated into the inmost heart of a thing; detected the inmost mystery of it, namely, the *melody* that lies hidden in it; the inmost harmony of coherence which is its soul, whereby it exists, and has a right to be, here in this world. All inmost things, we may say, are melodious: naturally utter themselves in song.[1] Browning, concerned with music like no other post-Shakespearean writer, also dallied with a melodic persona, declar-

[1] 'The Hero as Poet', *Heroes and Hero-Worship*, 1841.

ing, in 'Transcendentalism', 'Song's our art,' and depicting, in 'Thamuris Marching', a quite inspired version of the Orpheus legend, electrifying neutral reality:

> *And had the rooted plant aspired to range*
> *With the snake's license, while the insect yearned*
> *To glow fixed as the flower, it were not strange—*
>
> *No more than if the fluttery tree-top turned*
> *To actual music, sang itself aloft;*
> *Or if the wind, impassioned chantress, earned*
>
> *The right to soar embodied in some soft*
> *Fine form all fit for cloud-companionship*
> *And blissful, once touch beauty chased so oft.*
>
> *Thamuris, marching, let no fancy slip*
> *Born of the fiery transport; lyre and song*
> *Were his, to smite with hand and launch from lip—*
>
> (*Aristophanes Apology*, Con., 149–61)

Transported by heard melodies, the fond lover may kiss his marble maiden: 'there was no more near or far.' But even here, alas, Romantic hubris is perceived: Thamuris, rashly challenging the Muses, is destroyed, and

> *I have not spurned the common life,*
> *Nor vaunted mine a lyre to match the Muse*
> *Who sings for gods not men! Accordingly*
> *I shall not decorate her vestibule—*
> *Mute marble, blind the eyes and quenched the brain,*
> *Loose in the hand a bright, a broken lyre!*
>
> (*Aristophanes Apology*, Con., 182–7)

comments Aristophanes the humanist satirist (and note, again, the blindness associated with the self-worshipping state of subjectivity). And Browning too perhaps, for poetry 'is all teaching . . . and people hate to be taught. They say otherwise—make foolish fables about Orpheus enchanting stocks and stones, poets standing up and being worshipped,—all nonsense and impossible dreaming,' he wrote to Ruskin.[1] And with the discrediting of the creative musician, the entire house of

[1] 10 December 1855.

cards collapses:

> But if I would retrace
> Effect in Art to cause,——corroborate, erase
> What's right or wrong i' the lines, test fancy in my brain
> By fact which gave it birth?

(Fifine, 633–6)

queries Juan, subjecting the listener's subjective/objective synthesis to the positivist test,

> I re-peruse in vain
> The verse, I fail to find that vision of delight
> I' the Bazzi's lost-profile, eye-edge so exquisite.
> And music: what? that burst of pillared cloud by day
> And pillared fire by night, was product, must we say,
> of modulating just, by enharmonic change,——
> The augmented sixth resolved,——from out the straighter range
> Of D sharp minor,——leap of disemprisoned thrall,——
> Into thy light and life, D major natural?

(636–44)

Even the 'truest truth' of music, most persistent of all versions of revelation, fades with the rest into the light of common day.

### III   *The Didactic Resolution*

After his repudiation of Romanticism, Browning turned to early reading for positive alternatives and was able to evolve the 'prismatic' techniques of his mature oeuvre, history, satire, casuistry, etc. These he obliquely tabulates in *Parleyings*. But being—all the time, despite himself—a Romantic, he could not help projecting onto each a duplicate of his initial dualism; and being a Romantic, he could not help trying, secretly, to reconstitute, with their assistance, the subjective vision: which, being a Victorian, he had then to reject. Even the text itself, repository of all these modes, fell under suspicion, to question, in a self-immolating act of textual introspection, its own substance.

> *And then I heard a voice upon the slope*
> *Cry to the summit, 'Is there any hope?'*

> (Tennyson: *Vision of Sin*)

'One of the books he best and earliest loved was Quarles's *Emblemes*, which his father possessed in a seventeenth-century edition. . . . Its quaint powerful lines and still quainter illustrations *combined the marvellous with what he believed to be true.*'[1]

I

'An Emblem,' according to Quarles, 'is but a silent parable,' i.e. (according to *Bailey's Dictionary*) 'a painted enigma or representation of some moral notion by the way of device or picture.' Quarles's book is correspondingly based upon a series of quaint illustrations'—with, however, an *explanatory poem* alongside each 'enigma' (as had been the case with Elizabethan emblem-books); and it is this development which, I believe, mattered to Browning. For it sets up the polarization between an *image* which in Elizabethan terms represents an objective diagram of a universal truth, and an *explanation* which reduces this for the subjective apprehension of the reader. This 'subjectivity' in the text is accentuated by its tendency, in Quarles's hand, to take the form of an ironic monologue or short dramatic scene, in which the abstract truth represented by the enigma is particularized within the subjectivity of a protagonist. Some of these pieces could indeed be called dramatic monologues. Remove the picture, and one has 'The Bishop Orders his Tomb'—as indeed the first line of that poem, 'Vanity of vanities, saith the preacher, vanity of vanities!' could be called a sort of verbal enigma of which the remainder of the poem acts out the application.

Emblem, then, could and did represent a subjective/objective conflation; and its appeal to Browning is indicated by the presence in the library, besides Quarles, of an *Emblemata cum commentariis*, and other books containing emblematic plates. Browning's adaptation, like Donne's, involved transposing the scheme onto a purely linguistic plane: the metaphysical conceit is quite simply the systematic analogizing of a

[1] Orr, *Life*, 30.

*verbally* depicted abstract—'our two souls'—and a verbally enacted particular—'stiff twin compasses'; and 'revered and magisterial Donne' is
the most conspicuous influence on Browning's love-poetry.

Browning's 'conceit' took the form of what he called the 'instance'.
This resembles both conceit and its parent emblem in the adoption of an
analogizing mode for abstract truth: where it differs from them is in (1)
the circumstantial elaboration of the analogy and (2) the excision of the
initial abstract. Thus, Browning on the one hand developed a dense
machinery of detail in the analogy quite excessive to its purely illustrative efficiency, and on the other hand, in, as we have seen, the dramatic
monologue, removed the abstract premise altogether, leaving it to be
deduced from the meandering remainder.

He had precedents for both these tactics. In encrusting the analogy
with detail he was simply incorporating into it the *anecdotal* format of,
especially, Wanley's *Wonders*: there too some abstract quality, 'the great
goodness of some husbands to their wives,' receives illustrative representation, but the illustrations, being 'facts' affiliated to the real world, forfeit emblematic neatness for circumstantial veracity. Browning's
illustrations correspondingly extend themselves well beyond a purely
illustrative decorum.

This perhaps suggests an unwillingness to coerce reality into emblematic symmetry, which might also account for the next move of elimin-
ating any explicit emblematic reference. In order to understand how
Browning could see, say, a simple narrative in emblematic terms, it is
necessary to look at Lairesse's *Art of Painting*. This, too, turns out to be
emblematic: Lairesse explains that 'when I was under my father's instruction, and studying design, my chief gusto was for emblems' and
'Accordingly,' subjoins his editor, 'he pursued history, and its chief orna-
ment, emblematic learning . . .' But turning to the book itself, though
we do find emblematic plates (and Browning mentions 'the good I seem
to have got from the prints'), we frequently witness its 'wondrous text'
spilling quite out of the Quarlesian mould in such items as 'Innocense
surprised by Lewdness: an Emblem,' where, after searching in vain for a
picture, we find instead a protracted and circumstantial *narrative*.
Browning's debt to Lairesse turns on the latter's demonstration of how
emblem might be redefined as 'a moral fable or allegory such as might be
expressed pictorially.' Both 'The Statue and the Bust' and 'Gold Hair' fit
his category perfectly (especially the former, which first unweaves the

pictorial premise into its narratorial original, and then tells us that we have indeed been reading 'a moral fable').

I am saying that all Browning's techniques, analogy, narrative and dramatic monologue, are emblematic in the sense that they expound some anterior truth nowhere directly presented. But I do not mean that emblem-books are Browning's only source: this abstract/concrete, static /kinetic motif in fact pervades many of his other books which thus share the responsibility for prompting this manoeuvre. Very clearly related to emblem is Bunyan's *Pilgrim's Progress* (Bunyan also produced an emblem-book), where the relation between concrete narrative and explanatory marginalia enacts the emblematic split; and Ralegh's *History of the World* explicitly accommodates contemporary applications of its récits. And Wanley's *Wonders*, already affined, could, I think, have played a decisive role in shaping *The Ring and the Book*. That work, of course, displays emblem affinities in the initial Ring-figure; but the entire subsequent strategy of marshalling a series of independent and unselfconscious narrative strips to illustrate 'this lesson' that 'our human testimony (is) words and wind', echoes Wanley's disposition of his materials. A contributing variant of Wanley's method could have been Mandeville's *Fable*, which, in its final form, consisted of the original short poem, 'The Grumbling Hive' plus a stupendous aggregate of explanations, explorations, vindications, branching from that central premise.

But Wanley admits that 'some of these examples which I have set down seem utterly incredible, or at best but improbable . . .'; and Shaftesbury characterizes emblem as 'preposterous, disproportionate, gouty and lame forms. False *imitation*, *lies*, impotence, pretending. . . . *Magical*, mystical, monkish and Gothic emblems.' (my italics)[1] Suppose 'the ape Philosophy', enemy of all subjective/objective syntheses so far, should object that emblem too involved a lie? Would not the synthesis be split again?

2

To understand how, in this instance, Browning could slip the punch, and how the terms of his resolution influence earlier indecisions, let us examine 'Development' (*Asolando* 1889), his own description of his own literary childhood. We first see the child aimlessly playing. His Father (note

[1] Earl of Shaftesbury, *Characteristics*, 1711.

the capital) sets about recruiting these random energies by, in the first
instance, contriving an enactment of *The Iliad*. Next,

> *It happened, two or three years after wards,*
> *That—I and playmates playing at Troy's siege—*
> *My father came upon our make-believe.*
> *'How would you like to read yourself the tale*
> *Properly told, of which I gave you first*
> *Merely such notion as a boy could bear?*
> *Pope, now, would give you the precise account*
> *Of what, some day, by dint of scholarship,*
> *You'll hear—who knows?—from Homer's very mouth.'*
>
> ('Development' (*Asolando*), 24–32)

Browning is both introduced to the mediate idiom of Pope, and prospec-
tively seduced by the nicely-figured voluptuousness of the original:
'*tuphlos* which means "blind",/*Hedistos* which means "sweetest"'. And
he does learn Greek, and with it a mock-Gospel of 'facts' about Homer.
But

> *What's this the Germans say is fact*
> *That Wolf found out first? It's unpleasant work,*
> *Their chop and change, unsettling one's belief . . .*
>
> (63–5)

He finds there was

> *No actual Homer, no authentic text,*
> *No warrant for the fiction I, as fact,*
> *Had treasured in my heart and soul so long.*
>
> (71–3)

It is hard not to recognize here a final recapitulation of the dominant
module. The words 'fact', 'fiction', 'belief', 'authentic' all echo back over
Browning's career: the debate of *Dramatis Personae*, for example, is subsumed; but now, more relaxed, Browning can afford the tinge of farce
entailed in refashioning the dramatis personae into a pert lad and a
pedantic German. Yet the issue is grave enough: it implicates
Browning's own enterprise when we read in *Pauline* that his first efforts
derived from 'wisest ancient books'—clearly Homer, which furnished a
dream 'all halo-girt with fancies of my own.' It would be fair, I think, to

see the discrediting of Homer, and Renan's questioning of the existence of Christ, as reenactments of a formative dubiety, the polyseimic encroachment of 'shades of the prison-house' to spoil an Edenic dream, whether of God, Homer, or—can we say?—Shelley.

Its veracity discredited, the dream retains a kind of mythic efficacy, or at least 'Development' sets about claiming this; but it is not difficult to espy the misgivings of Browning's own inveterate objectivity in the wistfulness of '—ah, Wolf!' and the equivocality of 'No dream's worth waking.' He is really in an impasse. Now he involves the reader as a postulated speaker:

> *I, now mature man, you anticipate,*
> *May blame my father justifiably*
> *For letting me dream out my nonage thus . . .*

(86–8)

but this is where the shift begins, for via this voice which appears only to prolong his own defeated cogitations he effects the enharmonic rescue:

> *I might have—somehow—correspondingly—*
> *Well, who knows by what method, gained my gains,*
> *Been taught, by forthrights not meanderings,*
> *My aim should be to loathe, like Peleus' son,*
> *A lie as Hell's gate, love my wedded wife*
> *Like Hector, and so on with all the rest . . .*

(97–102)

The despondency of the rhetoric is diverted, Browning's oversimplification becoming ours whence he shifts to a new position where the dream —no matter if fact or fancy—is redeemed by virtue of its *didactic efficacy*. Factuality, it turns out, was never the issue, since *truth*, still its old Platonic self, must needs be realized in anecdote, instance or narrative, in order to be understood; and it is the poet's seraphic task to conduct the truth to our understanding *by any means*: these 'succeed if they bear the conception to you'[1]—and their success is, in a sense, their truth.

This, account implies, of course, that the Romantic vision really was truth all the time; and Hohenstiel-Schwangau shows how it is possible to quit the heights of self-sufficiency yet still acknowledge their sustained validity:

[1] *Ibid.* (see p. 37, n 1).

> *Did I believe one whit less in belief,*
> *Take truth for falsehood, wish the voice revoked*
> *That told the truth to heaven for earth to hear?*
>
> (*Hohenstiel-Schwangau*, 912–14)

No: the Romantic flaw is not its vision itself but the refusal to subject it to the didactic resolution, a reluctance or incompetence to translate it into bread and facts for 'those mute myriads':

> *Nature was made to be by Man enjoyed*
> *First; followed duly by enjoyment's fruit,*
> *Instruction . . .*
>
> ('Smart', 225–7)

Browning admonishes Smart. His fault is to 'please simply when your function is to rule—/By thought incite to deed . . .' He gives us the enigma without the explanation.

It is *this* module which dominates *Parleyings*. Carlyle exemplified

> *our mortal purblind way*
> *Of seeking in the symbol no mere point*
> *To guide our gaze through what were else inane,*
> *But things—their solid selves? 'Is, joint by joint,*
> *Orion man-like,—as these dots explain*
> *His constellation? Flesh composed of suns—*
> *How can such be?' exclaim the simple ones.*
> *Look through the sign to the thing signified . . .*
>
> ('Mandeville', 185–92)

Bartoli warningly illustrates the irresponsible application of this to history: which, too, offers a typology for contemporary edification, but being the doings of men, must not be transformed or invented—though why bother when Johnson's account so persuasively indicates how easily —as for Ralegh—a straight history yields us ample signification. Dodington ironically portrays the abuse of the didactic imperative:

> *You say 'Make shift*
> *By sham—the harsh word: preach and teach, persuade*
> *Somehow the Public—not despising aid*
> *Of salutary artifice—we seek*
> *Solely their good . . .*
>
> ('Dodington', 109–13)

'Furini' illustrates how emblem might have prompted this insight, for what Browning does is to take Furini's pictures as his enigma, an emblematic composite which he then expounds as he had the pictures of Lippi and Sarto (whose fundamentally didactic manipulation is glimpsed in Browning's insistence that these poems were written 'in order to get people to hear and see').

'Lairesse', I surmise, shows how the didactic redemption adapts the Romantic vision. Lairesse's neo-classicism, affirming though this does an essentially Romantic nostalgia, is not, like Arnold's mood, sterile, because it is used, in 'that prodigious book he wrote', to *teach* 'my pupils' how to cope with 'Dutch veritable earth.' This can become 'Dreamland' without peril, obedient to the instinct to

> *Supplement nature—not see flowers and weeds*
> *Simply as such, but link with each all*
> *The ultimate perfection . . .*
>
> (Lairesse, 159–61)

Classicism is not for Browning, true; but the didactic design, the insistence that 'Earth's young significance is all to learn' is advanced by Browning and Lairesse with self-vindicating vehemence against contemporary hedonisms.

Finally 'Avison' affords a highly significant revision of the earlier module in the light of this new one. You will recall that in each other Parleying, Browning calls up some anterior figure to 'confute for me' a modern instance of peevish ideality; well, the only modern protagonist in 'Avison' is John Relfe, who, being Browning's *teacher*, is, like Lairesse and for the same reason, in a state of grace. 'There is no truer truth obtainable/By Man than comes of music': Relfe by teaching it, Browning by performing and transforming it, activate its latent didacticism and save it and themselves.

And even more finally, 'Fust and his Friends', the 'epilogue' to *Parleyings*, fosters the module on Browning's own work. Fust's invention of printing—a transparent analogy to Browning's poetry—is redeemed by its power to disseminate—teach—the truth: there is an audacious pun:

> *Be sure that each new capture consigned*
> *To my types will go forth to the world, like God's bread*

> *Miraculous food for not body but mind,*
> *Truth's manna!*

('Fust & his Friends', 436—9)

Browning's 'types', his emblematic enigmas, are also 'truth's manna' for his work. And in the didactic thrust of his aesthetic he recovered, or at least patched up, a vision, at least for others' use. He might not believe in Adam, Lilith and Eve, but Mrs Fitzgerald must not 'turn from all the modern allusions to the marriage, priest, love-making, etc. which show it to be just a *modern instance*' or she will miss the point of the poem. As Browning told Ruskin, aligning himself with Rabbis ben Karshook, ben Ezra, Perida, Ferishtah, and the other pedagogues who dominate and direct the later works, 'it is all teaching.'

# 2: Browning and Romanticism

## MORSE PECKHAM

THE INTERPRETATION of the term 'Romanticism' governing my general orientation in this chapter is that it is a name for the attempt to resolve the crisis of European high culture of the late eighteenth century, that it was to be found, eventually, in all fields of high culture —philosophy, literature, painting, music, ballet, opera, religion, scholarship, science, and political theory—and that it took nearly a hundred years for what I call the Romantic tradition to recognize the only possible solution—at least so far—to the problem the crisis of the Enlightenment exposed. The recognition of that solution, which was the achievement of Nietzsche more than of anyone else, led to the extraordinary cultural redirection that took place in virtually all fields of high culture between 1905 and 1915. The names of Picasso, Schönberg, and Wittgenstein are enough to indicate what is meant here. Such a striking re-direction has been experienced by no other culture.

To understand the place of Browning in this tradition would obviously entail a much more extensive study of his work than is possible or even desirable here.[1] Rather I shall also use the term 'Romanticism' in a more restricted and traditional sense—the emergent culture of the first decades of the nineteenth century. Browning grew up in the second and third of those decades, and early in the fourth, when he was in his twenty-first year, he wrote the poem with which I shall be concerned, *Pauline: A Fragment of a Confession* (written in 1832 and published in March 1833). By 1832 the accomplishment of the Romantic tradition, or of Romanticism (if one wishes to think of it as dying away at about this time and yielding to something not properly called Romanticism) was already massive enough. The hypothesis of this chapter is that *Pauline* is

[1] I have made a tentative sketch of this in my essay 'Personality and the Mask of Knowledge', *Victorian Revolutionaries*, New York 1970.

the consequence of Browning's encounter with this accumulation. Apart from the famous passages on the 'Sun-treader', identified by Browning himself as Shelley, there are traces and echoes in the poem of Words-worth and Byron, almost certainly of Coleridge, possibly of Keats and Hazlitt, and also possibly, if the setting of 950–985, the description of the home-land of Pauline, is to be identified as Switzerland, of Senancour's *Obermann* (1804). However, I shall not be concerned with specific influ-ences, echoes, and traces, but rather with the indications *Pauline* may be with some justice said to yield about Browning's comprehension of that tradition, particularly with the problems it had raised and with the sol-utions so far available. None of them, to be sure, turned out to be viable for the advanced thinkers in the rest of the century, or for Browning himself, though they have by no means disappeared from the present cul-tural scene.

The first step is to construct a hypothesis of how the poem should be read. The usual hypothesis has been succinctly stated in a recent essay on John Stuart Mill's famous marginalia to *Pauline*.[1] The authors refer to Mill's 'distaste for Browning's self-indulgent confessionalism in *Pauline*.' This is Mill's own judgment, and there is no doubt that it has been pretty generally accepted. Its dissemination and the confirmation of Mill's hypothesis is probably owing to DeVane's discussion in his *A Browning Handbook*.[2] His interpretation depends upon a hypothesis that the poem is 'Browning's autobiography to his twentieth year.'[3] But if, as he says, Pauline is 'a mere lay figure', the phrase 'thoroughly autobiographical' seems somewhat exaggerated; if there was no Pauline in Browning's life, he can hardly be said to be writing autobiography. Furthermore, when Browning republished the poem for the first time in the 1868 *Poetical Works*, he asserted that it was his

> earliest attempt at poetry always dramatic in principle, and so many utterances of so many imaginary persons, not mine, which I have since written according to a scheme less extravagant and scale less

[1] William S. Peterson and Fred L. Standley, 'The J. S. Mill Marginalia in Robert Browning's *Pauline*: A History and Transcription,' *PBSA*, LXVI, 1972, 138.

[2] First pub. in 1935; 2nd ed 1955. As Browning scholarship develops, it becomes distressingly evident that DeVane's *Handbook* must be used with extreme caution and scepticism.

[3] DeVane, *Handbook*, 42.

impracticable than were ventured upon in this crude preliminary sketch—a sketch that, on review, appears not altogether wide of some hint of the characteristic features of that particular *dramatis persona* it would fain have reproduced.

The inadequacy of the Mill–DeVane hypothesis has been convincingly discussed by Roma A. King,[1] but something remains to be said, since Professor King does not exhaust the theoretical possibilities of his position that the speaker of the poem is situated between the objective *persona* of Browning's claim in 1868 and the purely subjective autobiographical speaker of Mill and DeVane.

The first step in constructing a hypothesis for interpreting the poem appropriately is to recognize it as an exercise in self-definition. Like most adolescents and young men, however, Browning had as yet very little in the way of a unique self to define. At this stage of life the young imagine they are defining a unique self when they are but defining themselves in terms of a culturally available and validated social role. That this is what Browning was doing is suggested very strongly by the line in which the speaker identifies himself as properly both 'priest and prophet' (l. 1019), a mode of self-definition that was already very nearly a Romantic commonplace, at least within the Romantic tradition. Thus insofar as the poem is autobiographical, Browning was identifying himself as an exemplification of the primary Romantic figure or role. But we may go a little farther than this. Culture in the full anthropological sense is a set of directions for behaving in interaction with the non-human world, with other humans, and with oneself, which amounts to the same thing, since the individual is most usefully considered as a social dyad. Just as culture institutionalizes behaviour in persistent patterns of behaviour known as social institutions, so the individual in issuing himself directions for his own behaviour institutionalizes himself and becomes a dyadic social institution. Thus in *Pauline* Browning was institutionalizing himself as a Romantic Poet, and in the standard Romantic way was presenting the development or historical emergence of that role as a means of organizing and directing his behaviour. In his personal history only those tendencies and events which contributed to the emergence of that role or which hindered it and frustrated it are considered important and related to his 'true self'. The process, of course, is no different for someone who defines himself in terms of the role of auto-

[1] *The Focusing Artifice*, Athens, Ohio 1968, 4–10.

mobile mechanic or literary scholar. The peculiar twist of the situation, responsible for the almost irresistible autobiographical impression the poem makes, an impression which must however be resisted, arises from the fact that a central ingredient or factor in the role of Romantic Poet (or any kind of Romantic figure) is the notion of self as opposed to role. (This is responsible for the various judgments that the poem is sincere or insincere, or partly one or the other, or, as Professor King suggests, that its insincerity demonstrates its sincerity. But since 'sincerity' is transparently a normative term, to raise the question of Browning's sincerity in *Pauline* and to resolve it is merely to terminate investigation.)

The problem of the first Romantics, such as Wordsworth and Coleridge, was to create a new social role, but since the problem emerged from the rejection of available social roles, the solution was to create an anti-role, i.e., a 'self.' Now it is true, to be sure, that each individual is a self, but only in the sense that in performing a role his performance is necessarily a greater or lesser deviation from the current conception of how that role should be played, a circumstance made more apparent by the fact that each individual differs in his judgment of what the essential factors of the role-performance actually ought to be. The two standard ways of justifying role-deviation are, first, to point out the unique factors in the situation eliciting the role which required that the role be adapted to a situation with novel factors; and, second, to point out the formative or historical factors in the individual life which are responsible, it is asserted, for the role-deviation. Both these justifications are to be found in *Pauline*; the speaker presents what he conceives to be the unique and distorting factors in his personality and life and uses the Sun-treader as a surrogate for his cultural situation.

Both of these strategies are to be found in the first Romantics, and were responsible for what can, I believe, be identified as subjective and objective historicization, the historicization of the personality as a strategy for identifying and justifying the resources for deviance into an anti-role, and the historicization of the situation as a strategy for identifying and justifying the necessity for that deviance. The two great exemplars in English literature are Wordsworth's *The Prelude* and Carlyle's *Sartor Resartus*, but neither of these works, though written before *Pauline*, was as yet published. In thinking about the problem Browning was undertaking in *Pauline* it is essential to keep in mind that these two works were as yet unknown, and that the other models,

*Childe Harold*, *Alastor*, *Endymion*, and the figure of The Solitary in *The Excursion*, were incomplete and in part as yet incomprehensible. (Indeed, *Endymion* is still inadequately comprehended, and very likely always will be.) The Romantic anti-role, then, was something by no means clearly outlined in the tradition of English Romanticism, insofar as it was available to Browning, nor unlike Carlyle, had he found additional and more firmly outlined exemplars in German Romanticism, particularly in German Romantic philosophy. What Browning was attempting to do in *Pauline*—this is the hypothesis proposed here—was late adolescent self-definition in terms of a recently emerged and incompletely and inadequately defined social role, the Romantic anti-role of poet-prophet-priest. We must turn, then, to the problem of why the Romantic anti-role was conceived in these terms, or why, more precisely certain attributes of each of these metaphors were combined in the Romantic anti-role, and to a clearer understanding of why that anti-role was identified as a 'self'.

In any culture the priest is the regular, customary human instrument by which the divine is made accessible. The prophet, who also operates under the aegis of the established religion, is the divine instrument at times of crisis. Insofar as both are not merely witnesses to the divine and channels of the entrance of the divine into the human but are also individuals who utter specific directions for behaviour in specific situations, that is, moral propositions, the difference is that the priest utters validated morality while the prophet innovates morality by extending the validated morality to meet what he perceives to be the novel demands of a novel situation. The position of the poet, as conceived in one tradition of European culture from the time of Plato, and perhaps before, is unstable, moving along a continuum from a validated notion of divinity to an innovative notion, and from a validated morality to an innovative morality. Lacking the authority of both prophet and priest, his position often permits the negation of dominant notions of divinity and dominant moral notions. Milton, for example, self-defined as a poet, permitted himself innovation in both areas of conceptualization. The priest asserts that redemption is always available for those who behave properly; the prophet asserts that redemption is available if the demands of an emergent situation are met as he recommends; the poet asserts that redemption is available through channels other than the normal or validated channels of the culture, and in this he may be anything between boldly innovative and utterly platitudinous. In using the metaphors of poet, prophet, and priest to define his anti-role the early Romantic combined the attributes of permissive innovation of the poet (which Plato justified by asserting that the poet himself does not understand his own utterances and therefore is not truly responsible for them), of crisis innovation of the prophet, and the priest's normality of being a channel for the divine. Thus Coleridge, for example, asserted the truth of Christianity, but on wholly novel grounds, by re-interpreting, for one thing, the theological meaning of the Trinity. This amounted to a claim that the socially validated grounds for accepting Christianity were false, or at least inadequate. He claimed to be not merely an alternative, secular channel for divine knowledge, but a channel that superseded the cognitive aspect of established religion. That was in the 1820s, but as early as 1798 in *The Ancient Mariner* he developed at least the beginning of a new mythology of redemption, the innovative character of which was brought out by the failure of the Mariner to be successful in demanding validation by a recognized instrument of grace of the established Church, and by the fact that he is condemned to repeat his story indefinitely. Perhaps we are to assume that the occasion of repetition is always to be an interruption of the religious validation of a social ritual, as it is in the narrative poem we have.

In defining himself as at once poet, prophet, and priest, the early Romantic was making the most extraordinary claims. He was doing something different from what Thomas of Münster, for example, had done. Innovative prophets, often claiming for themselves the status of priesthood, had appeared with considerable frequency in the history of European Christendom. Luther himself was one of such. His unique achievement was not religious but political. He was able to create for himself so powerful a secular support that he and subsequently his religion, although branded as a heresy by the Church, were able to resist the best efforts of the Church's secular arm, and to survive. Thomas of Münster's secular support was miniscule by comparison and easily overwhelmed and destroyed. The early Romantic, however, was in a different position and made a different claim. First, the rationalism of the seventeenth century, its notable scientific achievements, and the secularization of culture by the Enlightenment had already created a situation in which it was relatively safe to propose an alternative mode of redemption. Next, the French Revolution and subsequently the Napoleonic sweeping away of feudalism and the secular power of the clergy made it even safer. Ever since the Revolution and the Napoleonic cultural reorganization, Europe has experienced a permanent measle-like rash of strange religions. Nor are they always independent of the Romantic tradition. Yeats was interested in such phenomena because of fundamentally Romantic reasons. Next, the fact that philosophy had already become independent of religion gave to the early Romantic analytic instruments which he could and did use to dissolve the cognitive claims of established theology; he also could turn them against previous philosophy. The fact that most of the Romantic writers were not technically very good philosophers is of no importance. But the most important factor was that at the level of high culture there was a vacuum. For the most acute spirits of the time the traditional explanation of the world had dissolved from its own internal incoherence and from the failure to make its claims good.

The Enlightenment, it has long been recognized, was a secularization of the Christian scheme of redemption. Redemption was to be accomplished by the philosophical, rational, and sentimental fusion of man and nature, a fusion that became the channel for the entry of the divine into the world. Since philosophy, reason, and sentiment comprehended the character of that divine, it was possible to generate a set of moral propositions of such a character that, if they were used to direct and control behaviour, an adequate, or even a perfect, social order would be the result, the equivalent of Heaven. To be sure, a good many Enlightenment figures, especially towards the end of the century, had their doubts about all this, but generally speaking they were committed either to trying or to asserting, like Burke, that given the natural circumstances and human limitations, an adequate society already existed, or at least one existed that could be redeemed by rational reforms. The great moral force of the Enlightenment lay in the ease with which it could demonstrate that the traditional, Christian explanation of the world was responsible for social situations which could not possibly be reconciled with the attributes of deity. But that moral force was lost when the French Revolution and Napoleonic imperialism attempted to put Enlightenment redemptionism into effect.

To put it in different terms, according to the traditional Christian explanation of the world, the subject (the divinely illuminated reason of man) absorbs the object; that is, the categories of the subject exhaust the attributes of the object. That which cannot be absorbed or exhausted is defined as evil, in turn defined as the absence of divinity; it need not be absorbed or exhausted. The Enlightenment version was that the object (divinely created Nature) properly absorbs the subject, Man, or the natural reason; that is, the categories of the object exhaust the attributes of the subject. That which cannot be absorbed or exhausted is defined as error and ignorance, which the enlightened reason can eliminate. Through the analysis of Hume and Kant, arriving at results which others, such as Wordsworth, arrived at independently, and through the violent, chaotic, and dictatorial imperialism of the French Revolution and the Napoleonic enterprise, it became apparent, even before Napoleon for some English and German figures, that the Enlightenment version of the subject-object relationship was not a true negation of the Christian version but a mere inversion of it. If the subject claims that the object absorbs it and exhausts its attributes, it is nevertheless making a subjective claim. The boasted objectivity of the Enlightenment was thus transformed into a wilful self-delusion. This is the explanation for the ease with which certain adherents to the Enlightenment, such as Manzoni, returned to Christianity. From this point of view the Enlightenment was identical with Christianity; the only thing new was terminology. But for others, the failure of the Enlightenment in theory and practice, philosophically and politically, meant the failure of Christianity. To them there was no turning back.

Browning was perfectly aware of this development and describes it in *Pauline* with great accuracy. The relation of the speaker to the Sun-treader changes in the course of the narrative. At first he accepts the ideology of the Sun-treader (one who walks on the sun, often presented as the location of heaven in early nineteenth-century England); although he says that his 'choice fell / Not so much on a system as a man—' (ll. 403–404), this is not to disclaim that he accepted the system, as indeed he did. However, that system turns out to be a dream:

> First went my hopes of perfecting mankind,
> And faith in them—then freedom in itself,
> And virtue in itself—and then my motives' end,
> And powers and loves; and human love went last

(458–61)[1]

[1] 1833 text. The 1889 text is a little clearer: 'First went my hopes of perfec-

The next paragraph spells out the result:

> *My powers were greater, as some temple seemed*
> *My soul, where nought is changed, and incense rolls*
> *Around the altar—only God is gone,*
> *And some dark spirit sitteth in his seat*
>
> (469–72)

At the end of the poem the reason for emphasizing the man rather than the system becomes clear. In the last paragraph the Sun-treader is appealed to without any reference to his system. He is not even a role-model; he is reduced to a mere supportive function. It is fairly evident that in Browning's development Shelley presented primarily Enlightenment values which Browning had already rejected by the time he wrote *Pauline*. This is suggested even in the first and most famous Sun-treader passage:

> *And I, perchance, half feel a strange regret,*
> *That I am not what I have been to thee*
>
> (191–2)

At this point, since I am discussing in behavioural terms the Romantic problem of defining an anti-role, it is necessary to attempt to clarify in such terms the notion of the divine and of redemption. The definition of a role can be created only in language. That is why the other arts followed poetry in defining the artist in terms of the Romantic anti-role, and why painters and composers—and after a hundred years, scientists—claimed to be poets and controlled their artistic behaviour (and sometimes non-artistic behaviour) by literary utterances. Behaviourally the central and most important and crucial fact about language is that meaning is not immanent. The connection between word and meaning is not inherent, but conventional. If the word is categorized as stimulus, then the meaning is properly categorized as response. But if this link between stimulus and response is conventional (or a matter of human culture) then any word is capable of eliciting all possible responses, and likewise all words are capable of eliciting the identical response. Clearly interaction with the world, other humans, and oneself is possible only if

---

ting mankind, / Next—faith in them, and then in freedom's self / And virtue's self, then my own motives, end / And aims and loves, and human love went last.'

responses to words are limited and channelled. The fundamental way this limitation is carried out is the only way possible, by sheer, unlimited, arbitrary force, which in the form of social power is the necessary base of society, and is always the ultimate sanction. But there are endless numbers of ways limiting linguistic response before force has to be resorted to, so many that it is probably correct to say that the principal expenditure of human energy is directed towards limiting the range of response, i.e., of behaviour, as, to give a by no means trivial example, the vast energy that goes into dictionary-making is witness.

One of the most important ways of limiting linguistic response is explanation. From this point of view language is a closed system, and also an unstable one. Explanation is hierarchical. At the bottom are those words which are asserted to be concrete, or empirical, or phenomenal. It is alleged that they are words that refer to extra-linguistic phenomenal configurations. But since reference is subsumed by meaning, and since meaning is arbitrary and conventional, then reference is equally conventional and arbitrary. Rather, such terms are exemplary words, subsumed by more general terms which are conceived of as having an explanatory relation to them, as 'iron', 'copper', 'gold', 'silver', etc. are subsumed by the word 'metal'. This kind of subsumption begins a hierarchical ladder of explanation, properly termed an explanatory regress, 'regressive' because each level categorizes more of the world and is therefore vaguer. At the top of this regress are such words as 'God', 'Nature', 'Energy', 'Mind', 'Will', 'the Unconscious', 'the Eternal Mystery', etc., which serve merely to terminate that regress.

Two other points need to be made to clarify the Romantic's problem. One is that this explanatory hierarchy is carried by and is identical with the hierarchical structure of all social interaction involving more than two persons. (In a dyad, subsumption shifts back and forth between two persons.) In a social hierarchy the relation from the top down is a matter of giving instructions in words; at the top is the ultimate power-wielding role; at the bottom is the social role engaged in applying the various levels of instruction (or explanation and subsumption) in responding to and manipulating extra-linguistic phenomena. The second point is that what is true of words is also true of extra-linguistic phenomenal configurations, which must be regarded as signs, since there is no immanent or inherent link between them as stimuli and responses to them. Language, then, is a mode of signs of which the distinguishing attribute is hierarchical explanation.

From this point of view it is easier to understand what the failure of Enlightenment explanation involved. In the Christian explanation, strongly influenced by Platonism, and Neo-Platonism, meaning emanated from the subject to the object, that is, from language to the world. In the Enlightenment view meaning emanated from the object to the subject, from the world to language. If both the Christian and the Enlightenment view of the subject-object relation are abandoned, any immanent, necessary, and inherent link between language and the world is broken. And this is what Kant, stimulated by Hume, accomplished when he asserted that we cannot know the *Ding-an-sich*. And in the other direction he asserted that though we can know God exists, we cannot know anything else about him. This is tantamount to saying that 'God' merely terminates an explanation.

The consequences even now have been recognized by only a few radical and as yet unvalidated philosophers. The non-inherency, non-immanency of the link between a word and its extra-linguistic referent must also be applied to links between words, since a verbal reply to an utterance is the response to a stimulus. From this orientation logic is to be perceived as one of the many means for limiting the range of response to words, and the epistemological problem becomes a normative matter. At the beginning of the nineteenth century, however, these consequences were by no means apparent. What was apparent, at least to a few, was that the relation of subject to object was one of irresolvable tension. The history of Romanticism in the fuller sense, the primary sense indicated above, is the history of the gradual recognition of the consequences of sundering any necessary relation between subject and object, of the consequences of tearing language loose from the world.

We may now return to 'divine' and 'redemption'. A redeemed individual is one who returns from a deviant mode of behaviour to a validated mode. 'Deviant' is here used in two senses: one, behaviour that follows a well-established pattern, such as adultery, but is invalidated by instructions maintained by a social hierarchy supported ultimately by arbitrary power; and two, innovative behaviour that is not yet validated and perhaps never will be. Redemption, then, involves conforming to a validated mode of response to a particular category of situation, such as marriage, and to a particular set of either verbal or non-verbal instructions, or both, as when the individual is told to respond to his rosary by uttering certain prayers for a given period of time or a given number of repetitions. To be truly redeemed involves a change of heart. This means that the response to a given stimulus, it may be successfully predicted, will in the future not be deviant, in either sense. It is a change of heart because the individual imposes upon himself a limitation of response to the stimulus in question and sanctions it with a self-imposed application of the ultimate sanction, power. Hence in a wide variety of cultures redemption is maintained by self-inflicted flagellation.

In Heaven, however, the application of power is not required. Heaven is a place where there is no possibility of deviant behaviour; it is a place in which one always 'knows' how to respond. It is instructive that most visions of heaven are marked by a singular limitation of the range of behaviour. A place of eternal redemption is a place in which all behaviour is marked by the attribute of the individual who has been redeemed from one particular kind of deviant behaviour. To put it somewhat differently, if the bulk of human energy goes into the strategies for limiting the range of behaviour, in heaven the range of behaviour is limited without any expenditure of energy. Or, any expenditure of energy is immediately returned by emanation from the Deity who rules the heaven in question, as in Milton's vision of Heaven before the revolt of Satan.

God and the ultimate social role in a social hierarchy have a number of attributes in common, a not surprising fact if one is aware that the explanatory regress is identical in structure with and is carried out by the power regress of social hierarchies. The Divine Right of Kings is but one of innumerable instances of the interdependency of explanation and social power. Those conservatives of the seventeenth century who asserted that to deny the Divine Right of Kings was to head society towards a severe crisis were quite right. The first of these attributes, of course, is power itself. To be redeemed, whether on earth or in heaven, is to have immediate, intimate, and unquestioning contact with the ultimate source of power. An intimately related pair of attributes is made up of love (i.e., valuing) and chastisement. Absolute monarchs always chastise their people in the name of love: Gods and Kings are called fathers and sometimes mothers. The inseparability of love and chastisement, and the necessity for self-imposed chastisement for redemption gives the figure of Christ its immense charismatic power. A final attribute common both to God and ultimate social roles is creativity, which is the innovative adjustment of socio-cultural systems to emergent situations, sanctioned and validated by power. By establishing new modes of response and limiting and channelling those modes creativity becomes redemptive.

There are, then, two modes of redemption, in symbiotic relationship, verbal and political. By 'political' I mean redemption carried out by social institutions; thus even self-flagellation is political behaviour. Pre-Enlightenment societies found their ultimate verbal sanction in 'God', post-Enlightenment societies in 'Nature'. The United States of America used both, since it was founded during a transitional period; it was both Christian and Enlightenment, a source of endless confusion to this day, when representative assemblies, in spite of the separation of Church and State, employ chaplains and begin their deliberations with prayer. This is why when the social institutions charged with exercise of verbal redemption are discredited and are judged to be deleterious, destructive, and decadent (Voltaire's *l'infâme*) the institutions charged with political redemption, unless they dissociate themselves from the verbal institutions, are threatened; thus the Enlightened monarchs of late eighteenth-century Europe frequently downgraded the church and separated themselves from it. The Jesuits, on the whole a relatively harmless group and socially more valuable than many of the Catholic orders, were destroyed. But of course, as Voltaire's case shows, the discrediting of a mode of explanation exercised by verbally redemptive institutions necessarily involves the innovation of an alternative mode of verbal redemption. And this alternative mode, to maintain itself, necessarily must gain control of the ultimate roles in politically redemptive institutions. Hence the French Revolution and its Napoleonic aftermath. In Italy, for example, the unification of Italy, in reality the conquest of the rest of Italy by Piedmont, was made possible by the memory of the innovative verbal and political redemption introduced by the French conquest of Northern Italy, and of Murat's brief rule of the kingdom of Naples.

The Revolutionary-Napoleonic enterprise and liberation of Europe from feudalism and the Church also saw the ultimate source of political redemption, social power based on force, exposed in all of its nakedness and arbitrariness. To those who accepted the verbal redemption of the Enlightenment, the Revolutionary-Napoleonic enterprise was acceptable. To those who rejected the Enlightenment mode of redemption and still accepted the Christian mode, that enterprise was not acceptable. It was these who restored the Christian verbal and political modes of redemption after 1815 but who also incorporated in their political institutions a large share of the modes of Enlightenment political redemption, and in their verbal institutions even bits and pieces of Enlightenment verbal redemption. To that tiny group of Europeans, however, for whom the Christian and the Enlightenment modes of political and verbal redemption were seen as mere inversions of each other and not true negations (as, for example, the naked exercise of the Revolutionary-Napoleonic power made perfectly clear), both were unacceptable. Hence rose the Romantic alienation from both social institutions and explanatory modes available in the European tradition. The problem of the Romantics, then, was to draw the consequences of the true negation of the Christian-Enlightenment explanation of the world, the breaking of the link between subject and object, the sundering of any necessary tie between stimulus and response.

Now the history of Europe, and especially the history of the Enlightenment, demonstrated that any large-scale innovation must begin with verbal redemption, the reason being that political institutions find their sanctions in the extremes of explanatory regress when the directions issued down from hierarchically ultimate power are no longer effective in relating institutions to the extra-linguistic world, a fact that Hegel was the first to realize fully. It is why he asserted that history is the history of *Geist*. (Marx, in the 1840s, emphasized the relation of language to the world, but in failing to realize fully what Hegel was saying fell back on a Christian-Enlightenment pattern of redemption. He thought he was negating Hegel when he was merely filling out what Hegel had sketched.) Thus Hegel quite correctly placed philosophy higher than religion, since for him and a few of his European fellows religion as an institution of verbal redemption had clearly failed; it must, therefore, be subsumed by philosophy. Consequently Romanticism first emerged in literature and metaphysics. Furthermore, since these alienated individuals had no access and wished no access to political institutions (except for small groups of the like-minded), of the various attributes in common to deity and the ultimate power levels of political institutions, they chose creativity. The poet-prophet-priest figure emerged as the Romantic figure with access to the divine (ultimate explanation) and to the redemptive (an ultimate mode of limiting and channelling response), but unlike their predecessors the Romantics claimed the attribute of radical creativity. Since the innovative task was not to adjust political and verbal redemptive institutions, but to discover the foundation for new modes of redemption, the old modes having failed, creativity was located within the individual as the precondition for the innovation of verbal redemption and, it was hoped by some at any rate, eventually the innovation of political redemption. This is to be seen, for example, at the end of Hegel's *Phenomenology* (1808) when the fully self-conscious spirit, having transcended all modes of explanation and redemption, turns once again to the phenomenal world, the material on which to exercise its creativity.

The early decades of the nineteenth century were the early decades of Romanticism, or, if one wishes, were the period of Romanticism. Its history can be summed up very briefly. The implication of the breaking of the link between subject and object was not yet recognized, the implication being that final redemption, political or verbal, is impossible and that the explanatory and political institutions of man cannot solve the fundamental human problems. The significance of the irresolvable tension between subject and object, that is, the impossibility of redemption, was not yet recognized, even though the fact of that tension was accepted. The explanation for this failure is that overwhelmingly the European cultural tradition was founded upon the possibility of and necessity for redemption, verbal and political and final, as for the most part it still is. It was difficult and virtually impossible to imagine anything but an alternative yet innovative mode of redemption. (Senancour and Hegel were two of the very rare exceptions, perhaps the only exceptions. Neither was understood.) Consequently Romanticism, or the first stages of Romanticism, depending on how the term is used, was marked by an extraordinarily wide-ranging effort to create an alternative and viable final mode of redemption. That is, though the Christian and Enlightenment modes were seen as mirror-like inversions of each other, not true negations, it was still believed that a negation of that mode was to be another redemptive mode; it was not yet perceived that the possibility for final redemption had been culturally exhausted. But since it had been exhausted, the only possibility was to begin by locating the source of redemption in the self, as distinguished from the role, since the existent roles were necessarily part of the existent verbal and political redemptive modes and institutions. Further, only the existing redemptive fields of verbal and non-verbal high culture were available as institutions in

which creative innovation was possible. Hegel identified them as philosophy, religion, and art. The early decades of the century, then, were
marked by redemptive innovation in each of these fields. Browning was
born into and grew up in a cultural situation in which were to be found
available Christian, Enlightenment, and a wide variety of Romantic
redemptive modes. It was to define himself in this situation that he wrote
*Pauline*. Moreover, since he was a very young man, hardly more than an
adolescent, we cannot assume that he had mastered the full range of any
of these in anything like the great variety and confusing interrelation-
ships and interactions of all three possibilities. Given his extraordinary
intelligence and the rich culture of his upbringing, he could still do no
more than his best in an extraordinarily confusing cultural situation. It is
my own opinion that he did very well indeed, and that *Pauline* is by no
means the confusing failure it is usually judged to be. It is not merely, as
he was to claim in 1868, that it was the first of his dramatic monologues;
it is also the case that *Pauline* established the pattern of his use of the
genre, for the great monologues to follow were to be more than anything else exercises in self-definition by their speakers.

The sub-title of *Pauline* is *A Fragment of a Confession*. The poem, then, is
not to be read as a complete statement of an experience, but the word
'confession' is not ordinarily used unless there is something to confess, a
reason for feeling guilty, or, the word used in the poem, shame.
Deviance in either sense has been at work in the life of the speaker, but it
is not, it develops, a Byronic deviance, some violation of the validated
norms of behaviour, but rather verbal deviance, deviance, to use the
terms of the poem, of mind and thought. It is moreover, it appears, innovative deviance. The speaker condemns himself throughout for that
reason. In the second paragraph, for example, he speaks of a

> wandering aim
> *Sent back to bind on Fancy's wings and seek*
> *Some strange fair world, where it might be a law'*

$$(32-5)^1$$

Confession is the second step in the path to redemption, the first step, of
course, being the admission that there is something to confess, that
deviance has taken place. The sub-title establishes the redemptive theme.

---

[1] Unless otherwise indicated the text is that of the 1833 edition for all subsequent quotations, as derived from the variants in *The Complete Works of
Robert Browning*, Athens, Ohio vol I 1969 as I have corrected them.

The epigraph from Marot is equally important, for it asserts that an irreversible change has taken place. This again reappears in the poem several times, that the speaker cannot return to his former condition. This theme is of prime importance, for it explains why the confession is made to a representative of neither a political nor a verbal institution. Pauline, to whom we shortly learn the poem is addressed, is a redemptive figure but a completely secularized one, a woman who loves the speaker but who in return is 'to receive not love, but faith' (l. 43), thus emphasizing Pauline's redemptive function, a task facilitated by her beauty. Love, beauty, a beloved woman as instruments of redemption were already Romantic commonplaces, and through fiction, the drama, and the opera, as well as poetry with its more restricted circulation, were in the 1830s and 1840s presented as redemptive instruments to a more general non-Romantic public, which, however, had been sufficiently unsettled by the events of the preceding hundred years to welcome alternative redemptive modes, at least so long as they were not regarded as necessarily excluding the traditional modes. To the Romantic, of course, they were innovated because the traditional modes were unusable, culturally inaccessible. The possibilities of this triad for redemption arise from the fact that awareness of deviance is a source of tension, of a sense of internal incoherence. Whatever else redemptive behaviour might accomplish —and recidivism indicates that it does not necessarily accomplish much—at least it reduces tension. For the Romantic there were two sources of severe tension, one his cultural deviance, and the other the fact that that deviance when properly apprehended involved an irresolvable tension between subject and object. Since the whole tradition of redemption emphasizes tension-reduction as the highest human value, this was yet another reason for the desperate effort in the early decades of the nineteenth century to create alternative redemptive modes. It took nearly a hundred years of the Romantic tradition for a few individuals to arrive at the notion that tension is not of negative value but of positive. Erotic love, therefore, and eroticized beauty, both of which had long been used by religion as weapons in its arsenal of redemptive strategies, since both have as their goal total tension reduction, could easily be separated from religion in such a way that their redemptive attribute, gained from religion, could function independently of it. Although Goethe's *Faust II* and its *ewige weibliche* appeared in the autumn of 1832, perhaps while Browning was writing

*Pauline*, it is unlikely that he knew of it. Nevertheless, the cultural convergence is striking, because Pauline is given the same function as Goethe's 'eternal feminine': 'It draws us on'. Pauline's redemptive function, it turns out at the end of the poem, is to reintroduce the speaker to his tension-raising innovative deviance. Browning had already gone beyond Wagner, whose Senta can only redeem his alienated Wandering Dutchman from a life of alienation into what certainly seems to be a Christian paradise. The poem for *Der Fliegende Holländer* was written in its first form in May, 1841.

From this point of view the second epigraph, from Cornelius Agrippa's *De occulta philosophia*, is comprehensible.

> They will say that I teach forbidden things, lay the seeds of heresies, offend pious ears, and corrupt pure minds. . . . My book . . . is harmful and very poisonous. In this book is the gateway to hell; it speaks hard words.

In a note to this quotation published in 1888 Browning was to call it 'absurdly pretentious', but it should be taken seriously. It shows his clear comprehension that he was undertaking a deviant self-definition. In relation to the culture as a whole and even to high culture, Romanticism was in 1832 still a deviant mode; hence the fact that Romantic spokesmen are so often presented as wanderers, outcasts, Cains, poets with a curse on them, and so on, and that so often Romantic individuals acted out this self-definition in their personal lives. The only significant deviance in Browning's life at this point—at least that we know of—was his refusal to continue his studies in London University after a very brief trial. At the time the older Carlyle was still acting out the outcast role in Craigenputtock. Tennyson had acted it out at Cambridge and was to continue his Bohemian experiments for several decades to come. And even then he withdrew to the Isle of Wight. Browning, however, seemed to have as early as this that cultural objectivity towards his own self-definition which made such acting-out unnecessary. Instead, he developed his peculiar version of the dramatic monologue, disclaiming personal responsibility for his characters, and in life in the course of time, and perhaps—there is some evidence for this—even in the 1830s adopted that socio-cultural *doppelgänger* strategy in which in later years he was adept.

The opening paragraph of the poem establishes Pauline's initial function, to provide the traditional protection of the confessional. But what is to be confessed is not sins, but rather a

> *sleepless brood*
> *Of fancies from my soul, their lurking-place,*

(6–7)

These thoughts are clearly presented as dangerous, but it would be even more dangerous not to unlock them. Unlocking them is the precondition of song, that is, creative utterance. Sad confession of their presence in the soul must precede—what? 'Ere I can be—as I shall be no more' (l. 27). This reveals the purpose of the confession to create an unknown subjective condition. The second paragraph speaks of shame, but it is not the shame of harbouring such thoughts, but rather, it would seem, the shame of confessing that the thoughts, the 'wild dreams of beauty and of good', have not been allowed issue. What has to be confessed, it transpires in the next paragraph, is not guilt for deviance but weakness in not being deviant. It is Pauline's wish, he says, that he 'essay / The task which was to me what now thou art' (ll. 53–4), clearly a redemptive task. The fourth paragraph continues the theme of shame and weakness, and presents the initial confession to Pauline, which took place in the natural world in the spring.

This introduces a theme which recurs several times in the rest of the poem, and towards the end is crucial, the redemptive power of nature. But to put it this way is to offer the possibility of a confusion of the Romantic attitude towards nature with the Enlightenment attitude. For the latter, nature was exemplary; it provided non-verbal exemplifications of verbal propositions; the attitude towards nature was still allegorical, as the order of nature was an allegorical exemplum of the ordering power of God. For the Romantic the first important thing about nature was not so much the presence of nature as the absence of man. This in turn facilitated the 'aesthetic' response to nature, a tension-reducing feeling state elicited by the natural world and ultimately inexplicable. Not the explicability of nature, but the inexplicability of the response to the natural world indicated its redemptive power and made it not into an allegory of divine attributes but a symbol of the sense of divinity. Wordsworth was probably right when he traced it back to what we could call today the preconscious awareness of the infant in relation to its mother, the felt fusion of subject and object, a fusion from which, however, no further propositions could be deduced other than that of the divine character of that fusion; divine because it was a creative act of perception on the part of the subject. It is best understood as an eroticization of nature, or at least can be so understood if eroticism is seen as having its origin not in sex but in the pre-conscious fusion of subject and object which for most individuals is most successfully repeated and recalled—or regressed to—in sexual behaviour. From this point of view it is not surprising that Pauline's erotic function should first appear in a natural setting. Eroticized nature was, of course, a redemptive mode which by 1832 had been richly explored and well established. Browning had only to make use of it.

The paragraph concludes with an interesting passage beginning

> *thou art not more dear*
> *Than song was once to me; and I ne'er sung*
> *But as one entering bright halls, where all*
> *Will rise and shout for him. Sure I must own*
> *That I am fallen—having chosen gifts*
> *Distinct from theirs*

                                                                    (76–81)

This equivalence in value of Pauline and song indicates the redemptive function of song, and the next lines suggest the redeemer who is recognized as such. Yet the supportive group is only potential, and that potentiality has been sacrificed to other interests. In the concluding lines of the paragraph, however, that potential group is spoken of as having once actually existed. This is something of a puzzle, but it can be resolved—if at all resolvable—by the explanation that the self-created isolation of the Romantic alien or deviant was responsible for an inextinguishable longing for that support which any radical and innovating deviant always seeks. The personal history of the great Romantic figures shows a continuous record of gathering about themselves such supportive groups. Among lesser Romantic figures the same conditions were responsible for the emergence of the Bohemian sub-culture. Here again Browning turned out to be something of an exception. Insofar as he had a little group it consisted, it would appear, solely of Elizabeth Barrett, and that for less than two decades. Indeed it may be worth noting that the more one studies *Pauline* the more one is tempted to see Browning using Elizabeth in much the same way that the speaker uses Pauline. At any rate, in this passage the imagined group is spoken of as having existed. And of course it had. It was the audience for the traditionally redemptive poet, the audience in which the speaker refused to find his support, though he feels that he had the power to have done so.

The next paragraph, beginning with line 89 (not a paragraph in 1833), identifies the 'chosen gifts'. They were the dangerous gifts of total self-involvement:

> *my soul had floated from its sphere*
> *Of wide dominion into the dim orb*
> *Of self*

> (90–2)[1]

'Soul' seems, then to mean here the capacity to establish successful relations to the objective world. The isolated imagination, turned in upon itself, can only destroy the traditional values of beauty and divinity. The effect in the next paragraph is the sense of aging and of loss of value. The next section of the poem is concerned with how the Sun-treader rescued the speaker from this condition. Yet, as indicated above, the redemptive power of the Sun-treader fails; even though the speaker feels himself once again cast down into an abasement, he refuses to imitate him, to use him as a role-model for self-definition. The Sun-treader was only a temporary interruption of the value-destroying self-isolation already defined. The result has been the probing of 'life's vanity' (l. 237), a condition from which Pauline rescues him, 'won by a word again / Into my own life' (ll. 237–8). But still this gives him no sense of having 'part in God, or his bright world' (l. 251). All he can do is to sing, thoughtlessly, without confidence—of himself.

At this point the autobiographical narrative *of the speaker* begins. Five things, he says, formed his native endowment. First is

> *a consciousness*
> *Of self—distinct from all its qualities,*
> *From all affections, passions, feelings, powers; . . . linked . . . to self-*
> *supremacy,*
> *Existing as a centre to all things,*

[1] 'Wide' is so preferable to the 1868–1889 reading 'wild' that it is possible that the passage should be emended to its original reading. Work on the Ohio Browning Edition has revealed that Browning, though an earnest proof-reader, was no more successful at achieving perfection than anyone else is, and less successful than some.

> *Most potent to create, and rule, and call*
> *Upon all things to minister to it*
>
> (269–76)

It is hardly necessary to point out this attribute as the defining attribute of Romantic self-definition. The second of his native gifts is

> *a principle of restlessness*
> *Which would be all, have, see, know, taste, feel, all*
>
> (277–8)

This is obviously the central theme of Goethe's *Faust*, but it is also to be found in Fichte, and among English works in *Childe Harold*, *Don Juan*, *Endymion*, and *Prometheus Unbound*, and it was to be the theme of *Paracelsus*. Like the presentation of self-consciousness as a native gift of the speaker, Browning apparently believed that it was already so well-established as an ingredient of Romantic self-definition that it required no further explanation. Still, the use of the word 'restlessness' indicates Browning's rather remarkable insight that to want to know everything, to be forever restless, is to deny the redemptive power of tradition. Even the Enlightenment looked forward to a human condition in which such restlessness would be stilled. It is anti-redemptive because such behaviour exposes one, as Goethe makes quite clear, to a condition in which one does not know how to behave. It violates the basic principle of redemption, the limitation of the range of behaviour. It presents, therefore, a violently alternative redemptive mode, one which necessarily raises tension, rather than reduces it. In the next paragraph the destructiveness of such a desire is clearly understood; that which saves it from destructiveness is of his powers 'the only one / Which marks me'—imagination (ll. 283–4), defined by the metaphor of an angel, thus ascribing to it the attribute of divinity. The Romantic change of meaning for the term 'imagination' invariably, to quote from a passage above, indicates that divine 'creativity was located within the individual as the precondition for the innovation of verbal redemption'. The whole passage shows an interesting cultural convergence with Hegel, with whom it is unlikely that the young Browning was familiar. In short, the Romantic self definition as poet, prophet, and priest could not be clearer.

In what follows the speaker asserts that he has always yearned after God, even though neglecting his laws, and even though he came to doubt his existence, always felt his presence. It must not be imagined, as it often is, that the mere approving mention of God, even when it is clearly the Christian God, means that the Romantic writer accepts Christianity. An acquaintance with the cultural history of the period, especially the more obscure areas of religion and philosophy, not only among the Germans, indicates that one of the more common modes of innovative verbal redemption was a re-interpretation of Christian propositions, both theological and moral. God was retained, and it was claimed that it was a Christian God, yet the word terminated a quite different explanatory regress. Yet it is also perfectly true that a great many Romantic figures, in the interest of social safety and of being let alone, quite deliberately deceived a non-Romantic public by referring to God, or, as Carlyle did, seduced them into a Romantic redemptive mode. Hegel realized that God was dead (that philosophy subsumes religion), but he was almost alone. The persistence of the term is like the persistence of redemption. European culture overwhelmingly demanded both. On the other hand, the creation of alternative redemptive modes the explanatory regressions of which were terminated by 'God' was in the development of Romanticism one of the more important means by which the function of that term as a mere means of terminating such a regress was revealed. Kierkegaard, for example, within the next two decades after *Pauline* was to make that function almost painfully clear. His final refusal to accept the identity of Christianity and an established Church in symbiotic relationship with the state indicates his awareness of having created a deviant innovative mode of verbal redemption. Less clearly, this recognition also emerges in *Pauline*.

The final native attribute comes as a surprise: 'I can love nothing.' Yet 'sense supplies a love / Encircling me and mingling with my life' (ll. 310–12). This seems best interpreted as on the one hand a rejection of traditional modes for eroticizing experience and on the other the acceptance of the aesthetic mode, initially, in Romanticism, applied to nature, and subsequently applied to art. The passage appears to assert the autonomy of the self and by dissociating the self from sensory experience sunders the subject from the object, the self from the world. To ascribe love, the fusion of subject and object, to mere sensation is to assert more precisely what was asserted earlier, that affections, passions, feelings, and powers belong to the object and that any sensation of fusion of subject and object is an illusion. The importance of this denial of the capacity for love to Browning's future development can scarcely be overestimated. It was a factor in Romantic self-definition that did not emerge in the development of Romanticism until several decades after *Pauline*. Once again it shows Browning's remarkable grasp of the Romantic problem.

The next section of the poem presents the speaker's encounter with ancient literature and then, with a sense that his powers were bursting out, his encounter with the Sun-treader. His vowing himself to liberty and subsequent disenchantment, already discussed, was the central experience of those who originated Romanticism. The effect here is not despair but light-heartedness, wit, and mockery, shortly followed by the disappearance of God and the appearance in his place of a dark spirit. But the further effect was the effort to chain his own spirit down. Browning, then, is different from the early Romantics, who had to discover the true 'self'. The Romantic self-definition had been by his time at least well enough formulated and established so that he could postulate its five attributes as a native endowment. Thus shame at self-betrayal takes the place of the earlier guilt over violating established social modes. This stage is in turn succeeded by an elaborate rationalization for avoiding the vanity and suffering of genius, for such the speaker thinks himself. To abase himself before the remembered figure of the Sun-treader and 'feed his fame' (l. 588) is now his only ambition. The result was a defiance of all hopes for glory, but a corresponding reward in the return of music, 'my life' (1.565), and other 'old delights' such as classical literature. The importance of music in the Romantic tradition and its emergence in the nineteenth century as a major art lay in its simultaneous inexplicability and its somehow convincing meaningfulness. It was therefore interpreted as the most intimate and truest expression of the 'self,' and consequently as the best, perhaps sole, mode of redemption. This tradition contributed powerfully to the survival of art as the sole means of redemption, a position arrived at in the late nineteenth century and powerfully continued into the twentieth. Nevertheless, the speaker discovers, all faith had left him, and what he took for a returning spring was but a fading autumn, a sunset glow. It was in this condition that he encountered Pauline, as previously narrated (ll. 55–88).

The argument of the poem has proceeded in the classical way of justifying deviation, a unique personal history and a novel situation, represented by the Sun-treader. However, the shameful deviation is not from a socially validated but from a Romantically defined self. As Paracelsus later was to say, the crucial matter is to let out that which is within. But these inner attributes, as a result of personal history, have been frustrated and suppressed. The rest of the poem is the exploration of possible strategies for undoing these bonds. Nevertheless, a striking sentence indicates Browning's penetration into the Romantic problem.

> *I will tell*
> *My state as though 'twere none of mine*
>
> (585–586)

This de-subjectification of the personality is one of the most interesting notions of Romanticism, one, of course, immensely difficult to accomplish; furthermore, it is exactly what Browning was doing in *Pauline* and clearly indicates the origins of his peculiar use of the dramatic monologue. It is similar to Carlyle's distinction between the I and the me, between the noumenal and the phenomenal selves. The same impulse is behind Flaubert's objectification of himself in Madame Bovary, and it accounts for the peculiar impression that Browning's poems make that they are at once autobiographical and non-autobiographical. It was a notion that was to flower in the 1870s in Nietzsche and in Vaihinger, though the latter did not publish his philosophy of 'as if' until 1911. The term 'construct,' now so widely used, is a development of this factor of Romanticism, and amounts to an objectification of cognitive processes.

The speaker proceeds by asserting that it is impossible for him to maintain the frustration and suppression of his powers. Thus he defines the character of the redemption he seeks:

> *so my baffled hopes*
> *Seek out abstractions; I would have but one joy,*
> *Delight on earth, so it were wholly mine;*
> *One rapture all my soul could fill*
>
> (607–10)

This is the clearest possible indication that his undertaking is redemptive, his aim a single mode of limiting the range of behaviour, dominating and subsuming all others. One certainly suspects that the delight is necessarily linked to the singleness. Of his initial endowment, the factor now singled out is the restless craving after knowledge, which he has suppressed, for reasons already suggested. He calls it a 'sleepless harpy' (l. 624), a striking metaphor for the awareness that such an endowment must necessarily violate traditional redemptive modes, that it necessarily leads to innovative deviance. Admitting that he 'cannot but be proud of my bright slave' (l. 634), he goes on in the next paragraph first to assert that this gift must be freed, and then to indicate the source of his self-hate, the fear that to attempt satisfaction of this instinct, which involves soaring beyond the earth (the validated social modes of verbal and non-verbal behaviour) would be a vain effort and would entail the loss of normal earthly satisfactions. We now see the real source of his shame. He wants to eat his cake and have it too. He will not take the risks his gifts require. This is the spell that needs to be broken (l. 698).

Whatever else one may say about the works and the lives of the first two generations of Romantics—and there are still many who can have no sympathy with them—no one can deny that they took major risks. The recognition of their cultural situation, as I have outlined it, demanded either that they take great risks or suffer total collapse. Half-way measures were difficult and, to the degree each recognized the demands of the situation, impossible. In his struggle to achieve self-definition, Browning has clearly seen this attribute of his great predecessors. To abandon normal modes of limiting behaviour is to expose oneself to a degree of disorientation that can threaten sanity and undermine that steady continuity of behaviour that makes risk-taking possible. Browning is very accurate, then, in linking the craving after knowledge with the fear of risk-taking, but the example of his predecessors makes it clear that risk-taking is his only possible mode of redemption. The problem of risk-taking—and it was the central psychological or decisional problem of Romanticism—is that the direction that limits behaviour is one that directs expansion of behaviour. This is the true Romantic paradox, and it explains why so many Romantic lives were filled with disturbance.

That the speaker is capable of it, he asserts, his past behaviour shows, but defences against the disorientation of risk-taking are, he realizes, necessary, and this is perfectly true. One is the power of empathy, to cease temporarily being a self and to become a plant, a bee, a sunbeam, a bird, a fish, a flower, or a tree. The other is the standard method of social withdrawal. Just as Browning's task was made more difficult by his lack of access to *The Prelude*, so his investigation of the strategy of withdrawal was made more difficult by the non-publication of *The Recluse*, which did not appear until 1888. Nevertheless his imaginary construction of 'A home for us, out of the world; in thought—' (l. 730) is as much Wordsworth as it is Shelley. Even so, the imaginative construction of withdrawal proves unsuccessful: 'But my soul saddens when it looks beyond; / I cannot be immortal, nor taste all (ll. 809–10).' For this there are good reasons. Exposure to problems and postponement of solutions, i.e., verbal (intellectual, cultural, spiritual) risk-taking, requires both psychic insulation and social protection, in actuality, not in imagination. Imaginative withdrawal, which is what he attempts here at some length, leads directly to the awareness of death. Indeed, the opening request to Pauline, to 'bend o'er me,' introduces in the first line of the poem the principle of protection. But at this point, the awareness of death, Browning uses a strange device, a long footnote, in French, signed by Pauline herself!

Several things about this note are worth comment, apart from the suggestion that the genre of the poem is the literary epistle and that Pope's 'Eloisa to Abelard' may have been a primary model. The note clearly indicates the structure of the speaker's life, a succession of increasingly lofty plateaus, each with a more extended view of the circumstances of human existence. It is an interesting anticipation of what subsequent study of learning has shown, that we do indeed learn by sudden leaps to new plateaus. To this ascent forgetfulness and slumber, Pauline suggests, will put an end. This transparent denial of immortality is cautiously suggested by Pauline to be as incomprehensible to the speaker as to herself, yet the rest of the poem makes it fairly clear that the notion of immortality is in fact abandoned.

This denial of immortality leads to the next point, the desire of the speaker's soul to

> *rest beneath*
> *Some better essence than itself—in weakness;*
> *This is 'myself—not what I think should be,*
> *And what is that I hunger for but God?*

(818–21)

Two things are of note here, the desire for submissive dependency, and as the next paragraph shows, a non-mediated access to a clearly eroticized deity, as eroticization is defined above. Obviously it is verbal redemption that is at work here, a redemptive mode which dismisses all culturally available modes of a redemptive relation to the term 'God.' This submissive dependency, for all the talk about Romantic pride, well-founded, to be sure, is nevertheless an important ingredient in Romanticism, particularly in its early decades, since all redemptive modes involve a submissive dependency upon some stimulus which is responded to by limiting the range of behaviour. When in the course of the century the most important source of redemption came to be art, the relation of the 'aesthetes' of the nineteenth century to art was a submissive dependency upon it. Further, the submissive dependency which is inherent in all modes of redemption, whether verbal or political, was given a double strength by the psychologically regressive effort to eroticize the source of redemption, of which the eroticization of nature, as described above, was but one form. This accounts for the diffused sexual eroticism to be found throughout the Romantic tradition, but particularly in the period generally known as Aestheticism. As I have suggested, many religions, particularly Christianity, have used eroticized sexuality as an instrument of redemptive control. Romanticism frequently reversed the process and eroticized religion, as in this passage and in the ensuing discussion of Christ.

This is followed by a rapid transition from an assertion that the speaker can envision spending the rest of his life in teaching the faith to an assertion that he is Pauline's forever and that he does love her, a passage which is concluded with the reversal of their relative positions. Pauline is now beneath, looking up. Pauline now assumes the role of submissive dependence, willing to die for the beloved. What has happened here is that the immediate apprehension of God and the empathetic experience of Christ and the crucifixion has successfully accomplished an innovative redemption, utterly deviant from the traditional Christian modes. Consequently the speaker, who was self-defined as incapable of love, is now capable of it, but it is a love in which he is the dominant figure, thus indicating at last a sense of being in command of his own gifts and able to put them to use. This dominating dependence upon Pauline suggests that the best interpretation of 'love' in this passage is 'value—in the object's own right,' to value another's subjectivity. It is the love of a ruler for his people, as suggested above. Thus Pauline henceforward ceases to be a redemptive figure, or even a protective one, but becomes rather a supportive figure, the need for which was so great to the Romantic. The relationship, after this sudden reversal, changes to a relation of equality, rather like that of

Wordsworth and his sister Dorothy, or more precisely of the first among equals.

The speaker is thus able to turn his back upon the past and project a genuine withdrawal to Pauline's native country, evidently Switzerland. Nevertheless, he anticipates a return from his self-imposed exile to his native England, a return to be marked by strength and calm, since the retreat to Switzerland will involve a re-investigation of the cultural tradition and a new examination of the mental treasures of the speaker. But even, he goes on to say, should none of this happen, he has achieved a moment of 'perfect joy', a claim he repeats. The redemptive pattern, then, is a sequence of the discovery of his fear of risk, the taking of that risk in an immediate, deviant, and innovative relation to 'God,' the traditional termination of an explanatory regress, and the assumption of a dominant relation to an object valued in its own right, and to his own powers. He can therefore claim that he will be calmer and purer, that 'beauteous shapes will come for me to seize' and that 'unknown secrets will be trusted me', that in short he will be 'priest and prophet as of old' (ll. 1015–19).

The final paragraph is once again addressed to the Sun-treader, to whom the statement is made that 'I believe in God and truth / And love' (ll. 1020–21). The Sun-treader, like Pauline, is now reduced to a supportive role, as is to be expected, since the speaker is now prophet and priest in his own right. This subordination of the Sun-treader is made possible because the speaker has arrived at an innovative conception of deity, a conception of truth which entails the unknown and thus innovation and deviancy, and a conception of love in which is the source of valuing. Thus he is able to extend the range of his awareness and of a potential supportive group beyond the Sun-treader and Pauline, concluding the poem in an epistolary manner. He is therefore free of doubt and fear. The purpose of the poem is achieved, self-definition as Romantic poet-prophet-priest, a role with a genuine social function, even though the role and its function should be recognized and validated but by a small group of people. Even so, the possibility of creating a nucleus for an alternative mode of redemption suggests an alternative society. But most important, as the phrase 'moment's pride' suggests (l. 993), finality is grasped as the *sense* of finality, a psychological condition, a feeling state, not an absolute truth, not a goal. He asks his friends to 'wish me well' (l. 1031). The future is open; the goal is unknown. There is at least the faint implication of a goal-less existence, of the abandonment of finality and redemption as anything more significant than cognitive vacations. *Pauline* either marks the end of Romanticism, or, if one accepts the larger and more inclusive definition, the beginning of a new stage in its century-long emergence.

# 3 : *Browning and History*

ROGER SHARROCK

IT IS A TRUISM that a great body of Browning's poetry is deeply involved in history: for its settings he drew on a wide and often out-of the-way knowledge of historians, biographers and memorialists; the characters of his dramatic monologues, ancient, medieval or modern, are either real personages (Paracelsus, Fra Lippo Lippi and Clive) or credible imaginary ones who behave plausibly in situations that might have existed (the Monk of *Soliloquy of the Spanish Cloister'*, the Duke of Ferrara in *My Last Duchess*, or Karshish the Arab physician). Error and conscious tampering with documentary facts there may be. Judge Marshall Gest has shown how for his artistic purpose Browning converted into buffoons the two able and conscientious lawyers who opposed each other in the trial of Count Guido Franceschini (*The Ring and the Book*, Books Three and Four)[1] As modern commentary on the poems grows, no doubt other cases of inaccuracy or perversion of the facts will be revealed, but these seem unimportant beside a general effort which seeks to ground poetic perception on documentary truth on a scale not usually attempted in literature except in the historical and the realistic novel of the nineteenth century. It is significant that the historical colouring of some of the best-known of the dramatic monologues of the middle period is reminiscent of Scott, whereas the dryer psychological penetration of late poems like *Red Cotton Night-Cap Country* and *The Inn Album* is comparable to Balzac. On the whole Browning's attitude to historical fact may be said to be at the opposite pole to that of the imaginative writer who cuts through detail and circumstance and boldly embraces a glaring anachronism if it will enable him to catch at the essential spirit of an his-

---

[1] John Marshall Gest, *The Old Yellow Book, Source of Browning's 'The Ring and the Book'*, Boston 1925.

torical situation; for Browning the spirit always inheres in the detail.[1]

Browning scholars and biographers have explored and continue to explore his sources and his treatment of them. But to speak of history since the late eighteenth century is to be aware of our historical self-consciousness and of our post-Romantic view of history as process, not merely to consider the accumulation of our knowledge of the past. Since Vico and Herder the European mind has become ingrained with the concept of ideological thinking; man is seen as the product of interaction with historical circumstances, and culture and cultural change as historical creations. Browning's adaptation of historical themes and persons must be seen against the background of this revolution in human thought. To say this, however, is only to admit that none of us, including Browning, has been unaffected by the revolution; it is not to state that his treatment of history necessarily stands in any direct relation to the main tradition of German historiography from the classic/romantic polarity of Herder and Schlegel through Schleiermacher's work on hermeneutic and Hegel's dialectic of history to Strauss and Ranke. To be sure, he had read Strauss and Ranke in translation; to the former's *Das Leben Jesu* (in George Eliot's translation) he was partly indebted for the desiccating lecture of the Göttingen higher-critical professor in *Christmas-Eve and Easter Day*; the latter, among many other things, afforded him material on Pope Innocent XII for *The Ring and the Book*.[2] But in both cases he is interested in historical fact or opinion as it illuminates or gives precision to feeling. He does not meet Strauss's destructive arguments concerning the divinity of Jesus as an historical critic with a different point of view, but deplores the reduction of the Christ of the Gospels and appeals to a consensus of reverence in ordinary people throughout history:

[1] In any consideration of Browning's love of history reference should be made to his father and to the advantages he enjoyed from his early years in the use of his father's library. The senior Robert Browning had planned 'a sort of biographical novel' under the stimulus of Thomas Otway's *The History of the Triumvirate* (1686); the poet's uncle William Shergold Browning was the author of *A History of the Huguenots during the Sixteenth Century* (2 vol 1829) which was frequently reprinted. It is a careful and judicious political narrative, though inevitably committed to the traditional Protestant point of view, for instance in arguing against Lingard on St. Bartholomew, and in this respect is perhaps interestingly like some of the poet's historical recreations. See *New Letters*, 39, 343.

[2] See W. C. DeVane, *A Browning Handbook*, New York 1955, 335.

> *Each, that thus sets the pure air seething,*
> *May poison it for healthy breathing—*
> *But the Critic leaves no air to poison;*
> *Pumps out with ruthless ingenuity*
> *Atom by atom, and leaves you—vacuity.*
> *Thus much of Christ does he reject?*
> *And what retain? His intellect?*
> *What is it I must reverence duly?*
> *Poor intellect for worship, truly,*
> *Which tells me simply what was told*
>   *(If mere morality, bereft*
>   *Of the God in Christ, be all that's left)*
> *Elsewhere by voices manifold;*
> *With this advantage, that the stater*
>   *Made nowise the important stumble*
>   *Of adding, he, the sage and humble,*
> *Was also one with the Creator.*
> *You urge Christ's followers' simplicity:*
>   *But how does shifting blame evade it?*
> *Have wisdom's words no more felicity?*
>   *The stumbling-block, his speech—who laid it?*
> *How comes it that for one found able*
> *To sift the truth of it from fable*
> *Millions believe it to the letter?*
>
>                                     (909–32)

In this tumble of indignant questions, Browning's argument, if argument it can be called, is an appeal to the common facts of man's religious experience and an indictment of any form of intellectual analysis which attempts to discount the strength of human sentiment. One does, of course, from Coleridge to Michael Oakshott, encounter the sort of defence of a traditional religious or political position which rests in an acknowledgment of the over-riding force of things as they are or an established manner of proceeding. But such arguments are usually based on a prior sceptical critique of theory and it is this element which is absent from Browning's discourse. As is customary with such rhetorical devices, the questions barely conceal an ultimately firm retention of certain emotional assumptions about Christian belief: the Victorian honest doubt remains on the intellectual surface and the bedrock of intuition is not disturbed. In fact it is this prior emotional assurance which prepares for and justifies the ardour of the visionary climax of the companion poem *Easter-Day*: this section of the poem would only seem uncharacteristic if the very definite limits to the scope of Browning's free inquiry were ignored; Elizabeth Barrett Browning was wiser than the Browning societies when she declared at the time of the poem's publication: 'Don't think that he has taken to the cilix—indeed he has not—but it is his way to *see* things as passionately as other people feel *them*.'[1] Browning certainly saw and felt, but he did not think, or only within the precise limits of a carefully prepared programme. That is why his small stock of ideas changed hardly at all during his long poetic career.

It is important to draw attention to the limitations of intellectual interest in Browning when one approaches his attitude to history. For our present concern with historicism and the correspondence between certain stances of Browning's poetry and the insights of the German historiographical tradition may lead us to detect parallels where there are only accidental similarities in a field where vagueness of generalization makes similarity seem easy. Wilhelm Dilthey, in an essay recently republished, spoke of the nineteenth-century historical movement and how it had led to the development of a new theory of interpretation:

> Schleiermacher . . . had developed the new psychological and historical modes of thought into a new philological art of interpretation. With Schiller and Wilhelm von Humboldt, with the Schlegel brothers, the German spirit had turned its attention from literary production to a comprehension of the historical world. It was a movement of great breadth; Böckh, Dissen, Welker, Hegel, Ranke and Savigny were all influenced by it. Friedrich Schlegel became Schleiermacher's mentor in philology. The concepts developed by the former in his brilliant essays on Greek poetry, Goethe and Boccaccio, were those of the inner form of the work, of the evolution of a given writer and of Literature as a systematic whole.[2]

Now if one were to paraphrase Dilthey's conclusion so as to transfer his observations from the work of art or literature to man in history the result would be a statement that might be aptly applied to Browning's treatment of human character: he studies the inner form of the indivi-

---

[1] *The Letters of Elizabeth Barrett Browning*, ed F. G. Kenyon, 1897, i. 449.

[2] 'The Rise of Hermeneutics', *New Literary History*, Winter 1972, 241.

dual, he sees him in his historical evolution (the changes and self-discoveries of Sordello or the sudden conversion of Caponsacchi which throws his past into a new light), and when he turns from the single character to the sum total of individuals he again contemplates an organic process of evolution, though purposive and Lamarckian rather than blindly Darwinian. But if it is easy to recognize that Browning shared in the pervasive historical consciousness of the nineteenth century, there is less evidence that he was intelligently aware of the problems raised by entertaining such views.

The case for aligning Browning's method of poetic analysis with the contemporary school of historiography has been forcefully argued by Morse Peckham.[1] It is a strong case because he refers, not so much to German theory of the Romantic and post-Romantic period, but to the enormous body of historical work employing similar methods that was being published in England in the early—and mid-Victorian period. This included *The French Revolution* and *Oliver Cromwell's Letters and Speeches* of Browning's friend Carlyle as well as the work of Grote, Finlay, Froude, Masson, Spedding and Kinglake. He does however find most interest in the parallels with the approach of Leopold von Ranke because of the profound influence on other historians of Ranke's attitude to interpretation.[2] Ranke evaluated the sources of his documents by attempting an assessment of the personality of the author of the primary document. This was combined with a strenuous use of all available sources. In their assessment of evidence Ranke (and Froude) become aware of the personal element in their own cognitive processes as historians.

'Ranke endeavoured to cancel, or at least reduce to a minimum, the distorting interest, or surd, of the authors of historical documents in order to get at historical truth, *wie es eigentlich gewesen*. Browning aimed at creating historical situations so that the irreducible surd of the interest of the speaker might be located. This is why it is so difficult to decide if the monologuist speaks for Browning: in one, Browning might be seeking to identify his own interests; in another, to identify interests with his character . . . But the mono-

[1] 'Browning's Historiography in *The Ring and the Book*,' *VP*, 1968, 243–57.
[2] It is noteworthy that Browning's friend William Wetmore Storey attended von Ranke's lectures at Berlin in 1850 (*Browning to His American Friends*, ed Gertrude Reese Hudson, 1965, 252).

loguist and Browning always had one interest in common, to mani-
fest their uniqueness, or irrational surd, in the cognitive apprehension and interpretation of a situation. Thus, if the structural
identity of Ranke's and Browning's thinking is acceptable, the
explanation can be located logically in their common source in the
main Romantic line.'

Like the self-conscious historiographer, honestly acknowledging and
allowing for his own personal bias in a world of surds, Browning comes
to admit the bias of his own interests as well as that of his self-exposed
characters. There is an irresolvable tension between subject and object:
in *The Ring and the Book* Browning is both evaluating the relative worth
of his documents, as he sets the different personal accounts side by side in
book after book, and making clear his own fallible position as a seeker
after truth: 'the Robert Browning of Book I is to be conceived as interpreting the documents according to his own interests—necessarily
and ineluctably.' Peckham develops his argument with some subtlety,
finally expressing the complex relationship of speakers and subject
matter in *The Ring and the Book* as an algebraic equation, which it is not
necessary to reproduce. He distinguishes, with perhaps undue refinement, between the historical Browning who writes the poem and what
he terms 'the compromised Browning' who gives his own tendentious
interpretation of events in Book I and then again at the end; he has in
mind the manner in which the poet imposes his personal myth of the
chivalrous rescue of Elizabeth Barrett on the contents of the *Old Yellow
Book*. It is a myth which blends the legend of St. George with that of
Perseus and Andromeda; he even changes the day of Pompilia's rescue
by Caponsacchi from 29 April to 23 April, St. George's Day. Finally,
in a sort of coda to his main argument, Peckham suggests that in his
later long poems Browning abandoned historical subjects because in
the course of the composition of *The Ring and the Book* he had confronted the irreducible obstacle to interpretation by recognizing himself as fallible interpreter.

The argument is ingenious but not wholly convincing. It is possible
to accept the relevance of the analogy with historical method and yet
to draw quite different conclusions. *The Ring and the Book* responds
more easily to Peckham's approach than would any of the shorter dramatic monologues: only a work of multiple confession, and one in
which the author parades his own point of view alongside those of his
characters, can stand up to the parallel with the historian who has to

make allowances for his own prejudices and those of a number of sources. But when one turns to *The Bishop Orders his Tomb* and *Fra Lippo Lippi* there appears another parallel with the work of the historians which is neglected in Peckham's treatment; this is the discovery of the idea of the unified historical period or moment of culture, objectified in thought, art, and life-styles, and with it the concept of evolutionary transition from one age to the next, the life and death of epochs usually conceived in terms of biological growth and decay. There is a passage early in Ranke's *History of the Popes* which brings to mind both these poems as it describes the transition from the middle ages to the humanistic Renaissance:

> If the book of history lay open to our view in its authentic reality, if the fleeting forms of speech stood before us in the durability of the works of nature, how often should we discover in the former, as in the latter, amidst the decay we mourn over, the fresh and quick germ! how often behold life springing out of death!
>
> However we may deplore this contamination of spiritual things with things of earth, this corruption of the institutions of religion, yet, without these evils the human mind could hardly have received one of its most remarkable impulses—an impulse leading to vast and permanent results.
>
> It cannot be denied that, however ingenious, varied and profound are the productions of the middle ages, they are founded on a fantastic view of the world, little answering to the realities of things. Had the church subsisted in full and conscious power she would exactly have perpetuated this state of the human intellect. But in her present condition she allowed the spirit of freedom to unfold itself in a new manner and from a totally different point. . . . the revived acquaintance with antiquity was the power that burst these bounds, that opened a higher, more comprehensive, and grander view.[1]

In *Fra Lippo Lippi* Browning expands the account of the painter he had read in Vasari[2] by developing a suggestion in Baldinucci's *Delle Notizie de Professori del Disegno da Cimabue* that Lippi was one of the first painters to break with ecclesiastical conventions for painting the figures of sacred

[1] Leopold Ranke, *The Ecclesiastical and Political History of the Popes of Rome during the Sixteenth and Seventeenth Centuries*, tr from the German by Sarah Austin, Philadelphia 1841, i. 55.

[2] He came to recognize the mistakes of dating in Vasari as a later letter to Edward Dowden shows (13 October 1866, *Wise Letters*, 104).

story and to strike out towards a naturalistic style:

> *Why can't a painter lift each foot in turn,*
> *Left foot and right foot, go a double step,*
> *Make his flesh liker and his soul more like,*
> *Both in their order?*                          (208–8)

And in the close of the poem the sense of evolution or transition is strikingly caught in the suggestion that Lippi is handing on his new realistic
technique to Masaccio:

> *They call him Hulking Tom, he lets them talk—*
> *He picks my practice up—he'll paint apace,*
> *I hope so—though I never live so long,*
> *I know what's sure to follow.*               (277–80)

The personal story of Lippi the scapegrace caught out by the watch on
his amorous escapade is a vehicle for a parable of historical transition: the
painter's alienation from the pious restrictions of his convent upbringing
reflects his rebellion against a whole order of things thought to be medieval; he represents a swing of the pendulum from an impossible devotion
to pure spirit back to an appreciation of earthly joys; he is the fresh and
quick germ working within an old and sterile order to bring forth life
out of death, the new phase of human development embodied in the
Renaissance cultivation of the beauty of the senses.[1]

The full realization of the sensuousness of the Renaissance is achieved
in *The Bishop orders his Tomb at St. Praxed's Church*. Again, a pronounced
individuality serves to imply a whole movement of culture; but in this
case, instead of the character being in a state of tension with his society
and representing the germ of a new order struggling to be born, he is a
type of the achieved spirit of the high Renaissance; every aspect of life,
and incongruously enough, of Christian belief, is converted into physical
and aesthetic terms:

[1] The idea of a 'new man' linking the medieval to the Renaissance order of
things is admirably caught in Gerard, the father of Erasmus and the hero of
Charles Reade's *The Cloister and the Hearth* (1861), a novel which displays
other affinities with Browning's historical dialectic. Gerard's temptress,
the Princess Clelia, is a representative figure for the medieval spirit: '*This*
was your true medieval. Proud, amorous, vindictive, generous, foolish,
cunning, impulsive, unprincipled; and ignorant as dirt.' (*The Cloister and
the Hearth*, ii. chap. xv.)

> *And then how I shall lie through centuries,*
> *And hear the blessed mutter of the mass,*
> *And see God made and eaten all day long,*
> *And feel the steady candle-flame, and taste*
> *Good strong thick stupifying incense-smoke!*
> *For as I lie here, hours of the dead night,*
> *Dying in state and by such slow degrees,*
> *I fold my arms as if they clasped a crook,*
> *And stretch my feet forth straight as stone can point,*
> *And let the bedclothes, for a mortcloth, drop*
> *Into great laps and folds of sculptor's work:*
> *And as yon tapers dwindle, and strange thoughts*
> *Grow, with a certain humming in my ears,*
> *About the life before I lived this life,*
> *And this life too, popes, cardinals and priests,*
> *Saint Praxed at his sermon on the mount,*
> *Your tall pale mother with her talking eyes,*
> *And new-found agate urns as fresh as day,*
> *And marble's language, Latin pure, discreet . . .*          (80—98)

The poem depends on a sort of conceit; at the moment of death the Bishop remains extravagantly unaware of the contradiction between the earthly desires, with material texture and beauty: he will only wait happily in his own church for the resurrection of his body if he can have the great blue lump of *lapis lazuli* and so scorn his rival Gandolf for eternity. The aestheticism of the Renaissance has now run into decadence; the Bishop remains extravagently unaware of the contradiction between the hope of Christian prayer and his fleshly desires:

> *And have I not Saint Praxed's ear to pray*
> *Horses for ye, and brown Greek manuscripts,*
> *And mistresses with great smooth marbly limbs.*          (73—5)

The Bishop is a brilliantly realized grotesque. His sensual vision of life has become a mania. Many other speakers in Browning's dramatic monologues verge in this manner on mania; a blend of family pride and connoisseurship constitute the monomania of the Duke in *My Last Duchess*, but there again a personality driven to the extreme bounds of idiosyncrasy serves to illustrate the decadence of a way of life incarnated in an historical period. The subject is now the egomania of the aristocratic tyrant—'I choose Never to stoop'—but the Duke has something in common with the Bishop in his exquisite connoisseurship:

> *Notice Neptune though,*
> *Taming a sea-horse, thought a rarity,*
> *Which Claus of Innsbruck cast in bronze for me!*          (55–7)

The emphatic final pronoun reflects back on the whole relationship of the Duke with his duchess and gives his personality away to us or to the ambassador in a single flash of perception; incidentally it also exposes the impurity of the Duke's taste when it is compared with the Bishop's comments on different kinds of marble and his genuine feeling for their texture. Ruskin in the fourth volume of *Modern Painters* was the first to appreciate how the essence of the Renaissance Italian spirit was captured by this precise attention to a particular mountain stone.[1]

Browning may well have been indebted to Ranke for crystallizing the cultural moment of the late fifteenth century as a devotion to sensuous forms. The latter had written:

> 'It has been the exclusive privilege of a few favoured and golden ages of the world to conceive and to express pure beauty of form. Such was the end of the fifteenth, and the beginning of the sixteenth century. How were it possible . . . to give the faintest outline of the entire devotion to art, of the fervid love, the unwearied study of it which then existed?'[2]

What Browning particularly seizes on in this artistic consciousness is the paradox of spirituality deeply committed to the palpable and physical. The conception seems to be widely diffused in both philosophers and historians. It is possible that it emanates from Hegel's *Lectures on the Philosophy of History* where he relates the abuses of the late medieval church to the embodiment of the Spirit in a coarse material form;[3] but the idea is pervasive in Browning and need not be traced to any single source. We encounter it again in *The Laboratory: Ancien Régime* with the same application as in the poems on Renaissance themes; the woman procuring

[1] John Ruskin, *Modern Painters*, IV, part v, chap. xx, 'The Mountain Glory.'

[2] *The History of the Popes*, ed. cit. i. 58.

[3] G. W. Hegel, *Lectures on the Philosophy of History*, tr by Joseph Sibree, 1900, 429–30. There is some resemblance between the role of Caponsacchi as expounded by the Pope and Hegel's 'World-Historical individual' in the same work.

poison for her rival provides a statement on the decadence of an historical epoch. Similarly, the characters in *The Epistle of Karshish* and *Cleon*
represent a culture, Semitic and ancient Greek respectively, that is at its
extremities and moving into the phase when new life will spring from its
death and despair:

> It is so horrible,
> I dare at times imagine to my need
> Some future state revealed to us by Zeus,
> Unlimited in capability
> For joy, as this is in desire for joy. (323–7)

There are however two ways of regarding this immersion of men in
their historical limitations. The first is, as we have seen, to dwell upon
their grotesque self-deception and extravagance. This is the method of
some of the outstanding monologues in *Dramatic Romances and Lyrics* and
*Men and Women*. The historical dialectic of these episodes is in the main
tradition of romantic historiography; it has been briefly touched on by
Robert Langbaum[1] but otherwise not much discussed. The second
method of approach is when truth is conceived as residing in the life of
brute experience and contingency; it may emerge from its shroud of
matter in a moment of revelation or special self-knowledge, and it may
be elicited by a special imaginative effort on the part of the poet. The
poet is now dealing, not with relative historical truth, but with absolute
spirit imprisoned in forms. *The Ring and the Book*, Browning's longest
and most ambitious poem, is the great example of the second method.
Thus the poems in the first category are concerned with a purely historical truth though they hint at a dialectical movement which supersedes
worn-out systems with fresh and dynamic life; Browning, like so many
Victorian historians and literary critics, seems to cheat a little in his handling of the romantic dialectic (but does not Marx do the same over the
supercession of primitive communism?); Fra Lippo Lippi is ebullient and
healthful, the centre of life for the poem; there is a preference for realism
and naturalism as against more formal modes. For the same reason most
of the poems with an historical background are set at the end of a cultural
period when men are becoming conscious of crisis and contradiction in
their beliefs; the majority depict the Renaissance seen as an age of human
transformation and enrichment, or, as we have seen, that moment of the

[1] Robert Langbaum, *The Poetry of Experience*, 1957, 96–7.

early Renaissance when the new ideas were poised on the cusp of the
dying middle age; a few subjects are also chosen from the transition between the ancient world and Christianity or the period of the decay of
the *ancien régime*.[1]

In *The Ring and the Book* there is no suggestion of historical evolution
and the supercession of old forms by new until we come to the Pope's
speech. The last decade of the seventeenth century holds no obvious
appeal as a time of cultural change or transition. The stress is rather on
the past as past, a deposit burying truth under fact and hearsay. By revi-
vifying the past and making it once again present Browning believes that
truth may be found. The strongest objection to the argument put
forward by Morse Peckham, that Browning's voice within the poem is
that of a compromised witness and Browning the writer knows it, is that
in the first book in which he speaks in person the poet explains the
metaphor of his title: the goldsmith making an embossed ring out of a
fine sliver of gold must mix the gold with a brass alloy for it to bear the
file; when acid is applied, the alloy flies off, and the ring of pure gold
remains:

> *Just a spirt* ·
> *O'the proper fiery acid o'er its face,*
> *And forth the alloy unfastened flies in fume;*
> *While, self-sufficient now, the shape remains,*
> *The rondure brave, the lilied loveliness,*
> *Gold as it was, is, shall be evermore.*                    (23–8)

Browning finds in his tattered yellow book on the Florence stall

> *pure crude fact*
> *Secreted from man's life when hearts beat hard,*
> *And brains, high-blooded, ticked two centuries since.*     (35–7)

---

[1] For the idea of an individual carrying the tendencies of an age to their
utmost point one might also compare the final passage in the Life of Strafford in John Forster, *Statesmen of the Commonwealth of England* (1840) i. 411.
(a part of the life which was probably written by Browning during
Forster's illness): 'A great lesson is written in the life of this truly, extraordinary person. In the career of Strafford is to be sought the justification
of the world's "appeal from tyranny to God." In him Despotism had at
length obtained an instrument with mind to comprehend and resolution to
act upon, her principles in their length and breadth . . .'

Before he allows the different characters to tell their versions of the story Browning describes how he reads and recreates the book. There is no question of ironic self-consciousness here. Nothing could be more positive and confident than his assertion that he has probed the truth behind the conflicting narratives; nor is it suggested that his motives as a seeker after truth have been impaired by the correspondences with the story of his love for Elizabeth Barrett; on the contrary, the poet's imagination with all its personal concomitants is seen as the very acid to burn off the dross of words in the documents and reveal the full radiance of Pompilia's purity and Caponsacchi's strength:

> *From the book, yes; thence bit by bit I dug*
> *The lingot truth, that memorable day,*
> *Assayed and knew my piecemeal gain was gold,*
> *Yes; but from something else surpassing that,*
> *Something of mine which, mixed up with the mass,*
> *Made it bear hammer and be firm to file.*
> *Fancy with fact is just one fact the more;*
> *To-wit, that fancy has informed, transpierced,*
> *Thridded, and so thrown fast the facts else free,*
> *As right through ring and ring runs the djereed.*
> *And binds the loose, one bar without a break.*
> *I fused my live soul and that inert stuff*
> *Before attempting smithcraft . . .*
>
> (458–70)

In an unforgettable passage of the first book the poet describes how in the interval between reading the Yellow Book and beginning his poem he reconstructs the events. On the terrace with its cool 'lozenge-brickwork' he is transported, first to the Apennines and Arezzo, 'the woman's trap . . . and torture-place,' then to the scene of the murder at the squalid inn at Castelnuovo, finally to Rome and the climax, 'the ghastly goal'. He freely admits the intensely personal nature of his interest. He does so because it is that interest which directs light to the dark places in the story, 'made the inertness malleolable.' He asks, 'Are means to the end themselves in part the end?' and the answer is that in a sense they are. It is a long and complicated answer in Browning's knotted style of religious exposition where the slow accumulation of clauses, qualifying or concessive, reflects the struggle of evolutionary process. All things are made by

God and remain in God's power, but man, though he cannot of his own
initiative add anything to the created universe, may call back to life
something that is dead:

> *Creates, no, but resuscitates, perhaps,*
> *Inalienable, the arch-prerogative*
> *Which turns thought, act—conceives, expresses too!*
> *No less, man, bounded, yearning to be free,*
> *May so project his surplusage of soul*
> *In search of body, so add self to self*
> *By owning what lay ownerless before,*
> *So find, so fill full, so appropriate forms—*
> *That although nothing which had never life*
> *Shall get life from him, be, not having been,*
> *Yet, something dead may get to live again.*          (719–29)

The analogies he invokes are with Faust and Elisha, especially the latter
who breathed life into a dead body and 'the flesh waxed warm.' The religious explanation has a bearing on the dignity of the poet's part in the
work of recovering truth; it bears more obviously on the truth to be recovered, the moral beauty of Pompilia and Caponsacchi: there is the
hand of God in the action and so it is rememberable. But in the immediate context the poet is most at pains to stress his own God-derived power
to penetrate the darkness of existence, a faculty analogous to the gift of a
mage. I think the reason why Browning does this is to bind his own intensely personal vision to the world of facts; it is not that he is lacking in
confidence in his intuitive reading of the case, or feeling guilty of a personal bias in regard to marriage, as if he were to add another prejudiced
voice to Half-Rome and The Other Half-Rome. It is rather that his deepest poetic perceptions always sprang from an intense, undifferentiated
consciousness of life and vitality in general, before ever he succeeded in
projecting that consciousness on to other selves. Thus the treatment of
history as a shadow on reality which must be pierced, in *The Ring and the
Book*, like the treatment of history as a series of ideological masks or roles
in the monologues of 1842–64, can only fully be understood in the light
of what preceded it in the earliest poems of Browning. In *Pauline, Paracelsus* and Sordello he is attempting in the manner of Shelley to achieve a
fusion between his own spirit and ultimate reality without the mediation
of persons or facts.

His first poem *Pauline*, so unlucky in its reception, provides a parallel with this very passage in the first book of *The Ring and the Book*. For as Browning is concerned in the latter to state that his all-important personal intuition remains divine in its origin, so in the former poem his theme is the recovery of a belief in God after a period of revolt and the effort to reconcile this with his authoritative sense of personality: the young Browning after reading *Queen Mab* had thrown off his inherited Evangelical beliefs and cultivated a proud reliance on the pure light of his own mind. The rejection can not have gone deep or lasted long. It is not really extraordinary that Browning was able through his whole career to reconcile his poetic realism with Christian optimism, however much the Christianity may smack of what later came to be called modernism. He exhibits like any good missionary priest a respect for sinners, a sympathy with inadequacy and failure. It would be pedantically correct to note that his theology is unorthodox; he makes no clear distinction between the spiritual and the physical realms, and inevitably this undermines his conception of the Incarnation and leads to an ultimately vitalistic view of human redemption. But it would be pharisaic to judge him on these grounds, if only on account of the passionately personal acknowledgment of Christ's love for man, another Congregationalist inheritance, displayed in *Christmas-Eve and Easter Day* and other poems. The optimistic evolutionism may have worn badly in the twentieth century, but Browning is always consistent with his premises; if we consider their generous comprehensive sweep he could hardly fail to be. All disagreeables and tensions are finally resolved in a heaven which is not another realm of reality but a reward for participating in the vitality of a single cosmic principle: 'on earth the broken arch, in heaven the perfect round.' Browning may seem unusual among great poets of the nineteenth century but we should not really be surprised that he does not possess the 'alientated vision' of Arnold or Tennyson; he remains invincibly middlebrow, a Teilhard de Chardin of poetry, but a century after the Victorian crisis of liberalism there are more humanized Christians than there are Baudelairean agonized ones: even his overweening egoism could not make him irrelevant.

What is perhaps more surprising is that in *Pauline*, after his brief flirtation with infidelity, when his belief in a personal God is restored, he yet writes about that all-devouring self-consciousness which had produced the crisis:

> *I am made up of an intensest life,*
> *Of a most clear idea of consciousness*
> *Of self, distinct from all its qualities.*                    (268–70)

It is as if, when he addresses God and presents to him his feverish, sickly, but overpowering aims, there is nothing in the created universe more real than the two of them:

> *My God, my God, let me for once look on thee*
> *As though nought else existed, we alone!*
> *And as creation crumbles, my soul's spark*
> *Expands till I can say,—Even from myself*
> *I need thee and I feel thee and I love thee.*
> *I do not plead my rapture in thy works*
> *For love of thee, nor that I feel as one*
> *Who cannot die: but there is that in me*
> *Which turns to thee, which loves or which should love.*        (822–30)

From *Pauline* onwards Browning retains this drive towards an all-inclusive consciousness on the part of the poet. In this he is nearer to the great Romantics than any other Victorian poet (his homage to Shelley, 'the Sun-treader,' is a mere external badge of his allegiance); for in *The Palace of Art* and *The Lady of Shalott* Tennyson retreats from its terrible responsibility which entails a withdrawal into a wholly substitute world. Browning however perseveres, since his ambition for complete understanding is sustained by his belief in a benevolent cosmic purpose. *Pauline* is one of those preliminary soul-records, ruthless in their self-exposure, with which romantic artists begin their careers, seeking to throw a bridge between their alienation and a total knowledge of the world; *Alastor* and *Sleep and Poetry* are similar introspective exercises and Keats's poem in its anticipatory vision of 'the agony, the strife Of human hearts' forecasts the solution which Browning was working towards. He could project this seething psychological awareness on to the minds and cares of other men:

> *a principle of restlessness*
> *Which would be all, have, see, know, taste, feel all—*
> *This is myself . . .*                                          (277–9)

> *'Twas in my plan to look on real life,*
> *Which was all new to me; my theories*

> *Were firm, so I left them, to look upon*
> *Men, and their cares, and hopes, and fears, and joys.* (441–4)

The world of Browning's poetry is not a surrogate world like that of Keats or Shelley, or Mallarmé or Laforgue, where even the landscapes and the skies are theirs before they are ours; but there are times when his world comes perilously near to being like this, when the apparent solidity of the dramatic framework crumbles, and we begin to hear Lippo Lippi, the sweating disciples bearing the Grammarian's body, the Pope and Rabbi ben Ezra, all speaking with the same voice. Yet the effort to objectify began early. It is to be seen in *Pauline*. The poem may seem a sprawling monologue in the poet's adolescent voice but it has a dramatic frame. It is in the form of a passionate love speech to a girl who is in the poet's arms; John Stuart Mill easily saw through this device,[1] but there is another which is more suggestive for the future: Pauline actually edits her lover's poem and adds a long note in French at one point. The penetration of its self-criticism reminds one both of Keats on the stages of 'poesy' in *Sleep and Poetry* and of his remarks on the adolescent limitations of *Endymion*:

> . . . un certain examen . . . pour découvrir la suite des objets auxquels il lui serait possible d'atteindre, et dont chacun une fois obtenu devait former une espèce de plateau d'où l'on pouvait apercevoir d'autres buts, d'autres projets, d'autres jouissances qui, a leur tour, devaient être surmontés.

The stages of exploration are to be situated in historical periods. It is only a step from this, with the ideological monologues, to seeing the various periods as unfolding truth progressively. All-absorbing consciousness attempts to defeat time by a knowledge of total process; and in an imperfect world where Pompilia and Guido marry and die the climax of the total process must be delayed until the future in which the perfect circle is achieved.

Even as early as *Pauline* the manipulator of this dynamic consciousness feels that it enables him to pierce the secrets of the universe like a mage, for he prefixes to the work a long quotation from Cornelius Agrippa, *De Occulta Philosophia*, declaring that he is not responsible for what his readers make of what he truthfully reports, the apology of all magicians and literary realists from Agrippa to Flaubert. Thus we are returned to the

[1] J. S. Mill's review of *Pauline* for the *Examiner* is partly reproduced in Griffin and Minchin, 59–60.

crucial passage in Book I of *The Ring and the Book* where Faustus is invoked and where once again submission to God and proclamation of the searching consciousness are held together in uneasy balance. Again the poet disclaims self-sufficience—'Man's breath were vain to light a virgin wick'—while he dwells on his power to make history alive again:

> *I can detach from me, commission forth*
> *Half of my soul; which in its pilgrimage*
> *O'er old unwandered waste ways of the world,*
> *May chance upon some fragment of a whole . . .*      (749–52)
> *I enter spark-like, put old powers to play . . .*      (755)

In the earlier part of this remarkable passage there are two lines, occurring at some interval in the description of his meditation on the terrace when he has closed the book, which serve to sum up the whole personal problem of expression which led Browning to choose such historically-based themes and to treat them as he did:

> *I turned, to free myself and find the world . . .*      (478)

> *The life in me abolished the death of things.*      (520)

These lines have that singular purity of diction and simplicity of utterance which Browning is capable of when he wants something of crucial importance to stand out from the breathing and groping of his character parts (or indeed from the winding and doubling back of his own meditative manner when he presents himself in a character part). They are remarkable because, in the first place, occurring within forty lines of each other, they seem contradictory. The poet frees himself by entering imaginatively into the story he has read, or by finding truth in it. We are not told what slavery he frees himself from, but the passages we have been referring to in *Pauline* may afford us a clue. That poem shows the poet self-absorbed, caught in a solipsistic hall of mirrors in spite of his rather feverish religious belief and his highly literary passion for a woman. The mature man and poet seems to need the repetition of this act of liberation; the poet had been saved by the effort to understand history—'Men and their cares, and hopes, and fears, and joys'—; the man had found freedom in a marriage of love which is probably as famous (and some would say as aesthetically satisfying) as any of his poems. In contemplating in history a case similar to his own the two acts of liberation are united in a single act which combines psychic release and creative fulfilment. The poet has grasped the world and found it solid and redeeming. But the second line states that the redeeming power was in him to begin with and that it brought life to a dead world.

The apparent contradiction between the two statements lies only on the surface. The apprehension of truth is an instantaneous process, not an intellectual one. Truth, in this case truth of conduct and life, is like an electric charge passing between the self and the persons in the past; both parties are transfigured. There is a resemblance to the transformation of common life as it is seen in the first Romantics. There is 'a new heaven and a new earth' and when it is contemplated 'the heavy and the weary weight of all this unintelligible world' is lifted from the poet. The poet and the world are liberated in the same moment from the dead hand of custom. 'Things' reflects on all that documentary matter, the dross of detail that has to be sifted to get at the truth. But it also has a more striking application to contingent human life and to a conversion experience which provides an image of artistic creativity. For the line anticipates the equally simple and salient declaration by Caponsacchi in Book VI:

> *I paced the city: it was the first Spring*
> *By the invasion I lay passive to,*
> *In rushed new things, the old were wrapped away;*
> *Alike abolished—the imprisonment*
> *Of the outside air, the inside weight o'the world*
> *That pulled me down. Death meant, to spurn the ground,*
> *Soar to the sky,—die well and you do that.*
> *The very immolation made the bliss.*                              (946–53)

Transformed by his love for Pompilia, Caponsacchi sees a new world; experience is remade and he dies into life. It is too obvious to relate this to pure autobiographical reminiscence on Browning's part. What is significant is that he uses a similar form of words to that which he had employed earlier for the analysis, not of his love for Elizabeth Barrett, but of the creative genetics of the poem. The poet is intensely present in the conversion experiences of his historical characters because in doing so he can realize his identity as a poet without being oppressed by it.

Thus the introductory first book of *The Ring and the Book* leads us to expect a poem about the striving of human consciousness to recapture truth from the past, from any past, by an act of artistic perception. This is what Browning the poet does on that particular evening in Florence, and this is what the man Caponsacchi does when he sees Pompilia as she really is. As the poem unfolds we retain this sense of a recovered action that has been placed outside time. To be sure, Guido may be classed as a representative of a dying class, of an old aristocratic culture gone rotten. But this point is not laboured, and it is not central. Nor are we made to feel that the heroic Caponsacchi and the saintly Pompilia are heralds of a new order. Or rather, we do not feel any thing like this until the tenth book. It is in the speech of the Pope that we encounter a new emphasis.

In the figure of Innocent X, the just old man weary with experience and knowledge pondering at the end of his life an irreparable judgment, it is generally agreed that Browning has scored one of the great dramatic successes of the poem. Especially masterly is the theatrical stroke of the conclusion in which the Pope resists the plea for clemency which he knows will be entertained by the Roman establishment. Setting himself against possible unpopularity he finally signs the death warrant and sends it to the governor of the prison. But the preceding two-thousand line review of the case appears at odds with the method and aim of the rest of the poem. That aim as it is enshrined in the central metaphor is to allow the eternal truth of moral excellence to emerge from the chaos of human particularity: the particularity consists in the discrepant individual accounts which constitute the main divisions of the work; it also consists in the total mass of detailed incident embodied in the law reports, and, at another level, in the fallible human words which contain this mass of detail. In Book X, seeing the history of the case through the eyes of the Pope, we are made to feel that the Babel of human language acts almost as an obstacle to knowledge of the truth; and yet it is only through sifting that language that the Pope, or Browning, or ourselves can arrive at the facts. So we have the notion of the necessary interpreter. And who more significantly authoritative as interpreter than a just and infallible pontiff? Does not Browning abandon his own method by presenting us with an assayer of the value of his ring of truth to take the place of the humble and useful alloy of particularity, of *res gestae*? When he demanded that the materials of *The Ring and the Book* should be brought firmly under the control of a single point of view Henry James was reading the poem as a Henry James novel manqué; but he rightly detected that the Pope came as near as any character to providing a dominant viewpoint (writing as the creator of Strether, James would have preferred Caponsacchi as a character who was also a participant in the major action).[1]

If Browning seems to be undermining his method it is not because he lets Innocent be the arbiter of what has gone before but simply because he makes him talk so much about the problems of interpretation. After all, the strongest reason for accusing Browning of inconsistency in the application of his method is that he betrays that method in the first book. In fact he never gives it a chance. In the summary of the main events which follows his account of the *Old Yellow Book* and of his epiphany in Florence (I. 838–1329), Guido's wickedness, Pompilia's innocence and Caponsacchi's chivalry are all declared, and we are told that 'a great guardian of the fold' speaks out and silences all doubt. Browning is not naïve in thus apparently rejecting his method of truth-through-documentation before he has ever tried it. It is what happens between the reading of the *Old Yellow Book* and the writing of the poem that is crucial. Truth is perceived in a single flash in the epiphany of the poet; storms or lightning flashes recur in the imagery as indicators of the spontaneity and immediacy of conversion experience. Just as the poet had to direct the intense life of self-consciousness on to the variety of other selves, so in the greatest of his works of dramatization, when he had come to believe that he could rely on the amassing and disposition of 'pure crude fact' on a scale he had never attempted before, none of this could be made available without the spark of personal intuition. Now the Pope is not a wielder of intuitive powers but one who sifts and ponders. On to him the poet is able to project some of the doubt, the sheer despondency over the chaos of language and human self-deception which at times oppress him. Why should these doubts occur to the believer in an ultimately optimistic system in which all particular defects are reconciled on a universal plane? I would suggest tentatively that Browning was aware of the flaw in his claim to truthful historical recreation; he knew, not that he was a compromised observer, to be sure, but that his intuitive spark was necessary to charge any character or situation: he was present in them all and they could not live without him. If what is at issue is simply the facts of the case in the legal sense, then in his long monologue the Pope is merely underwriting the intuitive forecast of it all in the first book ('previews' as the annotator of the Penguin edi-

[1] Henry James, 'The Novel in *The Ring and the Book*' was first printed in *Transactions of the Royal Society of Literature*, 2nd Series xxxi, 1912, and later collected in *Notes on Novelists*, 1900.

tion has succinctly termed these sections).[1] His meditation serves much more to present the suppressed fear that if intuition fails there is nothing else on which to stand; realism or documentary is an illusion since the writer can never abolish himself as interpreter; indeed when he appears to be absent as interpreter of his fiction, or history, it is then when he is most present.

The Pope's speech begins with reference to a hideous and confused story of his predecessors in the ninth century. Stephen exposes the body of Formosus the previous pope and abuses it in order to condemn his heresy and schism. Then Stephen's judgment is reversed by successive popes. As a preface to a book which more than other books of the poem seems to present judgment rather than material for the reader's judgment we begin with a piece of history that seems likely to swallow us in an abyss of relative values. The Pope speaks with quotations as if he is reading from an official general chronicle of the papacy. The commentators on the poem have not been able to identify any such general history. Browning has invented a chronicle as he has invented other documents for other poems, for instance a medieval interlude for *The Heretic's Tragedy*. There he could speak of the story as 'distorted by refraction from Flemish brain to brain, during the course of a couple of centuries.' Here there is no question of distortion of fact, either in the case of Formosus or that of Pompilia; the doubt concerns motive and the nature of true righteousness:

> *Which of the judgments was infallible?*
> *Which of my predecessors spoke for God?*          (x. 151–2)

The refraction is that brought about by the different points of view of the interpreting minds. The Pope's deep melancholy springs from the fact that the official interpreters no longer seem able to recognize truth. One suspects that Browning's evolutionary idea of goodness has involved him in a considerable theoretical difficulty at this point; it is not a hopeless difficulty because this remains a dramatic poem and these hundreds of lines of speculation do after all represent a stage in a man's making up his mind about history, a stage leading to present action. In terms of the arguments however, the poet appears to have weighted the odds against himself. We are told (ll. 270f.) that God judges the seeds of an act, not

[1] Robert Browning, *The Ring and the Book*, ed Richard D. Altick, 1971, 645 etc.

'leafage and branchage.' But this would imply an almost impossible task for men in interpretation; for they must cut through the waste product of moral consequences to arrive at the moral seed or potential. Browning also seems, through the mouth of the Pope, to be disparaging his own colourful picture of historical reality. The imaginary chronicle, the judgments of the Romans read by the Pope himself, seems to stand in lieu of an authoritative conspectus of world history. But, having to record the scandal of schism, it can bring no comfort to the interpreter. It might be said that an ideal reading of the complete body of Browning's dramatic monologues would envisage them as fragments drawn from such a world-history, a history comprising all the individual histories, every speech made in excuse to the watch, every soliloquy in a Spanish cloister. Our faith in the unseen totality guarantees our acceptance of the fragment as authentic. In fact our appreciation of Browning's poetry on historical themes is only sustained by our belief in an historical continuum;[1] we must have that imaginative grasp of a total stream of life in time which when pressed too far gives us the joke about the Hollywood historical picture in which knights ride in crying that they are going on the *first* crusade. This is history as continuous revelation, the nineteenth-century dream to which the Whig view is but a parochial adjunct. But now in the Pope's speech the historical record seems to spell chaos, not continuity; it is the obstacle of human language, with all its deceits and confusions, which is most responsible and therefore most condemned:

> *None of this vile way by the barren words*
> *Which, more than any deed, characterize*
> *Man as made subject to a curse: no speech*
> *That still bursts o'er some lie which lurks inside,*
> *As the split skin across the coppery snake,*
> *And most denotes man! since, in all beside,*
> *In hate or lust or guile or unbelief,*
> *Out of some core of truth the excrescence comes . . .*
>
> *Therefore this filthy rags of speech, this coil*
> *Of statement, comment, query and response,*      (x. 349–56)

[1] *Cf.* 'How beautiful to see . . . as through a long vista, into the remote Time; to have, as it were, an actual section of almost the earliest Past brought safe into the Present, and set before your eyes' (Thomas Carlyle, *Past and Present*).

> *Tatters all too contaminate for use,*
> *Have no renewing: He, the Truth, is too*
> *The Word. We men, in our degree, may know*
> *There, simply, instantaneously, as here*
> *After long time and amid many lies.*                    (x. 373–9)

It is extraordinary to find such a sweeping condemnation of the word by
a poet. For this is not an attitude like that of Eliot (someone much less
optimistic than Browning about the confusions of history and language)
which believes in the need for a perpetual struggle with language for the
renewal of the word; this is much more radical, and in falling back on
passion and instinct without words Browning's Pope qualifies as a barba-
rian in the sense used of the poet by George Santayana.[1] Distrust of language is shared by other poets who accept the new post-Romantic
criterion of the validity of personal experience; but it is ironic when
expressed like this by a poet who had carried the revolt against literary
language so far and had deliberately cultivated 'this coil Of statement,
comment, query and response, Tatters . . .' in order to mediate a personal truth.

Only God and the saved in heaven can know 'simply, instan-
taneously', without the confusion of words, leaping straight to the inner
quality of the person or the act. But Browning has chosen to forget that
at the crises of his poem some men can move with this divine sureness of
perception: this is how Caponsacchi and Pompilia recognize each other,
and this is how the poet in his first book seizes on the truth of his Roman
murder story. Most dramatically of all, it is in such an instantaneous flash
of conversion that the unspeakable Guido turns to Pompilia's spirit to
save him at the end:

> *Abate,—Cardinal,—Christ,—Maria,—God, . . .*
> *Pompilia, will you let them murder me?*                    (x. 2426–7)

This might be read as a mere pathetic whine if it were not for the forecast
of hope for Guido at the end of the Pope's meditation:

> *For the main criminal I have no hope*
> *Except in such a suddenness of fate.*

[1] George Santayana, 'The Poetry of Barbarism' in *Interpretations of Poetry
and Religion*, 1900; the essay is reprinted in *Selected Critical Writings of George
Santayana*, ed Norman Henfrey, Cambridge 1968, i. 98–116.

> *I stood at Naples once, a night so dark*
> *I could have scarce conjectured there was earth*
> *Anywhere, sky or sea or world at all:*
> *But the night's black was burst through by a blaze—*
> *Thunder struck blow on blow . . .*
> *So may the truth be flashed out by one blow.*
> *And Guido see, one instant, and be saved.*                    (x. 2117–28)

The Pope's pessimism about language leads on to acknowledgment of the failure of the official representatives of the law, civic and ecclesiastical. However much Caponsacchi's rescue of Pompilia may be seen as standing in the main line of Christian endeavour, a repetition at the human level of Christ's victory over Satan, it is not likely to be commemorated as such (X. 666f.):

> *.No lamp will mark that window for a shrine . . .*                (666)

There is a gap between hidden truth and the public record of history; there is an antinomian streak in the thought here and elsewhere. Those who should have been the defenders of virtue, 'with cross on coat,' are absent from

> *. . . the outcome, the brave starry birth*
> *Conciliating earth with all that cloud.*                      (1154–5)

A 'quite new quick cold thrill' now enters the mind of the Pope as he has a premonition of the turning cycle of history. Perhaps a new age is on the way, differing from the Christian era as that era has done from the times of his beloved Euripides. Euripides is given a substantial monologue to expound the principle of gradually evolving knowledge of the good—'How nearly did I guess at that Paul knew?' (X. 1723). He does not doubt the truth of the Christian revelation but envisages an alteration in its character. There will be a death of God, a withdrawal of reality from the church in a new age of rationalism, and Caponsacchi appears as the avatar of the heroism proper to the new age:

> *What if it be the mission of that age,*
> *My death will usher into life, to shake*
> *This torpor of assurance from our creed,*

> *Re-introduce the doubt discarded, bring*
> *The formidable danger back, we drove*
> *Long ago to the distance and the dark?*                    (x.1852–7)
>
> *Here comes the first experimentalist*
> *In the new order of things,—he plays a priest;*
> *Does he take inspiration from the Church,*
> *Directly make her rule his law of life?*
> *Not he: his own mere impulse guides the man . . .*(x. 1910–14)

This splendid poem within a poem, the tenth book of *The Ring and the Book*, depends on a profound psychological anachronism, the assumption that Innocent X could talk like a disciple of Comte or like Browning, or, since poets are prophets, like some Christians, Catholic or Protestant, in the twentieth century. By this book we are invited to view the medieval and Renaissance poems of the earlier collections in a new light. Their Catholic background is brilliantly sketched, but always from outside, by an expatriate bringing with him his liberal-Protestant assumptions, achieving 'emancipation' from the narrowness of a parochial culture without any real adaptation to the new country. After all, the Brownings' contact with Italians was with servants, and they hardly had met a Catholic priest.[1] They lived in Italy in the sort of American expatriate community that has become much more familiar lately. In Mary McCarthy's terminology, he was an expatriate, not an exile, in Italy, and his associations are with the Victorian historians and novelists, not with Manzoni.

One might sum up crudely by saying that Browning never acknowledged his earlier transference by which an original solipsistic consciousness, painful in its intensity, was projected on to imagined historical figures. He tried to preserve both the immediate flash of conscience which was so important to him (and so Nonconformist) and the heavy documentation of the consciousness in time. Sometimes when the contradiction became apparent he saw that a way to solve it would be if there could be posited an end to time, either the nineteenth century as a time of struggle and resolution, or a coming final age (Caponsacchi's). It

---

[1] 'I who never spoke to any other priest than our little Abbe for two minutes in my life!' *Browning to his American Friends* ed Gertrude Reese Hudson, 1965, 135.

is a compliment to Browning if we can feel that he might be leaving the nineteenth century to Kingsley, Reade, and Froude, and be marching forward, however progressively and militantly, to a world beyond the temporal stretch of the Browning Societies.

# 4: *Browning and Philosophy*

### PHILIP DREW

T HIS CHAPTER FALLS into two parts. In the first I give a brief account of the general philosophical position from which most of Browning's poems are written and attempt in particular to show his alignment in the controversy between Intuitionism and Utilitarianism. In the second I consider some of the critical issues raised by the title. These are large topics: to simplify them I shall limit 'philosophy' to 'ethics' and begin my account in 1850. The poems before that date, though important in the evolution of Browning's characteristic *literary* stance are not of first importance in the history of his thought.[1]

The first poem which shows clearly his preoccupation with the problems with which he was to struggle for the rest of his life is *Christmas-Eve and Easter-Day* (1850).

It ends as follows:

> *Thank God, no paradise stands barred*
> *To entry, and I find it hard*
> *To be a Christian, as I said!*
> *Still every now and then my head*
> *Raised glad, sinks mournful—all grows drear*
> *Spite of the sunshine, while I fear*
> *And think, 'How dreadful to be grudged*
> *No ease henceforth, as one that's judged,*
> *Condemned to earth for ever, shut*
> *From Heaven'* . . .

[1] The major exception is *Sordello*, for which see Michael Mason, 'The Importance of *Sordello*' in *The Major Victorian Poets: Reconsiderations* (ed Isobel Armstrong) 1969. See also Thomas J. Collins, *Robert Browning's Moral-Aesthetic Theory 1833–1855*, Nebraska 1967.

> *But Easter-Day breaks! But*
> *Christ rises! Mercy every way*
> *Is infinite,—and who can say?*

What is most extraordinary about this poem is its closeness in religious position to Kierkegaard. The parallels between the two writers need not be laboured. Superficially they share a fondness for pseudonyms and an oblique ironic presentation of ideas, together with a delight in paradox. More important, they were both discontented with the Church and yet convinced of the importance of making a decision and taking a stand on matters of belief. The whole burden of *Christmas-Eve* is that however tempting it may be to 'trim the bark 'twixt shoal and shelf' and take refuge in a 'mild indifferentism' (XIX), a man must finally stop balking at the externals of faith and make a choice:

> *Meantime, in the still recurring fear*
> *Lest myself, at unawares, be found,*
> *While attacking the choice of my neighbours round,*
> *Without my own made—I choose here!* (XXII)

It goes without saying that for both men the choice is a difficult one, and is a deliberate election of a difficult way of life, what Bonhoeffer calls 'costly discipleship.' Each of them lays enormous stress on the responsibility which such choices place on the individual. The words of the Pope might be those of Kierkegaard: 'Never again elude the choice of tints! . . . Life's business being just the terrible choice' (*The Ring and the Book*, X, 1235–38). Kierkegaard's well-known anti-Hegelianism is reflected here: it takes the form of an insistence on 'real ethical alternatives' which impose on the individual the necessity of making distinctions and active choices as opposed to a contemplative neutralism. In *Christmas-Eve*, XIX and XX, Browning attacks the 'genial mood' of tolerance—'I watched my foolish heart expand / In the lazy glow of benevolence.' Again Kierkegaard holds, in opposition to Hegel, that 'the self in its making of decisions is one kind of reality that can be apprehended immediately.' From this two consequences follow, both of which Browning accepted. First, that rational thought as such produces irrelevant answers to spiritual problems, and secondly that the great duty confronting the individual is to hold fast to what it means to be a unique human being.

I draw attention to these elements which the two writers have in common, to their insistence on the simultaneous importance of the subjective and the objective,[1] not because it is in the least degree probable that either influenced the other—there is, as far as I know, no evidence that they even knew of one another's existence—but because the clearest way to express the development of Browning's ideas is in terms of its relation to his Christian beliefs, and the nature of these beliefs at their most intense is most easily understood in Kierkegaardian terms.

It is a difficult question to decide how long such an active and demanding faith was the animating presence in Browning's poetry. Certainly Kingsbury Badger,[2] Henry Jones and other commentators are right to point to 'Saul', in *Men and Women* (1855) as a powerful expression of Christian hope. Similarly the long poems Cleon and Karshish, also in *Men and Women*, are designed to force the reader to compare two ways of life—the life with Christ and the life without. Browning cannot dictate the reader's verdict, but I do not think it will be disputed that he expects the reader to reach a conclusion favouring Christianity and rejecting alike the material values of Karshish, who considers blue-flowering borage more important than the testimony of Lazarus, and the 'profound discouragement' of Protus and Cleon. I have previously suggested that 'Bishop Blougram's Apology', in the same collection, can be interpreted with equal confidence. I am now inclined to modify my earlier comments to take account of the ambiguity of the poem's final lines—'(He) started for Australia—there, I hope, / By this time he has tested his first plough, / And studied his last chapter of St. John.' I took this to indicate that the journalist Gigadibs emigrated and there lived a simple agricultural life 'the last chapter of St. John' meaning that he had studied the Gospels to the very end (alternatively that he had become at last a disciple without doubt). But it might mean that Gigadibs had taken Blougram's advice and stopped bothering his head any more with the sort of theological puzzles posed by St. John. If one gives full weight to this ambiguity at the most crucial point of the poem it is impossible to

---

[1] 'For him [Kierkegaard], inwardness, or subjectivity, is the way to gain true objectivity in ethical and religious matters, in that subjective faith (not empirical objectivity) is a response to and the means of apprehension of the objectively real, eternal, and transcendent God.' G. E. and G. B. Arbaugh, *Kierkegaard's Authorship*, 1968, 408.

[2] '"See the Christ Stand!": Browning's Religion,' *Boston University Studies in English*, I, 1955–6, 53–73.

maintain, as I previously did, that the poem showed the total discomfiture of the sceptical Blougram. I think that he is provided with the poorer side of the argument and I think it is significant that what Gigadibs is out to establish is the necessity for a total Kierkegaardian faith or none at all, but, as I say, I do not now feel the weight of the poem as being unequivocally on the side of Gigadibs.[1] I see it rather as a Janus-poem, looking backwards to *Christmas-Eve and Easter-Day* and equally looking forward to Browning's later poems on Christian subjects where earnest questionings are more in evidence than settled faith. The poem still indicates the desirability of belief with great power but explores also the resources open to the men who cannot command it. Although Gigadibs is the superior character, there is a suggestion that his notions of faith are too naïve to be adopted, and can only be envied.

If this implies a shift of interest from religion to philosophy it is perhaps relevant to note two points. First that Kierkegaard was himself accused of destroying Christianity by his constant insistence on the highest standards of Christian belief, so that at the last it seemed as though he regarded Christ as the only genuine Christian. Secondly that Kierkegaard considered that Christ came to give the world 'an anxious conscience'. The debate about faith, the doubts of Blougram are the products of an intense scrutiny by Browning of what it means to be a Christian.

I have emphasized these parallels between the two men, born within a year of one another and confronting a similar religious situation, in part, as I say, because I think they illuminate the nature of the Christian ideas in Browning's poetry, but, even more importantly, because the concept of human nature and the nature of human choice which Browning formed in his Christian years remained with him even when he no longer retained an active Christian faith. Even if we take the view that the poem involves an admission that *total* belief may no longer be possible it is plain that in taking the outward signs and abandoning the central keep Blougram is choosing the wrong part. It will be my argument in the rest of this chapter that for Browning the values of Christianity survived the shows.

[1] At the risk of being accused of forcing a parallel I cannot forbear to point here to Kierkegaard's attacks in *The Fatherland* ('a secular newspaper of wide circulation') on Bishop Mynster 'that liar of blessed memory' on the grounds that his worldliness was incompatible with a true Christian witness.

The issue then which dominates Browning's poetry after 1855 is not that of deciding the important values by which human life is to be lived, since the values of the good Christian life are sufficient, but that of deciding how these values are to be given force if revelation is to be set aside. The years from 1750 to 1900 form 'one of those ages . . . that walk by sight, not by faith, but yet have no open vision,' in Arnold's telling phrase.[1] One may see the history of the intellectual and spiritual changes of the period encapsulated in Browning's career from 1845 to 1889, for Browning, like almost all his contemporaries, was committed to the search for the authentication of the values that justify and give direction to human activity. It is tempting to say that in the absence of any general principle of authentication Browning simply presented his readers with a series of human beings living their own lives according to their lights, and thus his gallery of men and women symbolizes, indeed actualizes, the collapse of a shared faith and a world where each man's way of life is of equal value. This would be easy enough were it not in direct contradiction of the experience of actually reading Browning's poetry, an experience from which, if a single dominant impression had to be isolated it would be one of an unceasing attempt to bring human conduct to the test. 'All to the very end is trial in life' as the Pope says (*The Ring and the Book* x 1304). Behind this there is never very far away the sense that the test itself may be called in question on the grounds that the criteria employed lack any external or rational authority. If this happens, Browning is prepared sometimes to argue the case for his values, sometimes to deny the need for any external authority and sometimes to do both.

What values Browning in general is prepared to advocate or endorse is a fairly straightforward question to answer. I have suggested elsewhere that the qualities he looks for and approves of in human behaviour can be briefly summarized as love, courage, perseverance, hope and truthfulness. It is not hard to see how easily these can be assimilated to the traditional Christian virtues, but, when Christian faith has gone, why do they continue to function as moral impulses and has the idea of virtue any content at all?

At this point it is convenient to refer to one of the major controversies in nineteenth-century British philosophy—that between the Intuitionists and the Utilitarians, whose positions I now briefly

[1] 'Marcus Aurelius' in *Essays in Criticism* (First Series).

summarize.[1]

The Intuitionists held that no direct evidence was possible for moral judgements—either they are simply known at once by inspection or they can be deduced plainly from some general rule of conduct which is intuitively known. Sidgwick's account of the development of Intuitionism suggests that the essential elements were articulated in Butler, and continued in 'the Common Sense Intuitionism of what is commonly known as the Scottish School' (Introduction, xxvi). The tradition would thus include Richard Price (1723–1791), Thomas Reid (1710–1796), Dugald Stewart (1753–1828), Sir William Hamilton (1788–1856) and William Whewell (1794–1866). In Browning's time the most prominent spokesmen were James Martineau (1805–1900), Henry Mansel (1820–1871) and James M'Cosh (1811–1894).

The Utilitarians, represented by Jeremy Bentham (1748–1813), William Paley (1743–1805), and, in a modified form, by John Stuart Mill (1806–1873) held that moral judgements were calculable:

> Nature has placed mankind under the governance of two sovereign masters, *pain* and *pleasure*. It is for them alone to point out what we ought to do, as well as to determine what we shall do. On the one hand the standard of right and wrong, on the other the chain of causes and effects, are fastened to their throne. They govern us in all we do, in all we say, in all we think: every effort we can make to throw off our subjection, will serve but to demonstrate and confirm it. In words a man may pretend to abjure their empire: but in reality he will remain subject to it all the while. The *principle of utility* recognizes this subjection, and assumes it for the foundation of that system, the object of which is to rear the fabric of felicity by the hands of reason and of law. Systems which attempt to question it, deal in sounds instead of sense, in caprice instead of reason, in darkness instead of light.[2]

If the only motives for human conduct are pleasure and pain then men

[1] 'When the main interest turns again to the systematic determination of right conduct, we find the antithesis between the plain man's Conscience and comprehensive Benevolence . . . developed into the antithesis between Intuitional and Utilitarian morality, which has lasted on into our own time.' (Henry Sidgwick, *Outlines of the History of Ethics*, 1888; (with additional chapter by Alban Widgery, 1931) Introduction xxv.)

[2] *An Introduction to the Principles of Morals and Legislation*, 1789 (2nd ed 1823) chapter I, paragraph 1.

will necessarily act in the way that gives the most pleasure. It was held to follow that actions in general could be assessed by the application of a similar calculus, that action being best which produced, in Beccaria's phrase, 'the greatest happiness of the greatest number.' Thus actions are judged by their results, and motives and feelings must be evaluated solely in terms of their tendency to produce desirable results. The Intuitionists, on the other hand, attached much greater value to the feeling which prompted an action. Martineau, for instance, according to Sidgwick, 'insisted that genuine moral judgment is exclusively on motives and the inner springs of action as distinguished from its external consequences' (p. 303). Bentham of course had no time for such abstractions as the 'inner springs of action' and in a celebrated footnote to the *Principles of Morals and Legislation* satirically examines and rejects all conceivable principles that might be supposed to lie behind intuitive 'approbation and disapprobation.'[1] Sidgwick quotes with relish Bentham's characteristically trenchant comment: 'For diet nothing but self-regarding affection will serve; for a dessert benevolence is a very valuable addition' (p. 249).

It is hard to think of two men of the nineteenth century whose attitudes, public and private, were more sharply contrasted than were those of Bentham and Browning, and it is not surprising therefore that the first broad generalization that one can make about the philosophy of life that lies behind Browning's poetry is that it rejects most of what Bentham stood for and defends most of what Bentham consistently attacked. Conversely Browning's position is normally fairly close to the Intuitionists, especially as Intuitionism had recognizable links with ethical systems deriving from religious sanctions.[2]

A quotation from John Stuart Mill's essay on Bentham[3] directs attention to one of the central points of difference. In his essay Mill praises Bentham's contribution to philosophy in extremely high terms, while at

[1] Chapter II, section 14.

[2] Cf. Sidgwick *Ethics* (rev. Widgery): 'His [Martineau's] *Types of Ethical Theory* was akin in its main features to those traditional forms of British ethics which had a theological background.' Martineau is quoted as saying, 'In perception it is self and nature; in morals it is self and God, that stand face to face.' (p. 302) But other Intuitionists, such as Whewell, Hamilton and M'Cosh, were sometimes considered suspiciously agnostic.

[3] *London and Westminster Review*, August 1838.

the same time making a series of equally damaging reservations and criticisms, of which the following passage is one of the most penetrating:

> Man is never recognized by him [Bentham] as a being capable of
> pursuing spiritual perfection as an end; of desiring, for its own sake,
> the conformity of his own character to his standard of excellence,
> without hope of good or fear of evil from other source than his own
> inward consciousness. Even in the more limited form of Conscience
> this great fact in human nature escapes him. . . . If we find the words
> 'Conscience,' 'Principle,' 'Moral Rectitude,' 'Moral Duty,' in his
> Table of the Springs of Action, it is among the synonyms of the
> 'love of reputation.'

Among the other human attributes which Bentham ignores, Mill points
to 'moral approbation or disapprobation . . . either towards ourselves or
our fellow-creatures,' 'self-respect,' 'the sense of *honour*, and personal
dignity,' 'the love of *beauty*,' 'the love of *order*,' 'the love of *action*' and
'the love of *loving*.' The importance of these qualities to Browning does
not need stressing.

It is implicit in the presentation of most of Browning's dramatic
monologues that there is more to the judging of a man's act than a simple
inspection of consequences. As Rabbi Ben Ezra puts it,

> Not on the vulgar mass
> Called 'work' must sentence pass,
> Things done, that took the eye and had the price;
> O'er which, from level stand,
> The low world laid its hand,
> Found straightway to its mind, could value in a trice:
>
> But all, the world's coarse thumb
> And finger failed to plumb,
> So passed in making up the main account;
> All instincts immature,
> All purposes unsure,
> That weighed not as his work, yet swelled the man's amount:
>
> Thoughts hardly to be packed
> Into a narrow act,
> Fancies that broke through language and escaped;
> All I could never be,

> *All, men ignored in me,*
> *This, I was worth to God, whose wheel the pitcher shaped.*
>
> (XXIII–XXV)

or, in the words of David,

> *'Tis not what man Does which exalts him, but what man*
> *Would do*
>
> ('Saul' xviii)

Perhaps the most revealing comment is that made by Browning in his own person in an aside in *Red Cotton Night-Cap Country*, when he breaks off the story and reflects on his own narrative technique:

> *Along with every act—and speech is act—*
> *There go, a multitude impalpable*
> *To ordinary human faculty,*
> *The thoughts which give the act significance.*
> *Who is a poet needs must apprehend*
> *Alike both speech and thoughts which prompt to speak.*
>
> (IV, 24–9)

The poet's particular gift is thus his insight into human motives, 'which give the act significance.' The importance of an action being thus located within the individual, Browning's characteristic approach to an ethical problem is to dramatize it within the experience of a single character, emphasizing the internal nature of the moral impulse by presenting the poem in the form of a monologue.

The special skill of Browning in this form is his ability to provide in the same poem a man's account of his own conduct and the materials for a judgement of that account. This proceeding is comparatively straightforward as long as a common body of religious belief provides more or less explicit authentication for the values by which the speaker is to be judged. But Browning has eventually to face the challenge addressed to his Pope who has claimed

> *Through hard labour and goodwill,*
> *And habitude that gives a blind man sight*
> *At the practised finger-ends of him, I do*
> *Discern, and dare decree in consequence,*
> *Whatever prove the peril of mistake.*
>
> (*The Ring and the Book* X, 1248–52)

Suppose, however, a voice taunts him with walking round the world candle in hand, not having noticed that the sun has gone out, that is that the ultimate source of his values had disappeared. The Pope admits

> *all that I do and am*
> *Comes from the truth, or seen or else surmised,*
> *Remembered or divined, as mere man may:*
> *I know just so, nor otherwise. As I know,*
> *I speak,—what should I know, then, and how speak*
> *Were there a wild mistake of eye or brain*
> *As to recorded governance above?*
>
> (X, 1287–93)

Browning accepts the challenge to show that his moral impulses are not merely habits which have persisted long after the religion which inspired them and gave them meaning has become obsolete. For the later part of his poetic career, including many of his finest poems, he is concerned to scrutinize the central assumptions about moral activity on which his distinctive presentation of ethical questions depends. The shortest way of stating the case is that he is equally unable to accept an ethical system based on utility—

> *The Devil, that old stager, at his trick*
> *Of general utility, who leads*
> *Downward, perhaps, but fiddles all the way!*
>
> (*RCNC*, II, 261–3)

or on a rationalizing of primitive impulse, a proceeding which even Blougram repudiates with scorn—

> *quick,*
> *Down to the root of all that checks your will*
> *All prohibition to lie, kill and thieve,*
> *Or even to be an atheistic priest!*
> *Suppose a pricking to incontinence—*
> *Philosophers deduce you chastity*
> *Or shame, from just the fact that at the first*
> *Whoso embraced a woman in the field,*
> *Threw club down and forewent his brain beside,*
> *So, stood a ready victim in the reach*
> *Of any brother savage, club in hand;*

*Hence saw the use of going out of sight*
*In wood or cave to prosecute his loves:*
*I read this in a French book t'other day.*
*Does law so analysed coerce you much?*                    (820–34)

Browning's position is thus often very close to that of the Intuitionists, though it would be more accurate to classify him as an anti-Utilitarian than as an Intuitionist. This may be seen from a brief summary of the leading ideas which he employs, by which I mean not that he is directly advocating them but that his presentation of the world implies them.[1]

I distinguish four such leading ideas. It is not too far from the truth to describe them all as survivals of Christian attitudes or secularized versions of Christian concepts. First, and most characteristically, stands his belief in the immortality of the soul. The philosophical consequences of this belief place him in the anti-Utilitarian camp, for if this world is not all we have then pleasure in this world need not be our sole motive. Conversely, if there was no assurance of immortality what permanent value could there be in any human activity? This is a question plainly stated by Browning in *La Saisiaz*; he accepts the paradoxical conclusion that we must posit eternal life to give value to our activities in this life.[2] Secondly, Browning continues to be in the last analysis sceptical of rationality. This does not lead him to abandon all trust in the patient operation of the human reason,[3] nor does it prevent him from constructing poem after poem on a ratiocinative basis, so that the articulation of the argument furnishes the poem with a structure, but it means that he rejects a mor-

---

[1] 'If a work presents or reflects problems which have analogs among the conceptual difficulties of philosophy, it can only add a level to our understanding of what is in the work if we see the moral problems in the light of the conceptual ones.' (Jerome B. Schneewind, 'Moral problems and Moral Philosophy in the Victorian Period,' *VS* Supplement to vol IX, 1965, 29–46). I am happy to acknowledge my indebtedness to Professor Schneewind.

[2] *Cf.* Tennyson, 'Locksley Hall Sixty Years After':

Truth for truth, and good for good! The Good, the True, the Pure, the Just.

Take the charm 'For ever' from them, and they crumble into dust. (71–72)

[3] See, for example, 'Apollo and the Fates' and the 'Parleying with Bernard de Mandeville'.

ality based simply on calculation and rejects also any philosophical system which subordinates belief to knowledge, the sort of position, for example, exemplified by W. K. Clifford's celebrated dictum 'It is wrong everywhere and for anyone, to believe anything upon insufficient evidence.' What we have in Browning is not, as Henry Jones suggests, a pernicious and self-defeating scepticism about the operations of the intellect but an assertion that some primary certainties are intuitively known and thus defy rational analysis and assault.[1] Thirdly, as this world is only one of a succession of human states, so man's progress through it is marked by a series of stages. Browning characteristically presents life as a process of learning or probation, and thus exposes himself to the attacks of philosophers such as Santayana who see the ideal state of human existence as one of tranquility. Browning's point is made clearly in such poems as Development, Rephan and Reverie, and is an essential part of the argument of A Death in the Desert. A quotation from this poem illustrates the process by which man learns more as time passes. This 'progress, man's distinctive mark alone' since it entails a movement from ignorance to knowledge implies that lack of complete knowledge is an essential part of man's nature.[2]

[1] In effect Jones (*Browning as a Philosophical and Religious Teacher*, 1891) complains that, whereas in early Browning there is no sense of a conflict between the claims of faith and those of knowledge, there is such a conflict in the later poems and Browning then does his best to preserve his faith by conceding all the possible weaknesses of the intellect. Browning's 'agnosticism' and 'scepticism', of which Jones makes so much, are certainly less apparent in his early poems, not because he had a more elevated view of the intellect but because he had a more secure religious faith. Later, I suggest, he found that in order to preserve an Intuitionalist ethic he had to assert the limited powers of the intellect. The principal weakness of Jones's book is that he does not recognize that between 1850 and 1870 there is a profound change in the nature of Browning's positive beliefs: he merely observes the poet's increasing reluctance to be bound by purely rational arguments.

[2] With 'A Death in The Desert' cf. Pico della Mirandola on the dignity of man: 'The brutes bring from their mother's body what they will carry with them as long as they live; the higher spirits are from the beginning, or soon after, what they will be for ever. To thee alone is given a growth and a development depending on thine own free will.' The idea of life as a 'training and a passage' is worked out in some detail in *The Ring and the Book*, x, 1308–1450.

> *Man, therefore, thus conditioned, must expect*
> *He could not, what he knows now, know at first;*
> *What he considers that he knows to-day,*
> *Come but to-morrow, he will find misknown;*
> *Getting increase of knowledge, since he learns*
> *Because he lives, which is to be a man,*
> *Set to instruct himself by his past self:*
> *First, like the brute, obliged by facts to learn,*
> *Next, as man may, obliged by his own mind,*
> *Bent, habit, nature, knowledge turned to law.*
> *God's gift was that man should conceive of truth*
> *And yearn to gain it, catching at mistake,*
> *As midway help till he reach fact indeed.*

(600–12)

Browning is thus able to argue that the very fact that men are in doubt is a sign that mankind, unlike gods or animals, is capable of moral growth. Since there is no assigned terminus to this growth, the value of human activity must lie not in attaining but in striving. To travel hopefully is possible: to arrive is not only impossible, but, were it possible, would negate all moral activity. It is because the journey itself is the important thing that we find in Browning a profusion of observations which have the compactness and the cheerfulness of a calendar motto. 'The prize is in the process.' 'Success is nought, endeavour's all.' 'The incomplete / More than completion matches the immense.' His metaphors for life tend to be those of growth, travel, and fluidity. There is no reason to suppose that he would quarrel with the terms of Prince Hohenstiel-Schwangau's description of the true nature of glory:

> *Quite otherwise the cheery game of life,*
> *True yet mimetic warfare, whereby man*
> *Does his best with his utmost, and so ends*
> *A victor most of all in fair defeat.*

(p. 122, 1st ed)

Finally, if we see Browning in his later poems as endeavouring to write a Christian poetry without Christ it is clear that the values he is exercised to defend must find their justification in the experience of the individual. At this point Browning encounters the problem that he debates with dogged persistence in many of his later poems—that of the subjective nature of individual experience. This is the obvious objection to the Intuitionist position[1]—that it is impossible to point to any generally valid authenticating principle for moral insights (in the way in which, for example, Wordsworth could offer Nature). Browning thus is always on the defensive against attacks on the grounds that he is generalizing from his own experience and that his values have no objective validity.[2] In *Prince Hohenstiel-Schwangau*, in *La Saisiaz*, in *Fifine*, and in more than one poem in *Ferishtah's Fancies*, to name only the most obvious cases, he expresses uneasiness (or alternatively an uneasy defiance) at his consciousness of the weakness of an assertion of purely subjective values.

His problem is to proceed from the simple trust of 'I know the right place by foot's fall' to the more general shared moral impulse which he implies in the 'Parleying with Bubb Dodington':

> *Something inside us all and each, that stands*
> *Somehow instead of somewhat which commands*
> *'Lie not'? Folks fear to jeopardize their soul,*
> *Stumble at times, walk straight upon the whole.*

(Section VI, 1st ed, p. 117)

Henry Jones has already dealt at excessive length with Browning's subjectivism, and a more recent study by Paul F. Mattheisen has shown with extreme care the close relation between Browning's practice in *The Ring and the Book* and Kierkegaard's 'crucial principle that no ethical truth which depends for its value and meaning on real existence within an individual can ever become the content of communication.'[3] It is plain however that even a man who accepts a Kierkegaardian 'ethical silence' can nevertheless assert that moral experiences are objective (though incommunicable). This is distinctly easier if the standards involved are

[1] 'There is some justification . . . for the complaint . . . that he [Martineau] took the story which his own moral consciousness told of itself and assumed that the same would be true for all' (Sidgwick (rev. Widgery) *Ethics*, 302).

[2] Note a curious passage in 'Rabbi Ben Ezra' (XIX–XXII), in which the idea is put forward by the speaker that in old age one is able to identify 'the Right / And Good and Infinite / . . . With knowledge absolute, / Subject to no dispute.'

[3] 'Uproar in the Echo: The Existential Aesthetic of Browning's *The Ring and the Book*,' in *Literary Monographs*—3 (Wisconsin 1970) 127–84.

sanctioned by some external authority, such as a system of religion. Browning, however, sees how close the ethical silence of an agnostic can approach to subjective intuitionism, which can in turn lead to ethical nihilism, a position Browning is never willing to accept. Mattheisen qualifies the general position by observing that Kierkegaard allowed that communication of a kind was possible in, for example, a Socratic dialectic. It is notable that Browning's preferred form is the disputation about matters of current interest, whatever the ostensible subject. When one side of the disputation is implied rather than expressed we have a dramatic monologue, a form which can not only be used for satiric ends but suggests a possible way of objectifying the internal individual experience and finally of making through the agency of art the crucial transition from a personal to a common morality. A further poetic consequence of this is that Browning normally attempts to suggest the rhythms of conversation, partly to preserve dramatic propriety, partly to allow the ideas to be plainly expressed and judged on their merits.

Since, then, Jones and Mattheisen have imposed on this question of subjectivity all the weight it will bear I will not say more here about Browning's preoccupation with it. If his concern seems excessive it is worth considering the importance of the problem to him. For if he rejects Utilitarianism and is unable to derive any universally applicable standards from his own moral intuitions, he will find it difficult to reply with conviction to a challenge to attach any meaning or value to human life. He has available two possible answers, neither of which is completely satisfactory. First he may, as Tennyson was often tempted to do, conclude that the whole concept of progress is illusory and therefore abandon the idea of human actions as significant because they take mankind as a whole into a higher condition. Alternatively he may, as most people do, continue to strive and struggle blindly simply because it seems to be on the whole preferable to giving up in despair.[1] Browning, of course, when under pressure, follows the second course, though not

---

[1] The reality of this possibility and its close association with a subjectivist morality is well brought out in an article by W. H. Mallock in *The Nineteenth Century* (January 1878). That Browning does not decide without some misgivings that 'man is hurled / From change to change unceasingly' is clear from 'James Lee's Wife' VI: Browning does not necessarily agree with the speaker, but it is plain that he realizes that there are two sides to a very difficult question.

without profound doubts. Certainly those who persist in trying to do what they believe to be right come off better in Browning's poetry than those who try to make the slipperiness of the problem an excuse for evading the obligations imposed on man as his birthright.

But again and again he is plagued by the doubt which he expressed so memorably in the Epilogue to *Ferishtah's Fancies*. 'What if all be error—/If the halo irised round my head were, Love, thine arms?'—what if all intuitions about man's moral existence are purely subjective? How can the world be prevented from degenerating into a moral chaos where each man follows his own version of the good life and, like Johannes Agricola or Porphyria's lover, justifies his conduct by reference to private unanalyable insights?

Sophisticated *verbal* solutions to the problem are of no help. Browning is not looking for a formula which will be logically unassailable or one which will enable him to hold together all the fragments of a metaphysical system. He is presenting men and women as moral agents. To do so he must not only show the *actual* springs of action, and demonstrate *why* individuals continue to try to act humanly, but also suggest ways in which these impulses may be generalized. It is in order to satisfy this complicated set of requirements that he modifies the four leading ideas I have just mentioned. As each of the ideas is to be found in Kierkegaard, a comparison provides a convenient index of the effort Browning made to preserve a generally hopeful view of human existence.

Briefly he proceeds as follows. First, he posits as a necessary fact that there is life after death, a world beyond this, where success will be possible for those who have not succeeded here, where the incomplete intuitions of this world will be converted into certainties, and whose very existence provides a universal motive for effort which cannot be found if this life is all. For Kierkegaard the notion of eternal life carried with it also the idea of judgement, whereas the pagan notion of immortality meant little more than indestructibility. Browning makes nothing of 'the eternal separation of the just and the unjust': for him the concept of immortality is almost wholly benign, whether it operates as a stimulus to effort in this world or as the ultimate compensation for its disappointments.

> *On the earth the broken arcs; in the heaven, a perfect round.*
> *All we have willed or hoped or dreamed of good shall exist;*
> *Not its semblance, but itself* ('Abt Vogler', IX–X)

Secondly, he trusts that where intellectual effort fails, simplicity of heart may succeed, especially in matters of moral conduct—'Let him rush straight and how shall he go wrong.' The whole weight of *Red Cotton Night-Cap Country* is brought to bear on this point:

> *Hold a belief, you only half-believe,*
> *With all-momentous issues either way,—*
> *And I advise you imitate this leap,*
> *Put faith to proof, be cured or killed at once!*
> *Call you man, killed through cutting cancer out,*
> *The worse for such an act of bravery?*
> *That's more than I know.*

It is notable that although Browning has his reservations about Miranda's conduct (e.g. IV 757–9) he is nevertheless prepared to base a general moral principle on his crucial act of choice.

Thirdly, to accommodate the clash of conflicting interests in his picture of the world as progressing forward by stages Browning sometimes made use of the Utilitarian idea that public utility is best served if each man considers his own interests. Liberty for each man to pursue his own ends is of first importance to Bentham and to Mill: The Utilitarians are therefore optimistic—free speech, free trade, free markets necessarily produce the greatest benefits—and libertarian. Browning can without much difficulty appropriate the idea that

> *Be hate that fruit or love that fruit,*
> *It forwards the general deed of man,*
> *And each of the Many helps to recruit*
> *The life of the race by a general plan;*
> *Each living his own, to boot.*

('By the Fire-Side', L)

Thus he welcomes Mandeville's ironical *Fable of the Bees* because it can be interpreted to support the idea that perhaps 'every growth of good / Sprang consequent on evil's neighbourhood.'[1] My suggestion is that Browning adopted this line of argument not simply because it made it much easier for him to entertain optimistic thoughts about human pro-

---

[1] No doubt Browning fails to perceive the full satiric force of Mandeville, but I do not think that he misinterprets him as thoroughly as DeVane suggests (*Handbook*, 496–9).

gress but also because it seemed to suggest some way of making the difficult transition from private moral insights to a concern for the general welfare and thus to principles of general ethical validity.

Finally, I have mentioned Browning's insistence on the stages through which a man must pass. Kierkegaard distinguishes three possible states of life—the aesthetic, the ethical and the religious: to move from one to another a man must make a crucial and sometimes violent act of choice. Browning, as we have seen, sometimes attaches great value to a secularized version of Kierkegaard's leap. Sometimes however he prefers to accept a more gradual view of the individual's development and to relate it to a generally evolutionary account of the development of humanity.[1] This is of course yet another way in which the individual's experience can be seen as typical.

*Paracelsus* and *Prince Hohenstiel-Schwangau* show clearly what use Browning was prepared to make of the theories of evolution when they seemed helpful to his general position.[2] One consequence of Browning's frequent reliance on such a view of man's nature is that his position is sometimes hard to distinguish from that of an agnostic-evolutionary such as Herbert Spencer, whose *Synthetic Philosophy* (1862–93) offered to assimilate all scientific knowledge under general unifying principles.[3]

Ultimately in his view of life as process Browning is not too distant from the creative evolution of Bergson, for whom the life of the individual was a fluid continuum which only a misguided intellectualism leads man to break up into a series of fragments. 'Dive back into that flux itself if you really want to know what reality is.'

This collocation of Browning and Bergson points very clearly to the epistemological problems with which Browning grappled in the last thirty years of his life and to the tensions which they generated in his

[1] E. g. 'Reverie' stanza VI: 'I for my race and me / Shall apprehend life's law: / In the legend of man shall see / Writ large what small I saw / In my life's tale: both agree.'

[2] The 'Parleying with Francis Furini' suggests that Browning was not able to accept all the implications of evolutionary theory, especially in the presentation of men like Tyndall.

[3] It would be unfair to apply to Browning what Mill said of Herbert Spencer, that he 'throws himself with a certain deliberate impetuosity into the last new theory that chimes with his general way of thinking,' but there would be elements of truth.

poetry. He is emotionally in sympathy with a philosophy such as Bergson's, which embraces the reality of manifestations, rather than with any Idealist view. But at the same time he resists, fiercely even, the pressures to become a total relativist, accepting every kind of human conduct as equally justifiable. He is, that is to say, trying constantly to find some middle way which will allow him to hold fast to certain objective standards of human conduct, to certain ideals, without dismissing everyday life as a mere ephemeral veiling of immaterial essences. No doubt most people, consciously or not, are looking for this same way, and no doubt it requires a certain tincture of optimism even to hope that it can be discovered. In the same way we may point to Browning's ability to resist the depressing and oppressive conclusions of materialism by as stout an assertion as Kierkegaard's, and envy also his ability to shed, along with Kierkegaard's religious convictions, the *angst*, the fear and the trembling. It is this sense that Browning is able to have, as we say, the best of both worlds that leads people to label him an optimist, and thus, by implication, either no philosopher at all or a dishonest one.


II


It now remains to show how, if at all, this general pattern of beliefs which I have outlined finds expression in the conduct of individual poems. The problem is most easily seen as three related questions.

First, how important is the content of poetry in general and of Browning's poetry in particular? Isn't the important thing to read it as Poetry without worrying about what it says? Secondly, if the answer to the first question entails attaching importance to content is it therefore necessary to be fully informed of the philosophical background? Is it, for example, essential to know who Martineau was before you can make anything of *Fifine At The Fair*? Further, even if it is not necessary, is it at least helpful? Thirdly, how important is Browning as a philosopher? Did he, for instance, make any useful contribution to the great nineteenth-century debate about the nature of man, and are any of his contributions now of more than historical interest? On the whole I shall be relieved to discover affirmative answers, for if the answer to the first question is 'Not important at all' then clearly there is no point in trying to connect the philosophy as such with the poems, and the value of this chapter is, to say the least, questionable. If the answer to the second question is that a knowledge of the philosophical background is neither essential nor helpful for a reading of the poems this again suggests very strongly that there is no connection between the two.

The third question does not require an affirmative answer in quite the same way, except that it is hard to justify attaching importance to philosophical speculations which were never part of the general intellectual fabric of the age and are now no longer of any interest.

There are obviously those who would answer 'Not important at all' to the first question. Their reasons for this answer would not be identical but they would presumably all agree more or less with Mallarmé's celebrated remark 'Ce n'est point avec des idées, mon cher Degas, qu'on fait des vers. C'est avec des mots.' This, perhaps through a slight misinterpretation of the word 'vers,' has been greeted as a declaration of the nature of poetry and transmuted into such familiar shapes as 'A poem should not mean / But be' and 'The dominant medium of modern poetry is the IMAGE.' The same idea lies behind McLuhan's 'The medium is the message' and Christopher Ricks's more cautious formulation 'Verbal achievement is an essential issue *whenever* a poem is quoted.' I am not concerned here to argue for or against the general aesthetic position that lies behind these statements. My concern is to decide whether they or some alternative theory of what poetry is enable us to understand more clearly what Browning's poetry is.

The obvious alternative to consider is the poetic theory of Browning's own century, especially the major critics of the age. The opposite case is clearly put by Goethe when he writes '. . . what is really deeply and fundamentally effective—what is truly educative and inspiring, is what remains of the poet when he is translated into prose,' but such an extreme statement is not necessary for the argument. For example, when Coleridge says 'No man was ever yet a great poet, without being at the same time a profound philosopher,' or when Wordsworth says 'Every great poet is a Teacher: I wish either to be considered as a Teacher or as nothing,' or when Byron describes the ethical as 'the highest of all poetry', they are not locating the entire value of poetry in its content, but they indicate unambiguously that the content of poetry is not negligible. Similarly Carlyle, after giving due weight to 'music', decides that 'a *musical* thought is one spoken by a mind that has penetrated into the inmost heart of the thing . . . Poetry, therefore, we will call *musical Thought*. The Poet is he who *thinks* in that manner. At bottom, it turns still on power of intellect; it is a man's sincerity and depth of vision that makes him a Poet.' Elsewhere he writes, 'On all hands, there is no truce given to the hypothesis, that the ultimate object of the poet is to please. Sensation, even of the finest and most rapturous sort, is not the end but the means.' Perhaps the most impressive witness is Ruskin. In the second chapter of the first section of the first part of *Modern Painters* (1843) he is concerned to define greatness in art. He does this by appealing to poetry as an illustrative parallel. This implies that he regards the position of the poet as not being in dispute. The entire tenor of Ruskin's argument is that the ideas expressed are what determine greatness, not the vehicle of those ideas. His conclusion may be fairly represented by two sentences—'It is not by the mode of representing and saying, but by what is represented and said, that the respective greatness either of the painter or the writer is to be finally determined.' 'He is the greatest artist who has embodied in the sum of his works, the greatest number of the greatest ideas.'

Arnold is more inclined to vary his definition of poetry according to the needs of his argument, but a passage from his essay on Heine in the first collection of *Essays in Criticism* (1865) will perhaps be accepted as representing a view of poetry which he never explicitly repudiates and is consonant with a large part of his critical writings. He points out that the men who can influence the poets can influence mankind' 'for poetry is simply the most beautiful, impressive, and widely effective mode of saying things' (p. 161).[1] This concurrence of testimony encourages me to accept the following statement of the general position by A. H. Warren:

> If one had to choose, one would probably say that modern criticism is characterized by its interest in the poem as a self-contained structure of meaning, in form, in other words, and in the techniques by which forms are produced. It is understatement to say that this inter-

[1] Even critics who are in general concerned to minimize the didactic element in poetry nevertheless make significant concessions e.g. 'A right moral state of heart is the formal and scientific condition of a poetical mind' (Newman, 'Poetry, with Reference to Aristotle's *Poetics*' 1829); 'The avowed object of the poet is pleasure; but he has laid in ambush other ends as mighty and as earnest as any that rule mankind' (E. S. Dallas, *Poetics: an Essay on Poetry*, 1852, 273).

est, particularly in so far as it is exclusive, is quite foreign to Early Victorian poetics.[1]

When we set Mallarmé's observation against this body of opinion it may appear as an unhelpful truism equivalent to saying that a mathematician operates with symbols: of course it does not follow from this that he does not also operate with ideas. Alternatively it may be seen as a description and justification of a certain type of poetry, perhaps resembling that of Mallarmé. If so, such a view of poetry is not necessarily applicable to all poetry and may very well obstruct our understanding of poetry written on different principles. At this point I may as well abandon this sketchy pretence at impartiality and say firmly that for nineteenth-century poetry, at least before the Symbolists, the aesthetic that is represented by Ruskin seems to me appropriate and revealing while the aesthetic represented by Mallarmé is inappropriate and informative only partially and by chance. Browning's own support of the earlier theories is amply documented.

If this is granted, the second question can be answered fairly briefly. There are not many of Browning's poems which *require* a detailed knowledge of current philosophical argument. *La Saisiaz* is typical of many of Browning's poems in this. Although it is designed as a contribution to a philosophical debate, and a reading of the symposium in the *Nineteenth Century* on the Soul and Future Life adds to the interest of the poem, a previous knowledge of the argument is not essential, for an important part of the structure of the poem is an analysis and careful articulation of the terms that are going to be employed. The reader has no need to bear in mind the vocabulary or systems of other writers. The point of the poem lies in Browning's attempt to take the argument back to a series of axioms: the particular circumstances of the poem make it more likely that these will command ready assent.

The Christian poems require, of course, a reasonable acquaintance with Christian doctrine; I do not think that *Christmas-Eve and Easter-Day* and 'Development', for example, make much sense unless the reader understands the direction of nineteenth-century criticism of religious evidences. Similarly 'A Death in the Desert' is in effect a reply to the *Wesen des Christentums* of Feuerbach, which George Eliot translated. While this information is helpful and serves to clarify the argument, it is

[1] Alba H. Warren Jr., *English Poetic Theory, 1825–1865* (Princeton Studies in English, No. 29, Princeton, 1950) 214.

not essential: the poem can be read, understood and enjoyed by those who have never heard of Feuerbach, just as *Oliver Twist* can be understood by those who have never heard of the New Poor Law, or the old one.

The chief use of a knowledge of the philosophical positions that corresponded with Browning's and of the alternatives that were available to him is in heightening the reader's consciousness of the constraints within which he was writing, just as an understanding of dualism helps the reader to realize the heresies which Milton must avoid in *Paradise Lost*. Browning, in particular, is, as I have suggested, close to the Intuitionists in the sense that he is committed to judging actions by motives rather than by consequences. Yet, in order to maintain that men are justified in following their own intuitions he finds it useful to borrow the Utilitarian idea that the public interest must be furthered by conflicting private interests. If this is not to issue merely in measuring actions by their consequences, he has to assert his own ability to judge motives as being in themselves good or bad, with the obvious danger on the contrary side of falling into a sceptical subjectivism. Clearly fine distinctions have to be made and closely-bordering positions discriminated between by the operation of what is very near to casuistry. I think that there are places where Browning strikes an unhappy compromise, arguing point after point against himself—the familiar spectacle of Browning Q.C. on his feet before the Hon. Sir Robert Browning in the Chancery Division —until aesthetic pleasure is attenuated to a purely intellectual admiration of patient hair-splitting, yet stopping short of the logical rigour which alone could give complete intellectual satisfaction. Many of the poems in *Ferishtah's Fancies* seem to me to fall into this group. At other times the sense that the poet is walking a narrow line between two perils gives a tension and excitement to the unfolding of the argument.

As one would expect, this is partly of historical interest. The reader can see in the poet a representative figure of his age—an age in which many men, perhaps indeed most men, found themselves unable to accept any longer the assurances of the Christian church and were confronted with the alternatives of an unexamined persistence in Christian values and the deliberate rapacity of Benthamism. The first effect of looking at *The Ring and the Book* with these ideas in mind is to suggest how closely the poem, in spite of its seventeenth-century setting, bears on the central preoccupations of the nineteenth century. Perhaps the point where

Browning's understanding of and sympathy for the Intuitionist point of view is most evident is in a striking passage towards the beginning of the Pope's monologue, as he sits alone with the final responsibility for judging whether or not Guido shall die. Men might suppose that the importance of the act would make him irresolute, but, he says, the prospect of making a mistake does not daunt him in the least. Suppose he encountered a peasant in a fit and prescribed a certain treatment, as a consequence of which the man died, he would not be vexed, since he would know that his own motives were good, however lamentable the consequences. Similarly if he honestly judges Guido guilty and he is executed, the Pope will have nothing to fear even though it should prove that Guido was innocent after all:

> *I hold a heavier fault imputable*
> *Inasmuch as I changed a chaplain once,*
> *For no cause,—no, if I must bare my heart,—*
> *Save that he snuffled somewhat saying mass.*
> *For I am ware it is the seed of act,*
> *God holds appraising in His hollow palm,*
> *Not act grown great thence on the world below,*
> *Leafage and branchage, vulgar eyes admire.*

> (X, 268–75)

It would be possible to agree that this is a firm statement of Intuitionist ethics but still to maintain that it is ascribed to the Pope for dramatic reasons; similarly with his judging of Guido in terms of 'motive' (533) and 'impulse' (537). However not only is there no sign at this point of dramatic distancing or of anything that might lead us to suppose that Browning does not endorse what the Pope says, but also the entire structure of the poem corroborates the Pope's assessment of the correct way of judging actions. For the Pope continues

> *Therefore I stand on my integrity,*
> *Nor fear at all: and if I hesitate*
> *It is because I need to breathe awhile,*
> *Rest, as the human right allows, review*
> *Intent the little seeds of act, my tree,—*
> *The thought, which, clothed in deed, I give the world. . . .*

> (X, 276–82)

The Pope's monologue is his own review of the motives of his actions. The same is true of all the other main monologues in the poem. To operate at all, that is to say, it requires from the reader assent to the propositions that motives have reality and are discussible. The actions are known, but when Browning subjects them to the scrutiny of his poem it is their origins, the 'little seeds of act,' not their consequences which he offers to show.

Pompilia's innocence and charity are shown as infinitely desirable qualities, but closely connected with her unquestioning belief in Christ. The Pope (X, 1885) sees her kind of faith as something that may persist into the future, but only for a few. Caponsacchi has to move into the world and make decisions where faith cannot guide him. In particular he has to decide between Guido and Pompilia, not on the basis of their actions, but on his own inference of their motives

> *As I*
> *Recognized her, at potency of truth,*
> *So she, by the crystalline soul, knew me,*
> *Never mistook the signs.*
>
> (VI, 931–4)

> *Felt time's old barrier-growth of right and fit*
> *Give way through all its twines, and let me go.*
> *Use and wont recognized the excepted man,*
> *Let speed the special service.*
>
> (VI, 1127–30)

He concludes his plea:

> *I do but play with an imagined life*
> *Of who, unfettered by a vow, unblessed*
> *By the higher call,—since you will have it so,—*
> *Leads it companioned by the woman there.*
> *To live, and see her learn, and learn by her,*
> *Out of the low obscure and petty world—*
> *Or only see one purpose and one will*
> *Evolve themselves i' the world, change wrong to right:*
> *To have to do with nothing but the true,*
> *The good, the eternal—and these, not alone*

> *In the main current of the general life,*
> *But small experiences of every day,*
> *Concerns of the particular hearth and home.*

(VI, 2081–93)

Caponsacchi thus illustrates the main premise on which the whole poem is built—that *actions* are evident to all, but that they must be interpreted, because what is of importance for the moral judgement is the motives that have led to them. But the Pope is quick to point out that 'his own mere impulse guides the man,' that it is only chance that he has been guided in the right direction, and that he cannot 'teach others how to quit themselves.' If he simply says 'Ask your hearts as I asked mine' what reply can he possibly make to the man who says, 'My heart answers to another tune'?

> *I live for greed, ambition, lust, revenge;*
> *Attain these ends by force, guile: hypocrite,*
> *To-day, perchance to-morrow recognized*
> *The rational man, the type of common sense.*

(X, 1938–41)

The Pope comments wryly, 'There's Loyola adapted to our time!'

An ethical system based on intuition would obviously lack coercive force over anyone who prides himself on being a realist. Guido, for instance, dwells only on what can be established and on the values that pass current:

> *Honour of birth,—*
> *If that thing has no value, cannot buy*
> *Something with value of another sort,*
> *You've no reward nor punishment to give*
> *I' the giving or the taking honour; straight*
> *Your social fabric, pinnacle to base,*
> *Comes down a-clatter like a house of cards.*
> *Get honour, and keep honour free from flaw,*
> *Aim at still higher honour,—gabble o' the goose!*
>
> . . . . . . .
>
> *On the other hand, bid this buffoonery cease,*
> *Admit that honour is a privilege,*
> *The question follows, privilege worth what?*

*Why, worth the market-price,—now up, now down,*
*Just so with this as with all other ware:*
*Therefore essay the market, sell your name,*
*Style and condition to who buys them best!*

(V, 439–46, 459–65)

The standard unit of his apology is a recital of actions and of the legal
verdicts on them combined with a resolute refusal to examine motives,
whether his own or another's. In essence his defence is that law is a deter-
rent, which he has made more effective by punishing Pompilia.

*Anyhow, here the offence, being punished, ends*

. . . . . . . .

*[I] have simply . . . .*
*Blackened again, made legible once more*
*Your own decree, not permanently writ,*
*Rightly conceived but all too faintly traced.*
*It reads efficient, now, comminatory,*
*A terror to the wicked, answers so*
*The mood o' the magistrate, the mind of law.*

(V, 1939, 1995–2002)

Guido thus justifies his actions on the grounds of public utility.

When, in his second monologue, he reveals more of himself—'I have
gone inside my soul / And shut its door behind me' (XI, 2291–92)—it is a
self without understanding of the meaning of moral action. Essentially
his plea in Book XI is for the world to recognize that there is no such
thing as a sincere Christian life. In a world of hypocrites there can be no
sense of right or wrong: there are legal and illegal acts, and illegal acts
which are discovered and punished are blunders. This is the most Guido
will admit. His version of the origins of law has a familiar ring:

*I say that, long ago, when things began,*
*All the world made agreement, such and such*
*Were pleasure-giving profit-bearing acts,*
*But henceforth extra-legal, nor to be:*
*You must not kill the man whose death would please*
*And profit you, unless his life stop yours*
*Plainly, and need so be put aside:*
*Get the thing by a public course, by law,*

Only no private bloodshed as of old!
All of us, for the good of every one,
Renounced such licence and conformed to law:
Who breaks law, breaks pact therefore, helps himself
To pleasure and profit over and above the due,
And must pay forfeit,—pain beyond his share:
For, pleasure being the sole good in the world,
Anyone's pleasure turns to someone's pain,
So, law must watch for everyone,—say we,
Who call things wicked that give too much joy,
And nickname mere reprisal, envy makes,
Punishment: quite right! thus the world goes round.
I, being well aware such pact there was,
I, in my time who found advantage come
Of law's observance and crime's penalty . . .
I could not, for that foolish life of me,
Help risking law's infringement,—I broke bond,
And needs must pay price,—wherefore here's my head,
Flung with a flourish! But, repentance too!
But pure and simple sorrow for law's breach
Rather than blunderer's-ineptitude?[1]
Cardinal, no! Abate, scarcely thus!
'Tis the fault, not that I dared try a fall
With Law and straightway am found undermost,
But that I failed to see, above man's law,
God's precept you, the Christians, recognize?
Colly my cow! . . .
I say, if ever was such faith at all
Born in the world, by your community
Suffered to live its little tick of time,
'Tis dead of age, now, ludicrously dead . . .
Look in your own heart, if your soul have eyes!
You shall see reason why, though faith were fled,
Unbelief still might work the wires and move
Man, the machine, to play a faithful part.

(XI, 515–37, 542–53, 558–61, 610–13)

[1] Cf. 'Vice may be defined as a miscalculation of chances' *Deontology*, ed by Bowring from Bentham's MS, quoted by Sidgwick, *Ethics*, 244.

His debased standards for evaluating actions are in the end what reveal
him as damned. To the end he is convinced that he is dying because of a
'mistake' and insists 'I recognized no law I could not see' (**XI**, 2389).

It is notable that the Pope, whom one might expect to resolve the
issues in dispute by the light of a pure Christian faith, asks 'Where are the
Christians in their panoply?' and replies 'Slunk into corners!' He recognizes that while he personally 'has light nor fears the dark at all' there are
many 'who pace outside / this petty circle.' Therefore the climax of his
speech is not an affirmation of Christian certainties but a powerful questioning of the permanence of Christian values. To preserve historical
propriety this is put in the mouth of Euripides, who argues that it is possible to live a virtuous life in a world without Christ. Living when he
did, he says, he might reasonably have argued, 'Why not live brutishly,
obey brutes' law?'[1] Instead he claims, in words which might stand as
Browning's description of the ideal poet,

> *[I] adopted virtue as my rule of life,*
> *Waived all reward, loved but for loving's sake,*
> *And, what my heart taught me, I taught the world.*

(1711–13)

Euripides is able to justify what he did in the absence of revelation, and
by implication to indicate a possible way of life for men who were no
longer able to accept the authority of Christ:

> *Therefore, what gods do, men may criticize,*
> *Applaud, condemn,——how should he fear the truth?——*
>
> .     .     .     .     .     .     .     .
>
>                     *Thus, bold*
> *Yet self-mistrusting, should man bear himself,*
> *Most assured on what now concerns him most—*
> *The law of his own life, the path he prints,——*
> *Which law is virtue and not vice, I say.*

(1747–8, 1753–7)

At the end of his monologue the Pope rehearses a battery of imaginary
arguments in favour of releasing Guido, each of which resolves itself into
a prudential suggestion that an acquittal will bring about some favourable consequence. The Pope finally silences his imagined advisers by

[1] Cf. Blougram's 'Grant I'm a beast, why beasts must live beasts' lives.'

saying 'a voice other than yours / Quickens my spirit' (2099–2100).

This account of the relation between *The Ring and the Book* and contemporary philosophical debates is partly of historical interest as a kind of sample case of available attitudes to moral judgements, but the use of Utilitarian doctrines as an index of Guido's character is of more general application as a clue to Browning's satiric methods. Three ambiguous characters—Blougram, Sludge and Prince Hohenstiel-Schwangau—have a feature in common, that they expect to be judged and justified by results, not intentions. Sludge, for example, says, 'I cheat and what's the happy consequence?' The repeated contrast in the second half of *Prince Hohenstiel-Schwangau* is between the prudential advice of Sagacity and the instincts of the Head to govern realistically but by the same principles as hold good for private conduct. Thus Sagacity promises that

> *selfishness shall surreptitiously*
> *Do wisdom's office*

while the Head prefers to say to his subjects,

> *Hear the truth, and bear the truth,*
> *And bring the truth to bear on all you are*
> *And do, assured that only good comes thence*
> *Whate'er the shape good take! While I have rule,*
> *Understand!—war for war's sake, war for sake*
> *O' the good war gets you as war's sole excuse*
> *Is damnable and damned shall be.*                       (3146).[1]

In 'Bishop Blougram's Apology' the same standards are deployed and are related even more closely to the main themes of the poem. Blougram assesses his life in terms of its product

> *We want the same things, Shakespeare and myself,*
> *And what I want, I have.*                     (539–40)
>
> *I well imagine you respect my place*
> *(Status, entourage, worldly circumstance)*
> *Quite to its value—very much indeed:*                 (25–27)
>
> *In truth's name don't you want my bishopric,*
> *My daily bread, my influence and my state?*                 (903–4)

[1] It seems probable to me that this part of the poem was designed as a specific rejoinder to the advocacy of the virtues of war to be found in Part Three of *Maud* or in Ruskin's *Crown of Wild Olive*.

But more is at issue than rival philosophical systems. The part of the
poem that now seems to me of most interest is the following:

> *It is the idea, the feeling and the love,*
> *God means mankind should strive for and show forth*
> *Whatever be the process to that end,—*
> *And not historic knowledge, logic sound,*
> *And metaphysical acumen, sure!*
> *'What think ye of Christ,' friend? when all's done and said,*
> *Like you this Christianity or not?*
> *It may be false, but will you wish it true?*
> *Has it your vote to be so if it can?*
> *Trust you an instinct silenced long ago*
> *That will break silence and enjoin you love*
> *What mortified philosophy is hoarse,*
> *And all in vain, with bidding you despise?*
> *If you desire faith—then you've faith enough:*
> *What else seeks God—nay, what else seek ourselves?*

$$(621-35)$$

If this is not to be read ironically, and I see no shadow of justification for
doing so, it embodies a question which was to trouble Browning for the
rest of his life—'It may be false, but will you wish it true?' This passage, I
think, directs us to the central concern of the poem, which is an examination of the ways of dealing with unbelief. Blougram himself expresses
the point succinctly but ambiguously:

> *How can we guard our unbelief,*
> *Make it bear fruit to us?*

The rest of the poem turns on the meaning of 'fruit.' Blougram is ready
to advance the notion of 'fruitful unbelief' but it is clear that the fruitful-
ness he has in mind is of a firmly material kind. He finds that, whatever
his private thoughts, he must 'To suit the world which gives us the good
things' make an announcement of 'positive belief.' This, he says, 'bears
me fruit / In power, peace, pleasantness and length of days.' He claims no
special virtue for his way of living except in terms of its consequences—'You criticize the soul? it reared this tree— / This broad life
and whatever fruit it bears' and finally 'Suppose we die tonight: well,
here am I, / Such were my gains, life bore this fruit to me.'

Gigadibs, on the other hand, is shown as insisting that actions should correspond to beliefs:

> *You meet me at this issue: you declare,—*
> *All special-pleading done with—truth is truth,*
> *And justifies itself by undreamed ways.*
> *You don't fear but it's better, if we doubt,*
> *To say so, act up to our truth perceived*
> *However feebly.*
>
> (806—11)

Once again Blougram exploits a verbal ambiguity, converting Gigadibs' challenge to 'act up to our truth perceived' into an admission that moral judgements refer only to actions:

> *Do then,—act away!*
> *'Tis there I'm on the watch for you. How one acts*
> *Is, both of us agree, our chief concern:*
> *And how you'll act is what I fain would see.*
>
> (811—14)

This once granted he has no difficulty in reducing Gigadibs' life to the lowest terms:

> *You weigh your pleasure with their butts and bleats*
> *And strike the balance. Sometimes certain fears*
> *Restrain you, real checks since you find them so;*
> *Sometimes you please yourself and nothing checks.*
>
> (886—89)

One correspondence is worth noting. Blougram's

> *I act for, talk for, live for, this world now,*
> *As this world prizes action, life and talk:*
> *No prejudice to what next world may prove,*
> *Whose new laws and requirements, my best pledge*
> *To observe then, is that I observe these now,*
> *Shall do hereafter what I do meanwhile.*
>
> (770—76)

neatly anticipates Guido's

> *Is there a new rule in another world?*
> *Be sure I shall resign myself: as here*
> *I recognized no law I could not see,*
> *There, what I see, I shall acknowledge too:*

> *On earth I never took the Pope for God,*
> *In heaven I shall scarce take God for the Pope.*
>
> (XI, 2387–92)

A corollary, almost a necessary corollary, of Browning's refusal to measure men by conventional standards of achievement is the insistence that there is merit of a kind which the world does not recognize. Poems like 'Waring', 'The plight of the Duchess' and 'Popularity' all pivot on the contrast between fame or position on the one hand and human worth on the other. More obviously the same idea animates 'Apparent Failure' and 'A Grammarian's Funeral', a poem about which I have blown hot and cold in the past but am now inclined to take more or less at face value, particularly in view of the last eight lines, in which I can detect no trace of irony.

The third question I proposed to consider was Browning's importance as a philosopher. His reputation in his lifetime was extraordinarily high.[1] My impression is that this was due in part to the fact that ethical studies in the nineteenth century were strong in theory but were not particularly helpful as a substitute for the regulative element of Christian teaching. Browning was felt to express, what many moral philosophers were reluctant to express, standards by which a man might shape his way of living in the world and understand some of the principles underlying human conduct. The fact that his values corresponded more or less to the traditional Christian virtues was an extra recommendation. His principles were non-technical, non-calculating, generous, and consoling. Love and courage were demanded of the individual: the larger good would be taken care of either by a beneficent addition of private efforts or by a generally favourable law of development: in any case in the world to come it is 'God's task to make the heavenly period / Perfect the earthen.' Browning, that is, set experience against theory, just as he set Intuitionalism against Utilitarianism, the 'brave impetuous heart' against the 'subtle contriving head.'[2]

The proceeding was sufficiently popular to attract the displeasure of at least one professional philosopher, Sir Henry Jones. But, except to those who choose to regard moral philosophy as a pure discipline with no application to life, it is not in itself illegitimate to relate ethical speculation

[1] E.g. 'Browning was not born a mere man, but a Buddha on the highest peak of the Himalayas of thought' (Edward Berdoe).

[2] The phrases are taken from Arnold's *Empedocles on Etna*.

to actual conduct.

Taken at its simplest level Browning's poetry implicitly asks for the reader's assent to the proposition that simple-hearted, straightforward, loving, trustful behaviour is still possible and still the best for man even in an age of fear, doubt, casuistry and mistrust, a position which must be respected in any debate on man's ethical nature. There is more than this, however, as I have attempted to show. Browning's protracted struggles to define, defend and generalize his intuitively-held position touch his age and ours at every point. He is bound in this to reflect the actual dilemmas that confront all non-Christians who are unable to accept Utilitarianism in its extreme forms.

Moreover he suggests a possible answer to one of the central problems—that of communicating ethical experiences. I have already quoted Kierkegaard's dictum about the extraordinary difficulty of conveying ethical truths. Browning's dramatic presentations of men and women confronted by an ethical dilemma scrutinizing their motives and justifying their decisions indicate at least a partial solution, especially if, as is commonly the case, Browning presents the speaker as a man with limited insight and requires the reader to complete the poem from his own experience, thus involving the reader actively in the generation of an ethical judgement. This is one way in which, to quote Browning's own description of the poet from *Sordello*, 'the best / Impart the gift of seeing to the rest' (III, 865–6).

Finally, even if we estimate Browning's philosophical importance at its lowest and decide that his conclusions are of no value or interest to us, it is nevertheless true that he was asking questions that still need to be asked. In *Fifine at the Fair* (1872) and *La Saisiaz* (1878), to name only the most obvious examples, he undertakes a methodical scrutiny of the bases of man's moral life. In the earlier poem his speaker, 'one who loves and grasps and spoils and speculates,' offers a ruthlessly reductionist analysis of human values: in the second Browning reverses the process and attempts to construct a model of man's moral nature by the controlled addition of postulates judged to be essential. It is when Browning is moving in this territory that we notice the combination of sceptical premise and optimistic conclusion which deeply distressed Henry Jones, although we may perhaps receive it with understanding rather than indignation. Much will depend on the expectations with which we approach Browning. In many of his poems, especially his later poems, his chief concern is with the exposition and exploration of an abstract idea. The energy of these speculative poems comes from the interest of the idea: the articulation of the argument is the structure. Such poems are, in general, written for people who are interested in this kind of speculation —*Prince Hohenstiel-Schwangau* is a good example. Those who are not interested in the subject are not advised to read the poems in the hope that some of the incidental features of the poem will engage their attention. There are also those who admit to an interest in ideas but do not wish to encounter them except in a clearly labelled work of philosophy, preferably in prose. Again it is much safer for such people not to read Browning's speculative poems. Or *Paradise Lost*, or the *Essay on Man*, or *Gulliver's Travels*, or *Erewhon*.

Browning's dramatic poems have obviously more to offer the reader who does not wish to encounter ideas, but they too are not without their bearing on the philosophical issues which I have been discussing. Two examples must suffice. First, a noted difficulty of the Intuitionalist position is the awkwardness of explaining why, having intuitively perceived the proper course of action, we should then follow it. Bentham makes great play with this. Browning hints at the difficulty in *Christmas-Eve* XVII, a passage which brings together many of the themes of this chapter. First Browning, writing at this point as a committed Christian, stresses the importance of man as a witness to divine truth:

> . . . *Were no eye in us to tell,*
>     *Instructed by no inner sense,*
> *The light of heaven from the dark of hell,*
>     *That light would want its evidence,—*
> *Though justice, good and truth were still*
> *Divine, if, by some demon's will,*
> *Hatred and wrong had been proclaimed*
> *Law through the worlds, and right misnamed.*

Absolute though these divine qualities are it is man's perception of them which is their embodiment on earth.

> *No mere exposition of morality*
> *Made or in part or in totality,*
> *Should win you to give it worship, therefore:*
> *And, if no better proof you will care for,*

*—Whom do you count the worst man upon earth?*
*Be sure, he knows, in his conscience, more*
*Of what right is, than arrives at birth*
*In the best man's acts that we bow before.*

'Right,' that is, inheres in the 'inner sense' and not in the 'acts': 'true, but my fact is, / 'Tis one thing to know, and another to practise.' It is in this situation that the poet, using the word in its widest sense, has a particular part to play in the ethical world. If in a time of faith it was true to say

*And thence I conclude that the real God-function*
*Is to furnish a motive and injunction*
*For practising what we know already.*

one of the functions of the ethical philosopher in a time of doubt must be to supply men with motives for practising what they intuitively know to be true. This is a work which can be done with particular force by the poets; Browning takes up the challenge with a will, and some at least of the stirring cries to action which a hostile critic has represented as declarations 'that the exercise of energy is the absolute good, irrespective of motives or of consequences'[1] are justifiable as part of a serious philosophical enterprise, that of providing men with a motive for actually doing what they have decided to be right. 'She turned on her side and slept. Just so! / So we resolve on a thing and sleep' (The Statue and the Bust). But this insistence on the need for a man to 'contend to the uttermost / For his life's set prize, be it what it will' does not mean that Browning thinks that one set of motives is as good as another.

My second example may serve to confirm this last point by suggesting that Browning operates directly on our moral faculties by presenting dramatically certain principles of choice as being in themselves beautiful or ugly. Pompilia and Guido, Miranda and Clara in *Red Cotton Night-Cap Country*, the two men and women in *The Inn Album*, the innumerable men and women in love in his earlier poems—these present to the moral sense aesthetic reasons for deciding to act in a certain way, or for evaluating the acts of others.

Of course this is generally true of all literature—one could argue the philosophical importance of Jane Austen, for example, on similar lines. The point is, however, of particular importance in a discussion of

[1] George Santayana, 'The Poetry of Barbarism'.

Browning, since he characteristically presents his characters in the act of analysing their own behaviour or even investigating the source of their own moral impulses. His readers are thus encouraged to judge the beauty not simply of actions but of motives. In this chapter I have tried to provide some evidence for believing that this is not accidental but is closely related to Browning's general rejection of Utilitarian theories of personal behaviour. Like F. H. Bradley, but with different weapons, he was fighting against Utilitarianism not because he felt it to be 'insular and immature and cranky' [T. S. Eliot] but because he felt it to be selfish and loveless and sterile.

In conclusion I should make one point clear. Since I insist on the philosophical importance of Browning I must in fairness be prepared to indicate how I should meet criticisms of him as a philosopher. The two criticisms of this kind which I have encountered most frequently are that he wilfully devalues logical thought and that all he has to offer as a view of the ethical life of man is the cheery and sanctimonious assurance that it can do no harm to look on the bright side. I see the force of both charges. My reply would be as follows. First Browning is repeatedly at pains to make the point that crucial moral choices are *not* logical. Just as a man's fundamental moral assumptions are chosen for reasons which are ultimately alogical—the final considerations may, for example, be aesthetic— so when a man has a great decision to make he will have to perform an act of trust, a Kierkegaardian 'leap,' 'put faith to proof, be cured or killed at once.' In any philosophy that is not completely reductionist something must be taken on trust. Browning places enormous emphasis on the importance of the act of trusting, on believing where we cannot prove.

The second objection suggests that *what* he asks us to believe in is an inferior article, which implies in turn that it is impossible for any serious thinker to be genuinely hopeful. Browning is thus either not serious or not genuine. But Browning is engaged in the difficult task of looking at the possibility of hope after the Christian hope has gone.[1] Three things in particular save him from a banal and insensitive optimism. First, he carefully discusses the alternatives to his own position, often giving them a

---

[1] Cf. '*Hope, the paramount* duty *that Heaven lays,*
        *For its own honour, on man's suffering heart.*'
(Wordsworth, *Poems Dedicated to National Independence and Liberty*, XXXIII).

voice in his poems. Secondly, he scrutinizes his own position with care, pointing out and worrying at the places where reasoning ends and trust must take its place. This scrutiny is often a linguistic one—a testing and defining of a vocabulary for discussing human motives and actions. Thirdly, Browning recognizes that human nature is mixed, that individual moral decisions help to define that nature and that the command to 'act up to our truth perceived' is therefore not a complacent conventional motto, but a direction to a moral life of continual self-questioning and strenuous effort.

# 5: *Browning and Politics*

## TREVOR LLOYD

Browning can be considered as a poet who wrote about political experience, and also as a man with political principles that emerge in his poetry from time to time. As a poet of political experience he said many intelligent and observant things; as a man he had coherent and rational principles, though they shifted from one position to another under the broad umbrella of Victorian liberalism. Perhaps some of his poems suffer because his principles were not really deeply thought out: it is not essential for a poet writing on political themes to have worked out a scheme of political philosophy, but it is a great help for a poet of Browning's densely argued style if he does have a philosophy of his own.[1]

The line of distinction drawn here between the poetry of political experience and the poet with political principles can be illustrated briefly from 'The Lost Leader'. The emotion of a follower let down by his leader is expressed in a way that can be generally understood but, because the emotion is relatively specialized and is most likely to be felt by people who have been active in political parties or comparable organizations, perhaps the poem has a particular attraction for politicians:

> *Let him never come back to us!*
> *There would be doubt, hesitation and pain,*
> *Forced praise on our part—the glimmer of twilight,*
> *Never glad confident morning again.*

'"Never glad confident morning again"—so I hope the change will not

[1] An attack on Browning's political thought by J. McNally, *Queen's Quarterly*, LXX, 1970, 568, is not founded on detailed enough study of the texts, or on a wide enough knowledge of political philosophy, to provide anything more than a very general introduction to the subject.

be too long delayed"[1] puts the feeling of disappointed, still slightly in-credulous political bereavement that might be expected of an audience that faintly wished the brightest of the sons of the morning could be res-tored to his former place but is being convinced that this could never happen.

The moment of nostalgia comes after the first rush of lacerating accus-ation. Browning had considerable powers of denunciation and the first six lines open an unbridgeable gulf before the second six lines show memories of past devotion reawakening. The poem is of course an attack on Wordsworth, but the emotion is very much a political emotion: neither in the poem nor in later discussion did Browning suggest that it was a comment on literary developments, and he would probably have been very surprised if any of the Browning Societies of the last decade of his life had attacked him in similar terms when he left the Liberal party over Home Rule in 1886.

While no definition of a political leader's obligations to his followers would win universal agreement, nobody denies that political leaders have some obligations to their followers. On the other hand it is very hard to see why writers have obligations to their admirers in the way that is suggested under the surface of the poem: although 'we' have nothing but copper to give, Shakespeare (and other, more obviously left-wing writers) were 'of us' and 'we taught him.'

There may possibly have been a poetical tradition of politically left-wing writing, though it is not easy to find a common style that fits all the poets discussed in 'The Lost Leader'. The question would still remain: did Wordsworth's membership of this tradition impose on him the obligat-ions of party allegiance? His admirers may possibly have had obligations to Wordsworth, but he was free to change his mind. The emotion in the poem could be seen more clearly, and perhaps would be better justified, if the literary references were laid aside. The poem really conveys very well the feelings of, say, a member of the Labour party who learnt in 1931 that Ramsay MacDonald, exulting that next day every duchess in London would want to kiss him,[2] had agreed to become Prime Minister of a predominantly Conservative government. MacDonald's behaviour

---

[1] *Hansard*, 5th ser., vol 679, col. 99, 17 June 1963. Mr Nigel Birch was suggesting that Mr Harold Macmillan should resign from his position as Prime Minister.

[2] P. Snowden, *An Autobiography*, 1934, ii, 957.

may have been politically justified, but the emotions of his followers would naturally have been very like those in this poem.

Browning claimed that 'an artist takes one or two striking traits in the features of his "model" '[1] and he specifically said 'these [handfuls of silver and bits of ribbon] never influenced the change of politics in the great poet,' but he added that Wordsworth's 'defection . . . was . . . even to mature consideration, an event to deplore.'[2] Browning had been born a Liberal, in the sense that an intellectually conscious Nonconformist, kept out of the older universities by Church of England restrictions, was likely to be a Liberal, and the fact that his father was strongly opposed to slavery made it all the more natural to see the world in this light; for Nonconformists it was easy to see the ending of the Slave Trade and the abolition of slavery as measures passed by Whig governments in the face of opposition that came almost exclusively from the Tory side. The principle of setting people free from unjustified restriction was not the whole of the liberalism of the French Revolution or of Jeremy Bentham, but it was the basis of Browning's liberalism.

There was no definition in 'The Lost Leader' of what Wordsworth was deserting: there was just the strong expression of political emotion. By an odd coincidence, at just the time he was publishing it, another literary figure (who, like Browning, had been encouraged in the pages of the *Monthly Repository*) was expressing the same emotion:

> 'I advise therefore that we all, whatever may be our opinions about free trade, oppose the introduction of free politics. Let men stand by the principle by which they rise—right or wrong. . . . The Minister [Sir Robert Peel] who attained the position which he now fills is not the Minister who ought to abrogate the Corn Laws. . . . Do not then, because you see a great personage giving up his opinions, do not cheer him on—do not yield so ready a reward to political tergiversation.'[3]

The Corn Law crisis of October 1845 to June 1846 lies entirely within the period of the Barrett–Browning correspondence, and there is vir-

[1] Mrs Sutherland Orr, *Life and Letters of Robert Browning*, 1891, 133.

[2] *Wise Letters*, 1933, 166–7; letter of 25 February 1875 to Rev. A. B. Grant.

[3] *Hansard*, 3rd ser., vol 83, col. 122–3. 22 January 1846. Mr Disraeli was suggesting that Sir Robert Peel should resign from his position as Prime Minister. 'The Patriot' was published, in *Dramatic Romances and Lyrics*, on 6 November 1845.

tually no reference to the crisis in the letters. There was nothing about the merits of the measure for them to discuss; Browning made it quite clear in the last lines of 'An Englishman in Italy' how hard he found it to believe that anybody would waste time trying to defend the Corn Laws, and Elizabeth Barrett undoubtedly agreed with him. As a man of fairly left-wing Liberal principles Browning probably did not notice that the Conservative backbenchers were experiencing the same emotions about Peel as he had expressed about the 'lost leader.' The relationship between leaders and followers is the political experience examined most fully in Browning's poems and, if the ex-leader is denounced in 'The Lost Leader', he is praised in 'The Patriot'. Browning was much more likely to see Peel in the latter form, and the poem has some similarity in content to Peel's last speech as Prime Minister:

'In relinquishing power, I shall leave a name severely censured I fear by many . . . but it may be that I shall leave a name sometimes remembered with goodwill in the abodes of those whose lot it is to labour and to earn their daily bread by the sweat of their brow.'[1]

Peel's speech is duller, but then he had achieved something more substantial than the patriot.

This curious and fairly certainly unconscious echo of the English political scene apart, there is too much description and too little reflection for 'The Patriot' to convey political experience really well: being about to be executed concentrates the mind, but not necessarily on the reasons why one is about to be executed. The political situation of adulation followed by overthrow is common enough, but that seems to be all there is to the old story. Undoubtedly Browning realized that the bloody end to the story was natural in a more brutal society, but that the political dynamics by which the adulated leader loses power are the same at any period. Anyone hoping for a poet to add something to his understanding of political behaviour would welcome a word about what happened between 'thus I entered' and 'thus I go', and the pictures of the two journeys are clear enough to suggest that Browning could perfectly well have filled in the year's changes if he had wanted to write a long poem.

Browning's own political principles do not emerge in 'The Patriot' as they had done in several of his previous poems. Before his interest in politics, at least as a subject for poetry, began to fade he had moved from

[1] *Hansard*, 3rd. ser., vol 87, col. 1054–55. 29 June 1846.

'Nonconformist' Liberalism to Shelleyan Liberalism to Benthamite Liberalism. In the general gloom of *Pauline* it is not surprising to find some lines of political pessimism:

> *First went my hopes for perfecting mankind,*
> *Next—faith in them, and then in freedom's self*
> *And virtue's self, then my own motives, ends*
> *And aims and loves, and human love went last.*
>
> (458–61)

The political position whose collapse is described has clearly come, like so much of the rest of the poem, from Shelley. Despite the relative optimism of the closing section, it would be easy to conclude that Browning was in a state of political as well as emotional bankruptcy in the mid-1830s. The last section but one of Book Three of *Sordello* (from 'They sleep, and I awake O'er the lagune, being at Venice' to 'My English Eyebright')[1] implies that this bankruptcy went on until his visit to Italy: the section does not quite come up to the general level of clarity of the poem, but it does suggest that Browning had become aware of the possibilities of political action and social reform as a subject for poetry.

He had probably been intellectually aware of it for some time. *Pauline* was praised in the *Monthly Repository*, a magazine of a type familiar to readers of the *New Statesman*: politics somewhat to the left of the leaders of the main party of the left, and artistic criticism that laid considerable stress on the virtues of novelty. Browning became a close friend of the editor, W. J. Fox, and seems to have picked up a good many of the *Repository's* views, at least at an intellectual level, before they burst upon him emotionally and artistically during his visit to Italy: the political message of *Sordello* is so much along lines Fox would have approved that it is not really necessary to look further for its origins, though it is fair to say that the argument in *Sordello* lies firmly within the strand of Liberal thought which was intellectually dominant at the time.

Fox had made the *Monthly Repository* (in which Browning published five poems) into a magazine of left-wing Benthamism; a good deal of it was written in the spirit of Bentham's remark that 'only by making the ruling few uneasy can the oppressed many hope for a particle of redress.' The *Repository* published articles in favour of abolishing the House of Lords, repealing the Corn Laws, wiping out the 'taxes on knowledge'

---

[1] *Sordello*, III, 614–966.

(stamp duty on newspapers and import duties on paper), marriage as a civil contract with provision for divorce, votes for women, simplification of the legal system, establishment of the secret ballot, a large expansion of the franchise established in 1832, trades unions, the New Poor Law of 1834, progressive taxation and elimination of all legal discrimination against Nonconformists.[1]

Any young Liberal who had read and accepted the programme of the *Repository* in the 1830s would have been politically equipped until the 1880s: for forty years the legislative history of England was a series of battles about the proposals made by Radicals in the 1830s. Browning's ideas do not seem to have developed much after the 1830s; the point can be illustrated from the way he answered an inquiry from Furnivall in quite a different area of thought by saying that he certainly believed in evolution and that the idea could be found in his own poem *Paracelsus*.[2] Here can be seen the advanced thought of the young man of the 1830s, and also the failure to notice that Darwin had added quite a lot to the idea of evolution which had been current in the 1830s.

Alexandra Orr said 'He had been a Radical in youth, and probably in early manhood; he remained, in the truest sense of the word, a Liberal.'[3] This is reasonable enough, and is a natural result of starting off with advanced views which were steadily turned into the law of the land. In early manhood Browning was in roughly the position of Sordello:

> God has conceded two sights to a man—
> One, of man's whole work, time's completed plan,
> The other, of the minute's work, man's first
> Step to the plan's completeness.          (*Sordello*, V, 85–8)

Browning seems to have experienced at Venice a sight of man's whole work. His response was strictly Benthamite, and Sordello put 'the pure and wholesome doctrine of general utility ["the greatest happiness of the greatest number"], to which all other rules and all antique prejudice will gradually be made to bow'[4] into verse:

[1] See F. E. Mineka, *The Dissidence of Dissent*, Chapel Hill 1944, 261–71 and 286–8.

[2] *Wise Letters*, 199; letter of 11 October 1881.

[3] Orr, *Life*, 374.

[4] Junius Redivivus (W. B. Adams) in *Monthly Repository*, 1834, 721.

> *How render first these people happy? Ask*
> *The people's friends: for there must be one good,*
> *One way to it—the Cause!*
>
> (IV, 297–9)

and he went on from this, in a mood as amiable as unhistorical, to attribute the struggle of Guelf and Ghibelline to a competition in maximizing general utility:

> *Behold*
> *The secret, so to speak, and masterspring*
> *O' the contest—which of the two Powers shall bring*
> *Men good, perchance the most good: ay, it may*
> *Be that!—the question, which best knows the way.*　　(IV, 317–21)

Of course, Guelfs and Ghibellines were not rival Benthamite groups, and there is no particular sign that they cared in the least about the people's happiness. However, the fact that the idea of 'general utility' is anachronistic does not necessarily hurt the poem. Possibly its unity —always rather shaky—suffered further damage from the appearance of the idea halfway through; on the other hand the Benthamite theme is handled with good political sense and has something of a unifying effect on Books Four and Five.

Sordello goes on from the general statement that making people happy is 'the Cause', to say that laws and legislation are of primary importance:

> *Let Rome advance,*
> *Rome, as she struck Sordello's ignorance—*
> *How could he doubt one moment? Rome's the Cause!*
> *Rome of the Pandects, all the world's new laws*
>
> . 　. 　. 　. 　. 　. 　. 　. 　.
>
> *Rome typifies the scheme to put mankind*
> *Once more in full possession of their rights.*
>
> (IV, 1010–13, 1018–19)

The poetic rhythm survives with difficulty and in the last lines is almost buried under the Benthamite proposition that laws and law-making are the important thing in politics. This idea, like the principle of general utility itself, is now accepted as one of the tacit major premises of politics but in the 1830s it was a left-wing novelty, and none the more popular for that.

At first in the battle-scenes it appears that there is very little to choose between the two sides and that 'whoso shall enlist With either, ranks with man's inveterate foe.'[1] This must have reflected fairly well the way Browning felt about the Italian situation at the time, because Austrian and Papal domination, which could be seen as nineteenth-century versions of Ghibelline and Guelf rule, together held Italian freedom back. Whether it reflected the thirteenth situation accurately to describe 'Friedrich' so exclusively in German terms is another matter: Frederick II, the sceptical Holy Roman Emperor who obtained free right of access to Jerusalem by negotiation rather than a military crusade, was Sicilian by birth, upbringing and preference.

In the following Book, before his interview with Salinguerra, Sordello becomes convinced that the Guelfs, personified in Hildebrand (Gregory VII), are more egalitarian than the Ghibellines, personified in Charlemagne. This argument is reinforced by the more specifically Benthamite argument that the Popes deserve support because they have evolved devices like the Crusade, the Lombard League (made up of the anti-imperial North Italian cities) and the Truce of God in order to restrain irresponsible force.[2] Bentham and his followers spent a good deal of time working out devices, mechanical or moral, to get government to work properly; Sordello chooses the Guelfs partly because they are more Benthamite in working out plans for medieval society.

At the present day 'liberty' and 'the greatest happiness of the greatest number' are seen—even by people who recognize the left-wing origins of both principles—to be quite likely to run into conflict with each other. For the men of Browning's generation the distinction was much less clear-cut. There is no need to think that Browning intended to write a Benthamite Epic, or even that he saw any great difference between his Shelleyan views at the beginning of the decade and his Benthamite arguments at the end of the decade. Browning had already read at least one writer who had resolved this conflict: Bernard de Mandeville. In his much later 'Parleying with de Mandeville' Browning of course takes him as an advocate of the standard theologians' justification for God allowing

[1] *Sordello*, IV, 941–2.

[2] V, 192–204.

evil to continue to exist, which was much more of a pun on de Mandeville's main argument than a serious application of it. But Browning had demonstrably heard of the doctrine of 'private vices, public benefits,' and the political implication of the doctrine was that, if people were left to do what they wanted to do, the result would be the greatest happiness of the greatest number. Browning did not in fact need to go back to de Mandeville; the interchangeability of freedom and happiness was part of the intellectual equipment of anyone on the left, and there was no difficulty in reconciling Shelley and Bentham.

On the other hand Browning was a poet writing about political experience as well as a man of the left. It is one thing to say 'A poet must be earth's essential king'[1]—a sort of medieval version of the 'unacknowledged legislators of mankind'—but it would be something quite different and altogether less probable to make Sordello into a completely convincing orator. 'His accustomed fault of breaking yoke Disjoining him who felt from him who spoke'[2] is just what might be expected from a man of strong political feelings with no practice at expressing them publicly (in these terms it is the spontaneous poet of Book Two that is unconvincing: there were extemporizers in the Middle Ages, but they did not acquire the skill by remaining in solitude).

On the other side Salinguerra is not a man to be converted suddenly to a belief in equality. He is a well-drawn and convincing character of a type to which Browning often returned: a military and political commander, undoubtedly good at keeping up the spirits of his followers and likely to hold their loyalty. Like so many of Browning's political characters he is not a leader who can devise a policy as well as carry it out. His response to Sordello's appeal is to volunteer to serve him, if he will desert the Guelfs. As if to parody the general chronological obscurity of the poem, the story goes on:

> *Up in the midst a truth grew, without speech*
>
> .    .    .    .    .    .    .
>
>       *Palma was found there still*
> *Relating somewhat Adelaide confessed*    (V, 742, 748–9)

but it is undoubtedly established that Salinguerra is not only ready to

[1] *Sordello*, V 306.

[2] V, 333–4.

serve under Sordello but also that he is Sordello's father. This is enough for Salinguerra; he now has a comprehensible policy which he can start trying to carry out.

Sordello has harder problems. Granted that the Guelfs are in the long run the true friends of humanity, might he not do more good in the short run by taking a leading place among the Ghibellines and trying to change their policy for the better? And, more fundamentally, how logical a position is altruistic Benthamism?

> e'en though somewhat sweat the Crowd for this
> Contribute each his pang to make your bliss,
> 'Tis but one pang.

(VI, 344–6)

Perhaps the supreme happiness of one superior soul justifies making life a little less pleasant for everybody else.

Sordello (in the poem, though not in real life) dies; he rejects Salinguerra's offer but he has not solved his other problems. Browning condemns him:

> what he should have been,
> Could be, and was not—the one step too mean
> For him to take—we suffer at this day
> Because of.[1]

(VI, 829–31)

The implication—with the subsequent reference to Dante—is that Sordello should have accepted a post of political leadership and that this would have made subsequent generations happier.

Certainly the lines about Hesperian fruit show that Browning at this time believed that a poet ought to be 'committed'. In political terms he remained a man of the left, and in literary terms he continued until his marriage to write about political subjects, but the connection between his views and his writing was much less direct than anyone would have expected after reading the closing sections of *Sordello*. Pippa's lack of leisure may have been suggested to him by the Reports and the argu-

---

[1] There is a discussion of *Sordello* in John Lucas's 'Politics and the Poet's Role' in J. Lucas, ed, *Literature and Politics in the Nineteenth Century*, 1971. This essay concentrates on the problem of poetical inspiration, and does not consider the content of the political views put forward in *Sordello*.

ments about Factory Acts that occupied public attention around 1840. The story does not of course show that all's right with the world, but that things are very wrong with the world at all levels of society, with a suggestion that tyrants ought to be assassinated and that Pippa ought to get her rightful inheritance. This is not really a much more profound reforming attitude than the quietism of Pippa's song. And it is not intended to be profound; the approach to commitment in writing that is put forward at the end of *Sordello* did not survive, and in fact Browning seems to have written himself out of the Benthamite mood when he finished the poem.

His seven plays, which make up so large a part of his writing between *Strafford* and *A Soul's Tragedy*, are all—except for *A Blot in the Scutcheon* —about people in political situations. The love-story is of more importance than the political story in *Colombe's Birthday* and in *The Return of the Druses*, but obviously the political situation is of some importance, and the political plot matters more than the vestigial love-story in *Strafford* or *Luria*. Although the plays are in this sense about politics, they contain surprisingly few political ideas. The ideas that do occur are not particularly original, are not expressed with the coherence of the Benthamite views in the second half of *Sordello*, and may simply be part of the plot rather than an expression of Browning's own feelings.

Most of the views put forward in the political plays are of course still very much the views of a Liberal: pro-Parliament in *Strafford*, in favour of morality in foreign policy and 'We did the people right—'twas much to gain That point, redress our nobles' grievance too'[1] in *King Victor and King Charles*, pro-nationalist in *The Return of the Druses* and in favour of the common people (and probably the repeal of the Corn Laws)in *Colombe's Birthday*. Browning had not changed his principles, though he was less interested in them than before.

The plays did not succeed at the time or later; they were written and were generally regarded as serious candidates for commercial production (unlike *Paracelsus* or the closet-dramas of other Victorian poets), were reviewed respectfully and (unlike *Sordello*) did his reputation no harm, but there is not much more to be said for them. It was a period in English dramatic history when, to judge by results, it was very hard to write good plays; and political drama has always been very hard to write —again to judge by results, very few political dramas stand in the high-

[1] *King Victor and King Charles*, Part ii, 60–1, *Centenary Edition*, II, 196.

est class of plays in the way that, from *Birth of a Nation* and *The Battleship Potemkin* onwards, political films have stood in the highest class.

Browning found interesting political situations for his plots. However, several of his protagonists show a trait of personality noted in Salinguerra: they are not leaders who can lay down a policy. Strafford and Luria are the most clear-cut examples; the interest lies in watching men who are, in effect, faithful followers being treated badly by their superiors. Their political value and their claim to be well treated lies in the fact that they are something more than followers and can lead the Royalist or the Florentine forces successfully, but within the play their dramatic role is as subordinates to Charles and the Florentine Council. In *Strafford* Browning makes his own political sympathy with Parliament very clear; in *Luria* it is not so clear whether Florence is right or wrong in her struggle with Pisa, though the Florentine Council's habit of treating its subordinates badly is made clear (for example, at the beginning of Act II).

Because the plays are studies in loyalty—and loyalty that survives unbroken despite ill-treatment—the question of political belief is removed from the centre of the action. The poignancy of Strafford's position is heightened by the fact that he has fallen away from the better side and is exercising the virtue of loyalty in standing by the worse, but there is really no discussion of the reasons why he chose the Royalist side. In contrast to *Luria*, which is too much an elaborate exercise in personal obligation to discuss political experience adequately, *Strafford* shows some understanding of political development. Politicians sometimes have to put forward one line of argument in public after arguing the opposite line in private, and this can be considered a political activity although it happens in other activities as well. Thus, Strafford changes, when Pym and the Parliamentarians come in, from blaming the King for dissolving Parliament to defending the step; the point may be clumsily expressed (particularly in the speech starting 'Strafford, guilty too of counselling the measure'),[1] but it makes good political sense. Browning tended to assume that every schoolboy knew the course of English history from late 1639 to May 1641 and accepted the Parliamentarian view of history, and the play may be too obscure for most audiences as a result. Nonconformists thought of the 1640s as a vitally important decade for their faith, but the Tory interpretation of these events was still accepted and

[1] *Strafford*, II, ii, 256, *Centenary Edition*, II, 37.

Browning's point of view was probably a little hard to follow.

*Colombe's Birthday* may have been—despite its obviously sentimental and Ruritanian aspects—the closest that Browning came to writing political propaganda. There is something sentimental about the Duchess playing with her toy Duchy, ignorant of the fact that her people are starving. At a deeper level there is something very sentimental about Berthold's mood of weariness and regret when the Duchess surrenders the Duchy to him because she wants to marry Valence and live happily ever after; ambition not only should be, but usually is, made of sterner stuff. All the same, the play can hardly have been intended simply as a piece of medieval tushery; if, in the year 1844, one writes a play in which the 'clothiers' representative' (Valence) comes from the second city in the realm to the capital, is held back at first by the courtiers but finally gets the chance to put to the ruler the argument that his townspeople lack bread, one must expect to be taken as an anti-Corn Law propagandist, with Valence as Cobden-and-Bright, Cleves as Manchester, the courtiers as the Conservative government and the Duchess as Queen Victoria (the conversion of the leading courtier, and his retirement from political power at the end of the play, is the sort of development that makes critics think the play sentimental, and would make Browning Societies even more convinced of Browning's preternatural insight if they followed up this pattern of interpretation and identified Guibert with Sir Robert Peel).

In *King Victor and King Charles* there seems to be no comparable reference to contemporary events. No doubt good kings practise honesty in foreign policy and treat their subjects well; and a king's duty to rule well is more important than a son's duty to obey his father. But this is not a very revealing account of political experience, nor is it an impressive view of Browning's own political principles—Browning certainly subscribed to the general ideas exemplified in the play, but they are not relevant to any real situation and emerge as copybook maxims. The character of D'Ormea is an unusual attempt to show a man of bad principles who develops and acquires good principles during the play, and the other characters can all be described in terms that suggest they might be interesting, but the fact of the matter is that in this play they are dull.

*The Return of the Druses* touches on perhaps the most significant political principles—nationalism and oppression—to be discussed in

Browning's plays. However, the play is dominated by other themes which he normally handled better than political issues: love, religion and the frame of mind of a man undertaking an imposture for the sake of something that he can convincingly regard as a good purpose. The false Hakeem is in a very interesting political situation, but this is not the aspect of his problems to which attention is directed. Browning's sympathy with the Druses is what would be expected of any liberally-minded man, but it must be noted what an untypical variety of nationalism he chose; emigration, which might be considered an answer by Jews or by the nineteenth-century socialist colonies, would not be relevant for the type of nationalism he usually thought about. He may have oversimplified things when he approved of Italians assassinating Austrians, in *Pippa Passes* and in 'An Italian in England', but emigration would not have solved the problem any more than assassination.

The last of the dramas, *A Soul's Tragedy*, is still written with some sympathy for the leaders of revolt, but the emphasis is on the unsuitability for leadership of both Liutolfo and Chiappino; the weakness of Chiappino is obvious, but it is also clear why Liutolfo would not succeed as a leader though he might be well suited for a martyr. Ogniben's success comes a little too easily, but then he is hardly meant to be taken seriously.

When he wrote this satire on the enemies of the status quo, Browning had come quite a long way in six years from the commitment of *Sordello*. Elizabeth Barrett, whom he was courting at just this time, agreed with him on the main issues of concern to Liberals—the Corn Laws, Italy, the rights of Nonconformists—but she was somewhat to the left of him. They did not say much about politics in their letters, but she did try out some advanced views on him. When she suggested abolishing the House of Lords he made no comment; when she denounced duelling he offered a Blougram-like defence of it and, though he made it clear that he did not approve of it, he came closer to tolerating it than she did. Browning opposed votes for women at this stage, though later he seems to have changed his mind for a time.[1]

After 1846 and for the next twenty-five years he wrote relatively little that was concerned with political experience. In *The Ring and the Book* it is fairly deliberately excluded; the Venetian's letter in Book Twelve makes it clear that the Pope was subject to political pressure for and

[1] *Letters*, II, 40–52 and 281; Orr, *Life*, 397.

against execution, but in Book Ten the Pope pays no attention to this issue.[1] Deciding whether execution or clemency would have gained more support for a policy of reform would have been an interesting and important political question for the Pope to consider, but not one that could easily be fitted into the general scheme of the poem. One subsidiary theme in the poem is a study of a social principle and the way it affects society. The old yellow book was said, not completely accurately, to deal with a case

> *Wherein it is disputed if, and when,*
> *Husbands may kill adulterous wives, yet 'scape*   (*The Ring and*
> *The customary forfeit.*                          *the Book*, I, 129–31)

There is in fact no dispute about whether husbands may kill their wives, and not much about when they may do so; the argument is whether Guido's case fits within the reasonably well-defined rules.

These rules go practically unquestioned in the poem, and their dominance is reinforced in the one book in which they are not accepted, that of Bottinius. Part of the satire on the two advocates is that each of them puts his own client's case in a highly unfavourable light: by the end of Archangeli's speech Guido's defence looks very thin, but by the time Bottinius has finished it is possible once more to think Guido's suspicions were understandable even if unjustified. Bottinius is ready to concede a good many points; and eventually he suggests that possibly Pompilia and Caponsacchi went too far at the inn but that Guido made altogether too much fuss about it.[2] This is just what anyone at the present day would say, and Victorian England, though more concerned about adultery, was no more sympathetic to *crime passionelle* than we are. But by the stage in the poem that Bottinius puts the 'modern' point of view, the general pattern of life in a society sympathetic to killing unchaste wives has been built up so effectively that, partly because the lawyer's speech is phrased in a lax and morally undemanding manner, Bottinius's speech pushes the balance of sympathy back a little towards Guido. The whole structure of a coherent society within which the characters obey a well-defined social code has been created, and the strength of the poem sweeps away anyone who takes this social code lightly.

[1] W. DeVane, *A Browning Handbook*, New York, 1955, confirms there was political pressure on the Pope in 1698.
[2] *The Ring and the Book*, IX, 855.

The overall effect depends so much on the absence of effective questioning of the characters' social principles that the expression of Browning's own views and the exploration of political experience cannot easily be undertaken in *The Ring and the Book*. In *Prince Hohenstiel-Schwangau* the solitary character's principles are questioned, as part of the background to a study of political experience more ambitious than anything since *Sordello*. In the plays Browning had moved away from discussing substantive political principles, usually to praise the virtue of loyalty. With Napoleon, issues of substantive principle could not be avoided; he had, at least after 1851, no superior authority to be loyal to, and the only question was to see what he made of his principles. The poem is intended to say 'what I imagine the man might, if he pleased, say for himself.'[1] The phrase is ambiguous: does it mean that Browning would write the very best defence for Napoleon that he thought possible, or that he would write the sort of imperfect and inadequate defence which he may have believed was all that Napoleon could manage, and thus expose him to the criticism from which the poem is on the surface meant to defend him? The poem is not completely satisfactory: as a defence it has flaws, some of which could have been repaired, and as a masked attack it is too well masked to be really effective.[2] It can be argued, on the basis of one section late in the poem when Browning was no longer concerned with defence (or masked attack) that he did not really possess a full grasp of the historical circumstances, and this may explain why some earlier passages are hard to attribute to any fixed point of view; more particularly, Browning does not seem to have had the command of his material that would have been needed if he wanted to mishandle it subtly and apparently accidentally in a way that would expose Napoleon's defence. The weaknesses in the defence may be the result of Browning's mistakes, rather than errors invented for Napoleon by him.

The first part of the defence, from 'A conservator, call me, if you please,' to ' "Somnolency", clear enough,'[3] is straightforward and

---

[1] *Dearest Isa*, 1966, 372. Letter of 25 January 1872.
[2] P. Drew, in *The Poetry of Browning*, 1970, comments 'fair-minded satire leaves the reader with no sense of direction. Since Browning seems to be offering us something of the sort it is hard to agree with his favourable verdict on [*Prince Hohenstiel-Schwangau*]', 302.
[3] *Prince Hohenstiel-Schwangau*, 298–1198.

uncluttered in expression. The words put in the Prince's mouth were not Browning's own beliefs, but they are a point of view that could be taken perfectly seriously; maintaining law-and-order when it was threatened by extremists of the left and the right, and looking after the 'mute myriads', would be acceptable enough, and interference with free speech and the manipulation of elections could possibly be justified on the grounds that

> *'Not bread alone' but bread before all else*
> *For these; the bodily want serve first, say I.*[1]
>
>                                                                              (917–18)

A good radical would probably have refused to accept the idea that there could be a conflict between democracy and the standards of living of the poor, but Browning can hardly have meant to strike radical attitudes at this stage of his career. This part of the poem sounds more like a summing-up in favour of the defendant than a speech by a defending counsel.

The next part, from 'Something like this the unwritten chapter reads' to 'with a work to do Which no man helps or hinders,'[1] is harder to follow; the sentences are broken by parentheses more often, imaginary quotations are inserted, and the confusing figure of Sagacity appears. This section is intended to defend the *coup d'état* of December 1851 by which Napoleon broke loose from the constitutional requirement that he should retire from the Presidency in 1852. The argument is expressed with the regard for the truth that is expected of a respectable counsel for the defence. 'His fellow-servants one and all Were—mildly to make mention—knaves or fools'[2] is rather an extravagant criticism of the men of the Second Republic, but no doubt caused a conscientious ruler to feel that he could do the job better than any possible successor. To say 'they saw him walk straight down, Each step of the eminence, as he first engaged, And stand at last o' the level'[3] is a one-sided account of the *coup d'état*, when a few hundred people were killed and a few thousand were imprisoned. But his success in the plebiscite ('Whereon the people answered with a shout "The trusty one! no tricksters any more" ')[4] was some sort of justification for seizing power. But he comes back to the

---

[1] *Prince Hohenstiel-Schwangau*, 1231–513.

[2] 1241–42.

[3] 1382 in.

[4] 1410–11.

question of social policy, as though it was the best defence he could find. 'Equalise things a little': Englishmen in general could believe, on the basis of the Anglo-French trade treaty of 1860, that Napoleon had helped the French economy in a way that would benefit the poor.

It is impossible to tell how much irony at his own expense underlies Browning's lines in which the Prince notes that he has not been able to live up to his youthful principles, but it can certainly be shown that Browning had come close to the same ideals. The principles that Napoleon had professed before 1848, and had made some slight attempt to carry out after coming to power, were mainly Saint-Simonian in origin, and some characteristic achievements of the Second Empire, such as the Suez Canal and Haussmann's redesigning of Paris, had first been suggested by the Saint-Simonians. Surprisingly the Benthamites had been sympathetic to the Saint-Simonians, though Saint-Simon was much more in favour of government intervention than Bentham, and the moment of closest contact between the Benthamites and the Saint-Simonians was in the mid-1830s when Browning was meeting Fox and Mill: Browning could criticize Napoleon's neglect of his youthful principles only if he had forgotten his own political position. The poet, as well as the subject of the poem, had modified his principles, and this part of the poem can be read as a criticism only at the cost of attributing to Browning a certain insensitivity about his own position. Napoleon tries to defend himself against his more high-minded critics ' "Age and experience bring discouragement," You taunt me',[1] and denies that he has been discouraged, but the deeper irony is that, whether Napoleon had been discouraged or not, Browning certainly had been.

The discussion of foreign policy, from 'Witness that lie of lies' to 'So Italy was free',[2] is even more complicated; the ambiguous Sagacity intervenes more often, with quotations in several of his speeches. The admission, at the beginning of this section, that this is what ought to have happened rather than what did happen, is a warning of complications to come. Browning very possibly believed that the French were naturally bellicose and that anyone who ruled them would be likely to be pushed into war with other countries. This view of the French was widely believed in England, though Napoleon himself was less committed to the idea that the French wanted war; when he said *L'Empire*,

[1] *Prince Hohenstiel-Schwangau*, 1163–64.
[2] 1526–908.

*c'est la paix'* there is no sign that he expected it to be unpopular. The argument in the poem that Napoleon had followed a peaceful foreign policy interrupted solely to fight one preeminently just war for Italian freedom was certainly 'the life I might have led, But did not.' French involvement in the Crimean War, the attempt to impose Maximilian on Mexico and the Luxembourg negotiations of the late 1860s were fairly clear evidence that Napoleon was ready to follow an exciting foreign policy. The frivolity of the declaration of war at the end of the poem is a criticism, but most of Browning's readers (in the state of British opinion in 1871) would have been even more hostile to Napoleon than this; the ambiguity of the foreign policy section continues to the end.

One reason for thinking the weaknesses of the poem are the result of Browning's poor control of his material is his demonstrable failure to handle historical facts in the next section. Presumably in order to express his own views, he moved into an attack on the principle of hereditary succession. Perhaps taken strictly within the world expressed in the poem, this section might have made sense, but the poem is expressed so completely in terms of Napoleon's career that it is simply not possible to step out of the real world at this point. In the real world, though not in the poem, the Prince had not been 'picked out . . . by providence;'[1] he had come to this throne because of his name and his family. Napoleon Bonaparte could have opposed the principle of hereditary succession, but Napoleon III could never do so without cutting off the branch he sat on. And there is some vulgarity, as well as a failure to understand the arguments in favour of hereditary succession, in lines like

> *And prove there's nothing so unprovable*
> *As who's who, what son of what a sire.*

> (2056–57)

In short, the poem deteriorates as it goes along, and it seems to deteriorate not so much because Browning was handling his material in a way that reveals Napoleon's faults deliberately as because the task of constructing a defence for him becomes harder and the use that is made of historical material becomes increasingly confused. The idea of the poem as a dream has its advantages: at first it is clear and straightforward, but by degrees towards waking it becomes increasingly unsatisfactory.

Until the 1880s it was possible to be a Liberal simply out of a belief in

---

[1] *Prince Hohenstiel-Schwangau*, 2035–37.

freedom; and while this is not the attitude defended in *Prince Hohenstiel-Schwangau* there is no suggestion that the Prince was a liberal. By the 1880s there were hints that liberty was not enough. Matthew Arnold approved of 'the Liberals the friends of trade as well as the friends of liberty,' but he added 'Of inequality . . . as a sure cause of trouble, Liberal statesmen are very shy to speak.'[1] A Liberal as moderate as Trollope also spoke of Liberalism in terms of the increase of equality,[2] so there is no real justification for the idea that there was 'a conflict between liberty as represented by Liberalism and equality as represented by Radicalism,'[3] but Browning was certainly on the Liberal side of this proposed dividing line. Orr mentions an occasion when Browning expressed deep approval for an improving landlord, and seems to imply that this meant he was becoming a Conservative, but this is merely the result of a failure (common enough among Conservatives) to realize how moderate the Liberals really were. Gladstone himself said 'A free and well-conducted proprietary body is a mainstay of the state,' and Browning went no further.[4]

Gladstone had a high opinion of Browning. When the resignation honours were being drawn up in 1885 at the end of his second ministry, his private secretary noted 'A Baronetcy for Browning has also occurred to Mr G'; but he added his own comment 'I don't think the public generally would much appreciate that honour. A poet to be truly great ought to be intelligible.'[5] The idea got no further, which was perhaps just as well, because it might have been mistaken for a reward for a political service. Browning had accepted—along with 54 other Liberals—an invitation from Andrew Reid, a left-wing Liberal journalist, to explain briefly 'Why I am a Liberal,' and an honour for Browning would have looked as if it had something to do with his willingness to take part. The responses to the invitation appeared in a book with this title, designed as semi-official campaign propaganda for the general election to be held later in the year. Browning wrote a sonnet and it was placed at the beginning of the book, in front of the contributions of Gladstone, Rosebery, and

[1] M. Arnold, 'The Future of Liberalism,' in *The Nineteenth Century*, VIII, 1880, 6 and 17–18.
[2] A. Trollope, *The Prime Minister*, 1876, chapter 68.
[3] Lord Dunraven, 'The Revolutionary Party,' in *The Nineteenth Century*, X, 1881, 185.
[4] Orr, *Life*, 363. P. Magnus, *Gladstone*, 1954, 434.
[5] 13 June, 1885. Bahlman, ed, *The Diary of Sir Edward Hamilton*, 1972, 883.

Chamberlain, which were followed by the other 51, arranged alphabetically. His answer was clear-cut:

> *But little do or can the best of us.*
> *That little is achieved through liberty.*
> *Who, then, dares hold—emancipated thus—*
> *His fellow shall continue bound? Not I.*

(XI, 351)

Of the fifty-five, nineteen gave answers which stressed the Liberal contribution to progress, twelve replied in terms of freedom, nine spoke of equality and another nine wrote about the greatest happiness of the greatest number, three wrote about democracy and another three stressed Liberalism's contribution to a peaceful foreign policy. The distribution of opinions in the book may not indicate anything about the weight that particular opinions carried in the party, but more or less the full range of opinions found in the party was represented.

The contributors did not refer to Irish affairs, either because they did not realize how serious the situation was or because they *did* realize but did not want to touch an issue that could damage the party. Within a year, the party had split over the question: most Liberal MPs and a great majority of Liberal voters supported Mr Gladstone's proposals for Home Rule, but most Liberal peers and an important section of the rest of the party opposed them. The Liberal poets—Arnold, Browning, Swinburne, Tennyson—opposed it. Swinburne dashed off a poem denouncing Parnell and Gladstone in terms which implied a respect for established authority that contrasted rather sharply with his earlier political poems. Arnold wrote an essay declaring that Home Rule or local self-government for Ireland was intolerable because it would lead inevitably to her becoming a separate nation—a line of argument which took it for granted, in a thoroughly imperialist way, that the Irish were not to be allowed to choose for themselves about their future.

Browning did not part company with the Liberal party in any comparably conspicuous manner. He wrote nothing on the subject; Orr suggests he regarded Gladstone as a 'lost leader',[1] but when he said in a letter 'To my discomfiture sat next to [Gladstone]—nobody could be more agreeable', it seems simply that he was slightly embarrassed and that Gladstone—who had had far more experience of this sort of thing

[1] Orr, *Life*, 375.

—behaved calmly and politely.[1]

Some of the limits of Browning's Liberalism (and, it may be added, of Gladstone's) had been visible in 1882, when the British occupied Egypt on a temporary basis. Browning clearly approved, and had very few after-thoughts about liberty.[2] Some of the contributors to *Why I am a Liberal* could very easily justify the occupation of Egypt, and opposition to Home Rule, in terms of the principles they had put forward. A believer in progress might feel that Britain had a duty to improve under-developed countries; a believer in equality might feel that a British government would ill-treat the people at the bottom of the system in Ireland or in Egypt less than any conceivable alternative government; a believer in liberty might find his position a little harder to explain.

The energy of Browning's Liberalism had burnt out by 1886, but this did not mean he had become a Conservative, as he proved in his 'Parleying with George Bubb Dodington' the following year. The historical background to the poem is fanciful. Dodington is painted as a man who feathered his own nest in politics but failed to reach the top because he took the wrong approach to the problem of 'managing with skill the rabble-rout;'[3] Dodington in fact spent more on politics than he made out of it and, as the patron of James Turner and Edward Young, the friend of Voltaire, the defender of Admiral Byng and a minor poet on his own account, really deserved better treatment.[4] At a more serious level of discussion, he lived in an age when wooing the multitude was not considered by anyone to be the road to power. Dodington did hope to become Prime Minister, but he proposed to do so in the orthodox way, by winning the favour of the heir to the throne and of the country gentlemen in the Commons.

This historical background is not relevant to the rather slender literary merits of the poem, though it does show how historical knowledge and a regard for historical accuracy can be an obstacle to the enjoyment of Browning. The inaccuracies are irrelevant to the analysis of political experience as well. In the later sections of the poem Browning has some interesting things to say about the 'charismatic leader':

[1] *Wise Letters*, 291–2.

[2] Orr, *Life*, 363.

[3] *Parleying with Dodington*, 87 Centenary Edition, X 191.

[4] There is a sympathetic life of Dodington in J. Carswell, *The Good Old Cause*, 1954.

> each plays his part
> Submissive: why? through terror at the heart:
> 'Can it be—this bold man, whose hand we saw
> Openly pull the wires, obeys some law
> Quite above Man's—nay, God's?' On face fall they.   (336–40)

Or, in the less elegant language of the social sciences,

> 'the legitimacy of the norms enunciated by charismatic authority lies outside the norms practised in the existing society.'[1]

Political leaders who place themselves above human and divine law have become more common with the decline of religious belief and hereditary succession, and the failure of government based on contested elections to spread to many new countries in this century. As a description of the relationship between such a leader and his followers, the poem shows a great deal of insight. The comment that simple denials of 'selfishness and greed' help a politician very little, and that well-tried phrases like 'Hearth and Home, The Altar, love of England, fear of Rome' were losing some of their effectiveness was observant enough.[2] The point that the electorate has to be convinced that

> Win
> A master-mind to serve us needs we must,
> One who, from motives we but take on trust,
> Acts strangelier—haply wiselier than we know—
> Stronglier, for certain
>
> (280–4)

is a reasonable account of the relationship between ruler and citizens in all but the most educated of democracies.

The description of the technique by which this relationship is established has less claim to be generally valid, though it makes Browning's own political position very clear. The argument is that the ruler who wants to deceive the people needs

[1] Edward Shils, 'Charisma,' in *International Encyclopedia of the Social Sciences*, New York, 1968, II, 387.
[2] *Parleying with Dodington*, 314 and 319–20.

> *An imperturbability that's—well,*
> *Or innocence or impudence—how tell*
> *One from the other*

(236–8)

and must show

> *So slightly does he hold by our esteem,*
> *Which solely fixed him fast there, that we seem*
> *Mocked every minute to our face.*

(297–9)

Imperturbability and restrained contempt are undoubtedly methods that have been used to win and hold power,[1] but on the whole unrestrained conviction and violent commitment have been much more typical of charismatic leaders. Napoleon III in some ways fitted the approach suggested in the poem, and de Gaulle might be regarded as a later example of it, but there is no doubt that Browning had Disraeli in mind when he wrote the poem (There is a story about Browning and Disraeli at a Royal Academy dinner which is a good example of 'a touch Of subintelligential nod and wink').[2] Disraeli was not as dishonest as the poem suggests, and its publication certainly suggests that disagreement with Liberal policy to Ireland had not led Browning to see himself as a Conservative. Many Conservatives of the day would have agreed with the general criticism of the charismatic leader, but would have disagreed about the technique such a leader would use; their description of a charismatic leader would have sounded much more like a pen-portrait of Gladstone.

It may still seem odd that a Liberal who stressed liberty as an essential part of his belief should have opposed Home Rule. Probably he was to some extent floating along with the general current of London 'society', which was strongly opposed to it. Part of the explanation may lie in the

[1] Dodington himself had a different view of the virtues of imperturbability, and in his last poem, "Ere we drop into the Dark,' he wrote:

> *Envy's Censure, Flattery's Praise,*
> *With unmov'd Indifference view;*
> *Learn to tread Life's dangerous Maze*
> *With unerring Virtue's Clue.*

[2] Maisie Ward, *Robert Browning: Two Robert Brownings*, 138. The reference is to *Parleying with Dodington*, 268–9.

non-egalitarian approach he took to politics—and it may be remembered that, only a few years earlier, Gladstone told Ruskin 'I am an out-
and-out inequalitarian (sic).'[1] All the interesting political questions in
Browning's poems are concerned with the relations between leaders and
followers, and this naturally reduces interest in equality.

Any nineteenth-century thinker of Nonconformist background
always found the example of the seventeenth century and the great
struggle against royal power something of a political touchstone.
Browning expressed one aspect of that period in the 'Parleying with
Charles Avison':

> *Back to times of England's best*
> *Parliament stands for privilege*

$$(408-9)$$

'Privilege': the word is hardly one that is at present associated with the
left or the defence of freedom, but in the seventeenth century it was parliamentary privilege that gave MPs the right to resist the dangers of royal
autocracy. On a number of occasions the cause of liberty in England was
greatly helped by people who had special rights that were not available
to the rest of the community. This is a negative and defensive attitude,
and Browning had seen that it ought to develop into the more expansive
and more egalitarian approach of 'Who then dares hold—emancipated
thus—His fellows shall continue bound?' But in general his desire for
liberty did not express itself in a belief that everybody had an equal claim
to an equal amount of liberty; and this may make his willingness to deny
the Irish claim to self-determination.

As will have become clear, Browning's political interests were not of
primary concern in his work, but have some importance in considering
several of his poems of the second rank. Roughly the same thing can be
said about the type of opinion within Victorian Liberal politics which he
represented. When the old Victorian Liberal party, a wide range of
groups and interests that had ruled the country for most of the previous
fifty years, finally broke up over Ireland, the main groups that seceded
were the landholding Whigs and the Chamberlainite Radicals. Browning probably shared the Whig view that Liberal progress had gone about
as far as it should, rather than the Chamberlainite that it should continue,
in a new direction; but at the same time he was a long way from being a

[1] M. Drew, *Some Hawarden Letters*, 1928, 37.

Whig. He can best be placed among the anti-popular intellectuals who made up an important group within the Victorian Liberal party but must, in considering its fate, be put in the second rank.[1] It may not be too strained an analogy to suggest that his political poems could be described in similar terms.

[1] J. Roach, 'Liberalism and the Victorian Intelligentsia', *Cambridge Historical Journal*, 1957, XIII, 58–81.

# 6: *Browning in Italy*

## BARBARA MELCHIORI

Browning biographies from the first have been concerned with his connection with Italy, the country in which he spent almost the whole of his married life, in which much of his best poetry was written, and in which he died. The result of such comment has led, I believe, to a mistake of emphasis. Browning can in no way be regarded as an *inglese italianato*; his way of life remained remarkably English and his circle of friends in Florence, Pisa, Bagni di Lucca, Siena, Rome and Asolo were the small English colonies settled there. A few Italian hangers-on of this circle were acquaintances but hardly intimates, and Browning's closest relations with modern Italians were with his servants, particularly with Ferdinando the Italian cook who, as Elizabeth wrote, 'makes soups and creams and ice puddings and pastry to our uttermost satisfaction'.[1] Unfortunately he also seduced Wilson, her faithful chambermaid, and in 1855 the Brownings had to break a journey in Paris in order to see the two safely married.

The lack of any real Italian friendships may partly have been due to the extreme intimacy between Browning and his wife, and the fact that they were both very hardworking people. They had little time to spare for outsiders and were more than content with their own company and later with that of Pen. The fact remains that no Italian friends came anything like so close to them as the Storys or Miss Blagden. A touch of patronage creeps in very easily, particularly in Elizabeth's references to Italians, as in a letter written to the Storys: 'As soon as the rain ceases and I can get out, I will go and see your charming little Duchess.'[2] Not that the lan-

---

[1] Betty Miller, *Robert Browning. A Portrait*, 1952, 176. Quoted from 26 July (1853) Huxley typescript.

[2] Footnote by EBB to a letter of Browning's to the Storys, dated Florence, Monday [29 Oct.—Nov. 1859 by editor], in *Browning to his American Friends* ed G. Reese Hudson, 1965, 53.

guage was in any way a barrier. Both Robert Browning and his wife were excellent linguists and they accustomed their little son to speak in Italian rather than in English. Their segregation was a deliberate choice, and it allowed them to live in a foreign country without getting involved, giving them the freedom their work required.

They followed, naturally, the events which were rapidly leading up to the unification of Italy, followed them with sympathy for the cause of Italian freedom, but with very little attempt at participation. Philip Drew comes to a different conclusion, writing of Browning's poem 'Italy in England' (later called 'The Italian in England') that

> 'it had its origin in the intense interest that Browning took in the fortunes of the Italian nation, an interest which found frequent expression in his verse, at least till 1871':[1]

and a few pages later he adds

> 'even when he writes about Italy he does so in a way that emphasizes the immediacy of his subjects. He brings before the reader day-to-day life in nineteenth century Italy, as in "Up at a Villa" and "De Gustibus". In particular he brings to life Italian politics, a subject in which he shared his wife's unfailing interest.'

I have quoted Mr. Drew at length because it seems to me serious that the most perspicacious critic at present engaged in writing about Browning is perpetuating in these words a common fallacy of Browning criticism. These short poems he mentions (he has already quite rightly dropped the romantic 'Pippa' from the list) and some passages in *Prince Hohenstiel-Schwangau* are practically all that Browning has to say about contemporary Italy. Their proportion to his work as a whole is infinitesimal. When Browning was deeply interested in a subject he reverted to it over and over again, worrying it as a dog worries a bone, introducing it into similes in the most surprising contexts. He simply does not do this about Italian freedom. He took the stand which was common among English residents in nineteenth-century Italy, the stand that was also that of the English Liberals at home, that Italian unification was to be desired (as was the final disruption of the Austrian empire); he sympathized for the space of 162 lines with the predicament of political exiles in England, and here he had the stimulus of knowing personally of

[1] Philip Drew, *The Poetry of Robert Browning. A Critical Introduction*, 1970, 285, 288.

the case of Gabriele Rossetti, the father of his friend Dante Gabriel, whose nostalgia for Italy could not fail to move all those who came into contact with him. 'The Italian in England' was first published in 1845, before Browning had met the most famous of the Italian exiles of the Risorgimento, Giuseppe Mazzini. This meeting took place during a visit to England in 1852, and Mrs. Carlyle, who introduced them, records it rather dryly: 'Oh such a fuss the Brownings made over Mazzini this day'.[1] The fuss seems to have been mutual, for Mrs. Orr tells us that Mazzini informed Browning that he had read the poem to his fellow exiles to show them how an Englishman could sympathize with them.[2] The mood of the poem was probably in fact inspired by talk with Angelo Cerutti, Browning's Italian teacher, a political refugee, and probably also by the plight of Gabriele Rossetti. De Vane writes realistically of the poem that it 'is one of the few expressions of Browning's intense sympathy with the cause of Italian freedom!'[3] Nobody, so far as I know, has drawn particular attention to the fact that it was written *before* Browning began his fourteen years' residence in Italy: later he no longer wanted to become involved. Elizabeth Barrett was a much more ardent sympathizer with the cause of Italian freedom, but then she had a weakness for causes (ranging from the fate of factory children to Louis Napoleon) which was notably lacking in her husband.

It is difficult to avoid a comparison with the situation of Byron in Italy some forty years earlier: Byron the aristocrat who yet lived among the people in a way undreamed of by Browning. It is impossible not to suspect that if Browning had spent his Italian years in the company of Teresa Guiccioli instead of Elizabeth Barrett his attitude to Italian affairs would have been more *engagé*. But then an Italian mistress would have changed a great deal more for Browning than his attitude to Italian politics—almost certainly much of the contorted puritanism which so complicates his poetry would have disappeared. As it is, living in a small Anglo-Saxon community which seems to have contained more women than men, there are touches from time to time in the correspondence (though not the poetry) of the Brownings which seem to regard modern

[1] See Maisie Ward, *Robert Browning and His World. The Private Face*, 1968, 203.

[2] Mrs. Sutherland Orr, *A Handbook to the Works of Robert Browning*, 1913, 306, n. 1.

[3] W. C. DeVane, *A Browning Handbook*, New York, 157.

Italians as 'natives' much in the way that E. M. Forster's characters were later to do.

The period in which Browning showed most affection for Italy was, understandably enough, during the first year in England after his wife's death. It is then that he wrote to the Storys in Rome:

> And for me,—my end of life, and particular reward for myself will be—one day—years hence—to just go back to Italy—to Rome —and die as I lived, when I used really to live. If you knew—but you *do* know and can conceive how precious every mud-splash on the house walls of Rome is: how every minute of those last six months in Rome would *melt up* into gold enough for a year's use now, if I had it![1]

It is noteworthy that he is here using a metaphor which was always, in both his prose and poetry, indicative of considerable emotional involvement. There is no doubt that at this time Italy was closely connected in his mind with his married life, and the nostalgia he felt was part of his bereavement. From the same period we have letters which, at last, mention Italian acquaintances:

> I would send my kind remembrances to M. Boncinelli—if he cared to have them, and he may, in his good nature. Have you to do still with that clever Lombard artist? . . . By the bye—Mrs. Cholmeley wrote the other day and mentioned the death of poor Gajassi: if there is a sale of his effects, and the cast of Byron's head by Thorwaldsen, (with his 'points' on it) is to be sold for what you consider a moderate price, I should be glad to have it . . .[2]

The Italy which really mattered to Browning was the Italy that he found in his library, the Italy of the past. This Italy and the Italian scenery which surrounded him and of which he was such an accurate observer and recorder were the source of much of his work. The fact that he was living in Italy among the people, that he heard daily the variety of dialects and observed the age-old gestures (some of which Pen soon picked up), blended the present with the past in his imagination and brought alive the ancient stories with their records of crime and passion, helping him to find motives and clothe the bare ribs of his source-books with flesh and blood. Yet one is constantly struck, as always in Browning's poetry, by two conflicting forces at work: a participation which enables

[1] G. Reese Hudson (ed), *Browning to his American Friends, cit.* 95.
[2] G. Reese Hudson (ed), *cit.* 96.

him to become temporarily identified with his characters, tracing the inner play of motives and passions behind their actions in a way which few writers apart from Shakespeare have been able to do, and a refusal to become involved, which was in its way typically Victorian. If Browning did not go as far as the Lady of Shallott and weave his web from the reflection in a mirror, yet he outlines his position as an observer very consciously in one of his finest passages where he describes, at the beginning of *The Ring and the Book*, his discovery of his source-book, his instant recognition of its rightness, and steps out onto his balcony in Casa Guidi in Florence to view the world below him:

> *And from the reading, and that slab I leant*
> *My elbow on, the while I read and read,*
> *I turned, to free myself and find the world,*
> *And stepped out on the narrow terrace, built*
> *Over the street and opposite the church,*
> *And paced its lozenge-brickwork sprinkled cool;*
> >                    *. . . Beneath*
> *I' the street . . .*
> *The townsmen walked by twos and threes, and talked,*
> *Drinking the blackness in default of air—*
> *A busy human sense beneath my feet.*                    (I, 476—93)

I have written more fully elsewhere of the artist in his ivory tower which this passage suggests, but it seems so relevant to the whole of Browning's detached attitude to Italy, that I have wished to return to it here. Because here surely lies the reason for his choice of historical subjects, his preference for the Italy which he found in Baldinucci[1] and Vasari,[2] in Bartoli[3] and above all in 'The Old Yellow Book'.

Much has been said about Browning's fondness for art and music, and it has been argued from this that Italy for him was a natural home. Yet it should be remembered that his reason for settling in Italy in the first place was simply because the climate of Pisa had been recommended to Eliza-

---

[1] Filippo Baldinucci, *Notizie de' Professori del Disegno*, Florence, 1767—74.

[2] Giorgio Vasari, *Le Vite dei più Eccellenti Pittori, Scultori, e Architetti*, Florence, 1550, 1568.

[3] Daniello Bartoli, *Dei Simboli Trasportati al Morale*, Rome, 1677.

beth Barrett by her doctor. When Mr. Barrett, her tyrannical father, refused his permission for this journey, Elizabeth finally admitted to herself that her father's affection for her was almost wholly egotistical and agreed to place herself in Robert's hands and to fly with him after a secret marriage. Robert had long been pleading with her to take this step and when she finally consented their destination was inevitably Pisa. Had the doctor prescribed the Swiss Alps that is undoubtedly where they would have gone. Except for two or three trips to Paris and London, the whole of the Brownings' married life, from 1846 to 1861 was spent in Italy. After Elizabeth's death in Florence Robert returned to live with his sister in London and henceforth only visited Italy at intervals, finding for a while more inspiration from the northern coast of France. His visits became more frequent when his son Robert Wiedermann (who had always felt exiled in England) married a rich American girl and purchased the Cà Rezzonico in Venice. Browning was enough of a snob to enjoy staying in a palace and an unpublished letter of his, now in the Vatican library, shows his aspiration to give his London house in Warwick Crescent a palatial appearance by fitting out the dining room with Italian marble columns.[1] Marble had always fascinated Browning and his poems are decorated with the rarer marbles ('The Bishop Orders his Tomb' is the best example, but there is plenty of marble in *The Ring*) in the way in which other poets adorn their work with gems. This was almost certainly a taste acquired in Italy where the richly marbled churches were an integral part of the life of the cities—and many of them are built up to and into the adjoining houses forming a single architectonic agglomeration, a unity which forced itself on the attention of Browning.

Browning's attitude to the Catholic religion, which for him was so much a part of the Italian background, and a moving force behind the characters of the chronicles on which so much of his narrative poetry was based, must, I believe, be taken into account if we are to see what Italy meant for him. Rome, when in 1853 and the winters of 1858, 1859 and 1860 Browning and his wife lived there, was still a Papal city, and Browning, writing *The Ring and the Book* welded together the seventeenth-century Rome of his source and the mid-nineteenth century Rome

[1] Unpublished letter of Robert Browning to his son Pen, dated 1889, in the Vatican Library (original mss. + typed translation). Vat. lat. 12899 b, ff. 3–16, Biblioteca Vaticana.

with its Carnival and its Corsa dei Berberi as he describes them in his letters. Because Rome was still the city of the Popes, its basic traditions had not altered. Rome, the capital of Italy and the city of the bureaucrats had still to be born. The Quirinal palace had not yet replaced the Vatican as the centre of power and intrigue.

Browning's attitude to Catholicism, as to most things, was contradictory. He is very much and very often concerned with it, sometimes in open discussion, more often in passing references or in long-drawn-out and elaborate similes when he is professedly dealing with some quite other subject. What is really surprising in an attentive reading of his works is the depths of bitter anti-Catholic prejudice underlying his frequent attempts at broadmindedness.[1] What has caught the attention of most Browning commentators have been the attempts to understand the Catholic religion made by a non-Catholic in *Christmas Eve*, or again in Book X of *The Ring and the Book*, a dramatic monologue attributed to Pope Pius X recounting his spiritual struggle as to whether he should pardon Guido. Yet even here, in the passages which are usually quoted to illustrate Browning's sympathy, there are a number of revealing lines showing how deep-rooted was his suspicion. A wholly unconscious example can be seen in 'An Englishman in Italy' where he seems on the surface to be merely painting in a gay if slightly supercilious tone a popular religious festival:

> And then will the flaxen-wigged Image
>   Be carried in pomp
> Thro' the plain, while in gallant procession
>   The priests mean to stomp.
> All round the glad church lie old bottles
>   With gunpowder stopped,
> Which will be, when the Image re-enters,
>   Religiously popped;
> And at night from the crest of Calvano
>   Great bonfires will hang,
> On the plain will the trumpets join chorus,
>   And more poppers bang.

[1] Even Kingsbury Badger in his essay (1955–6) '"See the Christ Stand" Browning's Religion', republished in *Robert Browning*, ed Philip Drew, 1966, 72–95, has failed to note the extent of Browning's anti-Catholic prejudice.

> *At all events, come—to the garden*
> *As far as the wall;*
> *See me tap with a hoe on the plaster*
> *Till out there shall fall*
> *A scorpion with wide angry nippers!*                        (269–85)

The scorpion seems innocent enough here, he is introduced as a fragment of *natura viva*, as part of the garden scenery, and has nothing to do with the Church festival Browning has just been describing so gaily. Or so it would seem until we read, in *Prince Hohenstiel-Schwangau*

> *. . . Peter's Dome,*
> *The scorpion-body with the greedy pair*
> *Of outstretched nippers, either colonnade*
> *Agape for the advance of heads and hearts!*                 (862–4)

The scorpion which walks into the earlier picture as it were of its own accord (though it is significant that Browning had chosen this moment to tap it out of its hole in the wall) is the Church of Rome in its supreme embodiment, as he had been taught to see it as a child when he attended the Nonconformist church with his mother in York Street.

The main grounds on which Browning attacks the Roman church are precisely those encountered so regularly in Nonconformist teaching The chief of these is undoubtedly the wealth of the Church, which Browning loses no opportunity of describing as both ill-gotten and ill-spent. As an artist he could and did enjoy the riches and splendour; 'the Jesu church so gay' with its colourful marbles could give him pleasure, but underneath there was always the echo of the text 'sell all thou hast and give to the poor'. In 'The Bishop Orders his Tomb' the lump of lapis lazuli which the Bishop had actually stolen and hidden becomes a symbol of the riches hoarded in Rome, extracted from the faithful, as he shows in *Red Cotton Night-Cap Country*, by dubious pressures:

> *The faithful of our province raised the sum*
> *Preached and prayed out of—nowise purse alone.*
> *Gentle and simple paid in kind, not cash*                   (469–71)

Elsewhere in the same poem we have nuns and priests gathering money
for the church. The 'golden grist' of Monsieur Léonce Miranda's charity
pours

> *From mill to mouth of sack—held wide and close*
> *By Father of the Mission, Parish-priest,*
> *And Mother of the Convent, Nun I know.*        (III, 3153–55)

And their activity is significantly enough compared to the loading and
unloading of dung.

> *. . . the couple yonder, Father Priest*
> *And Mother Nun, who came and went and came*
> *Beset this Clairvaux, trundled money-muck*
> *To midden and the main heap oft enough.*        (IV, 4131–34)

Setting aside any psychological reading of this passage, it makes
Browning's basic objection to the Catholic religion extremely clear, and
helps us to understand why he was so cut off from the Italians who professed it. There was in the nineteenth century a strong and growing
movement of liberal anti-clericalism in Italy, but respect was preserved
for the traditional forms of worship and few would have subscribed to
Browning's definition of 'the raree show of Peter's successor'. His anti-
clericalism had different roots: while the Italian criticisms were based
rather on the misuse of temporal power, Browning's were directed
against many of the basic tenets of the religion, and always in those
points where the Catholic and Protestant forms of Christianity differ.
Even Pompilia, the most truly pious of his creations, questions most im-
probably the value of patron saints:

> *One who has only been made saint—how long?*
> *Twenty-five years: so, carefuller, perhaps,*
> *To guard a namesake than those old saints grow,*
> *Tired out by this time,—see my own five saints!*
>                    (*The Ring and the Book*, 'Pompilia', VII, 104–7)

Or again he deliberately makes fun of faith in relics

> *The blessed* Umbilicus *of our Lord,*
> *( A relic 'tis believed no other church*
> *In Rome can boast of).*

(*The Ring and the Book*, 'The Book and the Ring', XII, 184–6)

For Browning the whole history of the Catholic Church was based on corruption and ill-doing. In the Italian source-books for his many historical poems Browning finds and uses much material on which to found his attacks, specifically that of torture as an instrument of the Inquisition, and the burning of heretics, a theme which was not only the subject of his 'Heretic's Tragedy' but which recurs over and over again in his imagery, and runs right through from his earliest to his later work. In *Paracelsus* we already find a mocking reference:

> *The prince was pleased no longer to defer*
> *The burning of some dozen heretics*
> *Remanded till God's mercy should be shown*
> *Touching his sickness.*
>
> (III, 462–5)

Another strictly Protestant criticism of the Catholic church was that of the chastity enjoined on the clergy. Browning takes every possible occasion to reveal how far practice fell short of precept, at times subtly as in the 'Nephews—sons mine' of the Bishop of St. Praxed's, and the soft white mouse who is the Prior's niece in 'Fra Lippo', at times quite openly as in the description of Fra Lippo's own amorous escapades, and his gay *stornelli*.

What I want to draw attention to particularly is this peculiar blindness in Browning, an area of insensitiveness in a man who was hypersensitive. Because for all his subtlety in reading the motives behind the actions of his Italian characters, yet owing to his employment of the dramatic monologue technique these characters have to speak for themselves, and Browning's strongly prejudiced criticisms of the Catholic Church and of the Catholic religion are constantly voiced by them in the most improbable contexts. I have only been able here to give a sprinkling of examples (also because Browning's diffuseness makes illustration extremely difficult), but it is misleading to take, as is so often done, his broad-minded and open declarations in *Christmas Eve* as being his last word on the subject.

> *Though Rome's gross yoke*
> *Drops off, no more to be endured,*
> *Her teaching is not so obscured*
> *By errors and perversities,*
> *That no truth shines athwart the lies:*
>
> .   .   .   .   .   .   .   .
>
> *I see the error; but above*
> *The scope of error, see the love.*

> (*Christmas-Eve and Easter-Day*, XI, 614–18, 647–8)

Yet even in the above passage, the operative word is 'error'.

If he failed singularly to understand or appreciate the Italian religion, Browning was wholly in sympathy with the Italian landscape, which was of the greatest importance for his poetry. He was a tireless and accurate observer and enjoyed giving not only the general effect but the precise names and detailed descriptions of the flora and fauna which surrounded him. And he brought all a scholar's delight to the natural detail of his poems, many of which seem to be literally overgrown, like the Roman campagna 'by the caper overrooted, by the gourd overscored'. Nothing could be further from the landscapes of his predecessor, Byron, which were either tourist set-pieces such as the Colosseum by moonlight or rough though effective background:

> *. . . vines (not nailed to walls) from tree to tree*
> *Festoon'd, much like the back scene of a play.*[1]

Browning's artistry was more Victorian and less romantic in its precision—like Millais or other Pre-Raphaelites he would place his plants in detail in the foreground of a picture. In 'Two in the Campagna' his description of the spider's web reminds us of those beautiful Victorian hand-drawn botanic specimens:

> *First it left*
> *The yellowing fennel, run to seed*
> *There, branching from the brickwork's cleft,*

[1] George Gordon Byron, *Beppo*, 1818.

> *Some old tomb's ruin: yonder weed*
> *Took up the floating weft,*
>
> *Where one small orange cup amassed*
>    *Five beetles,—blind and green they grope*
> *Among the honey-meal: and last,*
>    *Everywhere on the grassy slope*
> *I traced it.*

(IV–V)

Nor has any other English poet mentioned so many birds by name as has Browning in *The Ring and the Book* where their importance as flight and annunciation symbolism is lost sight of in the sheer pleasure of their enunciation. The naturalist takes over at times from the poet in enriching the texture of the verse with a multiplicity of first-hand observations, interwoven with literary and Biblical quotation.

Some of the more patiently elaborated details, such as

> *And the leaf-buds on the vine are woolly,*
>    *I noticed that, today;*
> *One more day bursts them open fully*
>    *You know the red turns grey.*

('The Lost Mistress', II)

give us the measure of the time at his disposal, the sense of infinite leisure for observation—one of the undoubted advantages of his residence in Italy, cut off from the claims (which became more and more exacting during his later years in London when he allowed himself to be lionized) of society and free to dedicate himself to observation, meditation and leisurely excursions into the countryside with his wife and other Anglo-Saxon visitors and residents. Elizabeth's invalidism helped to limit the scope and pace of such outings (although it is always surprising to find out how much she did undertake) and a sense of blue skies and tranquil unelaborate meals in the open breathes from many of their letters during the Italian period, and from much of the poetry born from it.

Tedium is wholly avoided in Browning's many and long landscape descriptions by his consistent tendency towards symbolism. The landscape is detailed, it is almost invariably extremely precise and correct, but it is as symbolically charged as a Leonardo painting. Browning lived so much in his work that a ruined tower could become loaded with un-definable but undeniable menace—a tower glimpsed near Massa Carrara which is said by Mrs. Orr to be the source of 'Childe Roland' would blend with the ruined towers of the Campagna against which the shepherds built their huts, and with the literary towers of legend.

Or again the description already mentioned of the insects drowning in the cup of the flower nectar can carry a heavy sexual symbolism which is re-established in 'Women and Roses' in quite unambiguous terms. What I want to stress is that the Italian landscape, like everything else in Browning's poetry, underwent a process of fusion in his mind like the famous ring—it is transmuted into art. A double process is at work, a process which can be seen very clearly in *The Ring and the Book* in the flight of the 'lovers' from Arezzo to Rome: the passing landscape (familiar to Browning from his own journeys) is photographed in rapid and accurate frames and yet at the same time symbolic details such as the menacing tower (in Browning both a sexual symbol and suggestive of death) and the young woman with the babe in her arms (the birth theme which becomes stronger throughout the poem) are picked out in a special light.

The inaccuracies in Browning's Italian background understandably enough all belong to the relatively early poems before he settled in the country. Two are to be found in the well-known 'The Bishop Orders his Tomb', for the ninth-century church of St. Praxed's is dedicated to the female Santa Prassede whom Browning clearly took to be a man, and is one of the few Roman churches without a dome, whereas the Bishop speaks of looking 'into the aery dome where live the angels'. Likewise in *Sordello*, written after his first brief visit to Italy, we have inaccuracies. 'Goito's mountain cup' is at best a very big saucer, for the walls of Goito castle still stand on the wide Mantuan plain and only the distant Alps, visible on a very clear day, could justify such a description. If, as seems possible, Browning was referring to a map, then the mountains would have appeared much nearer and have seemed partly to ring the township. This kind of mistake disappeared altogether from his later poetry, when his long residence in Italy and familiarity with the language enabled him to make free with it and ring the changes on its diminutives in the innumerable forms of the name Giacinto: Cinone, Cinozzo, Cinoncello, Cinuolo, Cinicello, Cinino, Ciniccino, Cinucciatolo, Cinoncino, Cinarello, Cinotto, Giacintino, etc.

It would be surprising to note how little of Browning's poetry was concerned with contemporary nineteenth-century Italy if this did not exactly correspond to the amount of his poetry concerned with contemporary England. Contemporary Italy, just because he was so familiar with it, comes under the same kind of psychological censorship which prevented him from dealing openly with the problems of his own time and country. It did not offer him an 'exotic' background or the possibility of evasion: this he had to search for in the past, and the Italy of his poetry is above all the Italy of books, of paintings, of historical reconstruction, and no writer has ever excelled him in this art. What is particularly interesting is to see the use he makes of his source-books, his eye for details which could make his characters live, and his eye above all for the universal rather than the period flavour.

After the Romantic taste for false classicism and false medievalism, and at the time of Ruskin's and Morris's theorizing, Browning, without apparently theorizing at all, set to work to bring out of old books and manuscripts the universal types he found hidden there. Nor is Browning's way of looking at paintings any different from his treatment of his prose sources. He looked for the artist at work behind the painting, and at his problems as a creator, often reading his own problems as a writer into the biographical details which he found in the gossipy 'Lives' of Vasari and Baldinucci. Because Browning could render Masaccio familiarly as 'hulking Tom' and mentions by name at least thirty-four Italian painters with the air of knowing all about them, it has become customary to treat him as an authority on Italian painting. In fact his interest in these painters was almost exclusively psychological, moral and sociological. Even in his discussion of technical details in drawing and painting, details which he found in Vasari and Baldinucci, what interests him is always the psychological repercussion, the rightness or wrongness in moral rather than artistic terms. The best single example of this is the discussion in 'Andrea del Sarto' of the arm which Raphael drew wrongly and which Andrea hesitates to correct. What had impressed Browning above all about Andrea was the epithet 'pittore senza errori' which he found in Vasari and used as a sub-title of his poem. This appellative and details of the biography, in which Andrea is shown to be far from faultless, being guilty of peculation towards his munificent patron Louis XV, allowed Browning to introduce one of his favourite themes: the moral value of art. To this theme which he never exhausted to his own satisfaction, he constantly recurred. In 'Fra Lippo Lippi' and the parleying with 'Francis Furini' he examined the question not so much of the nude

in art as of the flesh and sensuality in painting. In the character of Fra
Lippo, the monk with an eye for the girls and with a certain experience
in the scaling of convent walls, Browning shows the artist as sensualist
and allows him to speak in his own justification. Browning's real difficulty seems to be not with the attitude of the artist, but with that of the
Roman Church. He found it hard to understand how the frankly sensual
treatment of religious subjects could be accepted by the Church, and he
even introduced disapproving old clerics shaking their heads over them
in a thoroughly Puritanical fashion:

> *'Your business is not to catch men with show,*
> *With homage to the perishable clay,*
> *But lift them over it, ignore it all,*
> *Make them forget there's such a thing as flesh.*
> *Your business is to paint the souls of men.'*[1]

('Fra Lippo Lippi', 179–83)

Certain aspects of the Church's tolerance brought out the innate Puritanism in Browning. We are reminded that after all Browning was a Victorian, and that just as Tennyson in 'The Lady of Shallot' introducing
two lovers strolling by moonlight hastens to reassure his readers that all is
well, that they are 'two young lovers *lately wed*', so Browning takes similar comfort in 'Andrea' in the reflection 'But still the other's Virgin was
his wife', even though the touch of irony suggests a fuller awareness, a
sense that moral values can get extremely mixed, for La Fornarina was a
much better influence on Raphael than was Lucrezia on Andrea.

A subtler examination of the same problem is to be found in the later
poem, the 'Parleying with Francesco Furini' a painter censured by Baldinucci for his naked paintings, in which Browning defends the painter's
'all too frank triumph of flesh' as the struggle of art to imitate nature and
the process of creation 'Striving to match the finger-mark of Him, the
immeasurably matchless', implying that also God saw fit to create man
naked. What we should not lose sight of is that these are the problems of
Browning himself, of a Victorian poet writing in a century which produced Buchanan's attack on Rossetti and the fleshly school of poetry.
The Italian painters about whom Browning is writing are being used as
vehicles for his own ideas, and, for all his careful documentation, it is a
mistake to consider him an authority on Italian art. This in no way
detracts from the value of his art poems: 'Andrea' and 'Fra Lippo' are

among the best and most popular dramatic monologues and psychological studies that Browning ever wrote.

In conclusion, the much quoted lines which the Roman municipality
put up (in an Italian version) on a tablet on the wall of the house in Via
Bocca di Leone where Browning had for a time resided

> *Open my heart and you will see*
> *Graved inside of it, 'Italy'*[1]

are misleading. Elizabeth, who knew him better than anybody, had
written to a friend in 1851: 'I do believe he would have been capable of
never leaving England again, had such an arrangement been possible for
us'.

Robert Browning was temperamentally disposed to make the best of
any place in which he found himself—nobody was less given to wasting
time in vain regrets—but his long residence in Italy was, though he
never admitted it, an exile, brought about by Elizabeth's health and her
peculiar family situation. The unsalted bread eaten in Dante's Florence,
and the books he gathered at Casa Guidi, proved together to be excellent
nourishment for his verse.

---

[1] Philip Drew, *Critical Introduction, cit.* 287, n. 1, has traced them back to a
French guide book to Venice: 'Voici la Ca' Rezzonico, où mourut le poète
Robert Browning en disant, Ouvrez mon coeur et vous y verrez écrit
"L'Italie".'

# 7: *Browning and Painting*

## LEONEE ORMOND

AMONG THE FIFTY WORKS in *Men and Women*, the two painter-poems, 'Fra Lippo Lippi' and 'Andrea del Sarto', have often been given pride of place. Quite apart from their quality as poetry, many have found in them Browning's most revealing exploration of his own creative beliefs, expressed imaginatively through the monologues of these exponents of a different art. The uniqueness of the poems is unquestioned, for the other great dramatic monologues of the age, Tennyson's 'Ulysses' and 'Tithonus', or Rossetti's 'Jenny', for instance, make no attempt to introduce 'real' people whose lives are extensively documented elsewhere. The closest literary parallel, significantly enough, is Browning's own musician-poem, 'Abt Vogler', another attempt to describe an act of artistic creation through the medium of poetry.

In the dedication to *Men and Women*, 'One Word More', Browning succinctly expresses both his desire to achieve a synthesis between two different art forms, and his awareness of the fact that he is unable to achieve it. He gives two examples of artists more fortunate than himself in having such a double gift: first Raphael, whose infrequent sonnet-writing Browning exaggerates by inventing an imaginary collection of one hundred poems, in order to make the point more strongly,[1] and secondly Dante, whose ability as a draughtsman is demonstrated by his drawing the head of an angel in celebration of Beatrice.[2] Then, addressing his wife directly, Browning writes:

[1] G. Willis Cooke, *A Guide-Book to the Poetic and Dramatic Works of Robert Browning*, Boston 1891, 227.

[2] D. G. Rossetti's pen-and-ink drawing of this subject, *The First Anniversary of the Death of Beatrice* (City of Birmingham Museum and Art Gallery) is dated 1849.

*I shall never, in the years remaining,*
*Paint you pictures, no, nor carve you statues,*
*Make you music that should all-express me;*
*So it seems: I stand on my attainment.*
*This of verse alone, one life allows me;*
*Verse and nothing else have I to give you.*          (109–14)

Five years before the publication of *Men and Women*, in January 1850, Dante Gabriel Rossetti had written in *The Germ* of his belief in the possibility of relating art and literature more closely in the work of the Pre-Raphaelite Brotherhood. Rossetti himself put this belief into practice by writing poems to accompany his pictures, and by repeatedly painting literary subjects, in particular those from Dante and Malory. In theory, Rossetti and Browning might be seen as working towards the same end, but, placed in juxtaposition with Rossetti's literary paintings, Browning's painter-poems are seen to be essentially historical, literal and factual. They belong to that popular Victorian genre, illustrating the lives of the old masters.

From the end of the eighteenth century, subject-pictures about the lives of early painters became popular throughout Europe. In a scholarly and revealing article on the French exponents of this genre, Professor Francis Haskell traces its history through the first half of the nineteenth century.[1] Between 1830 and 1860 as many as twenty such works were exhibited annually in the Salon, and the vogue only began to wane in the 1860s. Significantly, most artists chose to illustrate the success and fame achieved by their subjects, especially the deference shown to them by the great men of their day: Raphael with Cardinal Bibiena; Leonardo dying in the arms of Francis I; or Benvenuto Cellini being visited by the same French king. The experience of the nineteenth-century artists who painted such scenes was, of course, very different, and their treatment of their sources was just as fanciful as in other historical genre pictures. Browning does not directly depict scenes of adulation in his poetry, but he touches on them indirectly in 'Andrea del Sarto', where Andrea remembers his period of favour at the court of Francis I:

*And that long festal year at Fontainebleau!*
*I surely then could sometimes leave the ground,*

[1] 'The Old Masters in Nineteenth Century French Painting', *The Art Quarterly*, XXXIV, No. 1, Spring 1971, 55–85.

> *Put on the glory, Rafael's daily wear,*
> *In that humane great monarch's golden look—*
> *One finger in his beard or twisted curl*
> *Over his mouth's good mark that made the smile,*
> *One arm about my shoulder, round my neck,*
> *The jingle of his gold chain in my ear.*                    150–8)

This 'golden' passage is used to make a direct contrast with Andrea's present 'grey' situation, and it could be argued that, both here and in 'Fra Lippo Lippi', Browning is looking forward to a later tradition, which Professor Haskell characterizes as: 'the modern equivalent of the pictures under discussion—that the great masters were all misunderstood geniuses who starved in garrets when not drinking themselves to death' (p. 73).

Two other facets of the lives of the old masters appealed to contemporary artists. One was childhood scenes, which Browning introduces into 'Fra Lippo Lippi', and the other was touching love-stories, found both here and in 'Andrea del Sarto'. In the paintings of the period, Lippi is invariably represented with Lucrezia Buti, the nun he is said to have seduced; the best-known example is Paul Delaroche's painting of 1824 at Dijon. Andrea del Sarto was not a very frequent subject in nineteenth-century painting, but, had he been so, attention would doubtless have been concentrated on the anecdotal incidents of his career, as in Browning's poem, his disastrous marriage, and his relations with the king of France. Browning's references to Raphael and the Fornarina, in 'One Word More', correspond with Professor Haskell's statement about Ingres: 'It is curious that even Ingres should have paid so much more attention to Raphael's relationship with the Fornarina than with his work' (p. 64).

The dramatic monologue, of course, allows for more lengthy discussion of an artist's work than does a picture, and Browning is able to introduce the question of style into most of his painter-poems. Characteristically, however, he is most deeply concerned with two things. First, the way in which style reveals the man, and second, the relation of the painter's work to Browning's own belief in the artist's duty to 'paint man, man, whatever the issue'.[1]

[1] Old Pictures in Florence' XIX, 148.

Interest in the lives of the painters was only one part of a general enthusiasm for the past. It was fed chiefly by translations from Vasari's famous *Lives of the Painters*, and by bastardized versions of it. The first complete English translation, by Mrs. Jonathan Foster, was published in 1850. Browning, who read Vasari in the original Italian, was not dependent on popular or truncated translations, and he was therefore able to delve into the lives of little-known Florentine artists of the thirteenth and fourteenth centuries, usually omitted in anthologies of Vasari. Like the genre painters, Browning read Vasari first, and looked at the pictures afterwards. His interest in Renaissance painting was a natural extension of his passion for exploring Italian history. The two interests appear together in an early poem built up around a painting, 'My Last Duchess' of 1842, apparently inspired by a general notion of Italian court portraiture rather than a specific picture.

When he wrote 'My Last Duchess', Browning had been in Italy only once, in 1838, and his trip had been significant art-historically for one thing, a visit to the Accademmia in Venice when he suddenly discovered the richness of Venetian painting. Not only did this enthusiasm inspire a passage in 'In a Gondola', in which Browning describes an imaginary series of Venetian paintings by Titian, Giorgione, Schedone, and Luca Giordano, but it also led Browning to 'worship'[1] that most Venetian of English contemporary painters, William Etty. In a letter to Etty of 1849, he wrote to express his joy that 'a great Painter and Poet could realize his conceptions, as exquisitely in London, at this latter day, as in Venice, when the Doges were there'.[2] It was not until his second Italian journey, in the autumn of 1844, that Browning went to Florence, and began his study of Florentine painting.

His initial response to Florentine art-history is expressed in his dramatic monologue, 'Pictor Ignotus', written in 1845, in which he explored the situation of a minor Italian painter. Pictor Ignotus, as the title suggests, is one of the many painters for whom the nineteenth century knew no name, and whose religious frescoes were then thought to be indistinguishable from countless others. Browning may have been stimulated to write the poem by a particular series of frescoes, but it seems far more probable that the poem resulted from a general impression of religious art in Florence. Reading his own reactions into the painter's monologue,

[1] *Wise Letters*, 6.
[2] *Wise Letters*, 26.

the poet writes:

> *If at whiles*
> *My heart sinks, as monotonous I paint*
> *These endless cloisters and eternal aisles*
> *With the same series, Virgin, Babe and Saint,*
> *With the same cold, calm, beautiful regard,*
> *At least no merchant traffics in my heart.*               (57–62)

Pictor Ignotus declares that he has deliberately chosen the path of obscurity in order to avoid selling his work to an undiscerning public. He boasts that he could easily have matched Raphael, 'that youth ye praise so', had he wished.

Several features divide this poem from those on related subjects written after Browning had moved to Italy in 1846. Although he had clearly seen frescoes of the kind he describes, his approach to them as works of art was still comparatively undiscerning. He imagined that the creators of such 'monotonous' works must totally have lacked ambition, and their choice of conventional religious subject-matter seemed to him to be a proof of this. Nor is the poem a plea for the recognition of undiscovered 'primitive' painters. The title, 'Pictor Ignotus: Florence 15—', places its subject in the Cinquecento, the High Renaissance, and not in the much earlier period evoked in 'Old Pictures in Florence', written in March 1853. The subject of 'Pictor Ignotus' is far closer to that of 'Andrea del Sarto', also of 1853.

In the period between 'Pictor Ignotus' and the other painter-poems of *Men and Women*, Browning had lived in Italy, and made a first-hand, if somewhat haphazard, study of Italian painting. Contemporary taste directed him to three schools or periods of art, the Bolognese, the Venetian, and the High Renaissance. Browning already knew and admired the Venetians, and he continued to do so. The Bolognese school, however, did not stand the test of familiarity. Travelling through Italy in the later 1840s, the Brownings made a point of seeing the works of Guercino, the Carracis, Guido Reni and Domenichino, the seventeenth century Bolognese masters who were then much admired by Anglo-Saxon tourists and purchasers alike. The taste for the Bolognese school, and Guido Reni in particular, had begun in the eighteenth century. Sir Joshua Reynolds had added his imprimatur by lauding their technique and style in his *Discourses*, praising the Bolognese at the expense of the

Venetians. Works by these artists were still fetching very high prices in England throughout the High Victorian period, and it is their names, rather than those of Botticelli or Piero della Francesca, which appear in the contemporary guide-books. The slow fall from popularity began in the 1840s, when Ruskin attacked the National Gallery for purchasing expensive Guido Renis instead of early Italian pictures, and when Sir Charles Eastlake resigned his Keepership as a protest against this buying policy. The tide did not finally turn against the Bolognese until the time of Browning's death, when the Florentines were taking their place in both the art market at home, and the tourist programme abroad. From Elizabeth Barrett Browning's letters, one can trace their changing attitude to the Bolognese, no doubt dictated by the general change in taste. At first, they were very shocked by Ruskin's blaspheming 'so against a great artist' like Domenichino, whose 'very expressive' David they had just seen in the Cathedral at Fano.[1] In Fano they found another work to their taste, Guercino's *Guardian Angel* in the church of St. Agostino (Plate 1). Mrs. Browning was particularly delighted by it, and she told the distinguished art-historian, Mrs. Jameson: 'We both cry aloud at what you say of Guercino's angels, and never would have said if you had been to Fano and seen his divine picture of the "Guardian Angel", which affects me every time I think of it'.[2] To modern eyes, the work seems sentimental and flaccid, and Browning's deeply religious poem about it is not one of his best:

> *Guercino drew this angel I saw teach*
> *(Alfred, dear friend!)—that little child to pray,*
> *Holding the little hands up, each to each*
> *Pressed gently,—with his own head turned away*
> *Over the earth where so much lay before him*
> *Of work to do.*
>                      (36–41)
>
> .   .   .   .   .   .   .
>     *since I care*
> *For dear Guercino's fame (to which in power*
> *And glory comes this picture for a dower,*
> *Fraught with a pathos so magnificent),*
>
> *And since he did not work so earnestly*

[1] *The Letters of Elizabeth Barrett Browning*, ed F. G. Kenyon, 1897, I, 384.
[2] *Domett Letters*, ed Kenyon, I, 441.

> *At all times, and has else endured some wrong—*
> *I took one thought his picture struck from me,*
> *And spread it out, translating it to song.*                    (46–53)

By the time of their later journey through Italy in 1851, the Brownings had begun to revise their opinion of the Bolognese School. From Milan, Mrs. Browning wrote:

> Then the Da Vinci Christ did not disappoint us, which is saying much. It is divine. And the Lombard school generally was delightful after Bologna and those soulless Carracci! I have even given up Guido, and Guercino too, since knowing more of them. Correggio, on the other hand, is sublime at Parma; he is wonderful.[1]

Like the Venetians, the great masters of the High Renaissance, Raphael and Leonardo, never disappointed Browning. Much as he admired them, however, neither artist provided him with a pictorial image for poetry, suggesting that his visual impression of them was not a strong one. His eye was more effectively caught by Correggio's *Virgin of St. Jerome* in the art gallery of Parma. In 'Bishop Blougram's Apology', Blougram fills the imaginary cabin of Gigadibs with some of the best things that the world offers, and includes amongst them:

> *Parma's pride, the Jerome, let us add!*
> *'Twere pleasant could Correggio's fleeting glow*
> *Hang full in face of one where'er one roams.*        (113–15)

The passage is typical of the way in which Browning introduces painting into poems other than those directly concerned with painters. The brief reference to 'Correggio's fleeting glow' conveys enough to enlighten those familiar with his work, but offers only the vaguest of impressions to the uninformed reader, who would certainly imagine that the painting was of St. Jerome alone. This allusiveness is common in Browning's elliptical poetry.

Opposite Casa Guidi, the Brownings' home in Florence, stood the Pitti Palace, then still a residence of the Tuscan Dukes. The galleries are rich in sixteenth-century Italian pictures, and Mrs. Browning wrote of their delight at the prospect of studying Raphael so close at hand. Browning had touched obliquely on the subject of Raphael in 'Pictor Ignotus', and he was now to approach him again, equally indirectly, in

[1] *Domett Letters*, ed Kenyon, II, 9.

'Andrea del Sarto', his major poem about a High Renaissance artist. Raphael's spectacular success fascinated Browning, but, characteristically, he seems to have been less interested in the great painter's genius than in his effect on less fortunate rivals. If Raphael's unchallenged primacy was one stimulus to the writing of 'Andrea del Sarto', another was the anecdotal quality of Andrea's own story, as Browning discovered it in Vasari. According to W. Hall Griffin, Browning's interest was first aroused in the Pitti Palace, by the so-called self-portrait of Andrea with his wife, holding what was then thought to be a letter from Francis I.[1] (Plate 000.) The identification of the sitters and letter is now discredited, but at the time the portrait, with its romantic overtones, was one of the most popular paintings in the collection. The Brownings' patron, John Kenyon, asked the poet to commission a copy for him. In a letter of 17 March 1853,[2] Browning reported that it was impossible to get a good copy of the picture within a reasonable time. The dramatic monologue was apparently written as a form of compensation for Kenyon.

Whatever the truth of this story, the poem is typical of Browning's work at this period, when, as he told Joseph Milsand in February 1853: 'I am writing—a first step towards popularity for me—lyrics with more music and painting than before, so as to get people to hear and see'.[3] Browning sets his poem at a precise date, 1525, six years before the painter's death. Andrea, at thirty-nine, is seated in the window of his studio, speaking to his faithless and avaricious wife, Lucrezia di Baccio del Fede. Browning's source for the relationship between Andrea and his wife was the first edition of the *Lives*, where Vasari, formerly Andrea's pupil, writes from close knowledge of the couple. He describes the proud and haughty character of the beautiful Lucrezia: 'She delighted in trapping the hearts of men, and among others ensnared the unlucky Andrea, whose immoderate love for her soon caused him to neglect the studies demanded by his art, and in great measure to discontinue the assistance which he had given to his parents'.[4] On her first husband's death, Andrea married her, to the horror of his friends: 'the respect and affection which his friends had previously borne to Andrea changed to con-

[1] Griffin and Minchin, 200.
[2] Wellesley College Library.
[3] Griffin and Minchin, 189.
[4] *Lives of the Most Eminent Painters, Sculptors and Architects*, tr Mrs. J. Foster, 1910 edition, III, 194.

tempt and disgust, since it appeared to them that the darkness of this
disgrace had obscured for a time all the glory and renown obtained by
his talents'.[1]

Browning does not repeat all the precise facts given by Vasari, but a
hint of Lucrezia's character, and of Andrea's weary jealousy, emerges
early in the monologue, when the painter looks upon his wife's face:

> *My face, my moon, my everybody's moon,*
> *Which everybody looks on and calls his.*            (29–30)

In the form of a reverie, Andrea gradually unfolds the story of his life and
of his infatuation with her, while Lucrezia sits by the window looking
out for her lover. The irony of the story emerges in the contrast between
Andrea's total absorption in Lucrezia, and her indifference to him. There
is no narrative progression except at the end, when Lucrezia extracts a
promise of money from Andrea, intending to give it to her lover, whom
she presumably goes downstairs to meet.

Browning explores Andrea's personality in some depth, basing his
characterization on Vasari's statement that Andrea 'displayed no great
elevation of mind in the actions of his life, and contented himself with
little'.[2] Browning continually stresses the painter's sense of guilt, his
awareness of his own weaknesses, as in the passage where he describes his
conduct towards his parents:

> *My father and my mother died of want.*
> *Well, had I riches of my own? you see*
> *How one gets rich! Let each one bear his lot.*
> *They were born poor, lived poor, and poor they died:*
> *And I have laboured somewhat in my time*
> *And not been paid profusely. Some good son*
> *Paint my two hundred pictures—let him try!*            (250–6)

Vasari, too, provided Browning with the source for the idea that
Andrea seldom used any model other than his wife: 'he rarely painted the
countenance of a woman in any place that he did not avail himself of the
features of his wife; and if at any time he took his model from any other
face, there was always a resemblance to hers in the painting'.[3] In the

[1] Foster, III, 194.

[2] Foster, III, 235.

[3] Foster, III, 203.

poem this becomes:

> *you must serve*
> *For each of the five pictures we require—*
> *It saves a model.*                    (23–5)

Proof of Vasari's statement could be found in the many pictures by Andrea in and around Florence, where the same female type is endlessly repeated. Characteristically, Browning became interested in the human aspects of the story of Andrea's double dealing with the French king, which Vasari describes in detail. Vasari states that, after working for Francis I, Andrea returned to Florence with money to buy works of art for the king, and promised to return within a limited time. Corrupted by his wife, however, he kept the money and never returned to France. Modern scholars have not only doubted the attribution of the double portrait in the Pitti Palace, but have suspected the accuracy of Vasari's statements about the artist's relations with Francis I. Browning, on the other hand, makes the French incident the crucial act of Andrea's life, the main source of the painter's disillusionment, as he wistfully contrasts his present situation with the years of prosperity and fame at the French court.

Professor DeVane believes that Browning's attitude to the painter's work was based, not upon Vasari's brief critical comment: 'Andrea del Sarto, who may be said to have been remarkable, were it only because his works were free from errors',[1] but upon a reading of Filippo Baldinucci, who writes at length of Andrea's faultless perfection, marred only by a lack of inspiration.[2] Browning paraphrases a passage from Bocchi's *Bellezze di Firenze*, quoted in the notes to the Milanesi edition of Vasari, to prove that Michelangelo held a high opinion of Andrea del Sarto: '"There is a bit of a mannikin in Florence", observes Michelangelo, [to Raphael] "who, if he chanced to be employed in great undertakings as you have happened to be, would compel you to look well about you".'[3] Browning's version reads:

> *'Friend, there's a certain sorry little scrub*
> *Goes up and down our Florence, none cares how,*

---

[1] Foster, II, 362.

[2] W. C. DeVane, *Browning's Parleyings*, New Haven 1927, 174.

[3] Foster, III, 232.

> *Who, were he set to plan and execute*
> *As you are, pricked on by your popes and kings,*
> *Would bring the sweat into that brow of yours!'*          (189—93)

In Browning's poem, Andrea quotes Michelangelo with a feeling of pride. At the same time he is bitterly aware that faultless skill of hand is not enough, and that Raphael and Michelangelo possess some quality lacking in himself:

> *There burns a truer light of God in them,*
> *In their vexed, beating, stuffed and stopped-up brain,*
> *Heart, or whate'er else, than goes on to prompt*
> *This low-pulsed forthright craftsman's hand of mine.*
> *Their works drop groundward, but themselves, I know,*
> *Reach many a time a heaven that's shut to me.*          (78—84)

> .       .       .       .       .       .       .
> *Ah, but a man's reach should exceed his grasp,*
> *Or what's a Heaven for? all is silver-grey*
> *Placid and perfect with my art—the worse!*          (97—99)

In the poem, a Vasari copy of a Raphael drawing hangs in Andrea's studio, and Andrea points out an anatomical error in the execution of one of the arms. Taking chalk, he corrects it, but, as he anticipates, the new perfection destroys the soul of the work. The precise human detail is Browning's own, and is typical of the way in which he moves on from Vasari, and makes the subject vivid and alive. This part of the monologue represents Browning's chief comment on the life of Andrea as an artist, but, compared even with 'Fra Lippo Lippi', the work is curiously remote from the actual paintings, of which Browning must have seen so many examples in Florence. The painting on which the poem is based was misattributed to Andrea, and there is no precise reference to any single work of the painter in the poem. The smoothness of his style, and his habitual use of the same female model, are evident enough in his work, but Browning could equally well have learnt about these features from Vasari, who summarizes his comments on Andrea in his preface to Part III of the Lives, pointing out Andrea's debt to Raphael: 'In the same manner, but softer in colouring and evincing less force, there followed Andrea del Sarto'.[1]

[1] Foster, II, 362.

No reader of 'Andrea del Sarto' could claim that the poem is evocative of the painter's art, or shows much critical discernment. Browning, indeed, attempted to fit Raphael into his favourite category of realistic artist, on the doubtful grounds that he presented man as he is. The poem as a whole suggests that Browning's visual sense lagged far behind his human perception. He was on safer ground in the two poems which he wrote about earlier artists, also published in *Men and Women*, 'Old Pictures in Florence' and 'Fra Lippo Lippi'.

These two poems represent Browning's interest in a period of art disregarded by most English tourists, the Florentine school of the thirteenth and fourteenth centuries. Browning became interested in it while tracing the history of Italian painting from its origins. His wife wrote to a friend from Pisa in 1846:

> I mean to know something about pictures some day. Robert does, and I shall get him to open my eyes for me with a little instruction. You know that in this place are to be seen the first steps of art, and it will be interesting to trace them from it as we go farther ourselves.[1]

These 'first steps' were the series of frescoes in the Campo Santo at Pisa, begun by fourteenth century artists, including Spinello Aretino and Taddeo Gaddi, a disciple of Giotto, and completed by the fifteenth century painter, Benozzo Gozzoli. Early Florentine masters were little regarded, and the examples in Pisa were among the few to which English tourists were directed in their guide-books.

When the Brownings settled in Florence, Robert continued his study of earlier schools, exploring the churches and monasteries of the city:

> *empty cells of the human hive;*
> —*With the chapter-room, the cloister-porch,*
> *The church's apsis, aisle or nave,*
> *Its crypt, one fingers along with a torch,*
> *Its face, set full for the sun to shave.*

('Old Pictures in Florence', 36–40)

Browning already knew Vasari's *Lives of the Painters* when he wrote 'Pictor Ignotus' in 1845, and paraphrased the passage from the 'Life of Cimabue' where Vasari describes the triumphal procession which carried the Rucellai Madonna: 'with the sound of trumpets and other festal

[1] *The Letters of Elizabeth Barrett Browning*, ed F. G. Kenyon, 1897, I, 307.

demonstrations, from the house of Cimabue to the church'.[1] In a later comment, Vasari mentions the fact that the place where the picture was shown to Charles of Anjou was rechristened the 'Borgo Allegri', the 'joyful district'. In Browning's poem, Pictor Ignotus describes a procession of the same kind, even adding the detail about the naming of the area:

> *Flowers cast upon the car which bore the freight,*
> *Through old streets named afresh from its event,*
> *Till it reached home.*[2]                                              (31–3)

Browning's studies in the earlier sections of Vasari, from Nicolo Pisano and Cimabue to 'Ghiberti and Ghirlandajo' ('Old Pictures in Florence' XXIII), became more intensive once he had settled in Italy. Both Brownings had been struck by the singular appropriateness of their taking lodgings in Pisa 'in the great Collegio built by Vasari'.[3] Elizabeth told R. H. Horne: 'We live here in the most secluded manner, eschewing English visitors, and reading Vasari'.[4] Browning's historical researches continued to excite him for several years. In April 1853, Elizabeth described him as 'as fond of digging at Vasari as I am at the Mystics, and goes to and from him as constantly, making him a betwixt and between to other writers'.[5]

Basing his conclusions on his reading, Browning began to follow up Vasari's references to these early painters, even attempting to attribute works by them. The state of knowledge about the primitives was still fairly rudimentary. One of the few art-historians with any real discrimination was Sir Francis Palgrave, who edited the first edition of Murray's *Handbook for Travellers in Northern Italy*. Palgrave's own introductory section on Tuscan art was an outstanding feature of this 1842 edition, but, significantly, his passage on Taddeo Gaddi, Spinello Aretino and Fra Angelico, as well as on the later artists Benozzo Gozzoli,

---

[1] Foster, I, 41.

[2] The painter, Frederic Leighton, one of Browning's closest friends in his later years, exhibited a picture of this subject, *Cimabue's Madonna being carried in triumph through the streets of Florence*, in the 1855 Royal Academy.

[3] *Domett Letters*, ed Kenyon, I, 306.

[4] G. W. Cooke, *A Guidebook to the Poetic and Dramatic Works of Robert Browning*, Boston 1891, 218.

[5] B. Miller, *Robert Browning: A Portrait*, 1952, 175.

Botticelli, Filippo Lippi and Baldovinetto was omitted in subsequent editions.[1]

The reasons for Browning's interest in the early painters are many. Loving painting, and living in Florence, he was inevitably fascinated by what he saw around him. He could not afford to buy the works of the acknowledged masters, and so purchased pictures which interested him and cost less. More important still is his life-long love of the unusual and the curious, which led him to bypass the great artists in his poems, and write about less well-known figures. Although Browning's work can be seen as part of the tradition for painting the lives of the artists, yet his interest in minor painters makes his approach radically different from that of contemporary artists. Where they concentrate on Raphael, Michelangelo, Titian and Leonardo, Browning, in 'Old Pictures in Florence', has the idea that Raphael and Michelangelo can rest quietly on their laurels in heaven, while earlier painters have still a reputation to make:

> can they be quit
> Of a world where their work is all to do,
> Where you style them, you of the little wit,
> Old Master This and Early the Other,
> Not dreaming that Old and New are fellows:
> A younger succeeds to an elder brother,
> Da Vincis derive in good time from Dellos.        (VIII, 58–64)

Browning's exploitation of the primitives as a quarrying ground for his poetry gives him a small place in the history of taste. His approach was largely antiquarian. Like most of the early collectors of primitives, he was originally interested in them only in so far as they shed light on Raphael, Michelangelo, and the other masters of the High Renaissance. It was only slowly that he came to have any affection for early panel pictures, or 'goldbacks', as they were often called, in and for themselves. The vogue for primitives had been given impetus in the early years of the nineteenth century by the Napoleonic edicts which led to the large-scale sale of works of art from churches and monasteries. They were brought into England by private collectors and dealers, and were soon appearing

[1] A letter from Elizabeth Barrett Browning, dated 26 May 1847, recommends Murray's *Guide*, and, although she may be referring to the 1847 (3rd) edition, it seems likely that Browning had an earlier copy, perhaps bought on his second journey to Italy in 1844 (*Domett Letters*, I, 330).

in sale-rooms with fairly rudimentary attributions. Among the very early English collectors were Edward Solly and William Roscoe. Later came Prince Albert, the Rev. Walter Bromley-Davenport, William Fuller-Maitland and Lord Northesk, all of whom began to build up important collections of primitives, and who were far more sensitive and knowledgeable than their predecessors. At the same time, the pioneering studies of art historians like Charles Eastlake, the keeper of the National Gallery, Lord Lindsay, the author of *Sketches of the History of Christian Art*, Sir Francis Palgrave and the young John Ruskin, were helping to place the whole history of Renaissance art in a more objective and revealing perspective. Even so, popular taste lagged far behind. In 1847, the Government refused to acquire the notable Young Ottley collection of primitives for the National Gallery, where it would have filled a complete gap. It was not until 1848 that the trustees acquired, by a bequest, their first two primitives, a pair of works then thought to be by Taddeo Gaddi, but now attributed to Lorenzo Monaco.

By contrast, Browning was already forming his own collection of early Italian masters in 1850. Elizabeth writes:

> Robert has been picking up pictures at a few pauls each, "hole and corner" pictures which the "dealers" have not found out; and the other day he covered himself with glory by discovering and seizing on (in a corn shop a mile from Florence) five pictures among heaps of trash; and one of the best judges in Florence (Mr. Kirkup) throws out such names for them as Cimabue, Ghirlandaio, Giottino, a crucifixion painted on a banner, Giottesque, if not Giotto, but *unique*, or nearly so, on account of the linen material, and a little Virgin by a Byzantine master. The curious thing is that two angel pictures, for which he had given a scudo last year, prove to have been sawn off the sides of the Ghirlandaio, so called, representing the "Eterno Padre" clothed in a mystical garment and encircled by a rainbow, the various tints of which, together with the scarlet tips of the flying seraph's wings, are darted down into the smaller pictures and complete the evidence, line for line. It has been a grand altar-piece, cut to bits.[1]

Seymour Kirkup's wild attributions are an indication of the state of knowledge in a field which had, as yet, attracted more antiquarians and connoisseurs than art-historians. Twenty-five years before, the Hon.

[1] *Domett Letters*, I, 448–9.

1. *The Guardian Angel*, by Guercino

2. Work once attributed to Andrea del Sarto, and said to be a double portrait of the painter and his wife. This painting in the Pitti Palace may have inspired Browning to write 'Andrea del Sarto', his major poem about a High Renaissance artist

3. *The Salone at Casa Guidi*, by George Mignaty

*A* Pollaiuolo, *Christ at the Column* *B* A tall-back carved wood settee, plush upholstered *C* An open-fronted carved wood bookcase *D* Centre of Triptych: *Crucifixion* and four side wings: Single figures of male and female saints *E* Ghirlandaio (attributed), Altar piece representing *God the Father* with an angel on each side *F* A large wood gilt mirror *G* Tuscan school, *St Jerome*, attributed by Browning to Taddeo Gaddi *H* Tuscan school, *Portrait of a Bishop J* Two small busts of a man and a woman *K* A large carved wood bookcase *L* An Italian ebonized table *M* A North Italian walnut table *N* A North Italian walnut marquetry-topped table *O* A deep-back plush upholstered armchair *P* A lady's maplewood work table *Q* A folding armchair *R* Writing case in dark blue leather, tooled with gold *S* A mahogany writing-table *T* An Italian ebonized table.

4. *Christ at the Column*,
by Pollaiuolo

5. *Virgin and Child and St Hilarion* (detail of St Jerome) by Filippo Lippi

6. *The Coronation of the Virgin* by Filippo Lippi

William Homer Fox-Strangways, then secretary to the embassy in Tuscany, and later the fourth Earl of Ilchester, had found pictures in much the same way, apparently taking Walter Savage Landor with him to hunt them out. He gave the first part of his collection to Christ Church, Oxford, in 1828, and the second part to the Ashmolean Museum in 1850. When Browning, with even less expertise than Fox-Strangways and Landor, set about attributing his works, he settled for some less exalted names than those suggested by Kirkup, but even these were changed when the bulk of the Browning collection came up for sale at Sotheby's in 1913. A *St Jerome*, which he thought to be the work of Taddeo Gaddi, was then simply described as 'Tuscan School', together with a *Portrait of a Bishop* and a series of panels showing a crucifixion and four saints. Browning had optimistically attributed the latter to Margheritone of Arezzo. The named works in the Sotheby's sale were by later masters. An altar piece representing God the Father, with an angel on each side, was given to Ghirlandaio, and *Christ at the Column* (Plate 4), the only work reproduced in the catalogue, to Pollaiuolo.[1] Browning made some attempt to relate the works he purchased to other pictures and frescoes available in Florence. His poem, 'Old Pictures in Florence', written in March 1853, is the fruit of this amateur research. The poem is also an expression of fury against the Florentine authorities who were allowing works of art in their care to disintegrate. Like many of his generation, he was conscious of the picturesqueness of decay. In 'By the Fireside', of 1853, he writes of a ruined chapel near Bagni di Lucca, with its

> bit of fresco half-moon-wise,
> Set over the porch, Art's early wont:
> 'Tis John in the Desert, I surmise,
> But has borne the weather's brunt—            (XVIII, 87–90)

This pleasing quaintness was very charming, but Browning could also imagine the ghosts of painters watching over acts of vandalism committed on their work in churches:

> each fresco flaked and rasped,
> Blocked up, knocked out, or white-washed o'er
> —No getting again what the church has grasped!
> The works on the wall must take their chance.            (XXIV, 186–89)

[1] Now in Lord Harewood's collection. Browning gave an unattributed *Virgin and Child* to D. G. Rossetti, but no more details of this work have come to light.

Browning had evidently heard the Florentines complaining about the export of their art treasures, and he quotes complacent voices rejoicing that the frescoes, at least, were 'Works never conceded to England's thick clime!' Responding in his own voice, he writes sarcastically:

> *I hope they prefer their inheritance*
> *Of a bucketful of Italian quick-lime.*

(XXIV, 190–2)

In his view, the treatment which the pictures were receiving rendered their removal almost essential. To make the point, he refers directly to a work by Giotto, which had been much praised by Michelangelo:

> *But Giotto, you,*
> *Have you allowed, as the town-tongues babble it,—*
> *Oh, never! it shall not be counted true—*
> *That a certain precious little tablet*
> *Which Buonarroti eyed like a lover,—*
> *Was buried so long in oblivion's womb*
> *And, left for another than I to discover,*
> *Turns up at last! and to whom?—to whom?*

(XXX, 233–40)

Investigation of this passage, which must be virtually incomprehensible to most readers of the poem, presents another problem. Browning is referring, in his most oblique manner, to a picture which he later described to Hiram Corson:

The little tablet was a famous *Last Supper*, mentioned by Vasari, and gone astray long ago from the church of S. Spirito; it turned up, according to report, while I was in Florence, and was at once acquired by a stranger. I saw it, genuine or no, a work of great beauty.[1]

As so often, Browning's reference to this picture in 'Old Pictures in Florence' is based upon a subtle confusion. The painting which Michelangelo so much admired was not a *Last Supper* but a *Death of the Virgin*, painted for the church of the Ognissanti in Florence, and now in Berlin. This painting was in the collection of the Rev. Walter Davenport-Bromley, before eventually going to Germany. Either Browning had

[1] G. W. Cooke, *A Guidebook to the Poetic and Dramatic Works of Robert Browning*, Boston 1891, 222.

simply forgotten the correct reference, or, more probably, strengthened his case by deliberately confusing these two small pictures with each other.

Browning's interest in human nature led him to see the early painters as kindred spirits. Like himself, he felt, they rejected Hellenic idealism, and set themselves to explore man as he is:

> *On which I conclude, that the early painters,*
> *To cries of 'Greek Art and what more wish you?' —*
> *Replied, 'To become now self-acquainters,*
> *And paint man, man, whatever the issue!*
> *Make new hopes shine through the flesh they fray,*
> *New fears aggrandize the rags and tatters:*
> *To bring the invisible full into play!*
> *Let the visible go to the dogs—what matters?'*

(XIX, 145–152)

At first sight, Browning's reference to the visible and invisible here seems to contradict the mood of the poem. In fact, he is reiterating his belief that man's soul appears in his oddities, in the quirks of nature, all of which he found abundantly represented in early Renaissance painting.

'Old Pictures in Florence' reflects Browning's reading of the first two sections of Vasari, covering the period from Cimabue to Signorelli. It is a difficult poem, relying on background information to which Browning makes only allusive reference. It is sometimes hard to tell whether he is simply recounting what he has read, or whether he has any actual knowledge of the works of these painters. His reading, supplemented by the visual evidence of the engraved portraits, with which, where possible, Vasari illustrates his text, seems to have left the strongest impression. Each of the sixteen early painters he mentions is the subject of a separate chapter in Vasari. Especially with the minor painters, Browning seems to have relied exclusively on this source. For example, writing of Stefano in his poem, he quotes almost directly from Vasari, to whom he actually refers by name:

> *What, not a word for Stefano there,*
> *Of brow once prominent and starry,*
> *Called Nature's Ape and the world's despair*
> *For his peerless painting? (see Vasari).*

(IX, 69–72)

A note in the Browning Society Papers, presumably the response to a question put to the poet, reminds readers that Dello, Stefano and Margheritone of Arezzo actually existed.[1]

Other passages in the poem reveal that the artists who most intrigued him were either those whose pictures he believed he owned, or those with interesting psychological peculiarities. He sometimes seems to be making a case at the expense of the facts. His praise of the lively and bustling work of the sculptor, Nicolo Pisano, is a natural enough outcome of his theories, but his choice, in the next line, of Cimabue as the supreme painter of this school, is entirely arbitrary; like so many of Browning's opinions, it was conditioned by historical and biographical factors, and not by a critical examination of the art in question. Cimabue's pictures are far more hieratic and inhuman than the sculptures of the Greeks to which Browning contrasts them.

Giotto, Cimabue's pupil, is introduced into the poem as the artist of the small tablet admired by Michelangelo, and as the architect of the campanile of the Florentine Duomo. This was still incomplete, and Browning was actively campaigning to have it finished. The story of the campanile and Giotto's role in it, occurs in Vasari, and, at the opening of the poem, Browning pictures himself gazing down on it. Giotto's reputation scarcely rests on his architectural work, but it is typical of Browning's attitude that he does not attempt a comprehensive survey. Instead of making the expected reference to Giotto's frescoes, Browning alludes to a well-known anecdote about him, also found in Vasari. This is the story of the perfect circle which Giotto drew and sent to the Pope, who invited him to Rome on the strength of it. Browning was not a historian, and had no responsibility to be complete. At the same time, he was writing about painters well-known to his audience, and exploiting the fact, in an arbitrary, one-sided, fashion:

> *Thy one work, not to decrease or diminish,*
> *Done at a stroke, was just ( was it not? ) 'O!'*
> *Thy great Campanile is still to finish.*

(XVII, 134–6)

Another early painter whom Browning names is Taddeo Gaddi, to

[1] No. 2, 169.

whom he had attributed one of his own pictures, a St. Jerome, on the doubtful authority of a passage in Vasari:

> In the same church of Santa Maria Novella, this artist painted St. Jerome robed in the vestments of a cardinal, he having an especial devotion to this saint, and having chosen him for the protector of his house.[1]

It is to this, which he believed was his St. Jerome, that the poet refers in his poem:

> *But are you too fine, Taddeo Gaddi,*
> *To grant me a taste of your intonaco—*
> *Some Jerome that seeks the Heaven with a sad eye?*

(XXVI, 205–7)

Linked with Taddeo Gaddi in the poem are Lorenzo Monaco and Fra Angelico, both painters represented in the Uffizi and the Accademmia galleries, and by frescoes in the churches of Florence. All three artists would then have been described as 'primitives', as would Margheritone of Arezzo, to whom Browning attributed one of his own paintings:

> *Not a poor glimmering Crucifixion,*
> *Where in the foreground kneels the donor?*
> *If such remain, as is my conviction,*
> *The hoarding does you but little honour.*

(XXVIII, 221–4)

From Vasari's statement that Margheritone was soured in his old age by jealousy of younger men, and from the evidence of the engraving of him in his edition of Vasari (based on a lost fresco by Spinello Aretino), Browning summons up a vivid image of the embittered and petulent painter:

> *Margheritone of Arezzo,*
> *With the grave-clothes garb and swaddling barret,*
> *(Why purse up mouth and beak in a pet so,*
> *You bald, old, saturnine, poll-clawed parrot?)*

(XXVIII, 217–20)

Most of the painters to whom Browning gives any sustained attention

[1] Vasari, *Lives*, tr Foster, I, 201.

in his poem are later in date. Alessio Baldovinetti, Filippino Lippi and Botticelli, Ghirlandaio and Pollaiuolo are fifteenth century artists, like Ghiberti, the sculptor of the baptistery doors in Florence. Details of Pollaiuolo's appearance are taken from the illustration of him in Vasari. Characteristically, the painting used to illustrate his art belonged to the poet (Plate 4):

> *Could not the ghost with the close red cap,*
> *My Pollajolo, the twice a craftsman,*
> *Save me a sample, give me the hap*
> *Of a muscular Christ that shows the draughtsman?*

(XXVII, 209–12)

He details Botticelli by a brief reference based on an anecdote in Vasari: 'Sandro . . . chivalric, bellicose' (XXVI).[1] Of all the Italian masters, Botticelli was the one whose reputation was to rise most noticeably during the course of the nineteenth century. The early editions of Murray scarcely mention a work by him, and completely ignore the *Birth of Venus* in the Uffizi, and the *Primavera*, then in the Accademmia. Ghirlandaio, on the other hand, was already beginning to achieve a certain popularity as a painter showing authentic glimpses of Florentine life, something which Browning acknowledges by calling him 'the great Bigordi' (XXVI).[2] But, if Browning mentions some later fifteenth-century masters, he restricts himself to those who are typical of their age, rather than praising artists whose work looks forward to a later period. The art market in England, as Gerald Reitlinger points out, had yet to reach this stage: 'Only very late fifteenth-century works with a strong sixteenth-century flavour, such as Mantegna, Perugino and Giovanni Bellini, were capable of real appreciation'.[3]

'Old Pictures in Florence' clearly reveals Browning's attitude to painting. He has all the natural interests of the collector and antiquarian, but subservient to his creative instincts as a poet, which always lead him to seek out the man behind the work. None of the painter-poems reveals Browning as a poet with a true 'eye for a picture', or with a pronounced visual sense.

Browning's attitude to the painters of the early Renaissance does not accord with the ideas of other critics of his time. Like the collectors, he

[1] 202.
[2] 201.
[3] *The Economics of Taste*, 1961, 122.

was intrigued by the historical significance of these works. They seemed to confirm his own belief that man is the true subject of art. Three years before Browning began his collection, Lord Lindsay had published his *Sketches of the History of Christian Art*, in which he affirmed that these early paintings were expressions of a supreme religious ideal. Far from seeing them as works in which the human being is portrayed, Lindsay looks upon them as evocations of an earlier age of simple faith. His views are closely in tune with the whole philosophy of the Gothic revival, and laid the foundations for the popularity of goldbacks among the English 'aesthetes' of the 1870s and 1880s. Like Lindsay, the 'aesthetes' loved early art for nostalgic and aesthetic reasons exactly opposed to those of Browning. To know that Botticelli was 'chivalric' and 'bellicose' was to them irrelevant, whereas, to Browning, this simple fact was infinitely more revealing than the painter's idealized evocations of a lost and beautiful world.

Browning's theories on the nature of art reach their culmination in his dramatic monologue 'Fra Lippo Lippi', his most imaginative treatment of a subject taken from painting. Without being a goldback painter, Lippi was among the earliest masters of the Florentine Renaissance, and he was still relatively neglected when Browning wrote about him, the Ashmolean Museum in Oxford being exceptional in owning a *Meeting of St. Joachim and St. Anna*, presented by Fox-Strangways in 1850.

Vasari's life of the fifteenth-century artist Filippo Lippi provided Browning with his *mis en scène* for the poem. The painter is caught by the watch while enjoying an amorous escapade. Appropriately, the scene takes place in the early morning, capturing the mood of the early Renaissance, while 'Andrea del Sarto' is set at twilight. Lippi's defence rests on an elaborate apologia for his way of life as an artist. In creating his dramatic situation, Browning combines Vasari's brief comment on Lippi's sexual reputation ('It is said that Fra Filippo was much addicted to the pleasures of sense, insomuch that he would give all he possessed to secure the gratification of whatever inclination might at the moment be predominant'[1]), with Vasari's description of a particular episode, ('having endured this confinement for two days, he then made ropes with the sheets of his bed, which he cut to pieces for that purpose, and so having let himself down from a window, escaped, and for several days gave himself up to his amusements').[2] This is given more vigourous expression

[1] Foster, II, 76.

[2] Foster, II, 77.

in Browning's poem:

> *Here's spring come, and the nights one makes up bands*
> *To roam the town and sing out carnival,*
> *And I've been three weeks shut within my mew,*
> *A-painting for the great man, saints and saints*
> *And saints again. I could not paint all night—*
> *Ouf! I leaned out of window for fresh air.*
> *There came a hurry of feet and little feet,*
> *A sweep of lute-strings, laughs, and whifts of song,——*                    (45–52)

This passage, and the account given of Lippi's early life represent Browning's most direct borrowings from Vasari. He does not hesitate to make alterations which suit his own intentions. His Lippi has been shut up for three weeks, not for Vasari's two days. Lippi's poverty as a child, and the circumstances which led him to the cloister, play an important part in Browning's unravelling of the painter's psychological background, while Vasari's dry and general introductory paragraphs are given life and meaning by introduction of precise and imaginative detail. Professor DeVane has suggested that Browning took the small detail of Lippi's age when he entered the cloister from Baldinucci's *Delle Notizie de Professori del Disegno*,[1] but Johnstone Parr argues convincingly that Browning took these details, not from Baldinucci himself, but from the footnotes of the Milanesi edition of Vasari.[2] The main source for the poem is, in any case, obviously Vasari.

Fra Lippo Lippi is not, however, a mere dramatization of Vasari. Through the mouth of the painter Browning explains his own aesthetic credo. Professor DeVane is inclined to see Baldinucci as a possible source for Lippi's committment to reality, and there is certainly no authority for this in Vasari. On the other hand, Browning's view of the early Florentines seems to have grown directly out of the theories expressed in 'Old Pictures in Florence', and bears a direct relation to Browning's own beliefs, and to his purpose in creating his fifty men and women:

> *For, don't you mark, we're made so that we love*
> *First when we see them painted, things we have passed*
> *Perhaps a hundred times nor cared to see;*

[1] W. C. DeVane, *Browning's Parleyings*, New Haven 1927, 172.

[2] 'Browning's "Fra Lippo Lippi", Baldinucci, and the Milanesi edition of Vasari', *English Language Notes*, III, 1965, 197–201.

> *And so they are better, painted—better to us,*
> *Which is the same thing. Art was given for that—*
> *God uses us to help each other so,*
> *Lending our minds out.*
> (300–7)

Whatever Browning's source, there can be no doubt of the voice behind Lippi's question:

> *Now, is this sense, I ask?*
> *A fine way to paint soul, by painting body*
> *So ill, the eye can't stop there, must go further*
> *And can't fare worse!*
> (198–201)

Browning's reading of Vasari does seem to have inspired him to look at one of Lippi's major works, *The Coronation of the Virgin*, in the Gallery of the Accademmia delle Belle Arti in Florence (Plate 6). The vigorous rendering of saints and angels who crowd the canvas has an immediate appeal lacking in the more hieratic images of Lippi's predecessors. While the picture is scarcely realistic, its earthy and human qualities could serve as an illustration of Browning's thesis.

As always, however, personalities as well as theories captured Browning's imagination. He refers in one section of the poem to Lucrezia Buti, the painter's mistress, and the mother of his son, Filippino Lippi. Here she is the prior's niece, who appears as St. Lucy in the *Coronation of the Virgin*, the saint on the right of the central group, and a figure usually associated with Lucrezia Buti. Lippi had met her when working for the nuns at Santa Margherita, however, not, as Browning says, in his own convent, nor at St. Ambrogio's, for which the *Coronation of the Virgin* was painted. Browning is again seizing on the anecdotal when he identifies the figure to the right of her with the painter himself:

> *Well, all these*
> *Secured at their devotions, up shall come*
> *Out of a corner when you least expect,*
> *As one by a dark stair into a great light,*
> *Music and talking, who but Lippo! I!—*
> *Mazed, motionless, and moon-struck—*
> *I'm the man!*
> (359–65)

Since Browning's death the identification of Lippi with the figure on the right has been conclusively refuted, but Browning's error is scarcely important to the effectiveness of this final section of the poem.[1]

Browning's mistakes, here as in 'Andrea del Sarto', reflect the anecdotal state of art history. Like most of his audience, Browning himself was more interested in men and their motives than in pure aesthetics. Not all his references are literary, however. He is referring to a precise picture in the following passage of the monologue:

> *I was stealing back again*
> *To get to bed and have a bit of sleep*
> *Ere I rise up to-morrow and go work*
> *On Jerome knocking at his poor old breast.*          (70–3)

The figure of St. Jerome, kneeling and beating his breast, can be seen on the left of Lippi's *Virgin Adoring the Child with St. Hilarion* in the Uffizi[2] (Plate 5).

When Lippi speaks of a painting of Herodias he once completed, and of one of John the Baptist's head, which he thinks of carrying out, Browning was probably thinking of the series of frescoes of the life of John the Baptist at Prato. Although no slave 'holds John Baptist's head a-dangle by the hair' in the Prato series, the subject was easily associated with Lippi. The same kind of association, with Prato itself rather than a particular subject, probably led Browning to write of a St. Laurence fresco at Prato, which seems to have been imaginary. Lippi did paint St. Laurence at least twice, once seated in state,[3] and once holding a gridiron,[4] but, in neither picture is the saint actually shown on 'his tcasted side', and it seems probable that Browning invented the picture in order to make a point about the life-like nature of Lippi's frescoes, and their effect on those who saw them.

[1] Montgomery Carmichael, 'Fra Lippo Lippi's Portrait', *Burlington Magazine*, XXI, 1912, 194–200. Carmichael points out that the figure on the right does not represent Lippi, but the donor, Francesco Maringhi, who ordered the picture for the Benedictine nunnery of St. Ambrogio. He traces the error back to Vasari, who uses the head of Maringhi as the basis for his own engraving of Lippi.

[2] This picture was once in the Medici collection, and is therefore an appropriate choice in this context.

[3] Palazzo Alessandri, Florence.

[4] National Gallery, London.

In one respect, Browning was more accurate than he knew. Vasari refers to an early series of Lippi frescoes, depicting the Carmelite rule, and Browning alludes to them in Lippi's reminiscences of the subjects he was allowed to paint by the prior:

> *First, every sort of monk, the black and white,*
> *I drew them, fat and lean.* (145–6)

These much damaged Lippi frescoes, which had received a coat of 'Italian quick-lime', have recently been discovered in the monastery of the Carmine.

On the whole, however, Browning makes little effort to be accurate in writing of Lippi's pictures. The paintings to which he refers were completed at a variety of dates. The St. Jerome, which Lippi describes himself as painting for Cosimo de Medici, is dated around 1455, while the *Coronation of the Virgin*, which he is planning to paint, was actually completed several years earlier in 1447.

Browning's most serious error of fact was the result of his own research work, which led him astray in his references to the relative dates of Lippi and Masaccio. Browning, like most of his contemporaries, believed the Masaccio frescoes in the Carmine to have been begun after 1440, whereas they are now known to have been painted from 1426–7. Masaccio was, in fact, long dead when Lippi came to paint the *Coronation of the Virgin*, which gives us the assumed date of this poem, but Browning believed that Masaccio, whom he calls 'Hulking Tom' on the evidence of Vasari, was a pupil of Lippi rather than vice versa:[1]

> *We've a youngster here*
> *Comes to our convent, studies what I do,*
> *Slouches and stares and lets no atom drop—*
> *His name is Guidi—he'll not mind the monks—*
> *They call him Hulking Tom, he lets them talk—*
> *He picks my practise up—he'll paint apace,*
> *I hope so—though I never live so long,*
> *I know what's sure to follow.* (273–80)

Twenty years after 'Fra Lippo Lippi' was published, early art was no longer neglected, and primitives and goldbacks had become an object of

---

[1] See *Wise Letters*, 104, for Browning's reply to Edward Dowden who had pointed out the error. Browning was unrepentant.

the aesthetes' cult. It is probable that Browning and his painter poems had their part to play in this, even though the poet's attitude was so different. Only once does he strike an 'aesthetic' note in his poetry, and this is in a single line in his poem, 'In three days,' written in about 1852, in which he says that the lady's hair is dark 'as early Art embrowned the gold'. The aesthetes affected passion for old and brown paintings was well-known, and 'embrowned' was a favourite word of theirs. Early art had, however, become academically respectable before they appeared on the scene. The National Gallery in London bought its first Filippo Lippi in 1854, the year before the poem was published, and others followed in 1857 and 1861.

Considering Browning's three painter-poems, 'Old Pictures in Florence', 'Andrea del Sarto' and 'Fra Lippo Lippi', as a group, one must conclude that Browning's attitude towards painting was idiosyncratic and intensely personal, and that the greatness of the two dramatic monologues does not result from any profound feeling for the fine arts. When Browning's exploration of Florentine painting finds a direct expression in 'Old Pictures in Florence', the result is a complex and somewhat fragmentary work, where the poet carries his learning a little awkwardly. 'Andrea del Sarto', by contrast, does not mention a single painting, and its relevance to the real Andrea del Sarto is almost entirely biographical. Browning catches the idea of a flawless artist, and explores it in general, not precise, terms. 'Fra Lippo Lippi' is a more interesting case. Here, Browning makes use of pictures which he has seen as well as biographical sources, but few readers would argue that the poem tells them much about painting as distinct from any other art. In the final analysis, each of these poems is about the craft of poetry, and about Browning as its practitioner.

# 8: *Browning and Music*

PENELOPE GAY

THE POEMS OF BROWNING which deal in more than passing manner with music are few, and all products of his maturer years. They are more directly concerned with the question of 'truth' than any comparable body of poems; and yet their final importance lies rather in clarifying one aspect of Browning's emotional make-up than in setting up anything approaching a Yeatsian system. It seems, moreover, fairly obvious that Browning was indebted to nobody for his musical philosophy: he hammered it out for himself as his emotional impulses demanded. The ideas incorporated in the poems were indeed current in the nineteenth century, and earlier, but not in forms that made them readily available.

The cardinal point of any investigation is that Browning was a man extraordinarily well educated musically; no other literary Englishman of the century had such a thorough knowledge of the science. Indeed, very few Englishmen born in the first half of the century had any musical education whatsoever; those who did generally joined the small band of professional musicians in face of heavy parental opposition. It was not until after 1850 that musical education was reintroduced into the public schools. Young ladies, as we learn from Jane Austen, were expected to gain solace and give pleasure by being proficient in the pianoforte or the harp; but young gentlemen were considered sufficiently accomplished if they could sing a popular air or play it on the flute. There were no native English composers of originality, except those writing church music.

Concert life in London in the first third of the century was exclusively social, and confined to the efforts of the Philharmonic Society and the Antient Concerts—the latter, by 1837, says Francis Hueffer, 'in a very attenuated condition. . . . Their programmes consisted mainly of detached choruses and arias from Handel's oratorios.'[1] More lively, though still exclusively upper-class, was the activity of the Italian Opera, with factions and theatres warring over prima donnas and tenors, and beaux fainting in their boxes as they heard the phenomenal warblings of the last of the castrati. Singing, indeed, was the only form of musical activity at all popular: the old eighteenth-century madrigal societies still flourished; few people were unacquainted with the three or four best loved of Handel's oratorios. The Royal Academy of Music was founded in 1822, almost for the sole purpose of teaching singing; all students were required to learn Italian. There was a dearth of instrumental music, a fact all the more amazing considering that on the Continent at this time the great symphonic masters Beethoven and Schubert were creating perhaps the most substantial body of orchestral and chamber music in the history of the art.

It is not surprising that the Germans scornfully called England 'das Land ohne Musik'; nor, in such conditions, that there was almost no theoretical writing about or criticism of music. For vocal music depends largely on the performer for its effect; only the pure wordless sound of instrumental music challenges the mind to attempt an explanation of its peculiar hold over the listener. In this respect, Browning's predilection for instrumental music should be noted. *The Times* did appoint a permanent music critic, J. W. Davison, in 1846, and H. F. Chorley, Browning's friend of later years, began writing notices for the weekly *Athenaeum* in 1833. Both, however, confined themselves largely to the criticism of performances, and were chary of new music. More adventurous was the periodical *The Harmonicon* (1823–33), which was at least aware of musical events on the Continent, but its readership was of course limited to those 'social outcasts'[2] the cognoscenti.

The social status of music other than the Italian Opera began slowly to improve with the accession of Queen Victoria and her marriage to that ardent musician Prince Albert. She welcomed foreign composers such as Mendelssohn and Liszt, and heard their music at public and private concerts; she was even, according to Francis Hueffer, 'The First English-woman to Recognise the Genius of Wagner'[3]. Be that as it may, some-

[1] F. Hueffer, *Half a Century of Music in England, 1837–1887*, 1889, 10.

[2] Hueffer, 134, quoting a *Times* leader, on the occasion of Liszt's second visit to England in 1886, 40 years after his first.

[3] Hueffer, Dedication to *Half a Century* . . .

time in the 1840s began that revival of interest in instrumental and chamber music, and in musical scholarship, which was to lead to the great English musical renaissance of the last years of the century. By the time Browning began his correspondence with Miss Barrett, there was enough music of high quality available in London to keep his eager mind satisfied.

Browning's unorthodox education in a Dissenting household was of immense benefit in saving him from the hidebound conventions of what a nineteenth-century gentleman should know. He evinced an early interest in music—one of his first memories being of his mother's playing Avison's 'Grand March'—and it was allowed, indeed encouraged, to develop. He said proudly in later life, 'I was studying the Grammar of Music when most children are learning the multiplication table, and I know what I am talking about when I speak of music.'[1] Mrs. Sutherland Orr thought that this neglect of the multiplication table led to a lack of mental discipline in her hero, but she seems to have been unaware of the elaborate quasi-mathematical agility needed to harmonize the simplest tune, much less compose a fugue. It was this science of music that Browning was taught by 'great John Relfe'; he also had tuition in practical music, singing, pianoforte, violin and cello. But evidently it was the faculty of musical construction and analysis which gave the young Browning most pleasure: he composed music for songs (later destroyed), and even contemplated an opera. His teenage tenderness for Miss Eliza Flower, the composer of sacred music for Dissenting chapels, seems to have been based on what Mrs. Orr called 'genuine appreciation of her musical genius'; as late as 1845 he was writing to Miss Flower about her music, 'I put it apart from all other English music I know, and fully believe in it as *the* music we all waited for.'[2]

He was, like all dedicated amateurs, peculiarly proud of his musical ability. Early in his correspondence with Miss Barrett he writes, 'I have always been jealous of my own musical faculty (I can write music).'[3] Later he quotes whole bars to her, to illustrate some obscure point—a habit perhaps not very helpful to the musically deprived Miss Barrett. But music had its uses too in expressing the inexpressible in that intense correspondence:

[1] Griffin and Minchin, 15–16.
[2] Mrs. Sutherland Orr, *Life and Letters of Robert Browning*, 1891, 136.
[3] *Letters*, I, 98.

. . . this morning a very ordinary *motivetto* in the overture to "Rabuco" seemed to tell you more than I ever *shall*. . . .[1]

During their married life in Florence Browning's opportunities for hearing music were not so great, and he entertained himself at home with painting and clay modelling, and of course the indispensable piano, in which he began to instruct the boy Pen. The Brownings did not entirely lack high quality music: one of their friends in Rome and Paris was Mrs. Sartoris, the famous opera singer Adelaide Kemble, who had retired from the stage on her marriage; they heard 'excellent music at Mrs. Sartoris's . . . once or twice a week.'[2] It was in his last years that Browning's passion for music found its fullest expression. Mrs. Orr notes that 'It would be scarcely an exaggeration to say that he attended every important concert of the season';[3] Dowden adds that 'the extraordinary range of his acquaintance with the works of great and even of obscure composers was attested by Hallé.'[4] Evidently to some extent this musical and social activity filled an emotional gap left by the death of his wife. As early as 1864 he could write,

> The infinitely best thing in London to me is the *music*,—so good, so much of it: I know Hallé, Joachim, and others, and make them play at parties where I meet them—the last time I saw Hallé, at his own house, he played Beethoven's wonderful last Sonata—the 32[d]—in which the very gates of Heaven seem opening.[5]

This sentiment was echoed in a sonnet he wrote in 1884 at the request of Joachim the violinist, as a tribute to Arthur Chappell, the director of the Popular Concerts of chamber music at St James's Hall:

> '*Sense has received the utmost Nature grants,*
> *My cup was filled with rapture to the brim*
> *When, night by night,—Ah, memory—how it haunts!*
> *Music was poured by perfect ministrants*
> *By Hallé, Schumann, Piatti, Joachim!*'[6]

[1] *Letters*, II, 81. Presumably Browning means Verdi's *Nabucco*, first performed in 1842.
[2] Orr, *Life*, 199.
[3] Orr, *Life*, 303.
[4] E. Dowden, *The Life of Robert Browning*, 1915, 276.
[5] *Dearest Isa*, 191.
[6] *New Letters*, 304.

Such a rapturous receptiveness to music is, however, indicative of the limitations imposed by Browning's amateurism; professional musicians are always sterner critics. It was one of the leaders of the new self-confident group of English composers, Charles Villiers Stanford, who turned a cold eye on the subject of Browning and music. An anecdote from his *Pages from an Unwritten Diary* clarifies a distinction to be made between the man to whom music is meat and drink and the poet to whom it is a useful emotional and quasi-philosophical prop:

> There was a most interesting gathering in Coutts Trotter's rooms at Trinity, when Joachim, Grove, Robert Browning, and Hueffer (destined to be Davison's successor as critic of the *Times*) had a warm controversy on the subject of Beethoven's last Quartets. The member of the party who talked most and knew least about the subject was, curiously enough, Browning. I remember remarking *sotto voce* to my neighbour that his arguments explained to me that the true reason of the obscurity of many references to music in his poems was the superficiality and exiguity of his technical knowledge. When Jebb was writing his masterly Greek translation of 'Abt Vogler,' he too became well aware of this weakness, and was able with infinite skill to gloss over the solecisms of the original. 'Sliding by semitones till I sink to the minor,' is indeed the refuge of the destitute amateur improvisor.[1]

Another critic, writing in the *Boston Evening Transcript* in 1887, was less severe (and more fair), though he questioned the appearance of 'diminished sixths' in 'A Toccata of Galuppi's' ('rather like casually speaking of breakfasting off roc's egg as a matter of everyday occurrence'). This anonymous writer distinguishes with pleasing accuracy the positive aspect of Browning's amateurism:

> where Browning shows himself most truly musical is where he speaks of music untechnically. In all the varied suggestiveness he finds in great music, and in the vivid way he embodies in glowing verse the mental picture it calls up in his poet's brain, he makes it clear that this suggestiveness is a personal matter between the music and himself—that the composer has little, if anything, to do with it. He does not try to impute his own fancy to the composer, and one feels instinctively that, when he listens to music, he listens musically, and not merely sentimentally. The music he mentions in his poems, too, is almost invariably of a high order; his sympathies are not with

[1] C. V. Stanford, *Pages from an Unwritten Diary*, 1914, 176.

the musical populace but with the aristocracy of the art.[1]

That he was a musical and not merely a sentimental amateur puts Browning on a par, not with his fellow English *littérateurs*, but with the great Continental writers of the previous hundred years: the Ecyclopédistes, Goethe, Schiller, E. T. A. Hoffmann; Schopenhauer and Nietzsche. These creators of a Romantic theory of art were musically educated men who gave music a high place in the new aesthetic; but this was to have almost no impact in England until the 1870s.

We may distinguish two, or perhaps three, attitudes to music on the Continent in the late eighteenth and nineteenth centuries. That which was the correlative of Romanticism claimed that music expressed the inexpressible, that it in some way echoed the structure of the organic universe; or that, conversely, it expressed nothing but its ineffable self. The older view was that promulgated by the 'modernist' French Encyclopédistes, that it expressed precise emotions and could thus be a vehicle of the starkest dramatic realism—a very high-class form of entertainment. In France there was a long and bitter controversy over the conventions of opera: whether it was to continue to be a spectacle of ballets, machines, and vocal combat, or whether it was to be refined to give exact expression to the emotions of love, hate, fury, joy, etc., which were the staple of the operatic plot. The various articles on aspects of music in the *Encyclopédie* emphasized the supremacy of melody in conveying these emotions; a reformed opera, in which everything, including words, was directed towards clarifying the dramatic situation, was self-evidently the highest form of musical art.

This opinion was of course exactly that expressed by Richard Wagner a century later. The idea of opera as *Gesamtkunstwerk* probably came to Goethe and Lessing via Rousseau and Diderot, leaders of the French debate. Instrumental music was still largely unregarded, but the legacy of Kant in Germany meant that the element of logical precision in the idea of words illustrated by music began to give way to a mystic unity, in which words, tune, and accompaniment together expressed some indefinable ecstasy or longing. Indeed, many of the early German Romantic poets wrote such musical verse that it seemed only natural that the

[1] Quoted in Herbert E. Greene, 'Browning's Knowledge of Music', *PMLA*, LXII, 1947, 1097. Greene also quotes the Stanford anecdote and an otherwise unpublished letter of Browning, about his musical knowledge, to the Rev. Henry Spaulding of the Browning Society of Boston.

beginning of the century should see the first peak of German Lieder composition. Friedrich von Schlegel, whose writings played a large part in introducing a Romantic view of art, as a poet wrote of music as a structural analogy to 'earth's dream':

> *Durch alle Töne tönet, im bunten Erdentraume,*
> *Ein leiser Ton gezogen, für den, der heimlich lauschet.*
>
> (*Through all the tones in earth's colourful dream there sounds a single soft note for him who listens secretly.*)[1]

But it was left to Arthur Schopenhauer to elaborate a philosophy of music—a philosophy that deeply depended on music—within the Kantian framework. His *Die Welt als Wille und Vorstellung* was published in 1819, but went almost entirely unregarded until the 1840s. Schopenhauer argued that it is only art which can deliver us from the endless drivings of the will; only in contemplation of the beautiful in itself do we engage in will-less perception. Works of art are 'representations', archetypes of the phenomenal world—except for music, the only non-representational art, which is 'a copy of the will itself', of the noumenal:

> a perfectly universal language, the distinctness of which surpasses even that of the perceptible world itself. . . . The composition of melody, the disclosure in it of all the deepest secrets of human willing and feeling . . . may be called an inspiration. . . . The composer reveals the inner nature of the world, and expresses the deepest wisdom in a language which his reason does not understand. . . . The unutterable depth of all music, by virtue of which it floats through our consciousness as the vision of a paradise firmly believed in yet ever distant from us, and by which also it is so fully understood and yet so inexplicable, rests on the fact that it restores to us all the emotions of our inmost nature, but entirely without reality and far removed from their pain.[2]

As Morse Peckham points out in *Beyond the Tragic Vision*,[3] it was Beethoven the great symphonist who first made the will itself the subject of

[1] F. Schlegel, 'Die Gebüsche', in *Sämmtliche Werke*, 15 vol., Vienna 1846, IX, 148.

[2] A. Schopenhauer, *The World as Will and Idea*, tr. Haldane and Kemp, 9th impression, 1950, 3 vol., 1883, I, 330, 336, 341 (i.e., para. 52).

[3] Morse Peckham, *Beyond the Tragic Vision: The Quest for Identity in the Nineteenth Century*, New York 1962, 150 ff., 259 ff.

his music, and it was Wagner who deliberately set out to present a Scho-
penhauerian drama in the *Ring* operas; but curiously enough, Schopenhauer heartily disliked Wagner's music, and much preferred the tuneful
Rossini to Beethoven. Rossini's music, he said, 'speaks *its own language* so
distinctly and purely that it requires no words, and produces its full effect
when rendered by instruments alone.'[1] Here he would have found an
ally in Browning, who, for all his eagerness for new music, was not one
of the English Wagnerites, and whose poems, almost without exception,
are about eighteenth-century, pre-Romantic musicians. One suspects
that for both men the most satisfying type of music was the Classical,
however momentarily overwhelming were the ecstasies of the Romantic
will. Certainly this was the case with Edouard Hanslick, the influential
German music critic, supporter of Brahms and opponent of Wagner: his
book *On Musical Beauty* (1854) took up Schopenhauer's argument that
music is a *Ding-an-sich*, and concluded that if it is so, it is not even a copy
of the will, but merely a set of pragmatic laws which bring ordered
sound out of chaos.

Hegel, in his lectures on aesthetics of 1836, had a great deal to say
about music as the 'central' Romantic art, neither as spiritual as poetry
nor as sensuous as painting. His attempts to define the effect of music,
though much less clear than Schopenhauer's, arrive at a similar goal.
Music is pre-eminently 'the art of the soul'; its independence of space and
its fleeting association with time speak to the soul of itself. The resolution
of discords parallels the dialectic of the self and objective reality; melody,
as with Schopenhauer, is 'the more supremely poetic aspect of music',
reflecting 'the free self-consciousness of soul-life'. Consequently, like
Schopenhauer, Hegel preferred Classical music to his own century's
Romanticism; words for songs should be simple and lyrical—indeed, he
had no objection to Italian operatic music's habit of entirely parting
company with its words: the 'object is the enjoyment of art by itself',
offering the listener a consoling tranquillity, 'a liberation of the soul'.[2]

But for Hegel poetry was the art most nearly approaching the ideal
representation of the universe; for the ultimate expression of music's
high Romantic status we must turn to Schopenhauer's erstwhile follower
Nietzsche. His long essay on *The Birth of Tragedy out of the Spirit of Music*

[1] Schopenhauer, 338.

[2] G. W. F. Hegel, *The Philosophy of Fine Art*, tr. F. P. B. Osmaston, 4 vol.,
1920, III, 394, 398, 407, 349.

(1872) defined that 'spirit' as Dionysian: it 'gives expression to the will in its omnipotence . . . the eternal life behind all phenomena', the self-contradictions of an amoral artist-God. Language can never adequately render this cosmic symbolism: 'The poems of the lyrist can express nothing which has not already been contained in the vast universality and absoluteness of the music which compelled him to use figurative speech.'[1]

It is pleasing to note that the scholars who were translating these philosophical works into English at the turn of the century occasionally could not resist the urge to footnote their work with a reference to Browning on music, generally 'Abt Vogler'. Certainly what the Germans had to say seems more relevant to Browning's music poems than anything written in England in the nineteenth century. But it seems unlikely (though not impossible) that Browning was actually acquainted with their work. His surviving correspondence does not mention them, and in general—apart from the propaganda work done on behalf of their favourites by Coleridge and Carlyle (neither of them musical men)—there seems to have been little attention paid by English thinkers to Continental developments. We know that Browning was studying German during the 1840s, but why read an obscure modern philosopher such as Schopenhauer when all the glories of German literature awaited one? Nietzsche and Schopenhauer were not in fact noticed in England until the Wagner craze and controversies began in the 1870s; then, indeed, articles began to appear in the periodical press speculating on the nature and function of music.

The Rev. Hugh Haweis had evidently read his German philosophers, when in 1871 in the *Quarterly Review* he discussed several books of musical philosophy and history in a long essay entitled 'Music, its Origin and Influence'. He asserted that art is 'its own justification. . . . In freeing his own soul the painter, the orator, the poet has freed mine; I shall not suffer in this direction from the void and the agony of the unattained, for it is there worked out for me and for all men to rejoice in and to love.' Only music can express the ultimate complexity of the modern spirit, since it alone among the arts has the quality of 'Movement or Velocity'.[2] Here,

[1] F. Nietzsche, *The Birth of Tragedy*, tr. W. A. Haussmann, in *Complete Works*, ed O. Levy, 18 vol., London and New York 1923, I, 127, 55.

[2] H. R. Haweis, 'Music, its Origin and Influence', *Quarterly Review*, CXXXI, 1871, 145–76.

in fact, the literary clergyman joins hands with the agnostic father of the Aesthetes, Walter Pater, who in his famous 'Conclusion' to *The Renaissance* 1868, gave voice to the modern spirit thus: 'those impressions of the individual mind to which, for each one of us, experience dwindles down, are in perpetual flight; . . . each of them is limited by time, and as time is infinitely divisible, each of them is infinitely divisible also; all that is actual in it being a single moment . . . art comes to you professing frankly to give nothing but the highest quality to your moments as they pass, and simply for those moments' sake.'[1] Music, according to Pater (no musician), is the art towards whose condition all the others aspire—that is, to a perfect oneness of matter and form. Art is 'always striving to be independent of the mere intelligence, to become a matter of pure perception'—momentary perception, that is, rather than timeless contemplation, desirable as that may be. In these 'consummate moments'—'music or music like intervals in our existence'—'we seem to be spectators of all the fullness of existence'.[2]

Other writers, inspired by the modern spirit, felt obliged to side with Hanslick and criticize Wagner's view that the union of music and words in opera produced the highest possible art-form. A writer in the *Edinburgh Review* claimed that 'The very power and pride, the very raison d'être of music, is that it expresses that which words are powerless to express, which can be expressed in no other way.' When he continues, 'Mr. Browning has put this well in one of the finest of his shorter poems, the reverie of "Abt Vogler" '[3] (published twelve years earlier), one begins to realize just how independent Browning's thinking about music was.

The fact must be re-emphasized that although there was a great revival of musical activity in England in the latter half of the nineteenth century, much of it was imported—composers, conductors, virtuoso performers. The old jibe, 'das Land ohne Musik', remained fundamentally true until the country could boast its complement of native composers writing English music. Theoretical writing about music does not flourish dispossessed of a living example: the contrast with contemporary Germany and

[1] W. Pater, *The Renaissance: Studies in Art and Poetry*, in *Works*, 8 vol., 1900, I, 235, 239.

[2] Pater, 'The School of Giorgione', *The Renaissance*, 138, 150–151.

[3] H. H. Statham (anon.), 'Wagner, and the Modern Theory of Music', *Edinburgh Review*, CXLIII, January 1876, 170.

France, and even with eighteenth-century England, where Burney and Avison published significant volumes, makes the point. Furthermore, the philosophical temperament of the English does not incline them to theory: pragmatic and protestant, rarely to be caught speculating about Ultimate Reality or the relation of aesthetics thereto, much more concerned with establishing a proper morality. Asa Briggs has commented on the immense moral fervour which accompanied the perennial performances all over England of Handel's and Mendelssohn's oratorios in the nineteenth century: the universal opinion was that no music could be more uplifting.[1] The reforming author of *A History of Music in England* remarked despairingly,

> The inferior composer of the quasi-clerical order has for more than two hundred years been a peculiarly Anglo-Saxon product; other nations have known bad religious music, but they have not, like us, been deluged with it. Nor have they suffered, to anything like the same extent, from the application to artistic matters of totally non-artistic canons of judgement; it is only in England that musicianship has been really seriously hampered by the unmusical seekers after edification.[2]

And the Rev. Haweis was forced to conclude his lengthy examination of 'Music and Morals' with the observation that

> although we are inclined to admit that the English are on the whole a Religious People, we come back again and again to the sad conviction that however improving and improvable, the English are not, as a nation, an Artistic People, and that the English are not a Musical People.[3]

Robert Browning was, however, musical, and musically well-educated. There are several important aspects of his musical thinking which are not touched on by any of the writers mentioned above, though there is evidently some general similarity of outlook. The first fact which Browning's pragmatism obliges him to deal with is that of

[1] Prof. Briggs's lecture on the Victorian Music Festival, 'Music as Message', was given at the 1970 Aldeburgh Festival.

[2] Ernest Walker, *A History of Music in England*, 1907, rev. J. A. Westrup, 3rd edn, Oxford 1952, 396.

[3] H. R. Haweis, 'Music and Morals', *Contemporary Review*, XVII, July 1871, 508. The essay's first two parts are in XVI, 89–101, 280–97.

musical fashion, the apparently inevitable change 'every thirty years'[1] in the style which creates a satisfying musical experience. Browning's emotional commitment to music enabled him to use this fact as an analogy for the changing nature of historical experience, and thereby of how we conceive 'truth'. Then there is the business of the mystical mathematics of music, the largely psychological effects of certain combinations of notes; all the music poems employ this science, and with an expertise which defies the non-musician. The theory has had, from Pythagoras onwards, a natural connexion with a philosophy of the harmonious motion of the universe; something even of this may be discerned in Browning: music *is* a logical language, though it may not speak of comprehensible concepts. But ultimately Browning insists that music serves 'man's cause', that its mystery is available, if necessary, even in the humble form of a rousing march ('Charles Avison')—a thing which one can imagine the eighteenth-century theorists contemplating rather more easily than the nineteenth-century philosophers.

Of Baldassaro Galuppi, the first musician in Browning's poetic collection, *Grove's Dictionary* makes two pertinent remarks: 'he had a firmer grasp of harmony, rhythm and orchestration than most of his Italian contemporaries. . . . As inquiries are often made by members of Browning Societies and others as to the "Toccata of Galuppi" [sic], to which Browning referred in his poem of that name, it is perhaps well to state that no particular composition was taken as the basis of the poem.'[2] From a letter of Browning's we do learn that 'As for Galuppi, I had once in my possession two huge manuscript volumes almost exclusively made up of his "Toccata-pieces" '[3]; it seems not unlikely that somewhere therein he found those diminished sixths, written by the adventurous harmonizer, that so worried Browning's American critic.

The poem (published 1855) uses the language of music fairly simply ('I can hardly misconceive you. . . . But although I take your meaning, 'tis with such a heavy mind!'). The sprightly verse rhythm is just that of a harpsichord piece written to show off the player's touch. The discordant intervals of which the toccata seems largely composed speak to the listen-

[1] *Letters*, I, 544.

[2] *A Dictionary of Music and Musicians, A.D. 1450–1880*, ed George Grove, 4 vol., 1879–89, 'Galuppi'. This monumental dictionary is itself one of the first and finest products of the English musical renaissance.

[3] Greene, 'Browning's Knowledge of Music', 1099.

ers of ' "Dust and ashes" ', but as this eighteenth-century music is only thought of as entertainment, the elegant audience is not obliged to take note of what is being said. Browning plays music's oldest psychological trick by closing the toccata with a strong perfect cadence (dominant to tonic), so that the audience's equilibrium, unconsciously disturbed during the piece, reasserts itself. The speaker, however, with the advantage of a hundred years' hindsight, finds the 'old music' 'cold music', since despite its conventional and passé form, it was and is so chillingly accurate in its prophecy. Here Browning first suggests the fascination which the phenomenon of music in history held for him.

'Master Hugues of Saxe-Gotha' is a poem deliberately denigratory of music's power to speak. Perhaps it arose as an answer to the pessimism of 'Galuppi', published in the same volume. The most significant thing about the poem in this respect is that Hugues is the only one of Browning's musicians who is an invention—something of a straw figure, in fact. Browning again corroborates in the Spaulding letter: 'As to "Master Hughes" [sic], had he been meant for the glorious Bach it were a shame to me indeed; I had in mind one of the dry-as-dust imitators who would elaborate some such subjects as'—he quotes an elementary five-note exercise.[1]

The poem's rhythm and its five-line stanza form are a brilliant imitation of the fugal manner, and stanzas xii–xix present a verbal analogy to Hugues's fidgety elaboration of musical theory. Browning's own 'interpretation' of the poem was that it was 'merely the expression of a fugue . . . an involved labyrinth of entanglement *leading to nothing*—the only allegory in it was its possible reflection of the labyrinth of human life'.[2] Hugues claims an esoteric 'intent' in his music, which the organist is willing to allow him, but he finds that the self-importance and difficulty of the fugue's manner of proceeding obscures whatever of 'truth and nature' may be glimpsed. The organist is eager that something positive should come of this vast labour and argument: indeed, 'where's music, the dickens?' By implication, what is lacking in this form of music or thinking is the rousing and expressing of a noble emotion—something that perhaps would accompany the *mode Palestrina*. This, by Browning's definition, 'was the name given by old Italian writers on Composition to a certain simple and severe style like that of the

[1] Greene, 1098.

[2] L. C. Collins, *Life and Memoirs of John Churton Collins*, 1912, 79.

Master.'¹ But that is not the concern of this poem.

Music's emotional power is undoubtedly the concern of 'Abt Vogler'. The poem presents a singleminded approach to the problem by identifying the composer and the performer (as in 'A Toccata of Galuppi's') *and* the speaker; and, principally, by restricting the music performed to a few minutes of existence without the possibility of repetition. Abt Vogler's improvisation is a work of intuition guided by a knowledge of the laws of music. It has no existence beyond the memories of Abt Vogler and his hearers, thus corresponding very precisely to the Hegelian definition of 'soul-language'.

The poem certainly sets one wondering also whether Browning could possibly have come across Schopenhauer's philosophy by this date; for the passages from Schopenhauer quoted above read uncannily like a gloss on some parts of 'Abt Vogler'. There is the same distinction between the status of music and that of the other arts: ' 'tis we musicians know' with a knowledge beyond reason; the same claim that music is a copy of the will itself, 'a flash of the will that can, Existent behind all laws'; even an identical concept of the vision of a paradise, in which the existence of good and evil is resolved by the absence of pain. But music's paradise is artificial, a 'palace' which does not survive the effort of the will; its creator is God-like ('for I was made perfect too'; 'consider and bow the head!'), but only momentarily. Abt Vogler distinguishes, in a pre-Romantic theology, between the transitoriness of his music and the permanence of God, whose 'eternity affirms the conception of an hour'.

Browning plays off a *general* Romantic conception, for which music happens to be a particularly sympathetic image, of the mystically exalted artist redeeming mankind through his art, against a realistic acknowledgement of the transitoriness of such experience. Abt Vogler, by the leap of faith, rests on 'the substance of things hoped for'. Yet it is the gnostic artist who finally commands the poem. The display of musical science in the last stanza recalls to us stanza vii's proud priest, the creator of mystic triads. He can create a similar experience at will, despite the formal claim of acquiescence in 'the C Major of this life'. (The choice of this key itself has an esoteric significance: called by the earliest theorists of western music 'modo lascivio', its use was forbidden in church music until about the fourteenth century. This most basic of keys simply sounded too earthy and comfortable.)

¹ Greene, 1098.

The historical status of Abt Vogler repays consideration, for he has curious connexions with others among Browning's musicians. He lived from 1749 to 1814; he was thus roughly a contemporary of Goethe and Beethoven and stood at the watershed of eighteenth-century Classicism and nineteenth-century Romanticism—very apt for the contrast of interior and exterior revelation which is the poem's concern. As *Grove* puts it, 'He evinced from an early age a religious cast of mind and an aptitude for music'.[1] The 'musical instrument of his invention' may have been the orchestrion, a compact portable organ containing a large number of pipes; he gave recitals on the instrument in London, and one still survives in the musical museum at Brentford in Middlesex. It may, however, simply have been one of the reconstructed organs which he built all over Europe, with additions to improve their range and power. *Grove* says that his extempore playing was phenomenal; it 'never failed to create an impression, and in the elevated fugal style he easily outdistanced all rivals.'

So much for Abt Vogler as an appropriate subject for Browning's poem; there is an important aspect of his life which is not mentioned in the poem, though it perhaps underlies it. He was an ardent advocate of a new system of harmony—i.e., of musical mathematics—more practical than the old complicated system of figured bass. Its fundamental principle, *Grove* tells us, 'was that not only the triad but also the discords of the 7th, 9th and 11th could be introduced on any degree of the scale without involving modulation. He went even beyond this, and allowed chromatically altered forms of these chords and inversions of them.' That is, he anticipated in theory what Wagner and Liszt did fifty years later. The theory was of course not well received, but it may in part have accounted for the effect of his improvisations. Certainly Browning sees the audacity of his chordal combinations as quasi-divine; and in the last stanza of the poem the chromaticism which Stanford criticized as the feeblest resort of the improvising organist is also the point of departure for spiritual adventure, 'Which, hark, I have dared and done'.

Browning's own instructor in counterpoint, 'great John Relfe', was a follower of Vogler's system; he wrote a treatise *Lucidus Ordo*, which 'was a proposal for substituting a "figured bass" of his own, for the barbarous contrivance in use at the beginning of the present century', Browning

[1] *Grove's Dictionary*, 'Vogler, Abbé George Joseph'—'one of the most curious figures in the annals of music'.

told Mr. Spaulding.[1] Here, in fact, is the poet's real connexion with musical theorists, and it is a connexion not with the nineteenth century but with the avant-garde of the eighteenth.

The simplified system of conventional harmony taught today was largely the invention of Jean-Philippe Rameau, whom the French Encyclopédistes took under their wing. The only two remarkable English writers about music in the eighteenth century were Dr Burney and Charles Avison, both ardent pro-Encyclopédistes, though they hardly agreed on their principal concerns, the rival claims of Handel and the Italian masters. Neither of these men was at all avant-garde in his musical interests, though Avison was the more eccentric: his support of the despised French music of Rameau seems to have been a move towards a 'doctrine of the affections', i.e., of the exact expression of specific emotions in music. But Avison could not accept the burgeoning change in sensibility which this doctrine heralded: he was shocked by the modern music of the Mannheim and Viennese schools, which seemed to him 'exactly parallel to the turgid or bombastic in writing, and to suit very ill with the native charms of melody, but still worse with those of harmony.'[2]

This same preface contains an *Analogy between Musical Air and Grammar*, which title, along with that of the famous *Essay on Musical Expression* (1752), is indicative of Avison's concern that music should speak, and that clearly and elegantly. His own simple 'March' certainly does that, as Browning acknowledges, but the deliberately conservative nature of both it and its composer make them doubly apt subjects for the poet's longest investigation into the relation of music to the human mind, the 'Parleying with Charles Avison' (1887).

In the elder Mr. Browning's library there were two editions of the *Essay on Musical Expression*, and Browning himself possessed a copy of the 'March' in his father's hand.[3] It had a nostalgic appeal for him, associated with his mother's playing of it in his childhood; this is evidently important for the associative method with which the poem begins. As in other great Romantic poems, Fancy is a starting-point for an analysis of the Imagination.

[1] Greene, 1098.

[2] Avison, Preface to Concertos, op. 9 (1766), quoted in Charles Cudworth, 'Avison of Newcastle, 1709–1770', *Musical Times*, CXI, May 1970, 483.

[3] Greene, 1099; and *New Letters*, 341 (to 'VernonLee').

Early in the piece Browning indicates the limitations of the eighteenth century's idea of expressible emotions, 'rough rage or soft desire' (*vide* the libretto of any English eighteenth-century opera). Yet in the poem's third paragraph we watch the poet's imagination lulled by this 'thinnish air' to a mystical experience reminiscent of Abt Vogler's. Thus awakened to the intrinsic value of the music Browning makes an effort to recreate in his imagination the appreciative spirit of the time of its composition. But he founders on the rock of changing musical fashion: how can this apparently supremely inspiring work of art have become obsolete? Why is it that Wagner's 'O du mein holder Abendstern' (from *Tannhäuser*, first heard in London in 1876—in Italian!), a merely conventional address to the evening star, is more moving than any eighteenth-century version of it?

The answer is given with astounding directness:

> *I state it thus:*
> *There is no truer truth obtainable*
> *By Man than comes of music*

—*but* music must change as the way of expressing truth changes, as, in fact, sensibility (or the Imagination) develops. Music is of all arts most closely analogous to that mysterious Romantic sea, the Soul. That is, it is the least conceptual of arts: its job is to clarify Feeling so that its expression shall 'match and mate' with the development of Knowledge. But whereas knowledge is fairly concrete, sensibility is essentially evanescent, and so inevitably must the music be which brings it to light. One might question this 'inevitably'; certainly Schopenhauer would have, whose theory Browning's otherwise so much resembles. For Browning is perhaps too involved in a Romantic, progressivist view of history to allow disingenuously for the fact that great music does survive its age with unabated power.

Browning's attitude to the ambiguous 'chance and change' was typically Victorian, and almost obscured his cooler appreciation of the great achievements of the musical past. This particular theme found early expression in a letter to Elizabeth Barrett (March, 1846):

I made myself melancholy just now with some "Concertos for the Harpsichord by Mr. Handel" . . . what were light, modern things once! Now I read not very long ago a French memoir of "Claude le

Jeune" called in his time the Prince of Musicians,—no, "Phoenix"—the unapproachable wonder to all time—that is, twenty years after his death about—and to this pamphlet was pre-fixed as motto this startling axiom—"In Music, the Beau Ideal changes every thirty years"—well, is not that *true*?[1]

But, after all, the starting-point for this elaborate pursuit of truth in music has been 'one—well, thinnish air'. Browning's musical and anachronistic games with Avison's air witness to the poet's sense of su-periority over this particular effort at musical expression. His imagin-ation triumphantly moulds the musical idea in 'man's cause': the playful metaphor of chemical science for Relfe's system of harmony is both magical and utilitarian. Music is not after all autonomous, nor self-creating out of chaos, as the German thinkers would have it, but subject to the all-creating imagination: 'Avison helps—so heart lend noise enough!' The truth that comes of music comes actually of the sensibility of its composer and interpreters. So Browning merrily sets words to Avison's tune, to be sung by the notoriously music-hating Roundheads —one hundred years before the tune was written.

Browning's Don Juan is evidently of the same musical cast of mind as his creator. About halfway through the vast monologue of *Fifine at the Fair*, he begins to call on music to assist him in his argument that only through a wide variety of experience can the truth beneath the changing façade of falsehood be established. One of his first points is an antici-pation of the conclusion of 'Charles Avison': 'in the seeing soul, all worth lies' (stanza lv). Even music, that God-like vehicle of spiritual en-lightenment, is simply a product of elaborate man-invented rules (stanza xlii). To imaginations similarly attuned, music can say things more 'truthfully' than the particularizations of words; but that is not much use when the very nature of Elvire is to be the eternal opposite of Don Juan. And Don Juan, like Browning, is quite obviously proud of his musical knowledge. His own private version of the world's structure finds its image in musical mathematics:

> *Clash forth life's common chord, whence,*
> *list how there ascend*
> *Harmonics far and faint, till our perception*
> *end,—*

[1] Letters, I, 543–44.

> *Reverberated notes whence we construct*
> *the scale*
> *Embracing what we know and feel and are!*
>
> (lxii)

In the same manner he turns to music to express his great dream-vision of life as a carnival; bidding the music reassure him, through its faculty of recording emotion, that the vision did indeed bear a measure of truth. The music which Don Juan chooses involves Browning in some interesting anachronisms: it is Schumann's 'Carnival', published in 1834. When Clara Schumann performed her husband's piano music in London in 1865, Francis Hueffer records, it was 'thought by the public and the press to be the abstruse effusions of the modern spirit'.[1]

The latest manifestation of Don Juan before Browning's had of course been Byron's; Browning brings him, arguing volubly, into the last half of the Victorian era. But one thinks of Don Juan as essentially an emanation of the Baroque spirit, of the Classical period as opposed to the Romantic; then again, within the formal intellectual trappings of Classicism, whether Molière's or Mozart's, the image of Don Juan is quite clearly a Romantic one. This inbuilt tension contributes strongly to the masterly quality of all four works. It is an essential part, too, of the artistic personality of Schumann, whose piano music, including 'Carnival', was an expression of the eternal arguments within him between 'Florestan' the passionate and 'Eusebius' the contemplative. 'Carnival' is, on the face of it, an objectively descriptive piece, but its key-relations, based on four cryptic letters, indicate its deep ambiguity: the 'objective' vision, like Don Juan's, is a dream whose underlying truth only the initiate can divine. Don Juan paraphrases Schlegel to conclude his argument from music ('since change is there The law, and not the lapse', stanza xcii):

> *For as some imperial chord subsists,*
> *Steadily underlies the accidental mists*
> *Of music springing thence, that run their mazy race*
> *Around, and sink, absorbed, back to the triad base,—*
> *So, out of that one word, each variant rose and fell*
> *And left the same "All's change, but permanence*
> *as well."*

[1] Hueffer, *Half a Century*, 17.

> *—Grave note whence—list aloft!—harmonics*
> *sound, that mean:*
> *"Truth inside, and outside, truth also; and between*
> *Each, falsehood that is change, as truth is*
> *permanence."*

(cxxiv)

Schumann's 'pretty piece' has served its purpose in delivering its consoling vision of something beyond 'change', a logical world-structure even if it only exists in the creating imagination. The music being intrinsically of greater imaginative power, it is more accurately judged and valued than Avison's trivial march. (It should however be noted that *Fifine* was written fifteen years before the overtly philosophical *Parleyings*.)

If, therefore, we are to assign Browning a place among contemporary thinkers about music, it will be with the early rather than the later Romantics; and with their eighteenth-century forebears. The facts of his education support this interpretation. What we witness is not the later nineteenth century's adulation of music, its Wagnerian exaltation to the status of a substitute religion, but rather a profound emotional attachment founded at once on respect for its technical mysteries and a sense of power in the manipulating of them. The fact of change in musical fashion primarily indicates one thing for Browning, the superiority of human sensibility over any means of expressing it. Even though that means of expression may 'speak' more truly than any words can, its communication is limited by subjective interpretation. The two aspects of Browning's approach to his sister art are shown quite clearly in his last poetic utterance on the subject, 'Flute-Music, with an Accompaniment'. 'She', the musical initiate, hears all the errors in the poor flautist's attempts; 'He', comfortably subjective, interprets them as the perfect expression of romantic love, and concludes, quite justifiably,

> *Is not outside seeming*
> *Real as substance inside?*
> *Both are facts, so leave me dreaming.*

Music, for Browning, is an instrument which reconciles these two classes of facts.

# 9: *Browning and the Dramatic Monologue*

## MICHAEL MASON

### I

EVEN A PARTIAL ACCOUNT of the background to Browning's dramatic monologues will be a suggestive possibility for anyone interested in the literature of Victorian England. For the impulse to forms that consist of an imagined utterance by some person other than the author seems so characteristic of—local to, and widespread in—this literature. So many of the innovations thrown up during this unusually experimentalist period—quite apart from dramatic monologues themselves—involve, or are original simply in respect of, the dramatic principle: the pseudo-translation and commentary of *Sartor Resartus*, the invented mottoes in the novels of Mrs Gaskell and George Eliot, the epistolary verse-narrative of *Amours de Voyage*, the lyrical diary of *Maud*, the interspersed songs of *The Princess*. And then there is the often-remarked way in which both Tennyson and Browning produce in the 1830s, fairly independently of one another, dramatic poems of a rather similar form and strategy.

The possibility that Browning's dramatic monologues have their roots deeply in Victorian culture seems to me to justify, and perhaps even make practicable, that rather dreary-sounding project, defining the dramatic monologue as written by Browning. Admittedly there is a very large body of texts (from Ovid's *Heroides* to 'The Lincolnshire Poacher' and 'Charlie is my Darling'; from the Anglo-Saxon 'The Dream of the Rood' to Wordsworth's 'The Thorn') that resemble the poems conventionally called dramatic monologues in a confusing variety of respects. Admittedly, even if we do not become as convinced as B. W. Fuson did of the hopelessness of sorting out the latter, the alternative might mean doing 'little better than describe the handful of Browning and Tennyson poems we are using as models'.[1] And admittedly the work of Ida Beth Sessions appears to offer an insuperably rebarbative instance of this approach.[2] But if we do not try for a definition in the sense of a list of *all* common or generally shared features of Browning's dramatic monologues (and certainly not go on to discriminate 'perfect' and less 'perfect' cases), and are guided in our choice of features by the idea that this genre might have deep roots in its contemporary culture, it might be possible to arrive at a list of features that are agreed to be prominent, that make Browning's dramatic monologues fairly distinct from anything written before about 1820, and are intelligible ones for poetry of Victoria's reign to possess. So we would in a sense simply 'describe the handful of Browning and Tennyson poems', but in such a way that their distinctness is interesting.

I shall simply propose such a list. Naturally all the features I mention are alluded to by other writers, but I have not thought it necessary to make detailed acknowledgement. (1) The sort of dramatic monologue Browning wrote is a poem of which the versified part is devoted almost entirely to the imaginary utterance of some person other than the author. (2) There is a distinct attempt to reproduce the characteristics of actual speech, even in the unusual case where the utterance is supposed to have been written, or the form of the poem is that of simple lyric. (3) The utterance is used to do a job natural to extended speech, namely, to express a state of mind, disposition, attitude, or set of beliefs. It is not used to express action for its own sake, and, where it does express action, the interest is that this is a characteristic action for the speaker. (4) The state of mind, or whatever, is treated seriously, in the sense that it is given a full and fairly eloquent expression; it is not obviously discredited. (5) It matters for a full understanding of the text that the reader should take it as the utterance of some person other than the author, either because the interest is in the expression of a state of mind that is historically or culturally remote, or because there are ways in which the speaker betrays rather than consciously expresses aspects of his state of mind. In keeping with the spirit of (3) the speaker will not give conscious expression to more aspects of his state of mind than is plausible.

[1] Robert Langbaum, *The Poetry of Experience*, 1957, 76.

[2] Ida Beth Sessions, 'The Dramatic Monologue', *PMLA*, LXII, 1947, 503–76.

About the first four of these features I shall make only a few remarks. The first excludes a large class of verse-texts that are utterances by inanimate objects or by the dead to the living, also dramatic works with more than one speaker, or speech that is included in non-dramatic verse. The second is obviously the ground on which one would wish to exclude a large number of songs, as well as most verse-epistles, and unspeechlike speech such as Byron's 'The Prophecy of Dante'. The third excludes a body of candidates generally rather near home: several works by Southey, Byron, Coleridge, Hallam, and by Browning himself (such as 'Count Gismond'). The fourth has a narrow but significant application; one important contender it excludes is Burns' 'Holy Willie's Prayer', but I come back to this case in connection with Browning's 'Johannes Agricola'.

The fifth feature needs much more discussion. It is the crucial one in the sense that it seems to implement the idea that these texts are dramatic,[1] and this is an area on which most recent treatments of the dramatic monologue have concentrated. The requirement, as I have put it, suggests that there are two situations in which it is necessary for a full understanding of a poem that we know it to be the supposed utterance of some person other than the author. One is when the supposed speaker belongs to a context, historically remote or otherwise exotic, about which facts made use of in the poem will be known to the reader in advance. The speaker may be Mary Queen of Scots, or a dying Indian, or a Celtic hero, or Moses, or, in Cowper's fine instance of the type, Alexander Selkirk. Burns is exceptional in illustrating a contemporary provincial context in several of his dramatic poems. A favourite version of the exotic poem from at least the time of Joseph Warton is the utterance, usually when stricken by love, grief, or death, of dusky natives of loosely specified origins. As these examples show, dramatic writing in this sense is well established in English long before the Victorian period. The only change it undergoes in the hands of Browning and Tennyson is one of degree, in

[1] I use the word 'dramatic' in the sense in which Browning almost always used it himself, namely, to denote the utterance of a person other than the author. There is an important exception to this habit in his preface to *Paracelsus* which I comment on later. Some writers on the dramatic monologues have inexplicably used the word in other, unhelpful senses, e.g. H. B. Charlton, 'Browning: the making of the Dramatic Lyric', *The Bulletin of the John Rylands Library*, XXXV, 1953, 349–84; R. H. Fletcher, 'Browning's Dramatic Monologs', *MLN*, XXIII, 1908, 108–11.

the greatly increased use of authenticating historical detail. Several of
Tennyson's early monologues, including 'Ulysses', are basically highly
developed versions of the exotic poem. Browning, on the other hand,
does not often use the dramatic principle in this way in poems which are
clearly imitative of speech (as opposed to songs like 'Through the
Metidja to Abd-el-Kadr'). Nearly always in these poems the reader's
consciousness that the utterance is that of a person other than the author
has an additional purpose.

This brings us to the second situation, where the dramatic procedure
matters because the reader has to gather more from the utterance than the
supposed speaker is conscious of expressing. In a word, the treatment is
ironical. The speaker *betrays* important aspects of his state of mind rather
than *articulating* them. Philip Drew argues that this is Browning's crucial
innovation,[1] and I am sure this is right, as long as we keep in mind that it
is this effect in conjunction with the fourth requirement in the list—the
requirement of serious treatment—that is the innovation. There are,
after all, plenty of dramatic poems in English that baldly, comically dis-
credit their speaker. Browning is at least among the first poets to construct imaginary utterances that are both eloquent and betraying.

What sort of impulse lies behind this innovation of ironic betrayal? An
understandable first stab at an answer is that the impulse is naturalistic.
The poet invites us to introduce to our reading a kind of interpretation
we exercise in real-life intercourse, but normally withhold for interpreting poems with a strong first-person element. Thus, as I mentioned, the speaker is not supposed to have an unlifelike degree of
conscious access to his own state of mind. W. Cadbury, protesting like
Philip Drew against Langbaum's neglect of ironic betrayal, makes this
view of the matter fairly explicit: the dramatic monologues involve 'an
imitation of character'; 'we must first feel the character who displays it,
not the attitude itself.'[2] One weakness of this as a reply to Langbaum is
that it does not really distinguish Browning's procedure from that of the
Romantics, as Langbaum understands the latter. In my terms, he argues
that Romantic poets do in fact also betray their states of mind rather than
articulate them. I think he would say, with some justice, that the proper
contrast to Cadbury's 'imitation of character' is the Shakespearean soliloquy (or Southey's monodramas, one of its descendants) rather than the

[1] In chap. 2 of *The Poetry of Browning: a Critical Introduction*, 1970.

W. Cadbury, 'Lyric and anti-lyric Forms: a method for judging Browning', *UTQ*, XXXIV, 49–64.

Romantic lyric. On the other hand Langbaum makes out his case too strongly. It is clearly possible to put the Romantic kind of betrayal to distinctly dramatic and un-Romantic ends, as Tennyson does with the device of pathetic fallacy in *Maud*.

Nevertheless, as I argue shortly, Browning scarcely ever uses pathetic fallacy as part of a true 'imitation of character', which suggests that his use of betraying devices may not always be naturalistic in spirit, not always directed at the imitation of 'character' rather than the expression of 'attitude'. One of the first monologues in which this suggestion starts to be confirmed is 'The Tomb at St Praxed's'. We have only to reflect on how incredulous and confused we would be if this poem were offered to us (suitably disguised in Italian prose) as an authentic transcription of a sixteenth century stenographer's MS to realize that in responding to its ironies we are doing more than simply interpreting the bishop's utterance by the rules we use for ordinary intercourse. Doubtless it is by analogy with betrayals in ordinary intercourse that we know how to interpret the ironies Browning has inserted, but we cannot escape the consciousness of the author's activity in the matter. While we know the speaker is not Robert Browning we do not forget that Robert Browning is the author. The idea that the speaker is 'other than the author' becomes peculiarly strengthened in such a case. *Whoever* the author is, he is not the speaker[1].

This is not in itself an adverse comment on 'The Tomb at St Praxed's'. Indeed it points to one of the characteristic kinds of satisfaction Browning's dramatic monologues can yield. When reading the bishop's utterance we recognize and applaud the representation of betrayal, rather than betrayal itself. We applaud it because of its deftness rather than its naturalism. We are satisfied by a piece of considerable virtuosity, as much as satisfied by having gauged the bishop's state of mind. This kind of pleasing virtuosity is very general in Browning's poems. In this case it is compounded when we recognize the other strands, the historical and elegiac strands, that Browning is sustaining, and how dexterously they coexist with the betrayal of a state of mind. The response is a kind of delight, or glee, that any virtuoso performance gives, and, as with virtuoso performances, there is a close bond between the performer and the audience, a happy conspiracy of display on the one hand and

[1] As T. S. Eliot said of Browning's monologues, 'We have to be aware that the mimic and the person mimicked are different people.' *On Poetry and Poets*, 1969, 95–6.

applause on the other. This element of happy recognition of Browning the virtuoso seems to me a much larger part of a normal response to many of the dramatic monologues than is commonly allowed. For example, I believe we applaud the Duke's brief reference to his bronze Neptune at the end of 'My Last Duchess' ('Italy' in 1842) for its deft colloquialism and its appearance of historical authenticity well before we construe it as psychologically accurate. And the first feature I listed—the giving of virtually all the monologue's content through the speaker—now becomes more intelligible. The writer's adroit negotiation of this self-imposed obstacle will enhance the reader's pleased approval.

Hence, unexpectedly, we might stand a better chance of passing off an exotic dramatic poem as the actual utterance of its speaker than some of Browning's dramatic monologues, despite the thoroughgoing verisimilitude the elaborate accumulation of historical detail in a poem like 'The tomb at St Praxed's' might suggest. For a correct understanding of the exotic poem we simply need to realize that the speaker is not the person we know to be the author of the poem. If we don't know who the author is, and hence are free to suppose he is the speaker, this has no effect on our reading of the utterance. Chatterton's Rowley poems provide a good instance. These are in effect dramatic poems about which there is nothing anomalous, as far as their sense is concerned, if they really are the utterance of Rowley. Interestingly, Browning took the forgery aspect of the Rowley poems in his 1842 essay to be merely a technical convenience for the young lyricist.[1] Of course another reason for the comparative viability of the Rowley poems as forgeries is that they imitate a poetic utterance and not actual speech. This shows how a naturalistic aim in one part of Browning's programme for the dramatic monologue will tend to make naturalism in other areas more difficult to achieve; the greater the colloquialism the more obtrusive the author's artistic, shaping activity is likely to be.

What is it in the ironic betrayal of 'The Tomb at St Praxed's' that brings Browning's activity so strongly to the fore? The effect is not inevitable for irony; more completely self-effacing ironies are available to the dramatic poet, as Tennyson shows in *Maud*, and as Browning himself shows in several of the earliest monologues: 'Johannes Agricola', 'Porphyria', 'Cristina', 'Pictor Ignotus'. But when Browning uses the predominant betraying device of *Maud*, pathetic fallacy, he almost

[1] *Browning's Essay on Chatterton*, ed Donald Smalley, 1948, 116.

always turns its quality of distortion and exaggeration into a means of simply distancing the reader from the poem's sentiment, not of contributing to an intelligible psychology for the speaker. Consider, for example, the concluding image of 'A Serenade at the Villa': 'the iron gate / Ground its teeth to let me pass!' The excessiveness of the image simply enforces an almost facetious resistance to the predominant emotion of the poem. Other lyrics exhibit the same resistance in other ways, perhaps in some touch of excessive eloquence or suavity that is enough to make the label 'dramatic' feel right for these poems but only in the negative, unfocused sense that the author is not identified with the sentiment.

As far as the comparison with the self-effacing ironies of, say, 'Johannes Agricola' is concerned there is clearly a qualitative change in 'The Tomb at St Praxed's'. There is a simplicity, both as an interpretation and an evaluation of the Bishop's state of mind, about the irony of religiosity versus secularism that is missing in the relation between what is articulated and what is betrayed in 'Johannes Agricola'. There is also the too-palpable historical irony whereby the Bishop illustrates, all unconscious, the values of his age. In other words, Browning is giving us his analysis and evaluation of sixteenth-century official Catholicism pretty unequivocally. It would be disingenuous of any reader to claim that Browning's attitude in this poem is not clear, and intentionally so.

So in some of the monologues in Browning's second batch (the *Dramatic Romances and Lyrics* pamphlet of 1845) such as 'The Tomb at St Praxed's', he is trying to solve the worry he several times expresses in his letters to Elizabeth Barrett, that he was not 'speaking out' for himself in his poetry. The anxiety is perhaps more significant for the wish it expresses than as an account of his work hitherto. Naturally enough he tries to implement this wish, partly by including less and less dramatic verse in succeeding collections, and partly by making sure his own beliefs, such as they were, are not effaced in the dramatic poems. I think T. J. Collins is absolutely right to detect a real dissatisfaction on Browning's part with his achievement so far, including the dramatic monologues, in 1846, and to suggest that he only gets a new lease of conviction when religious belief starts to be tied into his programme for poetry.[1] In the *Men and Women* volumes the dramatic poems (though

[1] T. J. Collins, *Robert Browning's Moral-Aesthetic Theory 1833–1855*, 1967, chap. 4.

proportionally fewer than in any previous collection) often use what we may call 'positive ironies', unlike the negative irony of 'The Tomb at St Praxed's' and 'Cloister (Spanish)'. When this happens Browning's basic unconcern, by this time, with the imitation of character rather than the expression of attitude becomes even clearer. In 'The Tomb at St Praxed's' the bishop's disparaged lack of self-knowledge (potential to any ironic betrayal) is perfectly interpretable as a trait in his character, since Browning's attitude towards his values is disparaging also. But once the irony is positive, and what the speaker says is better and truer than he knows, this unconsciousness can only become a sort of joke rather than a trait of character. Consider the irony of *Cleon* whereby Cleon mentions but dismisses the man, Christ, whose teaching would fill out his own speculations. The force of this is a kind of nudging, poker-faced and rather clumsy joke between Browning and his reader. Cleon has dropped out of the picture. Indeed his presence in the first place seems to be little more than Browning's way of avoiding the obligation to discuss Christianity and secularism in a lucid and unmealy-mouthed fashion.

To sum up this discussion of the fifth, or 'dramatic', aspect: it turns out that one of the situations in which it is necessary that the reader does not take the utterance as the author's, the exotic poem situation, is familiar in English poetry before Browning, and that the other situation of this kind means in some cases not simply that we don't suppose Browning to be the speaker, but that we also nonetheless know him to be the author. How intelligible does the full list now seem for a Victorian genre? Not surprisingly the genre has clear naturalistic lineaments. The features mentioned under (2), (3), and (4) are those of mimesis, disinterested observation, and plausibility; moreover, and this is worth stressing, the colloquialism specified in (2) is the most consistently distinguishing trait of Browning's dramatic monologues. But the first feature seems most readily intelligible alongside other virtuoso characteristics of the form, and the fifth requirement, as we have qualified it, also tells a rather different story. It points out that the verisimilar imitation of a plausible utterance (colloquialism apart) was achieved at least as successfully by writers in the eighteenth century, and that some of the best known of Browning's monologues are unequivocal expressions of the author's attitude.

Now the latter is also very much the character of some of those innovatory uses of the dramatic principle I mentioned at the outset, like George Eliot's invented mottoes. Indeed I would suggest that it is mainly because of this rather puzzling character in these innovations—that they are supposed to be someone else's utterance but simply express the author's view—that we notice that they are dramatic at all. After all *Wuthering Heights* is dramatic in its form, and indeed might stand a better chance than many of Browning's dramatic monologues of masquerading as the genuine utterance of Mr Lockwood and Nelly Dean. But somehow this is not what we are looking for in the Victorian use of the dramatic principle; it is rather like the use to which many Gothic novels put it. Perhaps when we suppose we are impressed by how much Victorian literature is dramatic we are really being impressed by how much of it is dramatic for no clear reason.

Browning moves slowly towards this puzzling, characteristically Victorian kind of dramatic writing in the period up to 1855. He passes from an empirical to an expressive use of the dramatic principle. He leaves behind the monologue as 'a living semiotical display . . . ascertaining some important psychical principle'.[1] He does not lose his interest in human psychology or his powers of subtle characterization, but the typical Browning procedure, betraying irony, is not put at their service; instead Andrea del Sarto's insight into his personality is as good as ours. Nor is there any longer that sense of a personality conceived as a *datum* from the real world—the homicide, the religious maniac—which it is the poem's difficult but rewarding job to explain, a problem, as Symons well puts it,[2] to solve. But Browning perhaps never got over his early and I think very natural feeling that dramatic writing was properly a means of objectivity, incompatible with 'speaking out', since, as I mentioned, the proportion of dramatic poetry in the three collections of short poems up to 1855 is progressively reduced; all but two of the poems in the 1842 pamphlet, *Dramatic Lyrics*, are clearly dramatic; the proportion is less than half in the 1845 collection, despite its title, and only about 2/5 in the *Men and Women* volumes, making the description in 'One Word More', 'fifty men and women / Naming . . . fifty poems', quite false.

The period of Browning's real commitment to dramatic writing runs up to about the end of 1844. There is also a brilliance, energy, and confi-

[1] This striking phrase is used about the role of the drama in general by Beddoes in 1825: *The Works of Thomas Lovell Beddoes*, ed H. W. Donner, 1935, 609.

[2] Arthur Symons, 'Is Browning Dramatic?', *Browning Society Papers*, No. 28, 1885, 5.

dent originality about the short poems of this period that I miss in Browning's later writing. So I now turn to consider some aspects of the background to the monologues of these years. After all it is here that part of the answer to the basic question 'Why did Browning write short dramatic poems?' must be sought. Whatever subsequent uses Browning put the dramatic principle to he clearly continued to exploit it partly because he had exploited it extensively in the '30s and '40s, and was associated by his public with its use. And to the question 'why did Browning write short dramatic poems in the '30s and '40s?' one answer is 'because he was primarily a playwright'. But to understand the nature of this connection we must consider the whole matter of the acted and unacted drama at the time, and Browning's views on the two forms.

## II

In 1841 a commentator could speak of 'the universal recognition of the division of the Drama of our time, into the Acted and the Unacted',[1] but the distinction was at least twenty years old. It was sufficiently automatic by the early 1820s for *Blackwoods* to entitle their theatre reviews 'Notices of the Acted Drama in London'. The grounds for the distinction are laid in the Romantic period, when every significant poet turned his hand to drama and none with any great theatrical success, and when good texts of the older legitimate drama, Shakespeare and his contemporaries, were familiar to literary men but not used in the theatre. On the other hand the accepted gap between the two types did not cause much disquiet until the agitation of the early thirties to restore legitimate drama to the stage. Lamb was more than happy with the idea that Shakespeare should never be acted. Scott, writing in 1819,[2] anticipates the lobbying of the 1830s in deploring the 'monopoly' in legitimate theatre of Covent Garden and Drury Lane, but he nevertheless proposes that 'minds of a high poetic temperature may . . . receive a more lively impression from the solitary perusal than from the representation, of one of Shakespeare's plays'.

[1] F. G. Tomlins, *The Relative value of the Acted and the Unacted Drama*, 1841, 3.
[2] In 'An Essay on the Drama' *The Prose Works of Sir Walter Scott Bart.*, 1834, V, 219–395.

Disquiet about the situation is a mark of a later period: roughly the period in which Browning was writing his plays. This fact is neglected by historians of the later agitation who see the legitimate drama of the twenties and thirties as disqualified for production by anti-theatrical attitudes inherited from the Romantic period. Probably it was these attitudes that disqualified the drama, but the playwrights and their supporters are perfectly genuine in their desire to get serious drama produced. There is a new wave of feeling among literary men, first effectively expressed in Lytton's Parliamentary campaign of 1832, that the existence of a body of serious, unacted English drama, both actual and, it was trusted, potential, was anomalous. The idea of a 'decline in the drama' starts to be voiced, as it will be for decades. And theatrical men like Macready, who were not in favour of all the proposed reforms, shared this desire to restore legitimacy to the stage. The chief aims in the Parliamentary effort were to give playwrights copyright for any performance of their works and to repeal the legislation, dating back to the reign of Charles II, which appeared to give a monopoly in legitimate drama to the 'patent' theatres of Drury Lane and Covent Garden. The alternative picture was of the other London theatres, the 'minors', joyfully abandoning their diet of burletta and melodrama for the legitimate drama which the vast, actor-dominated patent houses had rejected or misperformed. One can sense in the proceedings of the House of Commons Select Committee on Dramatic Literature of 1832 (chaired by Lytton) the pressure of this enthusiasm for the legitimate stage. The mass of evidence heard is against the expected renaissance, and even when favourable is often elicited by loaded questioning. Moreover the most enthusiastic prognostications tend to come from witnesses not directly involved in the theatre, even simply from keen theatre-goers. Yet the Committee endorsed the proposed reforms.

This wave of feeling was perhaps partly provoked into existence by the more vigorous attempts that were made in the twenties to enforce the patent theatres' monopoly,[1] but it was mainly, I believe, a spontaneous shift in literary fashion. It is the context of Browning's first venture in the drama in 1836 (the start of a ten years' campaign), and of Macready's excited hope that he might prompt in the young writer 'a spirit of poetry whose influence would elevate, ennoble, and adorn our degraded

[1] See W. Nicholson, *The Struggle for a Free Stage in London*, 1906, chap. 11.

drama'.[1] But Browning's failure in the theatre was not due to the 'monopoly', or to the copyright laws, or to the Lord Chamberlain's powers as
censor. Although his friend Arnould invoked those bugbears of the re-
formers, 'the miserable, great, chilly house' of Drury Lane and the
tyranny of the famous actor (in this case Macready),[2] in extenuating
Browning's final failure with *A Blot in the 'Scutcheon* it was not these factors that drove Browning from the stage. Nor were the obstacles that
Lytton sought to remove the ones that really prevented the revival of the
legitimate stage. The warnings are clear in the Select Committee's evidence, but were ignored: the 'minors' were seldom of intimate, Globe
proportions; they actually already had considerable freedom to perform
legitimate drama; provincial theatres not restricted by the patents were
not flourishing centres for legitimate drama; authors could make handsome sums from their plays without the protection of copyright. The
reforms were not fully achieved until 1843 with the abolition of the
patents (copyright to plays had been secured in 1833), but the lack of
result was predictable. If anything the 'decline of the drama' got worse.
Not a single theatre was built in London, for example, in the next
twenty years.[3] By the late fifties the deterioration was being put down to
the very measure that was earlier intended to be its chief solution, the
abolition of the patents.[4]

Clearly the difficulties for a legitimate stage went deeper. And as far as
the contemporary legitimate drama was concerned the trouble, as several writers have suggested,[5] lay in the aesthetic attitudes that inform it.

[1] *The Diaries of William Charles Macready 1833–1851*, ed W. Toynbee, 1912,
I, 277.

[2] *Domett Letters*, 1906, 65–6.

[3] For a useful survey of the continuing 'decline' see D. Ganzel, 'Patent
Wrongs and Patent Theatres: Drama and the Law in the early Nineteenth
Century', *PMLA*, LXXVI, 1961, 384–96.

[4] E.g. J. W. Cole, *The Life and Theatrical Times of Charles Kean F.S.A.*, 1859,
I, 9.

[5] See E. Reynolds, *Early Victorian Drama (1830–1870)*, 1936; Allardyce
Nicoll, *A History of the English Drama*, IV, 1955; H. W. Donner, *Thomas
Lovell Beddoes: the Making of a Poet*, 1935; R. M. Fletcher, *English Romantic
Drama 1795–1843*, 1966. The accounts of the attitudes involved given in
some of these books are extremely naïve; the best by far seems to me to be
Fletcher's. For very strained attempts to argue that the conditions of thea-

Some of the most acute and entertaining exposures of the self-disqualifying aspects of this drama are to be found in comment of the day, especially in the uninhibited comment of the melodramatist and manager, Edward Fitzball, and the even more uninhibited comment of Alfred Bunn, manager in his time of both Drury Lane and Covent Garden. Both give funny, persuasive pictures of the contemporary legitimate playwright and his wares from the managerial point of view. Here is part of Bunn's:

> A tragedy of nearly six hundred pages, written by an author totally unknown, and likely ever to remain so, was sent me by one particular friend of mine, and strongly recommended by three others. The first was a moonlight scene, and in the opening soliloquy thereof the hero, gazing on the unclouded glory of Diana, accused her, despite her beauty and alleged chastity, of intriguing—(with whom can the reader imagine?)—with the *Man in* THE MOON.[1]

There are also some amusing parodies of the legitimate drama in Gilbert Abbott à Beckett's *The Quizzology of the British Drama* (1846).

Even though the three volumes of Bunn's *The Stage* are effectively an extended defence of the non-legitimate theatre against the legitimate school, it is Fitzball who is the more analytical about the deficiencies of the latter's conception of drama. His main complaint is that this school does not sufficiently value action as opposed to poetry—neither for its expressiveness, nor for the satisfaction of a well-constructed plot.[2] This important criticism had been the substance (stretched rather thin by the end of the series) of Darley's lively and pointed 'Letters to the Dramatists of the Day', which ran in the *London Magazine* between July 1823 and January 1824:

> *Action* is the essence of drama; nay, its definition ... But that essence ... you, Gentlemen, seem, with one consent sedulously to avoid meddling with ... You seem to think that the whole virtue of

---

trical production really were to blame see U. C. Nag, 'The English Theatre of the Romantic Revival', *Nineteenth Century*, CIV, 1928, 384–98, and E. B. Watson, *Sheridan to Robertson*, 1926.

[1] Alfred Bunn, *The Stage: both before and behind the Curtain*, 1840, 79.

[2] Edward Fitzball, *Thirtyfive years of a Dramatic Author's Life*, 1859, I, 108, 217, &c.

tragedy lies in its *poeticity*.[1]

Darley is unusual in criticizing the unstageability of the legitimate drama when he himself belongs in the authorial rather than the managerial camp, but attitudes had not yet hardened in 1823. The complaint about lack of action must have been continuously voiced. Browning was evidently sensitive to it (if only because of what Macready thought about the lack of action in *Strafford*, and its necessity for good drama[2]) when he vainly tried to recommend *A Blot in the 'Scutcheon* to the actor:

> I have written a spick and span new Tragedy (a sort of compromise between my own notion and yours—as I understand it, at least) . . . there is *action* in it.[3]

If we go a little into the nature of this emphasis on 'poeticity', and indifference to action, we will see that it was not just an unfortunate aesthetic preference that made the contemporary legitimate drama a bit dull on stage, but the expression of a basically atheatrical notion of drama. To start with the taste for poeticity, as G. H. Lewes clearly recognized, was very largely due to the example of the 'Old Drama':

> Unhappily all our poets could learn in that Old Drama was precisely that of which (if they were poets) they stood in least need, viz. poetry; finding *that* there, they learned to think that poetry was enough to make a drama![4]

Of course the only channel for virtually the whole of the Old Drama was the printed page, so the legitimate dramatists were strongly influenced by models that they had only encountered as a reading experience, and never assessed as spoken verse combining with stage action.

More important, poeticity before action implies the assumption that the real creative and expressive activity in drama is the author's (which was usually thought of as private and Olympian). All the creation and expression intrinsic to a drama has been completed with the completion of the author's text; the manager and actors simply exhibit this text visibly. So naturally the author's medium, the words, receive the maxi-

[1] *London Magazine*, VIII, 1823, 85.

[2] *Diaries of Macready*, I, 389–90.

[3] *Wise Letters*, 5.

[4] In 'The Old and Modern Dramatists', 1850, *Dramatic Essays of John Forster and George Henry Lewes*, ed W. Archer and R.W. Lowe, 1896, 101–4.

mum heightening. That part of the performance which cannot be fully specified in the authorial activity, the action as opposed to speech, is either neglected or, perhaps more interestingly, assimilated into text. By this I mean the effect Beddoes very astutely spotted in *Strafford*, an effect apparently favoured by current opinion:

> the Examiner is quite rapturous about Strafford: altho' I confess that the extracts, he chooses and praises, appear to me not exactly drama- tic. One is a dialogue between two people describing Pym's appear- ance, action &c in a style which has been approved of by critics of late and considered highly graphic. But is it not very artificial?[1]

Beddoes is referring to the opening of Act IV Scene 2, a passage in which a group of spectators specify not only Pym's actions but also those of the King, Strafford, and some nearby curtains. The poet is reaching out with his text to try and impose an absurd degree of control on the play in per- formance. Moreover it is in the poetic text that this is done, not in stage- directions; the author's versifying and the play are virtually coextensive.

This important bias against the theatre is very clearly illustrated by Lamb in his essay 'On the Tragedies of Shakespeare considered with Ref- erence to their Fitness for Stage Representation' of 1811.[2] Indeed the lop- sidedness of his view must nowadays appear rather breathtaking. It hardly seems credible that the following passage describes, not what an actor has to do, but what the author does, and what it is impossible for any actor to emulate:

> To know the internal workings and movements of a great mind, of an Othello or a Hamlet for instance, the *when* and the *why* and the *how far* they should be moved; to what pitch a passion is becoming; to give the reins and to pull in the curb exactly at the moment when the drawing in or the slackening is most graceful.

All this is for Lamb unequivocally *in the text* of a great dramatic artist like Shakespeare. His view is obviously absurdly negligent of the perform- ative aspect of drama, but I shall argue soon that the complex and special response Lamb values in a reading of Shakespeare is very relevant to the aims of Browning in the dramatic monologues.

This anti-theatrical bias is still remarkably clear in the polemics of the second agitation, led by R. H. Horne, to abolish the theatrical patents.

[1] *Works*, 667.

[2] *The Works of Charles and Mary Lamb*, ed E. V. Lucas, 1903, I, 97–111.

This starts within a couple of years of the rejection of Lytton's bill by the Lords in 1832. With their continuing enthusiasm for a legitimate stage Horne and the others defend the necessity of performance, but invariably the triviality or inconsistency of the defence shows how unconnected the agitation is with a real feeling for drama on the stage. In one of the first shots in the new campaign John Denman feels forced to reply 'no' to the question 'Could not plays have the desired effect, by being confined to the study?' because 'the young may here [in the theatre] learn the world, without danger of incurring in reality the dear-bought experience of fools and knaves' and 'heedless and illiterate people would be totally unconscious of the existence of some of the finest compositions in the English language'.[1] In the little faction led by Horne (and sustained by endless admiring citations of each other's polemics) both the Mayhew brothers played a part. Here is Edward Mayhew's extraordinarily tepid defence of the theatre as a medium for drama:

> it does not follow therefore, that an author should despise the advantages to be derived from a judicious use of the properties and scenes of the theatre. The interest must be intellectual; yet on the stage the imagination of an audience . . . may be stimulated by the introduction of such accessories.[2]

The publisher and journalist F. G. Tomlins, almost as prolific on these matters as Horne, obviously felt the justice of complaints about lack of action in the unacted drama, and goes out of his way to declare himself a believer in its necessity: 'Action . . . is the essential and vital fibre that defines what is dramatic'. But the concession is only skin-deep. Within three pages he concludes his address with this unencouraging vision of the revived drama:

> You have listened to my lecture; why should others not sit in a larger room with you, and listen to a beautiful poem, recited with all the adornments that graceful elocution, fine painting, and energetic gesture could give to it?[3]

Despite the paradoxical enthusiasm for a legitimate stage the old anti-theatrical views, rooted in Romantic criticism, are still strong. A drama is coextensive with the author's activity, an expression of his 'strongest

[1] John Denman, *The Drama Vindicated*, 1835, 42.

[2] Edward Mayhew, *Stage Effect*, 1840, 57–8.

[3] *Acted and Unacted Drama*, 14.

impulses',[1] which he may or may not choose to make public:

> Such men may write an occasional tragedy for their own satis-
> faction, or that of a friend, but they do not deign to offer them to the
> be-devilled bear-garden of the royal patent theatres! They prefer re-
> tiring into the wilds of Yorkshire, Cumberland, or North Wales.[2]

A drama is identifiable with the author's text; it is essentially a kind of
poetry: 'The unacted Dramatist . . . is a poet, and not only a playwright
. . . This is poetry of the highest kind.'[3] Indeed drama needn't have the
literal form of a play:

> Stage-plays are not of necessity dramas, and more truly dramatic
> elements may be found in the novelist's works than in the theatrical
> writer's. The dramatic spirit of our age, of this very year, is to be
> found more living and real in the pages of Hood, Dickens, Mrs
> Gore, and Mrs Trollope, than in the playhouse pieces.[4]

Hence the essence of serious drama is not physical but ideal and intellectual—not necessarily requiring the intervention of the stage and its
physical accoutrements: 'The mechanist, the orchestra, and prop-
erty-man would be reduced to their proper level, and mind would be
left to compete with mind'.[5] Horne sums up the anti-theatrical drift of
the agitation in one sentence: 'The Drama is a root; a theatrical show is a
mere blossom'.[6]

Broadly speaking Browning's career as a dramatist is another expression of the paradox I have been trying to illustrate in the agitation for
a legitimate stage. Like Lytton and his followers, and later Horne, there
is a strong and genuine wish for a revival of legitimate drama on the
London stage, but the 'drama' is simultaneously understood in a sense
that disqualifies it for effective theatrical production. We have already
seen how some of Browning's plays provoked responses that more or less

[1] R. H. Horne, *The New Spirit of the Age*, chap. 16.

[2] R. H. Horne, *Exposition of the False Medium and Barriers Excluding Men of
Genius from the Public*, 1833, 43.

[3] Tomlins, *Acted and Unacted Drama*, 6.

[4] Horne, *New Spirit*, chap. 16.

[5] F. G. Tomlins, *The Past and Present State of Dramatic Art and Literature*, 24.
See also Mayhew above, and Horne's preface to A. W. Schlegel's *A Course
of Lectures on Dramatic Art and Literature*, 1840.

[6] *New Spirit*, chap. 16.

explicitly relate them to the issues of the day: Macready's hopes for *Strafford* and his disappointment at its lack of action, Beddoes' observation on its undramatic method, Arnould's extenuation of the failure of *A Blot in the 'Scutcheon* in performance. But what is the detailed story of Browning's views on the nature of drama, unacted and acted, and how does it bear on his turning to a special kind of unacted drama, the monologue?

At the 1846 anniversary dinner of the Literary Fund Browning was toasted by Talfourd as the representative of 'dramatic literature'. In his toast Talfourd betrayed that belief in the irrelevance of theatrical performance so typical of his time:

> whether he shall present those works his imagination may vivify, upon the actual scene, to touch our hearts and senses with electricity, or only on that ideal stage which all men erect in their own minds.[1]

Apparently Browning was too shy to reply at length. This is a pity, because we know he was planning to 'speak for about five minutes on the advantages of the Press over the stage as a medium of communication of the Drama',[2] and it would be interesting to have his reasons. Clearly Browning has gone beyond mere indifference to the theatre of the kind Talfourd exhibits. His hostility must surely be partly due to his galling treatment by Macready over *A Blot in the 'Scutcheon*, and its consequent failure in 1843. Perhaps Browning was also disillusioned by the failure of the repeal of the patents in 1843 to create in the minor theatres centres of legitimate drama.

But his hostility probably also owes something to his association with Horne. It was Browning who late in 1843 provided the motto for Horne's fighting chapter on the neglect of the unacted drama in *The New Spirit of the Age*, the Knowles and Macready chapter (the remark I have already quoted about drama and the novel occurs here).[3] Browning showed he well understood its purpose when he referred to it as 'The Dramatists and the Stage' chapter, and he suggests a quotation from Joseph Hall's fourth satire that is thoroughly apt for Horne's line of argument:

[1] *Royal Corporation of the Literary Fund, list of members &c* (1846), 33.

[2] *Letters*, II, 701.

[3] *New Letters*, 31–2.

> *Too popular is Tragic Poesy*
> *Straining his tip-toes for a farthing fee.*
> *Painters and Poets, hold your ancient right!*
> *Write what you* will—*and write not,*—*what you* might!
> *Their limits be their list,*—*their reason, will!*

Browning also proposes as a motto the lines from the Prelude to Part
One of Goethe's *Faust* where 'The "Poet", there, answers the solicita-
tions or requirements of the "Messenger"—that he should popularize
and degrade his style and matter'. It is clear, I think, from the way
Browning enters into the spirit of Horne's chapter, and from his considering Goethe's poet to reply 'famously', that he is in sympathy with
Horne's elevated view of the dramatic author's role, and with his indifference to, even contempt for, the performative aspect of drama. His
remark of a few months later about the relative value of actors and
authors is in keeping: 'The poorest Man of Letters . . . I ever knew is of
far higher talent than the best actor I ever expect to know'.[1]

Earlier in his career Browning had almost certainly held very different
views on the stage from those he betrays after February 1843. His enthusiastic plunge into writing for Macready in 1836 and his subsequent
tenacity in theatrical composition suggest this. And in the very interesting preface to *Paracelsus* he acutely questions the value of a reading
text that preserves the form of a drama; the implication is that drama is
for the stage and not for the study:

> I have endeavoured to write a poem, not a drama . . . I do not very
> well understand what is called a Dramatic Poem, wherein all those
> restrictions only submitted to on account of compensating good in
> the original scheme are scrupulously retained, as though for some
> special fitness in themselves.

Ten years later, at the Literary Fund dinner, Browning might have come
close to publicly contradicting this statement.

But we have already seen how in the climate of these years a real enthusiasm for the stage could consort paradoxically with the assumption
that performance was no essential part of a serious drama. There are signs
that even before 1843, while he was still ambitious of success in the
theatre, Browning could think as readily of the press as a satisfactory
medium for the drama. In this connection his remarks in the 'Advertisement' to *Pippa Passes* are revealing, for they clearly suggest that stage

[1] *Wise Letters*, 10.

drama and written drama are basically indistinguishable, both in their nature as works of art and in the relation they set up with their audience:

> Two or three years ago I wrote a play, about which the chief matter I care to recollect at present is, that a Pitfull of goodnatured people applauded it:——ever since, I have been desirous of doing something in the same way that should better reward their attention. What follows I mean for the first of a series of Dramatical Pieces, to come out at intervals, and I amuse myself by fancying that the cheap mode in which they appear will for once help me to a sort of Pit-audience again.

Moreover Browning will print in the 1842 *Dramatic Lyrics* member of the series a fragment from a projected play, 'Artemis Prologizes',[1] and this despite his comment on the illogicality of such a procedure in the *Paracelsus* preface.

So can we locate a shift to an acceptance of the 'unacted' drama as a genre sometime between *Paracelsus* and *Pippa Passes*? After all these two works seem generically rather similar, but Browning prefaces the first by calling it a 'poem', not a 'drama' (and indeed claiming not to know what a 'Dramatic Poem' is), and prefaces the second by saying it's 'in the same way as *Strafford*'. There is something of a shift, but the difference between the two descriptions is not as great as might appear. In the *Paracelsus* preface Browning is withholding the terms 'drama' and 'dramatic' from his work only in a rather special and untypical sense. On this occasion these terms connote an 'external machinery of incidents' (whereas in *Paracelsus* he has, in a famous formula, 'ventured to display somewhat minutely the mood itself in its rise and progress'). Browning does not exclude the possibility of a purely reading drama in the sense in which he habitually uses the word, namely, works consisting of imaginary utterances. Indeed in the same preface he clearsightedly, and portentously, recognizes the rich possibilities of drama in this sense when operating in the new medium of the printed page, the 'new facilities placed at the author's disposal by the vehicle'. So when Browning came to distrust the stage in the mid-forties the grounds of his distrust went back to 1841, and probably to the outset of his career. Prompted by his contact with Horne and by his own failure on the stage Browning developed an explicit recognition of the superiority of the press to the stage for his kind of drama,

---

[1] For the origins of this piece see Mrs Sutherland Orr, *Life and Letters of Robert Browning*, 1891, 13.

but the recognition was rooted in his earlier ambivalent feeling about the theatre, which was in turn rooted in a bias that had prevailed with many literary men in England from early in the century. What does this picture of a continuous but developing assent to a widely shared antitheatrical bias imply for the dramatic monologues?

On the one hand there can be little serious doubt that none of the dramatic monologues would be enhanced by theatrical production. I find the theatrical version of 'Porphyria' proposed by H. B. Charlton[1] almost completely inadequate to the interesting content of this poem. Much more important, I believe the long-standing bias that lies behind this untheatrical quality leads to definite and crucial features of the dramatic monologue as Browning used it, and not just to its general aptness for page rather than stage. First of all there is the general point that this bias had at its heart an exclusive emphasis on the author and his artistic activity. So the strong sense of Browning's agency in the dramatic monologues and, increasingly, of his attitudes is a natural enough development. It is implicit in views that disqualified the unacted drama in general for the stage. Virtuoso display by the author is not surprising in a dramatic genre that grew up at a time when even serious acted drama was thought to be a manifestation of its author's creativity alone. In particular, the first kind of virtuosity the dramatic monologue calls for, namely the giving of virtually *all* the facts within the versified text (the first feature in the list I proposed) is also the most literal manifestation of this emphasis on the author's activity. We have already seen it illustrated in the way the verse text of parts of *Strafford* performs the role of stage-directions.

Secondly, there is the most striking resemblance between Lamb's account of the essence of Shakespearean drama (which in Lamb's view is lost on the stage) and Browning's achievement in the dramatic monologues, particularly the early ones. I am sure the similarity cannot be fortuitous. Of course direct influence is not involved, but there must be a common source for the critic's ideas and the poet's work, a common stock of assumptions and insights about the drama. Not only does Lamb see the main function of speech in Shakespeare to be the revelation of 'the inner structure and workings of mind in a character' (a general Romantic emphasis which Langbaum rightly spots as a precondition of the drama-

[1] 'Browning as a Dramatist', *Bulletin of the John Rylands Library*, XXIII, 1939, 57–67.

tic monologue), but he feels the bare text, the words on the page, to be
dense with subtly controlled but unequivocal indices of this 'inner structure'. Whether or not we agree with Lamb that Shakespeare's text alone
does this enormous job of unambiguous character-revelation there is no
mistaking the suggestiveness of this idea for some of the dramatic monologues. Browning, we may say, tries to create in the dramatic monologue the rich notation of character that Lamb imagined he found in
Shakespeare. But the really startling anticipation is in Lamb's discussion
of the moral effect of this verbal revelation of character. He feels that it
can pull our moral judgement in the opposite direction from the action
because it extenuates, by explaining, otherwise deplorable or contemptible behaviour. Lamb's account of the kind of character that typically
results could almost be an account of Porphyria's murderer or of
Johannes Agricola (indeed all Lamb's examples of this effect in Shakespeare are characters who exhibit madness or homicidal violence):

> So little do the actions comparatively affect us, that while the
> impulses, the inner mind in all its perverted greatness, solely seems
> real and is exclusively attended to, the crime is comparatively
> nothing.

On the other hand Browning's distrust of the theatre is a shifting
affair. As his belief in what the stage can offer him narrows and is eventually extinguished so he makes his unacted drama do different jobs for
him. He felt the label 'dramatic' to be inappropriate in one sense for *Paracelsus* because of the absence of an 'external machinery' in that work, and
'machinery', 'incidents', 'circumstances' added to a 'mood' seems to have
been for Browning the special characteristic of the acted drama, at least
in his early years. This is clear in how he tackles the planning of *Luria*:
'give me your notion of a thorough self-devotement, self-forgetting . . .
What circumstances will best draw out, set forth this feeling?'.[1] The
unacted drama of these years—*Pauline* (which is dramatic if we accept
Browning's account of its composition), *Paracelsus*, 'Porphyria',
'Johannes Agricola', 'Rudel and the Lady of Tripoli'—is correspondingly naked, an illustration of the 'mood itself'. But once that blur-
ring of the distinction between stage drama and reading drama signalled
in the *Pippa Passes* advertisement sets in,'external machinery' is no longer
the mark of the theatrical writing alone. We get fully-fledged narrative

[1] Orr, *Life*, 104.

circumstance in association with dramatic procedure (notably in 'The Flight of the Duchess'), and generally much more indication of the physical conditions of the utterance. Once Browning has finally abandoned the acted drama, and decided on 'the advantages of the Press over the stage as a medium of communication of the Drama', the monologues become dense with circumstantial detail. The technique of giving such detail via the speaker, which Beddoes spotted as so adrift for an acted play, flourishes in its rightful place in the non-theatrical, virtuoso context of the most celebrated monologues.

But the naked dramatic writing of the thirties is of course not simply conceived in contrast to the circumstantial, theatrical drama. Browning had nothing planned for the stage when he wrote *Paracelsus* and *Pauline*. For this reason our question 'Why did Browning write short dramatic poems in the '30s and '40s?' is far from completely answered by reference to his work as a playwright. We have also to look at the origins of the two earliest dramatic monologues, 'Porphyria' and 'Johannes Agricola', which were written and published before Browning had even thought of his first stage drama. However much the impulse that produced these two remarkable poems was overlaid by new aims and the effect of new artistic ventures in the later monologues, they clearly have a special claim on our attention. Here Browning uses for the first time the genre for which he is most celebrated. In this sense these 120 lines in the *Monthly Repository* for January 1836 bring us to bedrock.

## III

The exact force of Browning's distinction between 'mood' and 'circumstance' is not really clear, but one important consequence comes out in a reflection on the interpretation of Strafford's character:

> *He was consistent to himself throughout* . . . those who carry their researches into the moral nature of mankind, cannot do better than impress on their minds, at the outset, that in the regions they explore, they are to expect no monsters—no essentially discordant termination to any 'mulier Formosa superne'. Infinitely and distinctly various as appear the shifting hues of our common nature when subjected to the prism of CIRCUMSTANCE, each ray into which it is broken is no less in itself a primitive colour, susceptible,

indeed, of vast modification, but incapable of further division'.[1]

The optics of the passage are a bit puzzling, but the drift is clear: 'circumstance' will make a person's motivations seem incoherent and unstable but when these are properly identified they will be found to be unified and permanent. In a word, a man's character will be 'consistent' if analysed in enough depth. This lesson of consistency is one thing the first two monologues try to enforce. Johannes Agricola's mystical sense of God's love and his vicious spiritual elitism are seen to be two aspects of the same disposition. The seamless transition in the poem from one to the other enacts this. Porphyria's lover becomes her murderer precisely because he loves, not because he has come to hate. In killing her he is even in a way her physical 'lover'. The distinction between the 'circumstances' of loving and murdering is dispelled when both are seen as the same 'primitive colour' in the soul's spectrum. The later title, 'Porphyria's Lover', draws attention to this in its unexpected refusal to denote the main narrative content.

The principle of consistency helps to make Johannes Agricola and Porphyria's lover the surprisingly sympathetic figures they are. Spiritual elitism and homicide start to feel venial, even justifiable because they flow out of motives we condone or approve. But this effect should not be mistaken for a defence of the speakers. Accounts of the two poems along these lines are not convincing; at any rate Browning is surely not, in 'Porphyria', trying to 'preach' a 'doctrine' of the superiority of death to a compromise in life.[2] The degree of sympathy is remarkable, but it arises from a remarkably bold illustration of the idea that human motives will be found coherent if analysed in enough depth. The natural way to illustrate such an assumption is to show that alien impulses are continuous with, even in a way logically continuous with, familiar and accepted impulses. And this creates another source of sympathy: an ugly impulse is treated dispassionately. But both sources of sympathy are due to a central endeavour which is empirical: the analysis, or proposed analysis, of a

---

[1] *Robert Browning's Prose Life of Strafford*, ed : H. Firth and F. J. Furnivall, 1892, 60–1. This passage is agreed on all hands to be Browning's. For a convincing high estimate of the extent of Browning's contribution to the biography in general see W. S. Peterson's article in *Browning Newsletter*, No. 3, 1969, 12–22.

[2] As argued by C. R. Tracy in 'Porphyria's Lover', *MLN*, LII, 1937, 579–90.

strange but plausible state of mind.

Recent opinion has, I believe correctly, turned against the idea that these poems are in part or wholly covert expressions of Browning's own beliefs. D. Eggenschinler's analysis of 'Porphyria' as an empirically minded study of its speaker seems to me particularly good.[1] In the present context of considering the background to the monologues' I want to take up the disputed question of the joint 'Madhouse Cells' title. In printings of the two poems between 1842 and 1863 Browning gave the pair this overall title, but did he conceive of his speakers as lunatics in 1836? If he did I would think it becomes ever harder to read the poems as expressions of Browning's beliefs. C. R. Tracy has to argue that the addition of the 'Madhouse Cells' title was a kind of cowardice. But if Browning had meant Johannes Agricola and Porphyria's lover for madmen in 1836 the addition of the title could be simply a guide to the reader, a protection, it is true, but against the misinterpretation of his poems rather than the exposure of his personality. I shall suggest later why Browning might have removed the title in 1863.

One certain fact about Browning's original intentions, a fact also obscured from 1863 but very clear in the *Bells and Pomegranates* format in 1842, is that the two poems are companion pieces. They are written in exactly the same form: twelve five-line stanzas in iambic pentameters rhyming ABABB, an exceptional form for Browning. Any proof that either of them was conceived as the utterance of a lunatic would create a strong presupposition (especially in view of the later joint title) that both speakers are thought of as lunatics. The facts about the origins of 'Porphyria' make it almost certain that Browning intended to portray a madman; at least we can be sure this possibility was strongly before his mind.

In 'Porphyria' Browning used at least two sources of fairly recent date. The first is a piece in *Blackwoods* for 1818, known to be by John Wilson, called 'Extracts from Gosschen's Diary'. This purports to be the transcript of the MS memoir of a German priest called to the death-cell of a young man condemned for the murder of his mistress. I quote the section in which the clearest similarities to 'Porphyria' occur:

> Do you think there was no pleasure in murdering her? I grasped her
> by that radiant, that golden hair, I bared those snow-white

[1] D. Eggenschinler, 'Psychological Complexity in "Porphyria's Lover"', *VP*, VIII, 1970, 39–48.

breasts,—I dragged her sweet body towards me, and, as God is my witness, I stabbed, and stabbed her with this dagger, forty times, through and through her heart. She never so much as gave one shriek, for she was dead in a moment,—but she would not have shrieked had she endured pang after pang, for she saw my face of wrath turned upon her,—and she knew that my wrath was just, and that I did right to murder her who would have forsaken her lover in his insanity.

I laid her down upon a bank of flowers,—that were soon stained with her blood. I saw the dim blue eyes beneath the half-closed lids,—that face so changeful in its living beauty was now fixed as ice, and the balmy breath came from her sweet lips no more. My joy, my happiness, was perfect.[1]

The claimed absence of suffering to the victim, and some of her physical traits—the white flesh, the golden hair, and above all the blue eyes still visible—are details that are strongly echoed by Browning. Interesting aspects of the murderer—the erotic nature of his act and his religious fanaticism—are also retained in 'Porphyria' in a subdued and modified form.

Browning's friend Bryan Procter ('Barry Cornwall') acknowledged this *Blackwoods* piece as the source of a passage in his poem 'Marcian Colonna'—the title piece in a volume which had considerable success when published in 1820.[2] Here Colonna sits beside his murdered mistress:

> He sate and watch'd her, as a nurse might do,
> And saw the dull film steal across the blue,
> And saw and felt her sweet forgiving smile,
> That, as she died, parted her lips the while:
> Her hand?—its pulse was silent—her voice gone,
> But patience in her smile still faintly shone,
> And in her closing eyes a tenderness,
> That seem'd as she would fain Colonna bless.
> She died, and spoke no word: and still he sate
> Beside her like an image. Death and Fate
> Had done what might be then: The morning sun
> Rose upon him: on him?—his task was done.

[1] '"Extracts from Gosschen's Diary" No. I', *Blackwood's Magazine*, III, 1818, 596–8.

[2] According to R. W. Armour, *Barry Cornwall*, 1935, 151.

> *The murderer and the murder'd—one as pale*
> *As marble shining white beneath the moon,*
> *The other dark as storms, when the winds rail*
> *At the chafed sea,—but not to calm so soon.—*
> *No bitterness, nor hate, nor dread was there;*
> *But love still clinging round a wild despair,*
> *A wintry aspect and a troubled eye,*
> *Mourning o'er youth and beauty born to die.*
>
> *Dead was she, and her mouth had fallen low,*
> *But still he watched her with a stedfast brow:*
> *Unaltered as a rock he sate, while she*
> *Lay changed to clay, and perish'd.*                    (III. xvi)

Procter omits some important features of Wilson's piece that survive in 'Porphyria' (it is rather striking that like Browning he retains the detail of the victim's visible blue eyes). Some of Procter's additions, however, are taken up by Browning: notably the traits of survival on the victim's face, and the all-night vigil throughout which the murderer is so immobile.

In both these sources not only is the murderer a lunatic, but his madness is described and discussed at some length. The Gosschen piece concludes with a plea by the murderer for mercy because of his insanity, while Procter gives over quite a lot of his poem to an attempt to convey the experience of madness, and he discusses this attempt in his preliminary 'Advertisement'. (I shall return to what Wilson and Procter have to say shortly.) Clearly Browning could not have failed to entertain the idea that Porphyria's murderer is a lunatic, as this is the essential character of his model in the two sources. But this is not tantamount to Browning's actually implementing the idea; indeed it might be that his murderer is, so to speak, an anti-lunatic, an illustration of how an act conventionally referable to insanity might be the act of a rational being. This possibility could gain support from the way in which both Wilson and Procter present insanity as a state of mind discontinuous with conscious, rational mental life, marked by delusion and frenzy. Wilson's murderer is an hereditary madman, periodically the victim of 'red-rolling dreams'. Procter's Colonna likewise snaps into maniac states: 'his soul / Rising in tumult, and his eye-balls roll / Wildly and fiery red' (III. xv).

There is none of this in Browning, but I do not think its absence need mean that Browning's murderer is any the less a madman of a different sort. To start with, these little sketches of delirium in his two sources are curiously irrelevant to the much more impressive and subtle portrayals of madness their authors give in the murder episodes. It is as if both writers cannot quite sustain their pictures of relatively cool, reflective homicidal lunacy, and have to fall back on the conventional idea of a madman's frenzy, an idea that solves all problems of motivation at a stroke. There is something particularly unconvincing about the abrupt self-diagnosis of Wilson's madman:

> 'I gazed on her one moment longer, and, all at once, I recollected that we were a family of madmen . . . Was I not once confined in a madhouse? Are these the first chains I ever wore? No'.

Also, as I have argued, Browning wants to illustrate fundamental psychological consistency in these naked monologues, and his belief that we 'are to expect no monsters' when we examine the 'moral nature of mankind' might easily have extended to his understanding of lunacy. Here also there might be a 'primitive colour' in a man's nature, not just discontinuous states of frenzy and rationality. There is reason to think that Browning could have been encouraged to such a view by contemporary ideas about insanity. I cannot offer any external evidence for his contact with these ideas, except the merely suggestive fact of his association with Procter,[1] who was one of the Metropolitan Commissioners of Lunacy from 1832. Procter's biographer, Armour, says that the appointment was a political one, and there is certainly no clear sign in Procter's writings after 1832 that his activities as Commissioner (which included visiting asylums) had any impact on Procter the literary dilettante. On the other hand the minutes of the permanent Commission (set up in 1842) show him to have been a most conscientious attender of the biweekly meetings (the minutes of the previous Commission do not appear to have survived). Definite evidence of Browning's contact with current work on lunacy is lacking but there are nonetheless suggestive similarities between certain prominent innovations in the psychiatric theory of the day and the notion of mind suggested by 'Porphyria'.

In 1836 British psychiatric theory was still undergoing a revolution

---

[1] It is not very probable that Browning actually met Procter until after the publication of the two first monologues. Griffin and Minchin say the men met 'early' in 1836.

that had been initiated in the last decade of the eighteenth century. This revolution had its various manifestations in most of the advanced European countries and in America, but the only country with which Britain maintained consistently close contact in this field was France. Both Philippe Pinel, the greatest figure in clinical psychiatry at the end of the eighteenth century, and his successor as director of the Salpétrière asylum in Paris, Jean Étienne Dominique Esquirol, exercised a profound influence on British psychiatry in the early nineteenth century through their writings and through personal contacts. As the century advances Pinelist views become increasingly automatic and increasingly implicit in British psychiatric literature. This was not simply a mark of French influence. The new French psychiatry itself owed a debt to English thinkers like Alexander Crichton, Francis Willis, and John Haslam, and continued to do so. And in the main clinical innovation of these years —the substitution of 'moral management' for physical restraint—the two countries were in step: William Tuke's humane private asylum at York, the Retreat, was founded in 1792, the same year in which Pinel made his historic gesture of unchaining at least some of the inmates of the Bicêtre.

The new thinking on the nature and cure of mental illness had practical and theoretical aspects that are naturally linked. Practically there was a new emphasis on clinical observation, on prudence and objectivity in theorizing (indeed this is one reason why theory and practice became more closely related than hitherto). Observation was also part of the new idea of therapy. The alienist must live as much with his patients as possible, talk to them without the appearance of contempt or disapproval, try to enter into their thinking, and ensure that they are treated in a decent manner physically. This is roughly what was meant by 'moral management' or 'moral treatment', and it was this innovation that had the earliest and most widespread support in Britain. The first practical move was the founding of the Retreat, and although it was not until 1839 that physical restraint was abolished in a large pauper asylum (by Conolly at Hanwell) it was generally felt to be an abuse; as early as 1814 a Select Committee of the House of Commons was conscientiously eliciting details of such extreme inhumanities as the chaining of patients to their beds for days at a time.

As far as the theory of mental illness is concerned the move towards moral treatment clearly reflects a broadly more humane view of lunatics, a feeling that they are victims of disease who deserve compassion and help, but the most important specific development behind the idea of moral treatment is an enlarged sense of the patient's rationality. This is first exhibited in two new categories in Pinel's classification of insanity: melancholia and *manie sans délire*. Pinel's use of this vocabulary is a genuflection to the ancient tradition that divided mental illnesses into melancholia and mania, but he applies it in a new way. Esquirol brought out the new sense of melancholia in coining the term *monomanie*; here is his definition of 1838 (my translation):

> The intellectual disorder is concentrated on one object alone or on a limited series of objects; the sufferers start with a false principle, from which they draw legitimate conclusions that modify their emotions and wishes; outside this partial delusion, they feel, reason, act like everybody else ... monomaniacs are not irrational, but their emotions, their personality, are perverted.[1]

So the new idea of monomania allows for a large area of the patient's mental life that will be completely rational.

The concept of rational lunacy is pressed even further in the category of *manie sans délire*, also called *folie raisonnante*. This category was probably the most celebrated single contribution Pinel made to contemporary psychiatric theory. The idea is that a lunatic may be disordered simply in his behaviour and, supposedly, in the impulses that prompt his behaviour; his intellectual powers are quite unimpaired; in particular he suffers from no delusions about the external world. The insight is an important one, though the elaborate route by which it is reached in actual exposition can make it sound rather artificial. What is involved clinically, I imagine, is the whole broad area of severe neurosis. Esquirol accepts the category and, interestingly from our point of view, applied it in 1827 to homicidal 'monomania'. In this area too there is a delusive variety of lunacy, when the murderer 'is urged on by a private belief, but a delusive one', and a rational variety:

> He is influenced by a blind instinct, by *an idea*; by *something indefinable* which drives him to kill ... even when his conscience makes him shun the horror of the act he is about to commit.

Both types will conclude their act in a manner reminiscent of Porphyria's murderer: 'After the murder he is calm, he does not think of

[1] J. E. D. Esquirol, *Des Maladies Mentales*, 1838, II, 1–2.

hiding himself'.[1]

As the preceding example might suggest there was a certain amount of lexical and conceptual confusion about these new categories, even among writers in a single language, but this twofold idea of rational lunacy is clearly traceable in British psychiatric theory from early in the nineteenth century. The notion of monomania as Esquirol defines it already had some countenance in Britain in Locke's dictum, much cited at the time, that lunatics, as opposed to idiots, reason correctly from false premises. Indeed the phrenologist Spurzheim seemed to think in 1817 that this was the full sense of Pinel's *folie raisonnante*.[2] Even an advanced psychiatrist like John Conolly—'the English Pinel'—would not allow for a degree of rationality in lunacy beyond that sanctioned by the category of monomania, but the fascinating thing about Conolly's book, *An Enquiry concerning the indications of Insanity* (1830), is how even this rather conservative view of delusion and rationality is enough to help erase any clear distinction between lunatic and sane. Indeed this is the main thrust of his plea for humane treatment:

> A strong and definable boundary between sanity and insanity [is] . . . imaginary, and . . . by being supposed to separate all who were of unsound mind from the rest of men, has unfortunately been considered a justification of certain measures against the portion condemned, which, in the case of the majority, were unnecessary and afflicting.[3]

The book has a long and remarkable opening discussion which tries to make this idea acceptable by going through the varieties of mental impairment—senility, eccentricity, and so forth—that fall below the arbitrary threshold marked 'Insanity', and suggesting that the difference is one of degree.

But the idea of a completely rational lunacy also had an increasing number of adherents in Britain. An exceptionally early advocate was the Edinburgh physician Thomas Arnold, the first man, I think, to use the important phrase 'moral insanity' to do the job of *folie raisonnante*. His

[1] J. E. D. Esquirol, 'Note sur la Monomanie-Homicide' in J. C. Hoffbauer, *Médecine Légale relative aux aliénés et aux Sourd-Muets*, 1827, 309–59. My translation again.

[2] J. G. Spurzheim, *Observations on the Deranged Manifestations of the mind*, 1817, 68.

[3] J. Conolly, *An Enquiry concerning the Indications of Insanity*, 1830, 295–6.

picture of this state nominally includes a residue of delusion, but it has clearly become rather hard to say what exactly this kind of madman is deluded about:

> That state of mind in which a person sees, hears, or otherwise perceives external objects as they really exist, as objects of sense; yet conceives such notions of the powers, properties, design, state, destination, importance, manner of existence, or the like, of things and persons, of himself and others, as appear obviously, and often grossly erroneous, or unreasonable.[1]

Arnold also saw that the idea of 'moral insanity' tended to dispel the distinction between the mad and the sane: 'In a moral sense, every fool is with propriety said to be insane'.[2] The category of *folie raisonnante* is more fully accepted some years later by P. S. Knight (in curious confusion with the idea of the lunatic's diabolical 'ingenuity', over which he 'slyly laughs'), by Thomas Mayo, and by W. B. Neville.[3] Its most important exponent was James Cowles Prichard. First of all in an article of 1833,[4] and then in an expanded version of this in the very influential *A Treatise on Insanity* (1835), Prichard argued for a crucial extension to the idea of moral insanity. The 'fact of the highest importance', discerned by Pinel and Esquirol, 'that insanity consists, in certain cases, in a morbid perversion of the affections and moral feelings exclusively' had been obscured, so Prichard believed, by the nature of the examples the Frenchman had chosen: 'in which the principal manifestations of insanity were violent fits of anger or rage'.[5] According to Prichard moral insanity can exist without even an accompanying 'excitement'. A man may be completely sane except in his one impulse to commit an 'atrocious act':

> Many instances are well known in which a sudden impulse to commit some atrocious act has arisen in the mind of a person other-

[1] Thomas Arnold, *Observations on the Nature, Kinds, Causes, and Prevention of Insanity*, 1806, 56–7.

[2] *Ibid*, 83.

[3] P. S. Knight, *Observations on the Causes, Symptoms, and Treatment of Derangement of the Mind*, 1827; Thomas Mayo, *An Essay on the Relation of the theory of Morals to Insanity*, 1834; W. B. Neville, *On Insanity*, 1836.

[4] 'Insanity', *The Cyclopaedia of Practical Medicine*, ed J. Forbes, A. Tweedie, and J. Conolly, 1833, II, 824–75.

[5] J. C. Prichard, *A Treatise on Insanity*, 1835, 5.

wise apparently sane, and certainly in full possession of his intellectual powers.[1]

We are close to the world of 'Porphyria'.

It is most interesting that John Wilson touches on the question of moral insanity at the end of the 'Extracts from Gosschen's Diary'. The murderer mentions being 'morally insane' as a possible extenuation of his crime, which, incidentally, also suggests that Wilson was conscious of the interest in the legal position of lunacy that was another practical concern of the Anglo-French psychiatric school. Procter acknowledged an anecdote from a recent book on the forensic aspect of insanity as the source for another of his studies in madness, 'The Girl of Provence'.[2] He also seems to have planned to make Marcian Colonna's lunacy partly just an intensification of the experience of a sane mind:

> To paint the fluctuations of a fatalist's mind,—touched with insanity,—alternately raised by kindness and depressed by neglect or severity,—ameliorated by the contemplation of external nature, and generally influenced by the same causes which operate on more healthful temperaments.

When Colonna does contemplate nature in section I. viii his misanthropy is presented as an intelligible shunning of the 'busy world' of urban life.

But Wilson's murderer rejects the plea of moral insanity in favour of that of hereditary delusive madness—'imposed, forced upon me, with all its red-rolling sea of dreams'—and Procter allows regretfully that his 'intention has been in some measure departed from'. So these two writers are conscious of how they are coming close to exhibiting madness in a light consistent with recent psychiatric ideas, to writing something like 'Porphyria', but, as I said before, they cannot somehow sustain the conception, and they fall back on the stock notion of lunacy as mania marked by delusions. Browning has written the study of homicidal lunacy that others had tried to write before him. Dickens, however, turning his hand to the same sort of subject at almost exactly the same time, is still undecided between the alternatives of rationality and delusion. His madman in Chapter 11 of *The Pickwick Papers* is apparently re-

[1] *Ibid.*, 22.

[2] The book is George Dale Collinson's *A Treatise on the Law concerning lunatics, and other persons non compotes mentis*, 1812.

markably cunning; he has some 'dreams', but his madness chiefly consists in his own consciousness that he is mad which he craftily conceals (thus outwitting the probate court), and in his moral perversion, his homicidal cruelty. Then very abruptly in the note 'in another hand' at the end of the tale the whole narrative is written off as the delusion of his 'raving madness'—the terminal state in a sequence of 'fever . . . delirium . . . delusion . . . settled gloom . . . marked insanity' that was set in motion by the 'riot, dissipation, and debauchery of his younger days'.

Everything points to Browning's having intended an analysis of homicidal lunacy in 'Porphyria', an analysis guided by his own theory of psychological consistency and by contemporary ideas of rational lunacy, especially the notion of 'moral insanity'. I cannot adduce evidence to support the strong likelihood thus created that Johannes Agricola is also thought of as a lunatic. His kind of ecstatic spirituality is only occasionally discussed as a species of insanity in the psychiatric literature of the day; religious insanity is more commonly understood to mean such things as the delusion of being possessed by devils, extravagant despair of salvation, and so forth—a traditional category of madness that owed much in the eighteenth century to distrust of the effects of Methodism. At all events Browning has created a religious fanatic of a type new to English literature in Johannes Agricola. Tennyson's poem 'St Simeon Stylites', written in 1833, can lay a false trail here, since it is natural to want to associate this work with 'Johannes Agricola'. Tennyson's procedure is in essence that of Burns in 'Holy Willie's Prayer', and earlier of Richard Corbet in 'The Distracted Puritan' (1660), humorous poems that illustrate an unconscious inconsistency between their speakers' fervour and Christian values. But in Browning's poem the gap between piety and charity, once it has dawned upon us, is frightening rather than funny, since it requires no amusing inconsistency to sustain it. To call 'Johannes Agricola' a 'scathing satire' confounds this clear distinction.[1]

If Browning's title 'Madhouse Cells' reflects his original plan for companion studies of lunacy there remains the question of why he removed the title in 1863. I suspect he recognized that in one way the title is inappropriate. It indicates that the speakers are lunatics, but also gives the impression that they are in an asylum. This is unlikely to have been part of Browning's original conception. He appended a note in 1836 which showed Johannes Agricola to have been a fairly important historical

[1] Tracy's term in the paper mentioned above.

character, and hence unlikely to be stowed away in a madhouse, and only if Porphyria's lover is grossly hallucinated can his utterance be consistent with such an environment. Moreover, if I am right about his particular species of lunacy, then hallucination is exactly the wrong sort of symptom for him to exhibit; it would shatter the delicate and startling portrayal of rational lunacy with the same sort of clumsiness as Dickens' note on his madman's MS. Having rejected the 'Madhouse Cell' title for these reasons there was no obvious alternative way in which Browning could establish the lunacy of his speakers in his heading, so he abandoned the attempt.

Browning's venture in 1836, as I understand it, was an extraordinary one, and it is undertaken with an extraordinary degree of success. He wished to achieve a deep and sophisticated analysis of alien states of mind wholly through the natural-seeming utterance of their imagined possessors. For a serious account in English letters of mental alienation given from the inside in this way we have to go back to the sixteenth and seventeenth-century tradition of the Mad Song for a precedent. The last true example is perhaps Herricks 'The Mad Maid's Song' (1648). Thereafter, in the Mad Songs of Thomas D'Urfey and Henry Carey, the madness consists of little more than intense emotion, and is reported on by its victims with the objectivity of an outsider. The one exception, crude though it is, is D'Urfey's 'Mad Maudlin' (1719). Later in the eighteenth century Cowper's 'Lines written during a period of insanity' constitute a serious, internalized treatment of madness that does come close to Browning, but the alienated state of mind is not a mysterious *datum* to be grasped and elucidated as it is for Browning.[1] As we have already seen, the idea of conveying the quality of madness from the victim's point of view attracted several writers in the early nineteenth century, but usually their attempts are vitiated by allowing the sufferer to report on rather than betray his mental alienation. Some of the most impressive experiments, like Wilson's, are due to the *Blackwoods* group. Lockhart makes insanity the predominant note of his novel *The History of Matthew Wald* (1824) by concluding it abruptly in the middle of a brutal madhouse-keeper's utterance, vividly recalled by the now sane hero. He also introduces a highly-wrought hallucination, which he valued sufficiently to select for

[1] The poetry of madness at the end of the century seems to have been uniformly unadventurous. Or so the examples listed by Thomas Mayo would suggest (PMLA, LXIX, 1954, 498).

special praise in his own anonymous review of the novel.[1] James Hogg's brilliant and little-known 'Strange letter of a Lunatic'[2] is mainly concerned with the ambiguities of magic versus lunacy, but it incidentally gives a powerful feeling of sanity shading into insanity. Darley's extraordinary poem 'Walter the Witless'——[3] which in some ways anticipates Browning's 'Caliban upon Setebos'—would surely count as the first true mad monologue since the Renaissance, were it not that Browning had published 'Porphyria' and 'Johannes Agricola' just three months before.

Our list of salient features for the dramatic monologue was Janusfaced; the dramatic monologue in Browning's hands was at once a naturalistic genre, and one that involved the author's self-expression and, more fundamentally, self-display. In the monologues between 1836 and 1855 the second aspect becomes increasingly prominent, and the two areas of background on which I have concentrated are a gloss on this change. They confirm that a strong naturalistic purpose in the very earliest monologues was absorbed into a different kind of purpose, one which grew easily for Browning out of widespread current assumptions about dramatic writing. They illustrate a truth that is entirely natural: that there will be a discrepancy between what a writer first supposes a form will yield and the possibilities he recognizes later as these are clarified for him by his own changing needs and situation.

[1] In *Blackwood's Magazine*, XV, 1824, 568–79.

[2] *Frasers*, II, 1830, 526–32.

[3] This poem is accessible in Norman Ault, *A Treasury of Unfamiliar lyrics*, 1938, 485–6. It first appeared in *The Athenaeum* in April 1836.

# 10: *Browning and Victorian Poetry of Sexual Love*

## ISOBEL ARMSTRONG

Sexual love becomes an important poetic subject in the Victorian period in a way that it had not been for the Romantic poets or, indeed, for poets of the eighteenth century. And this is so in spite of the taboo on overt sexual reference, or sexual explanations of behaviour, in nineteenth-century literature. Or perhaps the sensible view is that sexual love is a subject simply *because* overt reference was so difficult. The need to write about experiences which were so hedged round with confusions and fears must have been immense. At any rate, the taboo too easily persuades people to assume that in Victorian poetry sexual symbols will be naïvely concealed (Russell M. Goldfarb seizes upon rowing, for instance) or else that the writers were deeply unconscious of what was happening to them when they used sexual imagery, exploiting it in an unknowingly euphemistic underground way.[1] I think this is a poor way of putting it. The Victorians produced some really great pieces of erotic writing. One thinks of the hurtful tension, the bursting fruit, flaming skies and heavy scents in the chapter of Rochester's proposal in *Jane Eyre*, or the heated, febrile brilliance and intensity of some of the poems in *Maud*. There is something about the intuitive discovery of sexual imagery in *Jane Eyre* and *Maud* which enables their writers to use their discoveries with extraordinary richness and energy. What is moving about them is their openness, an almost painful frankness of commitment to feeling and passion which would be impossible now, in a more knowing and sexually self-conscious period. Of course the Victorians did not have our post-Freudian schemata, vocabulary or knowingness. They were not knowing, but they did know. When they succeed, they write of sexual experience out of a free erotic innocence, not naïveté. In fact, for me the greatest difficulties come when they write in open rebellion against the

[1] Russell M. Goldfarb, *Sexual Repression and Victorian Literature*, 1970.

conventions, like Swinburne in 'Laus Veneris', where the ostentatious picking of excitingly deliquescent forbidden fruits is embarrassing because it is all worked-up morbidly factitious naughtiness. Meredith creates the same difficulties for me. It is here that the blocks and contortions are most obvious.

We must assume an understanding, intuitive or not, of the *pervadingness* of sexual feeling in Victorian literature, felt the more strongly because it was less lucidly defined than now. The very absence of an acknowledged vocabulary leads to subtlety. The pervadingness of sexual feeling is described by Mrs. Gaskell in *Ruth*, significantly, as a 'brooding spirit with no definite form or shape', as a thing strongly sensed rather than defined. Ruth was

> too young when her mother died to have received any cautions or words of advice respecting *the* subject of a woman's life—if, indeed, wise parents ever directly speak of what, in its depth and power, cannot be put into words—which is a brooding spirit with no definite form or shape that men should know it, but which is there, and present before we have recognised and realised its existence.

This is no Victorian euphemism, but an attempt to account for the unrealised strength of sexual feeling.

Browning's poetry has a more than usually strongly felt awareness of sexuality, an awareness which Barbara Melchiori explores in general Freudian terms in her *Browning's Poetry of Reticence* (1968). His love poetry has the kind of confident erotic intensity, the openness of which I have been speaking. This is partly because he draws with freedom on sexual imagery, and partly because the thrusting, kinaesthetic movement of his verse, and his way of making a poem look as if it is spilling over unmediated sense-impressions with a kind of still-wet perceptual freshness, makes the poetry a peculiarly sensitive register of physical feeling. 'Meeting at Night' is an extraordinary poem. Its movement is frankly —and happily—orgasmic, from the 'pushing prow' of the boat quenched in the 'slushy sand' to the blue spurt of flame and 'the two hearts beating, each to each'. And yet to say that it is a poem about an orgasm is not to exhaust its meaning. It is a poem about living in sexual time, timelessly long *and* momentary. The pressure of the poem is all to the final intensity of its ending, and yet it does not hurry to its end. Included in the ending is the whole experience of the poem, which is the long, serenely steady journey, with its purposive, physically relaxed movement, the soft mutedness of colour and leisurely openness to sweet sensory detail—'Then a mile of warm sea-scented beach'. The poem is minute, and yet its space and time is huge. It narrows from a coastline on the horizon to the physical closeness of two people, and the time of the journey is almost endless. 'Parting at Morning', the sequel, and once part of the same poem, is also contained in the ending of 'Meeting at Night'. It is not an ironical rejection of 'Meeting at Night'. It charts the inevitable movement away from the moment of intensity. The rising sun re-establishes the quotidian time of the 'world of men', which is simply qualitatively different from the time of the first poem. And so the poem is about its own immediacy. Anticipatory time and desire is different from remembered time and desire. The acceptance of this, as the sun makes its path of gold, is a curious mixture of content, curt brutality, and pain.

'By the Fire-side' is another poem in which sensory detail felt with a special awareness defines erotic feeling. It accumulates a series of sharp, jagged, discontinuous visual detail which suggests thwarted, uncentred sexual feeling and aggression. The spear-head rocks of the alps 'charge' the insubstantial sky: 'small ferns fit / Their teeth to the polished block', and the chestnut shells are 'thorny balls'. There is a painful sense of destructive sexual energy both suppressed *and* out of control as the poem moves in stabs and surprising jerks of sensation. The visual disproportion, and the sudden, involuntary starting-out of sensory detail here, all suggest tension and defensiveness. November hours draw blood:

> *That crimson the creeper's leaf across*
> *Like a splash of blood, intense, abrupt,*
> *O'er a shield else gold from rim to boss,*
> *And lay it for show on the fairy-cupped*
> *Elf-needled mat of moss . . .*

I used to feel that the stanza describing the bulging nipples of the mushrooms, peeped at by the 'indulged' toadstools, was a gross failure of tact: now, knowing Browning better, I feel that it succeeds in miming rank, restless, rapidly growing sexual feeling which can find no direct expression and so becomes lewd and burdensome to itself.

> *By the rose-flesh mushrooms, undivulged*
> *    Last evening—nay, in today's first dew*
> *Yon sudden coral nipple bulged,*
> *    Where a freaked fawn-coloured flaky crew*
> *Of toadstools peep indulged.*

The sensory details of this landscape encompass an amazing range of feeling—rank desire, pain and aggression, a double lyric nostalgia for the decay of things (for this is a *remembered* desire), to the sheer dead emptiness of feeling implied by the husk of the church to which the lovers walk.

What, then, was Browning trying to achieve through his exploration of erotic feeling? For one could call it this; the proportion of poems on sexual love in *Men and Women* and in *Dramatis Personae* is very high. What he was *not* doing is perfectly clear. Throughout his marriage and up to the time of *The Ring and the Book* Browning seems to have been completely unconcerned with the image of a certain kind of woman very familiar to us—familiar to us as a cultural stereotype, although her relationship to Victorian reality will always be problematical—which dominated other Victorian love poetry and which was constantly inspected, whether favourably or unfavourably. Favourably regarded, this is the figure that comes surrounded by a haze of mild mysticism and milder sex in Coventry Patmore's *Angel in the House*. She is the figure of Tennyson's domestic idylls, part of the domestic scene at the end of 'The Two Voices', the reformed Princess Ida. Unfavourably regarded, found out, as it were, she is the subject of Meredith's sexual sulks in *Modern Love* and, as Guinevere, the object of Tennyson's compassion in the *Idylls of the King*. Clough's struggles with the idea of marriage come, I think, from the idea of marrying *this* figure. Browning continued to ignore the type until the late sixties, but after this time, most notably in *Fifine at the Fair* (1872), he gives an astonishing account of the fantasies and confusions which go to the making of it, an account which is set directly in a contemporary environment and which amounts to an examination of the assumptions behind contemporary sexual myths. He realized that the myth of the pure woman is a strangely ambiguous thing. If you accept it you struggle with contradictions, for an impossible female docility can only be given ultimate credence when it is seen as the product of artfulness or duplicity. Hence even in the most ingenuous of Victorian poets, such as Patmore, the pure woman is contemplated with an odd mixture of adulation and anger. From poet to poet the same pattern—docility, duplicity, anger—the same configuration of feeling, is struggled with, with varying kinds of self-consciousness and insight. I want first to set this struggle with a female stereotype against the concerns of Browning's earlier poetry, and to explain why he was so uninvolved with it. Then I shall suggest the reasons for his change of direction.

I shall start with Coventry Patmore, because *Angel in the House* is so very nearly inadvertently a subtle poem, but I want first to glance briefly aside at an influential medical treatise, Thomas Laycock's *Treatise on the Nervous Disorders of Women* (1840). I do not want to use Laycock to show that the literary stereotype was a cultural reality—all writers, whether they are poets or not, struggle with images. We know very little about the relationship between a stereotype and historical reality (these subtle and indirect connections were not fully recognized, I think, in a recent *Victorian Studies* special issue on Victorian Woman).[1] But what Laycock does show is that a coercive model of womanhood as pure and weak leads to an equally coercive notion of woman as cunning and artful.

Laycock's treatise is in fact extremely kind and well-meaning and very bold in its diagnosis of the origins of psychological disorders. He believed that a great many of the illnesses of middle-class women (labouring women did not suffer in the same way) were not physical, but psychological in origin, and his book was written to prevent the damaging continuance of false diagnoses and treatment. Moreover, he argued unequivocally for the *sexual* basis of all nervous disorders in women. 'Lastly, it may be remarked that the whole nervous system is excited by the sexual stimulus, as much as by opium or other powerful nervine alternatives.'[2] The whole being and senses of women during their reproductive life are shaped by sexual feeling. Poor women, they can suffer from nervous diseases of the kidneys, bladder, intestines,

---

[1] *VS*, 14 (September, 1970), 'The Victorian Woman, A Special Issue'. Two essays in this issue deal with the Victorian stereotypes of women: Jill Conway, 'Stereotypes of Femininity in a Theory of Sexual Evolution', 47–62: Kate Millett, 'The Debate over Women: Ruskin Versus Mill', 63–81. These essays amplify some of the suggestions I have explored in this paper, though neither deals directly with the question of female cunning.

[2] Thomas Laycock, *A Treatise on the Nervous Disorders of Women*, 1840, 74.

stomach, pharynx, tonsils, salivary glands, circulation, respiration. But
Laycock is most interesting when he comes to the varieties of hysteria
under the head of 'Mental Affections', which includes such things as
'Fidgets', 'Timidity', and 'Insane Cunning' as categories. Saddest of all is
'Erotomania', extreme disappointment after an unsuccessful love affair
(all the Brontë heroines must suffer from this), but the most important
category for my purposes is 'Insane Cunning'.

Earlier he had remarked on the extreme weakness of women, and
assumed that women compensate for their lack of strength and aggression by high intelligence or 'artfulness'.

> One of the most remarkable of the faculties developed during the
> generative nisus, and peculiar to the females of the higher class of
> animals, is their artfulness; and this seems to be given them in place
> of those weapons of offence and defence with which the males are so
> generally provided. Indeed the less muscular power, want of defen-
> sive weapons, and exalted perceptive faculties of females, would
> *naturally* [my italics] excite into action timidity and cunning. This is
> strikingly obvious in the human female in general; their sagacity
> and acuteness being usually remarkable, when well informed . . .[1]

Hence the pathological category of insane cunning. 'There is not much
ground for surprise at the grotesque forms which cunning assumes in the
hysterical female', he writes, and when this occurs, 'it is as much a symptom of hysteria as any corporal affection whatever. It is true monomania,
and is most likely to occur in the female who is hysterical from excess of
sexual development,—one possessing the utmost modesty of deport-
ment, and grace of figure and movement; for the modesty itself springs
out of that feminine timidity to which I have alluded.'[2] Laycock means
here that the more *feminine* a woman is, the more she is likely to be a
victim of insane cunning. A good-tempered writer, he permits himself a
moment of irritation at the 'astonishing' way in which a hysterical
female will behave, stuffing her vagina with stones, playing havoc with
nurses and parents, dominating those around her with 'the almost incredible acuteness of senses, and of cunning, developed in hysterical
girls'.[3] The transition from tenderness to cunning is writ large in
Laycock's work because he is dealing with pathology, but the paradox

[1] Laycock, 72.
[2] Laycock, 353.
[3] Laycock, 355.

puts him in difficulties. The same paradox reappears in the work of the poets, and when the Victorian poet writes of sexual love we see him writing in difficulties.

Hopkins accused Patmore's later poetry of 'telling secrets', but the secrets his poetry betrays are never quite the ones he intended to tell. The ambivalences come out clearly because he never realized that they might need covering up. He has a pleasant belief in the importance of physical love—'Ice-cold seems heaven's noble glow / To spirits whose vital heat is hell' (Book 1, Canto III, ii), but his view of women is full of contradictions. Woman, with her temple-like repose and countenance angelical, elevates man. She is the softener, soother and stabilizer. She is pure and chaste and yet she is a matron and a mother: she is 'infantine', childlike, and yet in order to preserve this child-likeness she has to resort to sexual cunning; she is totally submissive, and yet she maintains this at the cost of subverting any possibility of reciprocity. Here, of course, is a banal figure which seems to justify all banal views of Victorianism. What is remarkable is the blandness of Patmore's acceptance of the contradictions. His playfulness, the combination of tea on the lawn and the vocabulary of love subsumed under religious language, thrills over stolen gloves, and mystical feelings, would be merely trivially venial if it were not for the inadvertent ruthlessness of some of his observations. He observes that the courted woman *knows* that she should preserve a proper innocence or ignorance of sexual realities, and does so at the expense of the man, who takes the active, and therefore blameable role. I underline the significant lines.

> *His words, which still instruct, but so*
> *That this applause seems still implied,*
> *'How wise in all she ought to know,*
> *'How ignorant of all beside!'*
> *His skilful suit, which leaves her free,*
> *Gives nothing for the world to name,*
> *And keeps her conscience safe, while he,*
> *With half the bliss, takes all the blame;*

(Book 2, Canto II, i)

The woman has to *exact* reverence and respect from the man. She can determine to be thoroughly submissive to him only if she exacts this reverence. Patmore sees this as a real dilemma, but he is so certain that the woman will submit to 'her lord' that he can afford to feel sympathetic. There is a tone of benevolence here, and a certain pride in the lover's capacity to create this dilemma through the power to excite disturbing sexual feeling.

> *A touch, her hand press'd lightly, she*
> *Stands dizzied, shock'd, and flush'd, like one*
> *Set sudden neck-deep in the sea;*
> *And, though her bond for endless time*
> *To his good pleasure gives her o'er,*
> *The slightest favour seems a crime,*
> <u>*Because it makes her love him more.*</u>
> <u>*But that she ne'er will let him know;*</u>
> <u>*For what were love should reverence cease?*</u>
> *A thought which makes her reason so*
> *Inscrutable, it seems caprice.*
> *With her, as with a desperate town,*
> *Too weak to stand, too proud to treat,*
> *The conqueror, though the walls are down,*
> *Has still to capture street by street;*

(Book 2, Canto II, i)

Again, I have underlined the important lines. Patmore writes as if the ultimate submissiveness has to be a steely act of will on the part of the woman because she has no *choice*.

> *And she's to changed allegiance true;*
> *And prizing what she can't prevent,*
> *(Right wisdom, often misdeem'd whim,)*
> *Her will's indomitably bent*
> *On mere submissiveness to him;*

(Book 2, Canto II, i)

Ostensibly Patmore colludes with a view of woman as both child-like and knowing. The woman lives in a 'rapture of submission' to her 'dear despot'. She dies 'back to the babe' in his love and 'prattles like a child at play'. But the childlikeness is a ruse to disguise a cunning manipulation of the male, and Patmore can denigrate women for being simultaneously childish *and* clever. The appalling account of female cunning here, in which the woman thinks of her own attractions while the didactic husband reads her the news of a disastrous battle, the imagery of cunning snake and predatory trapper, associated with the girl's innocence in keeping the husband devout 'against his nature', is a dreadfully coy self-betrayal.

> *Perchance, when all her praise is said,*
> *He tells the news, a battle won,*
> *On either side ten thousand dead.*
> *'Alas!' she says; but, if 'twere known,*
> *She thinks, 'He's looking on my face!*
> *'I am his joy; what 'ere I do,*
> *He sees such time-contenting grace*
> *In that, he'd have me always so!'*
> *And, evermore, for either's sake,*
> *To the sweet folly of the dove,*
> *She joins the cunning of the snake,*
> *To rivet and exalt his love;*
> *Her mode of candour is deceit;*
> *And what she thinks from what she'll say,*
> *( Although I'll never call her cheat,)*
> *Lies far as Scotland from Cathay.*
> *Without his knowledge he was won;*
> *Against his nature kept devout;*
> *She'll never tell him how 'twas done,*
> *And he will never find it out.*
> *If, sudden, he suspects her wiles,*
> *And hears her forging chain and trap,*
> *And looks, she sits in simple smiles,*
> *Her two hands lying in her lap.*
>
> (Book 2, Canto VIII, i)

Perhaps Patmore is too ingenuous to be taken seriously, but he is important because his naïveté hits upon the consequences of this dove-snake manipulating submissiveness: of course, even Patmore sees through it, and so it is self-defeating, and brings upon the woman only anger and rage:

> *Of smiles and simple heaven grown tired,*
> *He wickedly provokes her tears,*

> *And when she weeps, as he desired,*
>   *Falls slain with ecstasies of fears;*
> *He blames her, though she has no fault . . .*

(Book 2, Canto VI, i)

In the later 'Eros and Psyche', Psyche begs Eros to punish her, take his revenge on her, as a way of squaring her guilt about enjoying sexual love. Her words are a wild invitation to sadistic feeling.

> *Shouldst thou me tell*
> *Out of thy warm caress to go*
> *And roll my body in the biting snow,*
> *My very body's joy were but increased;*
> *More pleasant 'tis to please thee than be pleased.*
> *Thy love has conquer'd me; do with me as thou wilt,*
> *And use me as a chattel that is thine!*
> *Kiss, tread me underfoot, cherish or beat,*
> *Sheathe in my heart sharp pain up to the hilt,*
> *Invent what else were most perversely sweet;*

Patmore understood without realizing it an invitation to sexual rage involved in the relationship he describes between men and women, and this makes *Angel in the House* a disturbing work. Anger is at the heart of *Modern Love*, published in 1862, the year of the last book of *Angel in the House*. Understood, but not kept under control, it emerges again and again as sadistic petulance. The wife, in love with someone else in spite of herself, is a witch, has eyes which are 'poison-cups'.

> *But still he spared her. Once: 'Have you no fear?'*
> *He said: 'twas dusk; she in his grasp; none near.*
> *She laughed: 'No, surely; am I not with you?'*
> *And uttering that soft starry 'you', she leaned*
> *Her gentle body near him, looking up;*
> *And from her eyes, as from a poison-cup,*
> *He drank until the flittering eyelids screened.*
> *Devilish malignant witch! and oh, young beam*
> *Of heaven's circle-glory! Here they shape*
> *To squeeze like an intoxicating grape—*
> *I might, and yet thou goest safe, supreme.*

(IX)

I find the appeal of *Modern Love* for some recent critics very difficult to understand (John Lucas, for instance, in Ian Fletcher's *Meredith Now: some critical essays*, 1971). I can find no honest human engagement, either with the woman of the poem, or the man. Compared with the spring and resilience of the novels, it is a nasty piece of work.

The confusion of Meredith's speaker, who sees his past self as 'the puppet of a dream' of loyalty, is reflected in the constant ambiguity of syntactic concord in the poem. In spite of claims to the contrary, the self-pity never introspects, never blames itself.

> Now, as then, the grace
> Of heaven seems holding earth in its embrace.
> Nor eyes, nor heart, has she to feel it strange?
> Look, woman, in the West. There wilt thou see
> An amber cradle near the sun's decline:
> Within it, featured even in death divine,
> Is lying a dead infant, slain by thee.
>
> (XI)

The imagery is extraordinarily self-betraying: the generalized erotic-religious language—the 'grace' of heaven embracing earth—slides to an identification of the wife as mother, guilty of child murder, having killed the husband's love and, by extension, the husband too. Meredith is more subtle, though no more likeable, than Patmore in his understanding of the aggression and competitiveness in sexual feeling.

> Just heaven! can it be true that jealousy
> Has decked the woman thus? and does her head
> Swim somewhat for possessions forfeited?
> Madam, you teach me many things that be.
> I open an old book, and there I find,
> That 'Women still may love whom they deceive.'
> Such love I prize not, madam: by your leave,
> The game you play at is not to my mind.
>
> (XIV)

Of course, in other poems Meredith struggled against the notions which he cannot help letting loose in *Modern Love*. In *The Sage Enamoured and the Honest Lady*, he attempts to strip away the religious language of sex.

> *Had he not wits to pierce the mask he wooed?*
> *All wisdom's armoury this man could wield;*
> *And if the cynic in the sage it pleased,*
> *Traverse her woman's curtain and poor shield,*
> *For new example of a world diseased;*
> *Showing her shrineless, not a temple, bare;*
> *A curtain ripped to tatters by the blast.*
> *Yet she most surely to this man stood fair:*
> *He worshipped like the young enthusiast,*
> *Named simpleton or poet.*

*Modern Love* is merely *Angel in the House* turned upside down, for all its apparent sophistication. One comes away from these poems with the sickened feeling of having looked into the wretchedness of the contradictions involved in the domestication of a thinly platonized femininity. I seem, at this point, to be moving in the same direction as Stephen Marcus, in his *The Other Victorians* (1966). It is true that some Victorian pornography seems to be written out of a miserable rage with women, yet I have strong reservations about his approach to Victorian views of sexuality, which I shall mention when I discuss Browning's *Fifine at the Fair*.[1] For the moment, I shall complete my present discussion by looking at Tennyson and Clough.

In these poets the same configuration of feeling is being struggled with —female docility creating female duplicity, and male fury. Tennyson, the greater poet, understood the contradictions at a deeper level, perhaps, than anyone: Clough, the more intelligent poet, analyses them with an awareness and subtle honesty not to be found until Browning turned to the problem in the late sixties. All of Clough's long poems, of course, 'study the question of sex', and particularly of marriage. Women, 'so loving, and so exacting', whether they are the 'pink-paper comfits' of Philip's immaturity in *The Bothie*, or patient, sensible, and genuinely stabilizing, like Elspie or Mary Trevellyn in *Amours de Voyage* (it is not Mary's fault that Claude is engaged in eroding the concept of

[1] H. S. Ashbee's catalogue of pornographic tales is particularly revealing from this point of view. One novel has a particularly fierce account of a husband's sadistic rage against his wife. See Ashbee's account of E. Sellon's *The Ups and Downs of Life*, 1867, in *Forbidden Books of the Victorians*, ed. Peter Fryer, London, 1970, 198–203.

stability as a virtue), are at the centre of his poetry. They and what is due to them are a constant puzzle, a constant irritant, but it is in the clear-minded satire of *Dipsychus* that Clough confronts the problem most sharply. This is achieved by separating out ambivalent, contradictory feeling and personifying the oppositions in the characters of Dipsychus and the Spirit. Dipsychus hopes women are pure: the Spirit knows they are cunning. Dipsychus is amazed and threatened when he finds that he cannot reconcile his views of chastity and marriage with an over-powering sexual curiosity for the Venetian prostitutes.

> *Why, why in wisdom and in grace's name,*
> *And in the name of saints and saintly thoughts,*
> *Of mothers, and of sisters, and chaste wives,*
> *And angel woman-faces we have seen,*
> *And angel woman-spirits we have guessed,*
> *And innocent sweet children, and pure love,*
> *Why did I ever one brief moment's space*
> *To this insidious lewdness lend chaste ears,*
> *Or parley with this filthy Belial?*

(Sc. IIA, ll.3–11)

The Spirit holds the nullifying, mean-minded view of sex and women held unconsciously by Patmore and discovered with such chagrin by Meredith. He interprets the idealism which Dipsychus struggles to maintain as mere high-minded timidity, prurience disguised as mystical feeling. Sex is no 'revelation' and the sexual wiles of women cannot sustain you through 'the emptiness of things'. Clough shows that this diminution of human feeling is as extreme as the sentimental idealism of Dipsychus, although, of course, Dipsychus *needs* this sense. The Oxford editors omit some passages which slightly amplify scene IIA. After l.41 Dipsychus asks whether sexual relief frees one from sexual desire. If only he could believe that women enjoyed sexual experience, taking pleasure as an equal with men, then the situation would be different, and he might take a prostitute. However, his argument is not a Blake-like one of mutual sexual health and freedom, as one might expect: he could take the prostitute because if she were his equal he would not be *morally* responsible for her fall.

> *Could I believe, as of a man I might,*
> *So a good girl from weary workday hours*
> *And from the long monotony of toil*
> *Might safely purchase these wild intervals,*
> *And from that banquet rise refreshed, and wake*
> *And shake her locks and as before go forth*
> *Invigorated, unvitiate to the task*
> *But no it is not so.*

But he knows this cannot be the case. He would be morally responsible for the 'coy girl' who 'turns to the flagrant woman of the street'. The Spirit's comments show clearly enough how self-regarding moral doubleness is the result of a pernicious differentiation between men's and women's responsibility, how ultimately *self*-gratifying it is to see women as totally 'innocent', because Dipsychus can see himself as morally superior.

> *Stuff!*
> *The women like it; that's enough.*

and:

> *That is the high moral way of talking*
> *I'm well aware about street-walking.*

It is easy enough to wish not to be corrupted by corrupting a woman and easier still to blame *her* for being corrupt when you have done so. Dipsychus does both things without knowing it. The Spirit is always partly right. Yet his own answer is in terms of thin, practical economics, haunted by Malthusian fears of over-population, in spite of its pose of earthy wit. Virginity, the 'once rent hymenis membrana', is a mere technical, not a moral matter: prostitution solves a practical problem.

> *it needs consideration*
> *By what more moral occupation*
> *To support this vast population?*

Dipsychus sees marriage with its corollory in the 'prattle' of children, as the only way of lessening the shame of sex. It is clear that this is no moral victory: the falling cadences betray that it is the resigned acceptance of timidity, an only half-wanted weary compromise.

> *O welcome then, the sweet domestic bonds . . .*
> *And permanence and habit, that transmute*
> *Grossness itself to crystal.*
>
> (Sc. IIA, ll. 80–5)

The comic inter-action of ironies, turning simultaneously against Dipsychus and against the Spirit, takes place with elastic rapidity in this poem. There is a brilliant, tough lucidity about Clough's way of showing that Dipsychus and the Spirit are not the opposites but the complements of one another in their different kinds of self-regarding feeling. It is a toughness which has the discipline to be both unkind and charitable to the appallingly muddled goodness of Dipsychus, to acknowledge and to undermine the sense of the Spirit. It is strange indeed that the much later 'Clergyman's Second Tale' in *Mari Magno* should be so guilty of treating prostitution with the self-regarding dishonesty Clough exposed in *Dipsychus*. I think that Robindra Biswas is quite right to see it as an extraordinary self-betrayal, in which Clough is transmuted into a Tennysonian poet without any of Tennyson's virtues.[1] Edward, in 'The Clergyman's Second Tale', is so anxious not to fall a second time when he sees that he is followed home by the girl who first tempted him, now a wretchedly emaciated woman of the streets, that he has no humane feeling to spare for her. Neither, so far as I can see, has Clough. Her badness sets off Edward's moral restoration.

If Clough's intelligence preserved him from a discharge of bemused anger against women's duplicity in *Dipsychus*, his tenderness preserved him from it in *Mari Magno*. This is not so with Tennyson: we see everywhere, of course, his desperate need to keep to the sweet domestic simplicities and his struggle to accommodate himself to a more complicated reality, from 'The Lover's Tale', through *The Princess* to *Enoch Arden*, and to poor Guinevere's confession that she found Arthur too good for her. Yet Tennyson understood sexual anger to its very sources. In *Maud* he saw that fury was near the centre of the speaker's erotic feeling. In this frightening lyric of passion, just controlled by the tenuous lullaby form, the idea of reddening, the flush of colour, associated earlier with the flow of the blood and the speaker's destructive feeling, is transferred to his passion, the 'cruel madness of love', as he has earlier called it, until the whole world glows in a lurid dawn-sunset of savage colour. The lullaby movement accelerates to a hectic beat.

[1] Robindra Kumar Biswas, *Arthur Hugh Clough: Towards a Reconsideration*, Oxford, 1972, 469.

*Pass and blush the news*
    *Over glowing ships;*
*Over blowing seas,*
    *Over seas at rest,*
*Pass the happy news,*
    *Blush it through the West;*
*Till the red man dance*
    *By his red cedar-tree,*
*And the red man's babe*
    *Leap, beyond the sea.*
*Blush from West to East,*
    *Blush from East to West,*
*Till the West is East,*
    *Blush it through the West.*

(XVII, ll. 581–94)

The speaker thinks that his former aggression and fear of Maud's coldness and cunning—'She meant to weave me a snare / Of some coquettish deceit' (V), has dissolved and is directed towards her brother alone, but this lyric suggests his judgment is vulnerably wrong. According to Christopher Ricks, this lyric was originally intended for *The Princess*. Was it removed because of its inappropriate violence?

I turn now to Browning: what made him so immune to the configuration of feeling that I have been describing? True, he is aware of a pattern of neurotic emotion governing relationships, but it is a different pattern, and he asks different questions about men and women. The most dramatic way of showing what his concerns were is to begin with the startlingly intense non sequitur of the second stanza of an early poem, 'The Lost Mistress'.

*All's over, then: does truth sound bitter*
    *As one at first believes?*
*Hark, 'tis the sparrows' good-night twitter*
    *About your cottage eaves!*

*And the leaf-buds on the vine are woolly,*
    *I noticed that, today;*
*One day more bursts them open fully*
    *—You know the red turns grey.*

This statement about the end of a relationship is suddenly followed by a wonderfully minute observation which would be almost Tennysonian but for the clotted sensory way it falls on the page. The key to the second stanza is the initial elliptical 'And', for 'and' implies continuance and sequence, that this is part of a *series* of observations which has a self-perpetuating life of its own. The description of the vine is made with the peculiar awareness that only an intense state of feeling can bring. Once generated, the feeling runs on in spite of events. Against the mechanical understanding that the love affair is over it sets the full weight of involuntary, living and continuing feeling which cannot be abolished by the woman's edict. The whole poem is an astonished, unbelieving statement of the poet's inability to deal alone with his feelings. He has been coerced into a painful privacy with them. The 'I noticed that, today', with its emphasis on the solitary 'I', and the implied contrast between 'today' and 'yesterday', makes it plain that he exists in self-aware loneliness with his feelings. The implied metaphor of the visual detail, too, has a painful associative life of its own, as if the speaker cannot help acknowledging his condition, because it becomes a dual metaphor of growth and destruction. The bud 'bursts', burst open, or shattered, by growth: the fresh blush of young colour turns 'grey' as it matures. There is a tight, tense economy about this poem, as with all the poems in attenuated stanzaic forms.

The meaning of the second stanza leads one to the heart of Browning's exploration of love, because the speaker is forced into solipsistic communion with his feelings when the affair is over. He is appalled by their vivid, solitary life. Browning's love poetry is about the tragic solipsism and privacy of love, with its corollary in fantasy and morbid erotic feeling. It examines and erodes the great human myth of continuing love, and the high Romantic myth of a continuing, stable identity with which it supports itself, exploring the wilful strains and conflations of past with present selves that go into the creating of a belief in continuity and stability. Though they combine a kind of virtuoso intelligence with sensuality, Browning's most obtrusively manipulating manner is absent from these love lyrics and so they have a special quality of passion among his poems. Yet they often have a double movement of seriousness and mockery or puzzlement. They are self-undermining, swerving into a countermovement of irony against passion, or into passion against mockery.

They twist and turn in order to display the complicatedness and vulnerability of any *beliefs* about loving, any formulations about feeling. If in the
end they return to and celebrate the great Romantic myths, they only do
so at the cost of an immense agnostic undermining of them. The affirm--
ation is a Pyrrhic victory, and Browning means it to be so. Lawrence was
quite right to make Birkin see 'Love Among the Ruins' as an apocalyptic
poem set in a disintegrating society when he quotes it to Gerald in
*Women in Love*. The girl waiting for the lover in the empty landscape of
'undistinguished grey', trying to pour all her energies into a single, solitary relationship, waits in the ruins made by a once vivid, aggressive and
expansive society. It was a crude society but the energy of the dead, historical past makes itself felt in the cross-cutting rhythms of vigour which
alternate with the muted languor of the descriptions of the present. Love
*is* best, surely, but Browning's point, I think, is that we should not have
to see the question as a choice at all. It should not be necessary to make a
choice between love and society. The speaker talks as if there is no society, now, only him and the girl. How can a love relationship placed in
an extra-historical, extra-social emptiness be made to bear the whole
weight of meaning and value, the total significance of being? As if to
enforce this point, 'A Lover's Quarrel' followed 'Love Among the
Ruins', which was the first poem in *Men and Women* (1855), a measure of
its significance to Browning.

   Browning's love lyrics turn out to be passionately about intertwined
emotional-epistemological problems, and this puts him directly inside
the Romantic tradition. His concerns are the concerns, transmuted by his
dazzling sensory intelligence, of his great Romantic precursors
—solipsism, fantasy, identity, the action and reaction of past with present. He is the most directly Romantic of all the Victorian poets, and so his
response to sexual love is coloured by Romantic ideas, rather than the
problems with which his contemporaries are concerned. And, of course,
he continued to be a Romantic poet until the sixties, for his marriage shut
him away from the immediate concerns of Victorian society. At the same
time it confronted him immediately with the puzzles of sexual love.
When he returned to England he became a Victorian poet and began to
scrutinize his society and its sexual myths at closer quarters.

   There is only one poem in the earlier period which touches upon the
rage of men with women so apparent in the poets I have discussed. This is
'A Pretty Woman' (from *Men and Women*), which is a dancing, satirical,

social lyric about the way in which men use women as commodities, as vehicles for sexual fantasies. Male fantasies trap women in conventional roles, and men take revenge upon women when they do not react to conventional expectations: 'Shall we burn up, tread that face at once / Into tinder?' when a girl refuses to respond to the sexual demands made of her? There is a quick-silver play of good humour and mordant feeling here, and in all Browning's best poems there is a complex play of qualifying, doubling back feeling. But this gay poem is an exception, and we are in a different medium of feeling in Browning's other love poems.

As with so much of Browning's poetry, *Sordello* is the source of most of the worries underlying the love poems and I want to extract four interconnected ideas from that poem and use them as a way of confronting the love poems. In the first place, Sordello is a Romantic poet, whose esemplastic imagination creates his own world in a triumphant fusion of self and externality. Both Wordsworth and Coleridge would have recognized in Sordello the poet who half perceives and half creates, in whose life alone Nature lives.

> *they are fain invest*
> *The lifeless thing with life from their own soul,*
> *Availing it to purpose, to control,*
> *To dwell distinct and have peculiar joy*
> *And separate interests . . .*

Browning seems to have believed that there were two alternatives for the poet. Some poets become, as it were, swallowed up by the external world, they 'blend with each external charm', 'Bury themselves, the whole heart wide and warm,— / In something not themselves . . .' Others reverse the process and take the external world into themselves and make it 'their own'—'So, homage, other souls direct / Without, turns inward . . .' This swallowing up or internalizing of the world is Sordello's way. He is able to exist in the isolation of his fecund imaginative world where 'fancies' 'wreathed / Luxuriantly', and his way of learning about reality is in terms of self-created myths and fictions. He has to construct possible actions, roles, people, to enact a drama within himself. Browning is unambiguous about the corrupting possibilities of this pattern and later in the love poems he recurs constantly to the possibility that the other, the loved person, is a solipsist creation of the lover, trapped by the role created for him or for her. Browning talks of the

whole creative process as 'love'—'exceeding love / Becomes an aching
weight . . .' if it is not allowed to flow out and invest the external world
with its energy: the nineteenth century liked to think of love as outward-
going, the highest form of empathy, a flood of imaginative energy
directed towards the other. One thinks of the lover of 'The Lost Mistress', painfully experiencing the aching weight of love which has no
outlet. But when the poet or the lover, is of the sort whose energy 'turns
inward', internalizing all phenomena, the possibility of his being unbur-
dened from the aching weight of feeling is small. What is constantly
required from Sordello, and later of Browning's lovers, is a stronger
sense of externality. Sordello fails to communicate with his audience and
his poetic life is a long struggle with communication. This struggle to see
himself in active relationship with the world is extended from aesthetic
to social and political questions. Sordello wants, but fails, to see himself
in meaningful relationship with his society. He wants, another high Romantic wish, to be inside society, inside history, not inorganically isolated from it in the way that Browning describes Sordello's arbitrary
creative life—like a spider at the centre of its 'waving mesh', making
random connections with its 'festooning' threads. Sordello wants to see
his being as a connected and continuous whole, but this is finally denied
him because he has to make a moral choice between Guelf and Ghibel-
lino which seems to fracture his connections between his past moral life
and his present, and he cannot contain the contradictions. Similarly,
Browning's lovers look for continuity through love, which seems a way
of consolidating their identity. As in *Sordello* Browning is more than agnostic about the possibility of retrieving wholeness in this way.

The privacy of fantasy, the nature of role-playing, the struggle for
communication and the struggle for continuity, these emerge as connected puzzles in *Sordello* and in the best of the love poems all four concerns are bound together. I want to look at some of the ways these
patterns occur and then particularly at 'A Lover's Quarrel' and 'Two in
the Campagna' (both from *Men and Women*, 1855) before I discuss the
later poetry.

A very frequent setting for Browning's love poems is a darkened,
often underground place. The speaker of 'Mesmerism' begins his conjuring 'at night, when doors are shut': the lover of 'Evelyn Hope' solilo-
quizes in a room where

> *The shutters are shut; no light may pass*
> *Save two long rays thro' the hinge's chink.*

The woman in 'Any Wife to Any Husband' envisages herself going into her husband's tomb, and the speaker of 'A Lover's Quarrel' wishes that he and his lover could be trapped in a crypt together, in order to perpetuate their love. Interestingly enough, the source of Sordello's corrupt imaginative life is seen as a font in a darkened crypt of the palace of Goito. This is always a sign that Browning is dealing with morbid, inward-turning feeling. In 'Mesmerism', the fact is obvious: the speaker's obscene conjuring up of the image and then the physical reality of his lover is clearly a monstrous act of the compelling will, a fantasy of total power. I am not sure that this is a good poem, simply because Browning's hatred for the act makes it so violent and invests it with a self-conscious creepiness. 'Evelyn Hope' is different. The morbidity is less on the surface because it looks like an exercise in gentle nostalgia. But the nostalgic feeling is both genuine and deceptive. Death should close up possibilities because it closes up action and the future. But instead Evelyn Hope's death liberates the speaker into a world of possibilities. Its very finality makes a self-gratifying fantasy about their union easier, more possible rather than less, now that he is not inhibited by the obstinate living presence of the girl's lack of interest in him. This poem, with its typical combination of kindness and cruelty of insight, looks forward to 'Too Late' in *Dramatis Personae*, with its curious combination of fond, warm, longing for the dead woman, and necrophilia. 'Too Late' ends with the speaker imagining himself almost literally taking the woman into himself, swallowing her up, and Browning has a whole range of poems, particularly early poems, where the lover is compelled to destroy the autonomy of his lover and cannot bear to contemplate her or his separate existence. In *Pippa Passes* (1841) Giles the sculptor attempts to reshape Phene so that she becomes virtually his human work of art. *Dramatic Lyrics* (1842), contains 'My Last Duchess' and 'Porphyria's Lover', both poems where the lover has found a woman's living existence unbearable, either because she is independent of him, or because her continued life would mean a falling away from the moment of perfection. The duke thinks that the picture of his wife is easier to control than her reality because it has turned her into an object. He does not reckon, of course, for the living continuance of his own hatreds.

Extremes of neurotic feeling interested Browning up to *Dramatic Romances and Lyrics* (1845) where 'The Laboratory' and 'Cristina' continue the earlier themes. After this the interest is fainter, but up to this point he seems to have made a fairly systematic attempt to examine many kinds of neurotic or insane behaviour, and in particular the pathology of sexual feeling.

I confess that these poems, like 'Mesmerism', puzzle me. They are wonderfully intelligent, written with all Browning's confident yet controlled flourish and display 'Porphyria's Lover' in particular has the puzzling virtuosity of many of the best monologues. We do not know whether Porphyria's provocative behaviour, baring her shoulder to entice the man from his withdrawn, almost catatonic state, was really an ordinary or a monstrous act, because her behaviour is being described by a man who is mad. These renderings of psychosis may be full of profound insight in one way, but because they explore states far beyond the dangerous edge of things, they seem to me lurid and inaccessible. I shall not say much about them here, except to say that I think they were written deliberately to challenge, shock and test the responses of the unthinking reader. I think Browning found better and more subtle ways to do this in the love lyrics proper.

Browning explores another way of limiting the autonomy of the person you love, which is to create an image which is offered to the loved one as a possible way of being, a possible role. Of course, all love requires and lives upon this act of imagination. Browning looks mostly at the vulnerability of this creative act of will, but he acknowledges the human need to create and recreate a person in the imagination, the need to make consistent wholes out of people. The serio-comic 'In a Gondola', an early poem, is concerned with the morbid extremes that go on in the acting out of roles. The lovers' sadistic fantasy is fortunately perfectly matched, and they make their huge gestures of self-conscious passion in a kind of erotic vacuum, acting each one to themselves and secondarily to one another. 'A Woman's Last Word' is another poem which traps a lover in a false role. Like 'A Pretty Woman' it is in a sparing, tense stanzaic form which Browning is so good at making both lyric and self-mocking. This one has a lullaby movement, deceptively soothing. The woman attempts to reconcile a quarrel by persuading the man to sleep, to give up words and analysis, which are destructive—'Hush and hide the talking, / Cheek on cheek!' Sometimes, she says, it is necessary to turn away from the truth, the ominous predatory 'creature', which is waiting to destroy them while they quarrel, because the truth is sometimes unbearable. The advice in the first four stanzas is sentimental and unrealistic, but innocuous. It is hardly possible to say 'All be as before', when the very fact of the quarrel has altered and modified the nature of that 'before'. But in the fifth stanza it becomes clear that her conciliatory advice is in reality a deep rejection of the man: don't pluck the apple from the tree of knowledge 'Lest we lose our Edens'. The 'we' here should mean the man and herself and the line break encourages these expectations, but she says, selfishly, 'Eve and I'. As the poem proceeds with offers of self-abasement and the sinking of her identity in his, she asks continually that they take the roles of clod and pebble, the strong and the weak, and the role-making carries a hidden reproach: 'Be a man and fold me / With thine arm!'—why haven't you been a 'man' before? Even this imposed role does not carry conviction, for she maintains her right to reserve her identity beneath it—'That shall be tomorrow / Not to-night . . .' Browning's virtuosity with metre here persuades the lullaby rhythms to move with a cruel, energetic stabbing motion, and one might feel, perhaps, that this is another of Browning's cruel, virtuoso ironies. This could be so, except that the poem's greatest virtuosity is to make one feel as a haunting after-image, the man's pain, anxiety and exasperation.

Browning's exploration of role-playing and role-creating in love acknowledges the paradox of the act of imagination: it is a necessary fiction; it actually nourishes and sustains, continually bringing the loved one into being with fresh splendour: 'So life's night gives my lady birth / And my eyes hold her!' Such re-creations in the imagination are proof against change, says the speaker of 'In Three Days'. At the same time it is the damaging, illusory element in dishonest love. Having to create the other person brings Browning against the appalling unknowableness of the other: the woman of 'In a Year' asks

> *Was it something said,*
> *Something done*
> *Vexed him? was it touch of hand,*
> *Turn of head?*
> *Strange! that very way*
> *Love begun:*

The greatest of his love poems are those which are full of fear that the other will continue to vanish before even the most passionate efforts of the lover's creating imagination. Even the confident, marvellously inarticulate hyperboles of 'Song' (an early poem published in 1845), based on Donne's hyperbole, Every thy hair is much too much for love to work upon, falls back on astounded repetition—'Aught like this tress, see, and this tress . . . Above this tress, and this . . .'. The mingled grudging, and elegaic, distrustfulness of 'Any Wife to Any Husband' springs from the knowledge that the man's imagination will not sustain a living memory of her when she dies. The speaker of 'By the Fire-side' builds a whole permanence on only a single moment of reciprocity. *James Lee's Wife*, in *Dramatis Personae*, 1864, charts the drying up of the generous acts of imagination between man and wife which sustained the original impulse of feeling, which was a miraculously arbitrary event, like a brilliant butterfly on bare rock. Perhaps the most concise expression of the strenuous imaginative search for the lover is 'Love in a Life'.

> *Room after room,*
> *I hunt the house through*
> *We inhabit together.*

The speaker hunts through ever-receding empty spaces. Rooms enclose space and only seem to define the emptiness more, and the search is a repeated greeting of emptiness, of contentless experience. No wonder the poet has to importune each alcove. It is a beautiful image both of loss and absence and the vacant constructs of the mind. Only Browning could talk of importuning an alcove and make the act have a yearning, endless lyric reverberation.

    To end my account of Browning's Romantic treatment of love I have chosen a poem which is not very much discussed, 'A Lover's Quarrel', and 'Two in the Campagna' because they seem to me to be microcosms of his concerns. In spite of being a poem of disappointment, 'A Lover's Quarrel' is written with gaiety and daring zestfulness. It opens with an energetic sensory response to spring, which ought to be in ironic contrast to the lover's mood, but it is not. He *seems* brisk and cheerful, as if still in the excitement of the experience he has lost. The winter world of the lovers was 'blocked up' with snow, withdrawn and barricaded, and inside it they played high-spirited, absurdly childish games. The point about these games is not that they were silly, creating factitious thrills, but that every one of them is a model of the continual, free, unabashed

creating of one another that goes on between two people. They draw
one another—'Free on each other's flaws'—they create images of violence for one another (the rearing horse on the Pampas' sheen), they try
mesmerism together, a type of the willing and colluding imagination,
they act out mock crises. The man exclaims while he creates the image of
femininity before him—'See, how she looks now, dressed / In a sledg-
ing-cap and vest!' Finally, they boldly exchange *sexual* roles. Maleness
and femaleness are mutually created and mutually exchangeable. The
lovers invent each other's sexuality. There is a strange mixture of flagrant music-hall drag, here, with tender androgynous feelings.

> *Teach me to flirt a fan*
> *As the Spanish ladies can,*
> *Or I tint your lip*
> *With a burnt stick's tip*
> *And you turn into such a man!*
> *Just the two spots that span*
> *Half the bill of the young male swan!*

(X)

A fine touch is the reference to the newspaper report of the Emperor
Napoleon's marriage, an old man and a young bride in Stanzav. News
from the outside, other people's love, always seems ridiculous, or even
faintly obscene, to people not involved with it. The lovers are to Napoleon what the readers of the poem are to them. 'I was you all the happy
past', the man says when the woman has left him, and in the sense that the
love was a mutual act of liberated imaginative invention, this is perfectly
true. They did invent one another.

The ideas of withdrawal and fantasy come together in the image of the
mesmerizer snow in stanza XI, but the image is not an explanation of the
ending of the affair: the experience of the lovers is allowed to stand up to
the end of the poem with an energetic resilience. There is and can be no
explanation for the failure. The lover is left 'aghast' in the privacy of his
memories, to beg for explanation and to try to recreate the mood of the
winter. If there is an explanation it is as subtle and minute as the faintest
sound which can 'Scratch'—a very precise word for this infinitesimal
and damaging thing—'the brain's coat of curd!' (XIV). The recreation
of glee and delight is strained as the man imagines the girl's impossible
return. There is something sad and thin about the imaginary crypt

where, in retreat from the world, they will be forced to cling together for protection. It suggests death, and there is a hollow satirical note in the reminiscence of *Romeo and Juliet*, which is typical of Browning's way of twisting from lyric to irony. Always in this poem the tripping rhythmical pattern asserts itself almost jokingly against the smooth, easy resolution of feeling which both speaker and reader *want*.

This poem is remarkable for its honesty to all the phases of feeling in the episode. However thin, the man's fantasizing is not diminished by its failure to match the life of the reality but shown as of the nature of our experience. Not all the love poems succeed as well. The mockery and the seriousness sometimes overbalance one another. 'Two in the Campagna', however, is another completely satisfying poem. I have written of this work elsewhere.[1] But I should like to add to what I said by comparing it to 'By the Fire-side'. Like 'By the Fire-side', 'Two in the Campagna' is built upon a rapid sensory recreation of an associative process—'I touched a thought . . .'—and the process is rendered in terms of the physical objects over which the speaker's consciousness is moving. Similarly, the memories which bud out of the speaker's mind in 'By the Fire-side' attach themselves, with broad movements from height to depth, to the mountain scene. But the difference between the two poems comes from the fact that what the poet in 'By the Fire-side' is describing is all in the past. True, the past is altered by the very fact of successive memories of it, but the moment of union which is the climax of the poem has a safety guaranteed by its narrative terms. It is trapped, and the triumphant risk of building upon a moment fully acknowledged as dangerously fragile, arising out of intense anxiety and a kind of swollen, destructive irritability, is justified by the future which spreads out from that moment to the speaker's present. In 'Two in the Campagna' the narrative is forward not backward, and the poem is entirely open. It begins, as I have said, with the speaker caught in a mesh of tenses, with the puzzlement stretching back into his life and forward in the continuous present—'I wonder do you feel today / As I have felt since . . .' The beauty of the achieved 'good minute' and the poignancy of its disappearance have made people see this poem as an elegy on the evanescence of such experience. But the rendering of evanescence carries with it a further undermining statement of the *involuntariness* of passion, and this is what seems ultimately to

[1] 'The Brownings', in *The Victorians*, ed. Arthur Pollard, Sphere History of Literature, vol. 6, London, 1970.

deprive it of value. The associative process lights upon things which are both growing and dying—'The yellow fennel, run to seed . . .'—a fine mimesis of evanescence, the quick life and quicker fading of random thought. More important, the thought process is a model for experience in the poem because it is not here coexisting with the conscious will—'Help me to hold it!' It goes on in spite of itself, as the consciousness does, escaping control and definition. This leads to the central question of the poem: 'How is it under our control /to love or not to love?' The good minute and its disappearance, the central action of the poem, follows, dramatizing in large climactic emotional terms the failures that the random thought processes and the questions have suggested. Necessarily, the whole ramifying process of thought-spinning and thought-seeking then begins again—'Off again!' The poem stops in the middle of the act of searching. Browning has turned a great nineteenth-century metaphor against itself here. Some Victorians saw the associative process hopefully as the means by which human beings are connected with their past and with each other. The outgoing tissue of thought makes organic 'threads of connection', in George Eliot's phrase, between us. Here the speaker spins his threads in isolation like the spider described at the beginning of the poem, the same image used of Sordello's solipsist thought. Yet the poem contains a negative vindication of the involuntary moment: these moments can never be 'primal' in the way of nature's instinctual easy life (stanza VI), for they are invested with value by the human energy and imagination poured into them. They cannot be controlled by the conscious will but they can be apprehended by it. The play of puzzlement and yearning is itself their justification, but the celebration is shot through with loss and defeat.

> *Only I discern*
> *Infinite passion, and the pain*
> *Of finite hearts that yearn.*

The great love poems do not continue after *Men and Women*. The poems of *Dramatis Personae* are written out of void and emptiness after the death of Browning's wife, but they do not build further on the strange affirmations and ironies of the earlier lyrics. I shall turn now to *Fifine at the Fair* (1872), where there seems to be a great disjunction between the earlier love lyrics, dominated by Romantic ideas and idioms, and this new Victorian poetry, dominated by immediate topical issues.

The difference, it seems to me, is fairly superficial, for Browning's long dialogue with the Romantic tradition equipped him to deal with Victorian problems, in particular the question of sex, in a way quite different from his contemporaries.

The tone of *Fifine* is muted in comparison with the virtuoso flourishes of the early monologues. The speaking voice is understated, naturalistic, subtly reflecting class idioms and assumptions. It is such a convincing rendering of a voice which speaks intelligently, sophisticatedly and authoritatively to itself that the temptation is to believe in Don Juan's good faith and to accept the terms of the problem-solving exercise he sets himself, which is to demonstrate that both Elvire, his chaste middle-class wife, and Fifine, the wanton circus acrobat, are necessary to him, necessary without incompatibility and without loss of real virtue on his part. He gives the confident impression of being able to resolve a paradox, but his stance is deceptively confident. It is easy enough to see the origin of Guido's sexual hate in *The Ring and the Book* when he tells Pompiia to 'occupy your private patch of snow': he is infuriated by her recoil from him and angry that his-fantasy of fulfilment with a child-wife has been baulked by the fact that she is really a child in experience. It is far less easy to see what Browning is doing in Don Juan's knowing analysis of Fifine. Don Juan sees her as one of the raggle-taggle outsiders who give 'society the slip'. She is carelessly promiscuous, returning again to the ogre-husband, the strong man who will beat her, 'Brute-beast-face', the man she prefers sexually to any of her upper-class lovers—'Oh she prefers sheer strength to ineffective grace' (**XXV**). But Don Juan's amusement at class refinements and hypocrisy—'You draw back skirts from filth like her . . .' (**XXIV**) disguises an only gradually revealed sentimentality about Fifine and her class: he *needs* to see Fifine as a liberated rejecter of society rather than a social outcast; he needs to see her as rejecting him sexually, because thereby he reduces any human claim she might have on him, and he is able to dwell with self-titillating indulgence on the brute, atavistic sexual appetite of the lower classes. He talks as if Fifine is part of the class realities he understands, but she is surely sheer fantasy, the creation both of simplifying sexual desire and sexual fear. It is a brilliant demonstration on Browning's part of a way class, sex and fantasy can be all indivisibly smelted together in a person's consciousness. By the same token the respectable, insipid, but exactingly jealous Elvire is also the creation of fear and fantasy: her cold chastity justifies Don Juan's interest in the vivid sexual slut he makes of Fifine, and yet it also enables him to condemn and diminish Fifine. Don Juan polarizes his women into whore and virtuous matron because this sexual dualism makes possible a subtle denigration of both women. He feels in control of the situation. They have the vices of each other's virtues. One is cold but faithful: the other is satisfying but unfaithful.

Don Juan, of course, could be seen as one of Stephen Marcus's other Victorians, but I have not found it helpful to use Marcus here or at any point in this essay because in spite of himself Marcus writes as if pornography explodes rather than reflects fears and hypocrisies: too often he writes as if pornography exposes a truth which the official literature refuses to contemplate. His model is the Freudian unconscious. He celebrates Victorian pornography as an underworld literature, as if it acts like a kind of unconscious to the collective official society, turning up truth-telling reality time and again. He makes gestures toward a more subtle notion, but in general he loses sight of the fact that pornography is as much, if not more, likely to reflect cultural fantasy as any form. What I find perceptive in *Fifine at the Fair* is the insight that the notion of the underworld is itself the result of fantasizing. But Browning's imagination went further than this because he saw that the polarization into whore and virtuous matron, one implying the other, both bolsters Don Juan's sense of his maleness and simultaneously erodes it. It is destructive in its simplistic falsity and destructive because it leads to emptiness and a sense of impotence. So instead of resolving the paradox Don Juan sets himself, the poem cracks open its contradictions: it replaces the paradox with another one; the dualism *is* necessary to Don Juan only because, as he half realizes, it is necessary to sustain his view of himself. And 'half realizes' is an important qualification, for this is a poem about a highly self-conscious man struggling to define himself. There is constantly a subtle movement towards honesty and then away from it, and the drama of this poem is that the argument is discovered by a man in intense difficulties with himself. The way Browning traces the movements of Don Juan's position is to use yet again the Romantic image of the lover-creator, whose imaginative act of creating the lover can be both life-giving or corrupt and debasing. The image slowly turns against itself as the poem moves along.

Don Juan's first description of Fifine is a tour de force, in its leisurely, insulting, and curiously sensitive appraisal (for Don Juan is an

intelligent, corrupt poet) of her sexual being. It is also a taunting of
Elvire, who is listening, because by implication it defines her sexual in-
adequacies and entices her to sexual jealousy. Don Juan's connoisseurship
is intrigued by the tawdry costume, the teasing androgynous ambiguity
of the spangled dress, and the sexual aggression of Fifine's response to
him. Fifine is half immense nubile female, half homosexual boy.

> *And then, her neck! now, grant you had the power to deck,*
> *Just as your fancy pleased, the bistre-length of neck,*
> *Could lay, to shine against its shade, a moonlike row*
> *Of pearls, each round and white as bubble Cupids blow*
> *Big out of mother's milk,—what pearl-moon would surpass*
> *That string of mock-turquoise, those almandines of glass,*
> *Where girlhood terminates? for with breasts'-birth commence*
> *The boy, and page-costume, till pink and impudence*
> *End admirably all: complete the creature trips*
> *Our way now, brings sunshine upon her spangled hips,*
> *As here she fronts us full, with pose half-frank, half-fierce!*          (**XV**)

The half-tender sensuality here is very slightly coarse—Pippa's beads are
vulgarly bloated, but so is the hyperbolic simile for them. The discussion
turns to a comparison between the two women, further goading Elvire.
Fifine is the lily, sterile and poisonous, yet exciting, and liberated from
moral standards—'self-sustainment made morality': Elvire is the respectable rose of English married love, 'No flavourous venom-bell', but
plucked and put 'I' the proper loyal throne (**XVIII**) on breast where rose
should be'. There is a wonderful assimilation of Swinburne's erotic language here to the muted sophistication of Don Juan's voice, and the
slightly over-stated, Swinburnian element enables Browning to be
ironic about Don Juan's ironies. The inversion of the usual symbol is
treated with mocking irony here, thoroughly enjoyed by Don Juan.
Fifine is not the lily of purity: Elvire is not the rose of flaming passion,
which, placed alongside the 'daisy meek' and 'maiden violet', is made to
seem insipid and without vitality. But later, on the evening walk they
take together, Don Juan is sensually moved and puzzled by Elvire's coldness, teased by the 'silken thrill' of her eyelash (**LXIV**). He is haunted by
her apartness from him, which calls out lyric feeling. Browning never
forgets that however false the polarization between whore and pure
woman may be, the difficulties the fantasy lands one with are real

enough. Yet on the whole, the imagery always works against Elvire: in another tortured sequence of explanation, she is the cumbersome, stable motherboat, and Fifine is the light skiff (LXXXI—LXXXII).

Don Juan constantly resorts to the notion of the lover as artist in order to convince Elvire of the power of love. In the early part of the poem these are confident assertions. By mythologizing you, creating you as ideal being, he says, I bring into being and make possible your sexual self, just as the gods made Helen's phantom bring into being the great events of Troy (XXVI–XXX). He celebrates the 'self-vindicating flash' (XXIX) which rescues and recreates each human being. In another long sequence about the lover-creator (XLIII–LX) life is 'stuff for transmuting'; the 'elemental flame' of love creates 'a new birth of life, the challenged soul's response / To ugliness and death' (LV), so that lovers release each other's self-hood (LIX). But this noble reciprocity does not last. Fifine's qualities, when dwelt upon in the imagination, only serve to accentuate Elvire's loyalty and goodness. When the lover-creator idea is reversed and transferred to Elvire, Don Juan says that she makes him feel *real*. Like Arion's porpoise, women 'bear—palpitating— / One proud humility of love', a man's selfhood (LXXVIII)—there are strong sexual overtones here. It is at this point that fear, self-disgust and desperation begin to rise against the confidence. Men respond only to hate and aggression (LXXIX). A woman is an 'Auxiliary' who 'Takes nothing and gives all': 'at least', he says 'convince unreasonable me / That I am, anyhow, a truth' (LXXX). The desperation mounts again in the night-terror of LXXXIV: 'Are you unterrified? / All false, all fleeting too!' But such dependence for one's sense of identity on women breeds a counter-reaction of rage and fear. Earlier he has said that men destroy, 'take light and heat' from those they love, but 'Women rush into you, and there remain absorbed' (LXXI). Women are like headlong streams prepared to annihilate their identity, but in doing so they can swamp a man's maleness. The image is exactly like the account of the 'gentler' creating minds in *Sordello* who can 'Bury themselves' in 'something not themselves'. But now the image has turned sour: the female habit of swampy self-effacement must be countered by the male's assertion, and a further pattern of self-effacement (LXXVI). The most one can do is to *pretend* that this does not happen, to fabricate a relationship of respect and reverence. No wonder that, with an identity which is both damaged by women's self-interested effacingness and yet supported by

their humility, men will go in search of Fifines in order to release themselves from this self-defeating paradox. The Fifines are the means for a
kind of existential, free, testing out of the self through sex. The heroic
voyage of self-discovery on a dangerous sea comes to Don Juan's mind as
he explains that he needs to live in danger, 'trusting to sea-tracklessness'
(LXXXII):

> *With those . . .*
> *Who dreaded no degree of death, but, with dry eyes,*
> *Surveyed the turgid main and its monstrosities—*
> *And rendered futile so, the prudent Power's decree*
> *Of separate earth and dissacociating sea.*

Don Juan's self-mocking ironies attempt to qualify the heroics as he
remembers the 'comfortable ode' of Horace to Virgil on a sea voyage. As
usual the ironies are never quite directed aright: the sea and its 'monstro-
sities' is an analogue for *sexual* experience. And in Don Juan's image it is
everything that is threatening and destructive. It hits at the core of his
identity. It is a comparison full of fear and anxiety, fear of impotence,
fear of emptiness.

Browning has here analyzed the self-gratifying but damaging myth of
women as either Fifine's or Elvire's, whores or angels, with extraordinarily subtle meticulousness. The sophisticated uncertainties of the
argument get into the fractures of the form, the clogged syntax of the
poem, with its constant feints at articulation. The convoluted, repeated
arguments, the doubling in and out of feeling are a fine miming of the
confusions of Don Juan. Other poems, such as *Red Cotton Night-Cap
Country* and the *Parleying* with Furini can claim to show Browning looking hard at contemporary sexual myths. But nowhere did he look
harder, or more rigorously, than in *Fifine at the Fair*. The intelligence of
his scrutiny transcends a merely journalistic, topical investigation of contemporary life. He was able to arrive at insights about the nature of a
social fantasy by exploring it through the surprising and subtle applications of his old Romantic assumptions about the nature of the imagination. Browning continued to grow as a poet because he continued
to explore and question with versatile scepticism the possibilities of his
longest-held positions.

# 11: *Robert Browning: A Reader's Guide*

## P. J. KEATING

SHORTLY AFTER BROWNING'S death on 12 December 1890, Henry James published in *The Speaker* an obituary article in which he attempted to justify Browning's burial with the great literary figures of the past. It was not the first time James had pronounced on Browning, nor was it to be the last: it is not even, perhaps, his most memorable utterance (that was to be offered in fictional form) but there is about 'Browning in Westminster Abbey' a considered quality, a determined attempt at this moment of death, to speak well of the poet who had fascinated him and temporarily to ignore the man who repelled him, which assures it classic status in Browning criticism. James praises Browning's 'irrepressible faculty for looking at human events in all sorts of slanting coloured lights'; his 'contemporary individualism'; and 'the extraordinary beauty of his treatment of the special relation between man and woman'. Even his reservations are advanced as though constituting praise. He indicates the 'wonderful mixture' in Browning of 'the universal and the alembicated', and 'the confused yet comprehensive utterance of which he was the great professor', while James's own uncertainty is expressed in the sentence:

'A good many oddities and a good many great writers have been entombed in the Abbey; but none of the odd ones have been so great and none of the great ones so odd.'

Eighty years after James's attempt to 'possess' Browning 'through the glass plate of death' he remains curiously unchanged, the same bewildering mixture of greatness and oddity. His place is undoubtedly assured, but it is hardly possible to indicate among scholars (even among scholars of Victorian poetry) a consensus of opinion on how to define or evaluate the nature of that place. Like most other major writers he has become the centre of a vast academic industry, yet the flood of articles, monographs, and scholarly volumes, seems rather to heighten than lessen Browning's elusiveness. Even the most intelligent and enthusiastic of his modern critics tend to stumble when faced with the necessity of making a final assessment. H. B. Charlton can proclaim him 'the greatest nineteenth century English poet after Wordsworth', and then add: 'That may be prejudice rather than judgement'. In 1950, W. O. Raymond could state: 'Though it is now sixty-five years since the death of Robert Browning, the time is yet unripe for a definitive estimate of his place amongst English men of letters'; and eighteen years later Park Honan echoes these words: 'We have yet to estimate his artistic strengths and weaknesses convincingly for our time.'[1] It is tempting to blame this hesitation on the general reaction against Victorian poetry brought about by 'the great redirection of energy in English criticism initiated in this century by Eliot, Richards and Leavis,'[2] but this is hardly the whole story. Browning has *always* evoked critical doubt and uncertainty, and in the counter-reaction of the 1950s and 60s, his fortunes have continued to fluctuate while those of his most important contemporaries among Victorian poets, Tennyson and Arnold, have settled impressively. It would be difficult to imagine a modern edition of Browning's poetry being received with the widespread approval and pleasure excited by Kenneth Allott's Arnold and Christopher Ricks's Tennyson.

This is not to force upon Browning an inferior position, but rather to recognize his special qualities. The years have not lessened the notorious obscurity and difficulty of his poetry, and although some readers will be happy to follow Chesterton in his belief that, '*Sordello* was the most glorious compliment that has ever been paid to the average man'; and quite a few more George Eliot's magnificent tribute: 'In Browning's best poems he makes us feel that what we took for obscurity in him was superficiality in ourselves'; most will probably follow Elizabeth Barrett: 'There are fine things in it—and the presence of genius, never to be denied! At the same time it is hard . . . *to understand*—isn't it? Too hard? I

[1] H. B. Charlton, 'Browning: The Poet's Aim', *BJRL*, XXII, 1938, 98; W. O. Raymond, *The Infinite Moment*, 2nd rev. edn. 1965, 3; Park Honan, 'Robert Browning', in Frederic Faverty (ed) *The Victorian Poets: A Guide to Research*, Cambridge, Mass., 2nd rev. edn. 1968, 98.

[2] Isobel Armstrong (ed) *The Major Victorian Poets: Reconsiderations*, 1969, 1.

think so!"[1]

While exegesis will serve to clarify specific problems, it can never persuade the unwilling reader of a poet's worth: only an overwhelming conviction of his central significance can do that, and whereas such persuasion has been effected for, say, Hopkins and Donne, the same cannot be claimed for Browning, though Robert Langbaum in *The Poetry of Experience* (1957) has gone as near to achieving this as anyone. Until this does happen the uncertainty and doubt will remain, and Henry James, with his honest evaluation finding expression in multiple paradoxes, will remain our touchstone.

### Collected Editions, Bibliographies, Handbooks, and Collections of Essays on Browning

Browning's *Poetical Works* (17 vol 1888–94), largely supervised by Browning himself and completed after his death by Edward Berdoe provides the basis for subsequent collected editions, the most important being the 'Florentine' (12 vol 1898) edited by Charlotte Porter and Helen A. Clarke, and the 'Centenary' (10 vol 1912) edited by F. G. Kenyon. Augustine Birrell's useful two volume edition was first published in 1896 and frequently reprinted, and in 1915, together with Kenyon, Birrell edited a 'complete' works in one volume. This edition incorporated some new poems first published the previous year which had come to light in the 1913 sale of Browning material.

There is clearly a need in Browning scholarship for a modern, complete, and carefully annotated edition of the works, and this has been undertaken by the Ohio University Press under the general editorship of Roma A. King. Three of a projected thirteen volumes have been published so far. Volume One contains *Pauline*, the sonnet 'Eyes calm beside thee', and *Paracelsus*; volume two, *Strafford* and *Sordello*; and volume three *Pippa Passes, King Victor and King Charles*, the *Essay on Chatterton, Dramatic Lyrics*, and *The Return of the Druses*. The publication of the first two of these volumes has provoked some strong criticism of the textual principles adopted by the editors. In a review published in *Victorian Stu-*

---

[1] G. K. Chesterton, *Robert Browning*, 1903, 38; George Eliot, review of *Men and Women* in *The Westminster Review*, Jan. 1865, repr. Boyd Litzinger and Donald Smalley (eds) *Browning: The Critical Heritage*, 1970, 174; Betty Miller (ed) *Elizabeth Barrett to Miss Mitford*, 1954, 78.

*dies*, Thomas J. Collins has claimed that so 'incompetent' is the editing
that the whole project should be temporarily suspended, while, in a
calmer mood, Rowland L. Collins in *Victorian Poetry*, has also expressed
disquiet at the break with the principles of textual editing established by
the Centre for Editions of American Authors.[1] These are obviously only
the opening moves in what is likely to be a long drawn out controversy
between two schools of thought on the matter rather than a simple case
of right versus wrong, the editors of the Ohio *Browning* having acknowledged in their preface that their methods are 'not entirely conventional',
and justified their choice of the 1888–9 *Poetical Works* as the copy-text on
the grounds that this establishes as far as is possible Browning's own final
revisions and intentions. Apart from this controversy (which clearly
cannot be resolved until the Ohio edition is completed) the first volumes
are very usefully annotated and handsomely produced.

The amount of published comment on Browning's life and work is
enormous, and appears to be increasing at a faster rate than ever before,
though now, as indeed always, Browning has been favoured with
devoted bibliographers who have made reference to this varied mass of
material relatively easy. The standard work is *Robert Browning: A Bibliography 1830–1950* (1953) by L. N. Broughton, C. S. Northup and
Robert Pearsall, which contains full details of works by and about
Browning, together with listings of verse parodies, musical settings of his
poetry, and a Calendar of Letters. For all general purposes it supersedes
the earlier work by T. J. Wise and F. J. Furnivall, by its comprehensive-
ness, and also because it is free from the taint of Wise which has existed
since the unmasking of his forgeries initiated by John Carter and Graham
Pollard in *An Enquiry into the Nature of Certain Nineteenth Century Pamphlets* (1934), which should be read in conjunction with Wilfred
Partington's fascinating biography *Thomas J. Wise in the Original Cloth*
(1946), first published in 1939 as *Forging Ahead*. Robert Pearsall's entry in
the *Cambridge Bibliography of English Literature*, volume III, 1969, lists,
without annotation, the principal publications down to 1966; while *The
Browning Critics* (1965) edited by Boyd Litzinger and K. L. Knickerbocker, contains a thorough bibliography covering the years 1951–65.
Park Honan's chapter in the revised edition of Frederic Faverty's *The
Victorian Poets: A Guide to Research* (1968) is a masterly guide through

---

[1] *VS*, XIII, 1969, 441–4; *VP*, IX, 1971, 351–6.

Browning scholarship. Useful annual bibliographies are published in *Victorian Studies* (from 1958), and *Victorian Poetry* (from 1963). The *Browning Newsletter* (from 1968), which continues the Browning tradition at Baylor University established by A. J. Armstrong, also contains an annual checklist of publications, as does *Browning Society Notes*, the journal of the newly revived London Browning Society.

The large number of handbooks, primers, and introductions to Browning which have been published (especially in the years immediately following his death) offers a striking testimony to his reputation for obscurity, as well as to the belief held by, and perhaps encouraged in, potential readers, that unaided communication is unlikely to occur. W. C. DeVane's *A Browning Handbook* (1935, rev ed 1955) is indispensable. A major work of scholarship, it contains discussions of all of Browning's poems, relating them to his life, offering sources, details of publication, and astute bibliographical guidance. The range and reliability of DeVane's *Handbook* set it apart from the many similar earlier works, though in one respect it does not entirely supersede them. Mrs Orr's *A Handbook to the Works of Robert Browning*, first published in 1885 and in many subsequently revised editions, gives prose summaries of the poems, and although her interpretations are often unlikely to satisfy modern critics, her book can still help the student who is confused by the train of events or line of argument in the more complex poems. Edward Berdoe's *Browning Cyclopaedia* (1891) also offers detailed summaries, together with an unwieldy bulk of arbitrarily chosen information and annotation, as does, in a more intelligently selective manner, G. W. Cooke's *A Guide to the Poetic and Dramatic Works of Robert Browning* (1891). The most historically interesting aspect of these early handbooks is the emphasis they place on Browning's thought rather than his poetry, an attitude which helps explain the widespread use of prose summaries. They represent, as Berdoe expressed it, in one of his many unhappy phrases, a 'serious attempt to suck each verse dry of its wonderful teaching'.[1]

For the modern student, collections of critical essays, presenting sometimes an historical survey of a writer's work, more often a variety of critical approaches, have in many respects replaced the 'primer' or 'handbook' of seventy years ago, and carry with them the same useful-

[1] *Browning's Message to his Time*, 1890, 194.

ness and dangers. In recent years three such volumes have been devoted to Browning: Boyd Litzinger and K. L. Knickerbocker (eds) *The Browning Critics* (1965); Philip Drew (ed) *Robert Browning: A Collection of Critical Essays* (1966); and Clarence Tracy (ed) *Browning's Mind and Art* (1968). Litzinger and Knickerbocker's volume is the most ambitious, and interpretative, containing important studies written between the years 1891–1964; Drew's volume combines general estimates of Browning and close studies of specific poems, while Tracy's volume is largely limited to near contemporary critical estimates. Considering the similar nature of these books there is surprisingly little over-lap, and taken together they offer an impressive, if necessarily fragmentary, range of responses to Browning's poetry. *The Major Victorian Poets: Reconsiderations* (1969) edited by Isobel Armstrong, although not devoted entirely to Browning, includes four critical essays on him.

### Life and Letters

Just as Henry James's 'Browning in Westminster Abbey' provides a valuable starting point for a discussion of Browning's poetry, so does his short story 'The Private Life' (1891) offer a more suggestive approach to Browning's life than any of the full-scale biographies which have been published. The central character, Clare Vawdrey, was, as James acknowledged, based on Browning, though he was also careful to describe the story as 'of course a rank fantasy'.[1] James's view is that Clare Vawdrey is in reality two people, each quite distinct from the other: 'One is the genius, the other's the bourgeois, and it's only the bourgeois whom we personally know.' While the bourgeois Vawdrey is chatting with the dinner guests, his phantom genius sits in the bedroom writing; his public life is nothing, his private life is all. This interpretation is often taken to refer solely to Browning's active social life during his later years, but the point James is making goes, at least by implication, far beyond this:

> The irritating certitude [was] that for personal relations this admirable genius thought his second-best good enough. It *was*, no doubt, as society was made, but there was a contempt in the distinction which could not fail to be galling to an admirer. The world was

[1] F. O. Matthieson and Kenneth B. Murdock (eds) *The Notebooks of Henry James*, 1947, 110.

vulgar and stupid, and the real man would have been a fool to come out for it when he could gossip and dine by deputy.[1]

It's a matter of communication: a fear that a genius which is 'all private and no public life', cuts itself off from a potential audience by a contemptuous rejection of any but private values, a solution which makes communication all the more difficult; it encourages perhaps that 'confused yet comprehensive utterance' which James noted as characteristic of Browning in his obituary article. Critics have remarked that in this story James is thinking as much of himself as of Browning, and this is possibly true as the similarities between the two men are often striking. There is, however, one crucial qualification. For Browning the public neglect which ultimately bred scorn had not applied to most of his great contemporaries (to Tennyson, Dickens, and George Eliot); in this, as in so much else, Browning is unlike the early and mid-Victorians. But for James, who belongs to the radically changed atmosphere of late Victorian England, public neglect of major writers was more common than adulation, and in Browning he saw the dangers and uncertainties of his own position. His interpretation of the two Brownings echoes in biographical studies of the poet to the present day. The basic facts relating to James's 'fantasy' study of Browning have been examined by Sidney E. Lind in 'James's "The Private Life" and Browning', *American Literature*, XXIII (1951).

In 'The Private Life' James was, of course, offering interpretation not detailed biography, and it is perhaps unfair to include him here; but the problem with the more orthodox biographies is that while they provide (in ever increasing quantities) the necessary detailed information, they are, in the main, rather thin on interpretation. Edmund Gosse's *Robert Browning: Personalia* (1890) divides into two parts: the first, a brief narrative of Browning's life up to his marriage, and the second a more interesting warm personal tribute to Browning's friendliness and open nature: 'The subtlest of writers, he was the simplest of men.[2] Mrs Sutherland Orr's *Life and Letters of Robert Browning* which was first published in 1891, and revised and corrected by F. G. Kenyon in 1908, is virtually an 'official' biography: she knew Browning well and had access to family

[1] Leon Edel (ed) *The Complete Tales of Henry James*, VIII, 1963, 189–227. 'The Private Life' was first published in the *Atlantic Monthly*, April 1892.

[2] *Robert Browning: Personalia*, 1890, 92.

papers and letters which at that time were unpublished. Her sympathy for Browning, and the central role she played in helping to formulate late Victorian attitudes towards him, give the biography lasting value, though inevitably there were some areas of his life of which she was unaware or which she diplomatically passed over, and, as in her *Handbook*, her responses to his poetry and the ways in which it relates to his life sometimes appear over-simplified. As a reliable, straightforward narrative Mrs Orr's *Life and Letters* was superseded by W. Hall Griffin's and H. C. Minchin's *Life* (1910: rev 1938), which has long been the standard biography. Lillian Whiting's *The Brownings* (1911), apart from the gushing style in which it is written, is good on the relationship between Robert and Elizabeth and on Browning's later social life.

Thin interpretation is not a charge which can be made with justice against Betty Miller's *Robert Browning* (1952), the most aggressive, readable, and irritating of the biographies. Betty Miller challenges the traditional view that Browning's father was the dominant parental influence on his early life and asserts instead the power his mother had over him, relating this to his marriage and the many (admittedly curious) close friendships he formed with other women. The problem with this intense kind of psychological interpretation is that the conscious artistic intelligence of the poet tends to get lost in the relentless drive at his subconscious; the dramatic monologues, for example, become 'adopted disguises'—one of the many means by which Browning tried to obliterate all record of the less attractive aspect of his life. Betty Miller's confidence in her conclusions is unlikely to be shared by many readers: 'The most successful disguise of all, of course, was language itself: there can be little doubt that much of the obscurity of Robert Browning was an involuntary form of self-protection.'[1] A great deal of doubt is, of course, possible about such statements, and Betty Miller's biography should be warily enjoyed.

A very similar approach is to be found in Richard D. Altick's 'The Private Life of Robert Browning' (*Yale Review*, XLI, 1951). Pursuing James's notion of the phantom poet, Altick argues that 'Browning was the victim of a tragic ambivalence. He wanted to be a philosopher-poet, but his genius dictated that he fulfil himself in quite another way.' The 'dramatic mask' is once again given a rather sinister interpretation, and

[1] *Robert Browning*, 1952, 105.

even Browning's profound religious belief in the 'glories of the incomplete' is seen as the result of a 'growing need to salve his awareness of failure.' Altick's article is the most succinct expression of this kind of attempt to find a solution to what so many writers since James have felt to be a personal mystery lying at the heart of Browning's poetry. But there is, as we have seen, an alternative tradition, and Kenneth L. Knickerbocker's 'A Tentative Apology for Robert Browning' (*Tennessee Studies in Literature* I, 1956) is a lively rejoinder to Altick. Both articles are reprinted in *The Browning Critics*.

Maisie Ward's *Robert Browning and His World* (2 vol 1969) is a sane, well-balanced corrective to Betty Miller's excesses. The phantom Browning is still strongly present, but Maisie Ward resists the temptation to pursue him. She writes: 'There is something about Browning that makes the temptation to "explain" him almost irresistible. But theorizing is dangerous when one has to deal with facts.'[1] The strength of this biography lies in its comprehensive attempt at a factual reconstruction of Browning's life, and through this to bring out those seemingly contradictory qualities (in this case an essential simplicity of character combined with an 'exceptionally complex intellect') which makes theorizing about him so 'irresistible'. It is, however, unlikely to satisfy those biographers and critics who are unwilling to surrender the two Brownings theory, without being offered a similarly attractive alternative to replace it.

The one part of Browning's life with which everyone is familiar—his courtship of and elopement with Elizabeth Barrett—has inspired a vast number of studies, highly romanticized, drawing heavily (sometimes almost exclusively) on the love letters, and furiously perpetuating the belief that, in Dallas Kenmare's words, here is 'one of the most fascinating love-stories in the world'.[2] The following volumes, in their slightly different ways, are characteristic of the genre: Dormer Creston, *Andromeda in Wimpole Street* (1929); Frances Winwar, *The Immortal Lovers* (1950), and Dallas Kenmare, *The Browning Love-Story* (1957). The classic work in this field is Rudolf Besier's *The Barretts of Wimpole Street* (1930), which enjoyed enormous success both as a play and film. A virulent condemnation of such books is to be found in Norman Lindsay's article 'The

[1] *Robert Browning and His World*, 1969, II, 264.
[2] *The Browning Love-Story*, 1957, 7.

Mask of Robert Browning' (*Southerly*, XX, 1959), though, indeed, his tirade is directed at all biographies of the Brownings. Lindsay attacks the 'great deal of sickening sentiment' written about this 'idyllic' marriage, pronounces Elizabeth a 'prunes-and-prism prude' who exercised an inhibiting effect on her husband's poetry, and argues that Browning enjoyed many love affairs both during his marriage and after Elizabeth's death. The tone of Lindsay's article is often more unpleasant than anything Browning probably had to hide (and there is a moment of unconscious irony for someone so busily stripping off masks in the description of Chesterton as a 'fat clown') but, as Park Honan has pointed out, Lindsay does tend to 'make explicit what is implicit in Altick's and Mrs Miller's probings.'[1] Whether he is right or wrong is quite another matter.

Of the many shorter studies with a strong biographical interest, two persuasively argued articles by W. C. DeVane are of special interest. In 'The Virgin and the Dragon' (*Yale Review*, XXXVII, 1947) DeVane examines Browning's obsession with the Andromeda myth, traces its recurrence in the poetry and suggests that in his marriage Browning played Perseus to Elizabeth's Andromeda. 'The Harlot and the Thoughtful Young Man' (*Studies in Philology*, XXIX, 1932) explores the circumstances surrounding Buchanan's notorious attack on D. G. Rossetti in 'The Fleshly School of Poetry' published in the *Contemporary Review*, October 1871, and the reasons why Rossetti felt that Browning's *Fifine at the Fair* had been in part an answer to his own poem 'Jenny'. Both of these articles are reprinted in *The Browning Critics*. While DeVane is concerned with the breakdown of this relationship, Arthur A. Adrian's 'The Browning-Rossetti Friendship: Some Unpublished Letters' (*PMLA*, LXXIII, 1958), traces its early development between the years 1847–59, and reprints some interesting letters from Rossetti which demonstrate his great enthusiasm for Browning's poetry and his eagerness to meet the poet.

Several articles clarify aspects of Browning's early life. Betty Miller's 'This Happy Evening' (*Twentieth Century*, CLIV, 1953) recreates the dinner party which followed the opening night of Talfourd's tragedy *Ion* (1836), at which Browning was supposedly toasted by Wordsworth, and inspired by Macready to turn dramatist. Joseph W. Reed's 'Browning and Macready: The Final Quarrel' (*PMLA*, LXXV, 1960) examines

---

[1] Faverty (ed) *The Victorian Poets: A Guide to Research*, 88.

the causes of the breakdown of the collaboration which began on that happy evening, and offers a close study of Macready's revisions of Browning's plays, especially *A Blot in the 'Scutcheon*. In 'The Séance at Ealing' (*Cornhill*, CLXIX, 1957), Betty Miller succeeds in her usual lively manner in making one biographical mystery even more mysterious. A more complete treatment of the Brownings' involvement in the spiritualist craze which fascinated mid-Victorian England is to be found in Katherine H. Porter's *Through a Glass Darkly* (1958).

Finally B. R. Jerman's 'The Death of Robert Browning' (*UTO*, XXXV, 1965) is an exceptionally thorough exploration of Browning's final days and his eventual burial in Westminster Abbey. Jerman makes great play with contradictory descriptions of the circumstances surrounding Browning's death and burial, drawing warily on the memoirs of Fannie Browning and Evelyn Barclay, and a large number of other Victorian reminiscences. Apart from the solid information this article contains, and the mood of scholarly enjoyment it evokes, it provides a timely warning that the possible biographical sources for a writer as famous as Browning are virtually inexhaustible.

Only a few of the many critical studies which have biographical importance can be mentioned. W. C. DeVane's pioneering book *Browning's Parleyings, The Autobiography of a Mind* (1927) is both a detailed examination of one of the later and most neglected works and a demonstration of how the sources of certain dominant ideas and obsessions in Browning's poetry can be traced back to his early life. F. R. G. Duckworth's *Browning: Background and Conflict* (1931) will be discussed a little later, but deserves to be listed here for the contribution it makes to the 'two Brownings' tradition; while more energetic psychological interpretations are to be found in S. W. Holmes, 'Browning's *Sordello* and Jung: Browning's *Sordello* in the light of Jung's Theory of Types' (*PMLA*, LVI, 1941), and 'Browning: Semantic Stutterer', (*PMLA*, LX, 1945); and more recently in Barbara Melchiori's *Browning's Poetry of Reticence* (1969).

There is at present no collected edition of Browning's letters though one is projected under the editorship of Philip Kelley and Ronald Hudson. More surprisingly there is available no brief representative selection which would be of great use to students likely to be distracted by the growing number of published collections of Browning's letters to individual, or groups of, correspondents. This fragmentation has probably been encouraged by the feeling, even among Browning specialists, that his letters are uninteresting and dull. Philip Drew has described them as 'unrewarding' because Browning 'never responded . . . to the challenge of expressing himself in prose';[1] and W. C. DeVane, in his introduction to *New Letters of Robert Browning* (1951), writes: 'His letters are, in the main, matters of business, the prose side of his life.' These statements are too inclusive, but the force with which they are made does not promise well for a vast comprehensive collection, but rather gives strength to Isobel Armstrong's view that, 'A manageable volume of letters' is one of the 'prime needs of Browning studies at the present moment.'[2]

*The Letters of Robert Browning and Elizabeth Barrett 1845–6* (2 vol 1899), which were preserved by Browning against his usual tendency to destroy letters, are the most important. They tell the story of his courtship better than any secondary narrative, and contain many valuable insights into both the man and the poet. Apart from a useful index, they were barely 'edited' at all, and it is only recently that a trustworthy text has been published, in the handsome edition published by Harvard University Press, edited by Elvan Kintner. A single volume of selections from the love letters has been edited by V. E. Stack (1969).

The standard volume of Browning's letters is that edited by T. L. Hood (1933) from the collection of Thomas J. Wise. It covers the whole of Browning's writing life, and contains as an Appendix, Hood's important article detailing Browning's proposal of marriage to Lady Ashburton, which was previously published in the *Yale Review* (Autumn, 1932). The principal supplement to this volume is *New Letters of Robert Browning* (1950) edited by W. C. DeVane and K. L. Knickerbocker. Here again letters are drawn from throughout Browning's life, but it is especially rich in material relating to his early and middle years, his career as a playwright, and his relations with publishers. Another valuable Appendix examines the breakdown of the relationship between Browning and Chapman and Hall.

*Robert Browning and Alfred Domett* (1906) edited by Frederic G. Kenyon, contains letters relating mainly to Browning's friendship with Alfred Domett and Joseph Arnould during the early 1840s in Camber-

---

[1] *VS*, IX, 1966, 210.
[2] *VS*, XIV, 1970, 209.

well. It should be read in conjunction with *The Diary of Alfred Domett 1872–85* (1953) edited by E. A. Horsman, which contains a great deal of interesting material about Browning's later life, when the friend of many years earlier returned to London from New Zealand as a distinguished politician eager now for literary fame, and also, more generally interesting, about London's literary scene in the 1870s. Also relevant in this connection is Donald Smalley's article 'Joseph Arnould and Robert Browning: New Letters (1842–50) and a Verse Epistle' (*PMLA*, LXXX, 1965).

Three volumes of letters to women correspondents are valuable for anyone with a biographical interest in Browning. Richard Curle (ed) *Robert Browning and Julia Wedgwood* (1937), reconstructs a friendship of the late 1860s which remains mysterious despite the conjecture and speculation of scholars. Writing with an unusual frankness and air of ease Browning discusses the composition of *The Ring and the Book*, explains how *he* would have written *Enoch Arden*, and confesses 'I believe I do unduly like the study of morbid cases of the soul.'[1] It is, however, the tone of the letters rather than the information they convey, which makes this collection so fascinating. Maisie Ward has written: 'Browning is at home in these letters—that restful and stimulating feeling one gets only with people who themselves are at home in a library and can toss ideas to one another as readily as gossip'.[2] This is fair enough, but there is also apparent an underlying personal tension which would seem to have little to do with an interest in books. *Dearest Isa* (1951) edited by Edward C. McAleer, consists of the letters Browning wrote to Isabella Blagden who met the Brownings in Florence and was an intimate friend of both. She was also probably Browning's closest friend after Elizabeth's death until her own death in 1872. *Learned Lady: Letters from Robert Browning to Mrs Thomas Fitzgerald 1871–1889* (1966) has less direct interest than the letters to Julia Wedgwood and Isabella Blagden, but nonetheless are valuable for Browning's memories of earlier days, and for what they add to our knowledge of his frame of mind during his final years.

*Letters of the Brownings to George Barrett* (1958) edited by Paul Landis and R. E. Freeman, contains letters from the Brownings to Elizabeth's brother, ranging from 1838 to 1889, with a break of five years from 1846.

[1] *Wedgwood Letters*, 158.
[2] *Robert Browning and His World*, II, 20.

Gertrude Reese Hudson (ed) *Browning to his American Friends* (1965) gathers together the letters exchanged between the Brownings, the Storys and James Russell Lowell, and reconstructs, in the words of the editor 'the story of an intellectual, three-way friendship'. It also establishes a reliable text for the letters which Henry James had used in his biographical study, *William Wetmore Story and His Friends* (2 vol. 1903).

## General Assessments and Critical Studies

Throughout his life Browning was haunted by what he considered to be the wilful misunderstanding of critics and reviewers, though from the beginning he also enjoyed, and was grateful for, the loyal support of a handful of admirers. The history of his reputation in the Victorian period has been documented in *Robert Browning: The Critical Heritage* (1970), edited by Boyd Litzinger and Donald Smalley. It makes, as one would expect, depressing reading: so much incomprehension, so many feeble witticisms about his obscurity, so little real communication between author and reader. Yet certain points of great interest do emerge. It is apparent from this volume that many of Browning's most perceptive critics were his fellow writers. Making a point of cultural history, Chesterton claimed that with the publication of *Sordello* there emerged that significant literary phenomenon—the writer one boasts of not understanding;[1] and as a corollary to this there may be added the clear divergence of response between reviewers and readers, on the one hand, and fellow writers on the other; a degree of understanding (even if unsympathetic, and, making an exception of Charles Kingsley, the arch-Philistine) which contrasts markedly with the public image created and perpetuated by second-rate journalists. In the face of this what also emerges is a degree of artistic courage on Browning's part that deserves a more central place in biographies of him than it is usually allowed. Here is the poet who could write to Julia Wedgwood:

> It is one of the facts of my experience that one limits sorrowfully one's pretension to influence other people for good: I live more and more—what am I to write?—for God not man—I don't care what men think now, knowing they will never think my thoughts; yet I need increasingly to tell *the truth*—for whom?[2]

[1] *Robert Browning*, 35.
[2] *Wedgwood Letters*, 53.

And here is the poet who in his work would snipe gently at the critics until the furious outburst in *Pacchiarotto* (1876); who was not averse to offering some retaliatory wilfullness of his own; and who was to accept the eventual adulation of the Societies formed to honour him with a kind of amused weariness. Finally, we have, of course, both Clare Vawdrey and Henry James.

There is no lack of studies of Browning's reputation in the nineteenth and twentieth centuries. The articles by Charlotte C. Watkins and M. B. Cramer, are now supplemented by a number of useful volumes, notably Louise Greer's *Browning and America* (1952), Boyd Litzinger's *Time's Revenges: Browning's Reputation as a Thinker 1889–1962* (1964), and William S. Peterson's *Interrogating the Oracle: A History of the London Browning Society* (1970).

The emphasis placed by Browning's admirers in the years immediately preceding his death on his qualities as a sage—the attempt in F. J. Furnivall's reported words to prove that, 'Browning is the manliest, strongest, life-fullest, deepest, thoughtfullest of our living writers'[1]—was to linger for many years, but with his death there came at least more positive attempts by critics to offer total assessments of his work, attempts which, characteristically, served to heighten the divergence of opinion already referred to, and to create a polarization which remains unbridged to the present day.

In his influential book *Browning as a Philosophical and Religious Teacher* (1891), Henry Jones acknowledged that, 'It is only as a poet that Browning can be finally judged,' but chose instead to treat him as a 'prophet' and to examine the philosophy of life he offered to his readers. Jones argued that Browning's reliance on the 'heart' and his contempt for the intellect created contradictions which he made no attempt to confront. Logically he should have been an agnostic; in reality he was an optimist whose view of life failed to offer the moral guidance one expects from great thinkers. Jones's rationalistic approach was extremely persuasive (for an age which paid serious attention to Browning's 'philosophy' or 'message'), and has been answered, in an equally convincing manner, by Philip Drew in 'Henry Jones on Browning's Optimism' *Victorian Poetry*, II (1964). However important historically, few readers today are likely to return to Henry Jones except out of a sense of scholarly duty, but

[1] Berdoe, *Browning's Message to his Time*, 31.

George Santayana's 'The Poetry of Barbarism' in his *Interpretations of Poetry and Religion* (1900), remains one of the most stimulating criticisms of Browning ever written. Against the least idealistic of poets, Santayana's Arnoldian idealism was a devastating weapon. Browning's poetry becomes discordant, his view of life truncated (lacking reason and discipline) and dominated by a faith in experience as an end in itself. For Santayana, the signs of Browning's 'failure in rationality and the indifference to perfection', are, 'the turgid style, weighty without nobility, pointed without naturalness or precision', and 'the realism of the personages, who, quite like men and women in actual life, are always displaying traits of character and never attaining character as a whole.' Browning's claim that Italy was his University is mocked because he was totally incapable of participating in the 'civilised heart' of the Italian Renaissance: 'He saw, he studied, and he painted a decapitated Italy. His vision could not mount so high as her head.'[1]

Of the more favourable general assessments published at this time, those by Arthur Symons (1886); William Sharp (1890); which is ostensibly a brief biography but is good on the early poetry; Stopford Brooke (1902); Edward Dowden (1904), also organized as a biography but containing some outstandingly intelligent criticism which covers the later 'problem and narrative poems'; and C. H. Herford (1905), sufficiently balance the negative criticisms of Jones and Santayana. There is also strikingly observable in these early studies a critical confidence which enables the authors to range widely and unselfconsciously over Browning's work, a quality which was soon to disappear. Pride of place, however, must go to G. K. Chesterton's *Robert Browning* (1903). Chesterton refers specifically to Santayana's essay and notes truly: 'He, in contradistinction to the vast mass of Browning's admirers, had discovered what was the real root virtue of Browning's poetry; and the curious thing is, that having discovered that root virtue, he thinks it is a vice.' The whole of Chesterton's book can be seen as a reversal of Santayana's conclusions. Santayana's idealism is rendered pointless because Browning is a great realist; his poetry (and his love poetry above all) draws its strength from the ordinary mundane world of suburbia: 'Browning's love poetry is the finest love poetry in the world, because it does not talk

---

[1] 'The Poetry of Barbarism', repr. Drew (ed) *Robert Browning: A Collection of Critical Essays*, 17–35.

about raptures and ideals and gates of heaven, but about window-panes and gloves and garden walls . . . It is the truest of all love poetry, because it does not speak much about love.' Browning's poetry may often be grotesque or barbarous but so is nature; and his optimism has got nothing to do with a facile acceptance of life: 'There is no pessimism, however stern, that is so stern as this optimism, it is as merciless as the mercy of God.'[1] Chesterton rejects out of hand those who would limit Browning by forcing upon him the role of philosopher, prophet, or theologian, and in a few brilliant pages characterizes the essence of Browning's religious belief and relates this to his fundamental individualism. There had been nothing like Chesterton's book before in Browning criticism and there has been nothing like it since. It can be faulted as inaccurate, extravagant, and as lacking detailed examination of the poems; later scholars have written volumes where an epigram satisfied Chesterton; but he soars while they plod and his book remains unsurpassed as a general introduction.

The contrasting views of Santayana and Chesterton recur throughout subsequent Browning criticism (often, in Chesterton's case at least, unacknowledged) in much the same way as James's interpretation of the two Brownings echoes through biographies of the poet; it would even perhaps be possible to divide the greater part of twentieth-century Browning criticism into two distinct schools, with Santayana providing the source for one of them, and Chesterton the other. Some of the divergent points have already been indicated, but one needs further emphasis. For Santayana, Browning's ultimate failure lay in his inability to structure and organize his abundant energy: 'The passion he represents is lava hot from the crater, in no way moulded, smelted, or refined . . . He did not master life, but was mastered by it.'[2] Whatever the fascination of Browning he is not, therefore, an Artist. But Chesterton, probably with Santayana in mind, rejects entirely such a view: 'No criticism of Browning's poems can be vital, none in the face of the poems themselves can be even intelligible, which is not based upon the fact that he was successfully or otherwise, a conscious and deliberate artist.'[3] It is a notable curiosity of Browning's fluctuating reputation over the past seventy

[1] *Robert Browning*, 49, 183, 189.

[2] Drew (ed) *Robert Browning: A Collection of Critical Essays*, 25.

[3] *Robert Browning*, 136.

years that Chesterton's assertion—which few critics today would even bother to make about, say, Hopkins, Tennyson, Eliot, or Yeats—still needs to be made by Browning's admirers.

The most important work in Browning scholarship during the years immediately following the publication of Santayana's and Chesterton's contrasting interpretations was biographical and scholarly rather than critical; a first movement away from entrenched positions (whether of blind hostility or adulation), and a step towards the accumulation of more specialized studies of carefully defined aspects of the poet's life and work which now seems inevitably to precede a full revaluation, though in Browning's case this has suffered an unusually long delay. In his survey 'Browning Studies in England and America 1910–1949', published in the first edition of *The Infinite Moment* (1950), W. O. Raymond wrote: 'In the sphere of literary criticism, as distinct from biography, there has been no outstanding book written on the poetry of Browning as a whole since 1910.'[1] If one places the required emphasis on the phrase 'as a whole', this statement still remains true, for while the quality of much Browning criticism over the past two decades has reached a high degree of sophistication, this has been achieved by an ever increasing fragmentation. Browning's poetry seems to offer, just as tantalizingly as his life, some insoluable mystery at the heart of it which makes James's story 'The Figure in the Carpet' as appropriate as 'The Private Life'.

Full length studies of Browning's work have, of course, been published since 1950, those for example by J. M. Cohen (1952), H. C. Duffin (1956), and Leonard Burrows (1969), but these illuminate parts rather than the whole. The same is true of one of the best of such recent studies, Philip Drew's *The Poetry of Robert Browning: A Critical Introduction* (1970), and of special interest here is Drew's own awareness of the difficulties involved in attempting an overall reassessment. In his Introduction, he points out that his book began as a 'simple handbook' which would help readers to an appreciation of Browning's poetry by examining its distinctive qualities, but as the work progressed the difficulties multiplied, misunderstandings needed to be corrected, and earlier hostile criticism demanded refutation. The result was that the 'simple handbook' became 'an attempt to reverse the Browning criticism of the last seventy years'. Yet this said, the value of Drew's study lies precisely in its

---

[1] *The Infinite Moment*, 1950, 203.

exploration of a whole range of central issues—the 'colloquial' nature of Browning's diction, the relationship between his 'thought' and poetry, his 'difficulty', and the narrative strength of his later philosophical works, as well as the confrontation with the more important of Browning's late nineteenth and early twentieth-century critics.

Two critics who began to publish essays on Browning in the 1920s and 30s deserve to be excluded from Raymond's strictures—Raymond himself and H. B. Charlton. Although their works consists of essays on specific aspects of Browning's work and are not therefore overall assessments, when these essays are gathered together they offer some of the most valuable and level-headed criticism yet published on Browning. Raymond's *The Infinite Moment* ranges over a wide variety of subjects, historical and critical, with outstanding studies of Browning's imagery, his religious beliefs, and his 'casuists'. For Raymond, 'It is the informing presence of a discursive, fully charged mind that is an unfailing source of enjoyment to the sympathetic reader of Browning's poetry',[1] and Raymond's critical response demonstrates similar qualities at work. H. B. Charlton's series of essays on Browning have never been collected into book form: they were published over a number of years, in the *Bulletin of the John Rylands Library*, and as separate pamphlets. Like Raymond, he pays serious attention to what Browning says, not in order to elevate Browning's status to that of a prophet, but because the thought is an integral part of the poetry. And like Chesterton, who is Charlton's principal critical precursor, he argues that for Browning, 'man's relation to God is infinitely more important than his relation to his fellow-men', and, in discussing how the failure of Browning's plays led to the triumph of the dramatic monologue, he stresses the crucial importance of Browning's individualism:

> Only occasionally can his imagination preserve a double focus. It is the artistic consequence of his constitutional individualism, his inevitable way of seeing man. It is a consequence which affects his thought too: his doctrine that most failure is most success is a purely individualistic tenet which leaves social and corporate obligations of little or no account in contrast with the supreme duty of self-realisation.[2]

If Charlton continued and expanded the Chesterton tradition, there

[1] *The Infinite Moment*, 2nd rev. ed. 1965, 18.
[2] 'Browning as Dramatist', *BJRL*, XXIII 1939, 43.

were also still critics arguing like Santayana, the most persuasive of whom, F. R. G. Duckworth, examined in *Browning: Background and Conflict* (1931), the tangled problem of critical responses to Browning's poetry in the periods 1850–59, 1890–99, and 1920–29. Duckworth is not concerned simply to establish patterns of critical response, but rather to seek the root causes of some of the stranger contradictions. In a fine concluding chapter Duckworth traces a central image in Browning's poetry—'the white light'—and decides that Browning cannot 'be classed with the very greatest poets' because he failed to 'rise above limited and partial expressions of the truth to a steady embracing view of the whole truth'.[1]

Critical approaches to Browning's poetry since Raymond's survey can be best indicated by looking at five important books published in the 1950s and early 1960s: E. D. H. Johnson, *The Alien Vision of Victorian Poetry* (1952), Roma A. King Jr., *The Bow and the Lyre* (1957), Robert Langbaum, *The Poetry of Experience* (1957), Park Honan, *Browning's Characters* (1961), and J. Hillis Miller, *The Disappearance of God* (1963). E. D. H. Johnson begins with the historical assumption that, 'Nearly all the eminent Victorian writers were as often as not at odds with their age, and that in their best work they habitually appealed not *to*, but *against* the prevailing mores of that age'; the poets who began to publish their work in the 1830s and 1840s (especially Tennyson, Browning, and Arnold) suffered from a split consciousness which is recognizable in their work as, 'a kind of tension originating in the serious writer's traditional desire to communicate, but to do so without betraying the purity of his creative motive even in the face of a public little disposed to undergo the rigors of aesthetic experience.' Despite this historical judgement Johnson's method is not to place the work of these three poets against the attitudes and values of the Victorian period, but to offer through a detailed examination of their poetry the different ways they came to terms with the 'double awareness' imposed upon them by the age. Realization of the limited introspective nature of his early works led Browning into, 'a succession of technical experiments expressly directed to the formation of a more objective manner', with *Pippa Passes* as a turning point in his artistic development.[2] Johnson's fine analysis of *Pippa*, and the kind of em-

---

[1] *Browning: Background and Conflict*, 212.
[2] *The Alien Vision*, ix–xi, 82.

phasis he places upon it recalls Chesterton's similar observation: 'In 1841 *Pippa Passes* appeared, and with it the real Browning of the modern world. He had made the discovery which Byron never made, but which almost every young man does at last make—the thrilling discovery that he is not Robinson Crusoe.' But Johnson's interpretation deepens at this point. He argues that instead of breaking with the past by this attainment of a new kind of objectivity, Browning's imaginative inspiration remained unchanged and his dramatic technique served instead as an agent of sublimation: 'By motivating the actors in his dramas with his own ideas and impulses, Browning could speak out with greater originality and boldness than would ever have been possible in his own person.'² Such an approach clearly has much in common with the psychological interpretations of Browning's biographers which have already been discussed; but the most striking contribution made to the subject by *The Alien Vision* is the way it draws attention to the anti-social implications in much of Browning's thought and poetry (the love relationships, his intuitional psychology, and extreme individualism) without lessening the force of his creative and technical purpose.

The books by Roma A. King and J. Hillis Miller are both, in their very different ways, anti-historical. *The Bow and the Lyre* concentrates mainly on five of Browning's most famous poems, four of which are dramatic monologues ('Andrea Del Sarto', 'Fra Lippo Lippi', 'The Bishop Orders His Tomb', 'Bishop Blougram's Apology', and 'Saul'). King's method is the close analysis or explication of specific poems, with a concluding discussion of the characteristic aspects of Browning's poetry: 'Browning's poetry . . . may be read on two levels: each poem may be read as an entity or in the context of Browning's whole work. The better poems contain within themselves all the parts essential to their total meaning, making it unnecessary for the critic to go outside the poem for his interpretation.' King shares with most modern critics a sharp distrust of the traditional view of Browning as a facile optimist, and stresses that, 'For the most part, Browning's men and women are confused, disturbed, tortured.' The great virtue of King's approach is that it is directed to creating an understanding of Browning's conscious artistry; how, for example, the monologue is a form which embodies Browning's individualism and is most suited to his 'multiple vision'; it is

¹ *Robert Browning*, 43.
· ² *The Alien Vision*, 92.

therefore also an approach which can bring out the distinctive quality of the poetry without recourse to psychological guess-work:

> Browning was not satisfied with narrow perspectives and dogmatic statements. Unwilling to fix permanently upon one "truth", he avoided the single point of view, preferring rather to approach problems from different intellectual and emotional positions, juxtaposing one against the other, holding in suspension a personal commitment to either . . . Browning's was a multiple vision inclusive of differing modes of expression.[1]

It is unusual, and refreshing, to find in modern criticism the view that Browning was capable of deciding between two possible kinds of poetry.

The chapter on Browning in *The Disappearance of God* appears at first sight to have nothing whatever in common with *The Bow and the Lyre*; indeed turning immediately from one book to the other it is tempting to feel that it is not even the same poet being discussed. The highly intelligent, conscientious craftsmanship that we find in Roma King's study is transformed by Hillis Miller: 'Massive substance, a seething diffused energy, a shaping force urging the shapeless bulk towards form— these make up the initial Browningesque self and the Browningesque world.' The difference, however, is a matter of method and style, rather than any fundamental departure in Browning studies, for most of the central ideas in Hillis Miller's essay—the attempted movement from subjectivity to objectivity, the poet's relationship with God as epitomized in 'How it Strikes a Contemporary', the emphasis on individuality and the incarnation—these look back, strange as it seems, to Chesterton. This is not, however, to belittle the essay, for, as we have seen, a great deal of the best modern Browning scholarship draws on the same source. The originality of Hillis Miller's approach lies in his astonishingly successful attempt to capture, or even to recreate, the feeling of turbulence and restlessness, the sense of constant growth and development, which characterizes so much of Browning's poetry. He writes: 'The universe, for Browning, like the self which coincides with it, is a struggle of immense irreconcilable forces locked in elemental combat'; and Browning himself is described as being, 'like a world-conqueror moving from

---

[1] *The Bow and the Lyre*, 129, 134, 132–3.

city to city.'[1] The principal aim of the essay is to explore the ways in which Browning's religious beliefs inform the poetry, and this is certainly done with great perception, but perhaps, incidentally, the lasting value of Hillis Miller's essay will be for the understanding it demonstrates of an even more difficult issue—the infamous nature of Browning's obscurity.

Robert Langbaum's *The Poetry of Experience* is both historical and critical: it is arguably the best study of Browning since Chesterton's and, beyond our limited interest in it here, a good example of modern literary history. Langbaum argues that the early twentieth-century critical reaction against the literature of the Romantic and Victorian periods has obscured the strong sense of continuity which exists in all English literature since the late eithteenth century. He acknowledges the tendency of Victorian writers to move away from what they so often felt to be the stultifying subjectivity of Romantic poetry, but finds this concern to be also characteristic of the Romantic poets themselves; Tennyson, Browning, Eliot, and Pound, are therefore regarded not as breaking with the Romantic tradition but with extending it:

> Having seen the poetry which set out to be different from romantic poetry, we can find in the core that remains unchanged the essential idea of romanticism. That essential idea is, I would suggest, the doctrine of experience—the doctrine that the imaginative apprehension gained through immediate experience is primary and certain, whereas the analytic reflection that follows is secondary and problematical. The poetry of the nineteenth and twentieth centuries can thus be seen in connection as a poetry of experience—a poetry constructed upon the deliberate disequilibrium between experience and idea, a poetry which makes its statement not as an idea but as an experience from which one or more ideas can be abstracted as problematical rationalisations.

In the dramatic monologue, as used by Victorian and modern poets, Langbaum finds, 'the articulation of a form potential in romantic poetry from the start'; it is a form which serves to establish a complex relationship with the reader and to invoke in him a crucial sympathy by offering 'facts from within', at the same time 'meaning' is derived from, 'the poetic material itself rather than from any external standard of jud-

[1] *The Disappearance of God*, 83, 84, 124.

gement', and this paradoxically heightens the reader's sympathy for even the most unattractive speakers, and lessens the desire to pass absolute moral judgements: 'We clearly adopt the speaker's point of view, both visual and moral, as our entry into the poem—the resulting limitation and even distortion of the physical and moral truth being among the main pleasures of the form.'[1] The individual poems by Browning which Langbaum discusses include, 'Childe Roland', 'Caliban', 'My Last Duchess', 'Mr Sludge', 'Abt Vogler', and *The Ring and the Book*. It is certainly possible to disagree with the inclusiveness of Langbaum's formulations, and to argue, as Philip Drew has recently done, against the view that, 'We are never able to bring to bear on the speaker of a dramatic monologue those standards by which we judge the actions of men',[2] but nonetheless *The Poetry of Experience* remains an enormously stimulating book.

Park Honan is another critic who finds Langbaum's approach unsatisfactory: 'His thesis itself does not suggest the uniqueness of the dramatic monologue or reveal "an effect peculiarly the genius" of the form.' Honan's own method, in *Browning's Characters*, is to trace Browning's development through his early works (paying an unusually detailed attention to the plays) in order to show how a constant interest in the portrayal of 'character' attained its finest expression in the dramatic monologues: 'By 1845 . . . Browning had perfected a kind of mesh for catching character that consisted of a remarkably intricate set of dramatic, prosodic, and verbal techniques.'[3] These component parts together with twenty selected monologues are carefully analysed in order to clarify the techniques which characterize Browning's best work. *Browning's Characters* shares with *The Bow and the Lyre* a determination to rehabilitate Browning the conscious craftsman and experimenter, while the welcome emphasis on the language of Browning's poetry expands the usefulness of earlier linguistic studies such as H. H. Hatcher, *The Versification of Robert Browning* (1928) and Bernard Groom, *On the Diction of Tennyson, Browning, and Arnold* (1939). A more recent book which usefully complements Honan's attempt to trace Browning's developing technique in the early works is Thomas J. Collins's *Robert Browning's*

[1] *The Poetry of Experience*, 16, 35, 79, 137.
[2] *The Poetry of Browning: A Critical Introduction*, 1970, 27.
[3] *Browning's Characters*, 4, 120.

*Moral-Aesthetic Theory 1833–55* (1967).

It would not be wise or indeed possible even to attempt here any kind of survey of work done on specific areas of Browning's poetry or on particular poems. DeVane's *Handbook* is invaluable for this purpose, and the many listings and bibliographies of current Browning scholarship which were mentioned earlier provide an up-to-date record and are readily available. My intention has been to indicate some of the main lines and tendencies of Browning criticism since his death, with the appended bibliography offering guidance for further reading, both generally on Browning and on a four-fold division of his poetry (Early, Middle, *The Ring and the Book*, Late), but something must be said briefly about the nature of this division and the direction of Browning studies at the present time. The four-fold division is traditional and although obviously open to criticism as being artificial, it is, I would argue, justifiable. Early is taken to mean everything from *Pauline* (1833) to *A Soul's Tragedy* (1846). These works have always received attention, though, with the exception of *Pippa Passes* (1841), *Dramatic Lyrics* (1843), and *Dramatic Romances and Lyrics* (1845), they seem to me to survive for the modern reader less well than any other of Browning's poems. Defences of *Pauline, Paracelsus* (1835), *Sordello* (1840) and the plays, are not difficult to find, but the fact that a defensive attitude is felt to be appropriate, signifies all too clearly that this period of Browning's work survives largely as academic property—of enormous importance for any understanding of Browning's development, yet bewildering for the non-specialist and justifying Sharp's famous description of *Sordello* as 'a colossal derelict upon the ocean of poetry'.[1] Middle is taken to indicate *Christmas-Eve and Easter-Day, Men and Women,* and *Dramatis Personae,* the period of the greatest dramatic monologues, with *The Ring and the Book* representing both the culminating achievement of the dramatic monologue technique and an impressive work in its own right. It has also been the traditional view to regard *The Ring and the Book* as marking a high spot in Browning's development, with subsequent volumes demonstrating a falling away of his artistic powers. Chesterton praises the later poems with his customary enthusiasm, especially *Prince Hohenstiel-Schwangau* (1871) and *Red Cotton Night-Cap Country* (1872), but it is noticeable that he doesn't linger over them for very long. Mrs Orr although always de-

[1] *Life of Robert Browning,* 1897, 92.

votedly fair to Browning was obviously ill at ease with the later poems; Dowden also struggled to find something good to say of them and in doing so drew a characteristically late nineteenth-century distinction between the message and the poetry: 'Although in his later writings Browning rendered ever more and more homage to the illuminating power of the affections, his methods unfortunately became . . . more and more scientific, or—shall we say?—pseudo-scientific.'[1] Nor did the resurgence of critical interest in Browning in the 1950s do much to change this low opinion of his later poetry. Collections of critical essays provide a useful guide to contemporary judgements on a writer's work, and in the four discussed earlier—containing a total of nearly sixty items on Browning—only one essay, F. E. L. Priestley's study of *La Saisiaz*, is devoted to the poetry written during the last twenty years of Browning's life. A similar imbalance is observable in the book-length critical studies of the 1950s. Robert Langbaum, surprisingly perhaps, gives to the later poems nothing like the attention he gives to the dramatic monologues of Browning's middle period and to *The Ring and the Book*. E. D. H. Johnson finds that, 'The obscurity in which Browning's sophistries too often involved him in such poems as *Fifine at the Fair* was in the nature of a return to the manner of *Pauline* and *Sordello*'; and Roma King is even more dismissive:

> Although Browning wrote some good poems in his old age, it seems to me that after *The Ring and the Book* there is an over-all decline in the merit of his work . . . In contrast to his earlier work, his later is too often emotionally deficient and conceptually overladen. Its quantities of thought are not sufficiently realised poetically.[2]

Despite the force these various judgements carry, it would still seem true to say that Browning's later work has been unjustly neglected, and the assumption that *The Ring and the Book* represents a kind of climacteric in his creative life has been accepted too easily. It would be misleading to speak of a great revival of interest in Browning's later poetry, but in the last decade, as the items listed in the bibliography indicate, there have been more serious attempts to come to terms with works such as *The Inn Album*, *Red Cotton Night-Cap Country*, and especially *Fifine at the Fair*

---

[1] *The Life of Robert Browning*, Everyman, 1915, 306.
[2] *The Alien Vision*, 139; *The Bow and the Lyre*, 7.

than ever before. The articles by C. C. Watkins, Lola L. Szladits, and Clyde de L. Ryals are now interestingly matched by the space given to the later poems in very recent books on Browning If, as seems likely, this interest continues to grow, it is impossible to prophesy what effect it could have on Browning's reputation in the future, but it can hardly be more curious than the present situation which breezily dismisses something like the last third of his creative output to oblivion.

Two further tendencies in recent Browning criticism need to be mentioned briefly—the attention paid to the dramatic monologues of his middle period and to *The Ring and the Book*. That the dramatic monologues published in *Dramatic Lyrics*, *Dramatic Romances and Lyrics*, *Men and Women*, and *Dramatis Personae*, represent Browning's greatest poetic achievement has been the most constant judgement of critics over the past hundred years, and there seems no likelihood that it will be disturbed in the future. They are the only poems of Browning's which carry a popular as distinct from an academic or professional appeal and, once again, this is likely to continue. Detailed studies of individual monologues are nothing new in Browning studies, but (apart from the various books discussed above which are obviously relevant in this context) the last two decades have seen a vast increase in the number of such studies published in academic periodicals. At their best—those, for example, by F. E. L. Priestley, Richard D. Altick, and John Howard —they demonstrate a concern with the ways in which the dramatic monologue works, heighten our appreciation of Browning's immense and varied skill in the genre, and proclaim, in this area at least, Chesterton's total victory over Santayana. It would also be true to say that emphasis is still mainly placed on Browning's psychological ability to create 'character', with, more recently, a growing interest in his use of language. What is perhaps surprising is the high degree of concentration on a handful of particular monologues, with possibly 'My Last Duchess', Childe Roland', 'Caliban', and 'Bishop Blougram' heading the list; less surprising, considering the elusive nature of the form itself, is how frequently these interpretations differ from, and frequently contradict, each other: some representative examples are listed in the bibliography. There can be no doubt that the safest prophecy it is possible to make about the future direction of Browning criticism is that detailed studies of individual poems will multiply; though it is to be hoped that the choice of subject will become more adventurous to include some of the lesser known

monologues, the lyrics, the later poems, and the still curiously under-
rated *Christmas-Eve and Easter-Day* which surely deserves to receive the
kind of critical attention now being paid to *Pippa Passes*.

In his fine summary of the sources, biographical genesis, and critical
reception of *The Ring and the Book*, DeVane describes it as, 'The apex of
Browning's career as a poet, and the epitome of all his thought and artistic habits . . . It was his *magnum opus*.'[1] Similar sentiments can be found
everywhere in Browning criticism, from the comments of his contemporaries to Park Honan's description of *The Ring and the Book* as, 'a final
reconciliation of his religion, his England, his Italy, and his poetic career
to his love for his wife';[2] and, as we have seen, this view is implicit in the
neglect of the later poems. Yet this great culminating achievement of
Browning's life has itself not received, until very recently, the kind of
critical attention which its acknowledged importance would lead one to
expect. It has devoted to it some important studies of its sources and historical setting, most notably Charles W. Hodell's translation of *The Old
Yellow Book* (1908), and A. K. Cook's *A Commentary Upon Browning's
The Ring and the Book* (1920) which is still enormously useful: and more
recently Beatrice Corrigan's *Curious Annals: New Documents Relating to
Browning's Roman Murder Story* (1956), and a modern style critical commentary by Richard D. Altick and James F. Loucks, *Browning's Roman
Murder Story* (1968). In 1968 *Victorian Poetry* celebrated the centenary of
the publication of *The Ring and the Book* with a special number containing both critical and historical essays, and, as with the dramatic monologues, there is a rapidly growing periodical literature dedicated to the
total explication of the poem. *The Ring and the Book* has been relatively
ignored for so long that this revival of interest must be welcomed. Yet
there remains a feeling that although no longer ignored, *The Ring and the
Book* has still not been placed in any significant way either. Perhaps the
view of it as a 'culminating achievement' is responsible, for this reminds
one of how often it has been 'used' rather than read. One thinks immediately of Henry James publicly rewriting the poem, and the abundant
biographical purposes it has been made to serve—the Pope's monologue
as conveying Browning's own religious views, the 'O lyric Love' passage addressed to Elizabeth Barrett, the fascinating story of Browning's

[1] *Handbook*, 346.
[2] 'The Murder Poem for Elizabeth', *VP*, VI, 1968, 215.

discovery of the Old Yellow Book on a book-stall in Florence, and the flight of Pompilia and Caponsacchi as recreating the flight of Robert and Elizabeth. Modern criticism, of course, tends to reject such uses, but nonetheless the curious thing about so many recent explications is that while they serve to place *The Ring and the Book* in relation to Browning and to Browning scholarship, that is all they do; there is little outward expansion, virtually no sense of Browning's culminating achievement having a place in, or any kind of significance for, Victorian or modern literature. This is not true of Chesterton, nor indeed of Santayana, whose views may once again be taken as typical of two distinct schools of thought. Santayana was contemptuously dismissive, finding that *The Ring and the Book* had no 'structure' merely 'singular mechanical division'.[1] Chesterton on the other hand saw the poem as 'the typical epic of modern times', and offered two reasons for his view. First, its 'enormous multiplication of a small theme', this being important because, 'The characteristic of the modern movement *par excellence* is the apotheosis of the insignificant'; and secondly because, 'It is the expression of the belief, it might almost be said, of the discovery, that no man ever lived upon this earth without possessing a point of view . . . it is the epic of free speech.'[2] Chesterton anticipates most of the concerns with *The Ring and the Book* which we find in modern critical studies—the multiple points of view, the poem's historical relativism, its epistemological issues, and the blending of minute detail and noble thought—but this in itself is of little importance; the massive detail demanded of modern criticism has long since replaced Chesterton's epigrams. What is important is that Chesterton was not writing for Browning specialists and was concerned to answer the question which the non-specialist might still justifiably ask, Why read *The Ring and the Book?*

And there is a relevance here which stretches beyond *The Ring and the Book*. Over the past twenty or thirty years especially, scholars have accumulated and offered to us a great deal of valuable knowledge of Browning: we know more than ever before about his life, religious beliefs, artistic theories, and his growth and development as a poet. This accumulation of knowledge applies similarly to other great Victorian writers, but it is on turning to modern criticism that one realizes just how

[1] Drew, 30.
[2] *Robert Browning*, 164–73.

different is Browning's case from that of, say, Tennyson, Dickens, George Eliot, or Arnold. They retain a readership outside of the professional academic world: their works are appreciated and perfectly well understood by undergraduates and even by readers who have no contact with university life. It matters little if the reader is not familiar with the latest critical study because while it may enhance his understanding of a particular text communication is in no sense dependent upon it. But with Browning's poetry—excepting a handful of poems from his middle period—immediate communication is a far less common experience. Chesterton, James, and Santayana, remain the most stimulating of Browning critics because they never lose sight of this problem; they direct themselves constantly to the question, why read Browning at all? Most modern Browning criticism does not ask this question (let alone try to answer it) because it speaks invariably to and for itself: the old Browning Society is not dead, but transformed and reorganized on a vast, academic, international scale. Readers who are on the outside are as bewildered and uninformed as ever; Henry James is still their best spokesman:

> I cling to the dear old tradition that Browning is "difficult"—which we were all brought up on and which I think we should, especially on a rich retrospective day like this, with the atmosphere of his great career settling upon us as much as possible, feel it as a shock to see break down in too many places at once.[1]

---

[1] 'The Novel in *The Ring and the Book*', *Notes on Novelists*, 1914, 386.

# Robert Browning:
# A Select Bibliography

## P. J. KEATING

*Note*

Place of publication is London unless otherwise stated. The following abbreviations have been used:

BJRL   *Bulletin of the John Rylands Library*
EC     *Essays in Criticism*
JEGP   *Journal of English and Germanic Philology*
MLN    *Modern Language Notes*
MLR    *Modern Language Review*
MP     *Modern Philology*
MLQ    *Modern Language Quarterly*
PMLA   *Publications of the Modern Language Association of America*
PQ     *Philological Quarterly*
RES    *Review of English Studies*
SP     *Studies in Philology*
UTQ    *University of Toronto Quarterly*
VP     *Victorian Poetry*
VS     *Victorian Studies*

Items which are printed for the first time or reprinted in the collection of essays edited by Isobel Armstrong, Philip Drew, Boyd Litzinger and K. L. Knickerbocker, and Clarence Tracy, are indicated by [A] [D] [LK] or [T] after the entry.

## 1. COLLECTED EDITIONS

*The Poetical Works of Robert Browning*, 17 vol. 1888–94.
*The Poetical Works of Robert Browning*, ed Augustine Birrell, 2 vol. 1896.

*The Complete Works of Robert Browning*, ed Charlotte Porter and Helen A. Clarke, 12 vol. New York 1898. The 'Florentine' Edition.

*The Works of Robert Browning*, ed F. G. Kenyon, 10 vol. 1912. The 'Centenary' Edition.

*New Poems by Robert Browning and Elizabeth Barrett Browning*, ed Sir Frederic G. Kenyon, 1914.

*The Complete Poetical Works of Robert Browning. New Edition with Additional Poems First Published in 1914*, ed Augustine Birrell, New York 1915. The 'Macmillan' Edition.

*The Complete Works of Robert Browning*, general editor Roma A. King Jr., Athens Ohio, in progress. Three of a projected thirteen volumes so far published, 1969.

2. BIBLIOGRAPHIES, HANDBOOKS, AND CONCORDANCE

Berdoe, Edward, *The Browning Cyclopaedia*, 1891.

Broughton, L. N., C. S. Northup and R. Pearsall, *Robert Browning: A Bibliography 1830–1950*, Ithaca, New York 1953.

—and B. F. Stelter, *A Concordance to the Poems of Robert Browning*, 2 vol. New York 1924–5.

Cooke, G. W. *A Guidebook to the Poetic and Dramatic Works of Robert Browning*, Boston 1891.

DeVane, William C. *A Browning Handbook*, New York 1935; rev ed 1955.

Furnivall, F. J. *A Bibliography of Robert Browning, from 1833 to 1881*, 1881.

Honan, Park, 'Robert Browning', *The Victorian Poets: A Guide to Research*, ed Frederic Faverty, 2nd rev. ed. Cambridge, Mass. 1968.

Litzinger, Boyd, and K. L. Knickerbocker, 'Bibliography 1951–65', *The Browning Critics*, Kentucky 1965.

Orr, Mrs Sutherland, *A Handbook to the Works of Robert Browning*, 1885.

Pearsall, Robert, 'Robert Browning', *Cambridge Bibliography of English Literature*, vol. III, ed George Watson, 1969.

Wise, T. J., *A Complete Bibliography of the Writings in Prose and Verse of Robert Browning*, 1897.

3. LIFE AND LETTERS

(a) *Biographical Studies*:

Adrian, Arthur A., 'The Browning-Rossetti Friendship: Some Unpublished Letters', *PMLA* LXXIII, 1958.

Altick, Richard D., 'The Private Life of Robert Browning', *Yale Review* XLI, 1951. [LK]

Barclay, Evelyn, 'Diary of Miss Evelyn Barclay', *Baylor University Browning Interests*, ed A. J. Armstrong, 5th Series, 1932.

Besier, Rudolf, *The Barretts of Wimpole Street*, 1930.

Browning, Fannie Barrett, *Some Memories of Robert Browning*, 1928.

Burdett, Osbert, *The Brownings*, 1929.

Creston, Dormer, *Andromeda in Wimpole Street*, 1929.

DeVane, William C., 'The Harlot and the Thoughtful Young Man', *SP* XXIX, 1932. [LK]

— 'The Virgin and the Dragon', *Yale Review* XXXVII, 1947. [LK] [D]

Domett, Alfred, *The Diary of Alfred Domett 1872–85*, ed E. A. Horsman, 1953.

Gosse, Edmund, *Robert Browning: Personalia*, Boston, 1890.

Griffin, W. H. and H. C. Minchin, *The Life of Robert Browning*, 1910; rev. ed. 1938.

Haight, Gordon S., 'Robert Browning's Widows', *Times Literary Supplement*, 2 July 1971.

James, Henry, 'The Private Life', *The Complete Tales of Henry James*, vol. VIII, ed Leon Edel, 1963.

Jerman, B. R., 'The Death of Robert Browning', *UTQ* XXXV, 1965.

Kenmare, Dallas, *The Browning Love Story*, 1957.

Knickerbocker, K. L., 'A Tentative Apology for Robert Browning', *Tennessee Studies in Literature*, I, 1956. [LK]

Lind, Sidney E., 'James's "The Private Life" and Browning', *American Literature* XXIII, 1951.

Lindsay, Norman, 'The Mask of Robert Browning', *Southerly* XX, 1959.

Miller, Betty, 'The Child of Casa Guidi', *Cornhill* CLXIII, 1949.

— *Robert Browning: A Portrait*, 1952.

— 'This Happy Evening', *Twentieth Century* CLIV, 1953.

— 'The Séance at Ealing', *Cornhill* CLXIX, 1957.

Orr, Mrs Sutherland, *Life and Letters of Robert Browning*, 1891; rev. by F. G. Kenyon 1908.

Porter, Katherine H., *Through a Glass Darkly: Spiritualism in the Browning Circle*, Lawrence, Kansas 1958.

Reed, Joseph, 'Browning and Macready: The Final Quarrel', *PMLA* LXXV, 1960.

Reese, Gertrude, 'Robert Browning and His Son', *PMLA* LXI, 1946.
Shackford, M. H., *The Brownings and Leighton*, Wellesley, Mass. 1942.
Smalley, Donald, 'Joseph Arnould and Robert Browning: New Letters (1842–50) and a Verse Epistle', *PMLA* LXXX, 1965.
Sprague, Rosemary, *Forever in Joy: The Life of Robert Browning*, Philadelphia 1965.
Ward, Masie, *Robert Browning and His World*, 2 vol. 1968–9.
Whiting, Lillian, *The Brownings: Their Life and Art*, 1911.
Winwar, Frances, *The Immortal Lovers*, 1950.


(b) *Letters*:
*The Letters of Robert Browning and Elizabeth Barrett Barrett, 1845–6*, 2 vol. 1899; ed Elvan Kintner, 2 vol. Cambridge, Mass., 1969; Selection by V. E. Stack, *The Love-Letters of Robert Browning and Elizabeth Barrett*, 1969.
*Robert Browning and Alfred Domett*, ed F. G. Kenyon, 1906.
*Robert Browning and Julia Wedgwood. A Broken Friendship as Revealed by their Letters*, ed Richard Curle, 1937.
*Letters of Robert Browning, Collected by Thomas J. Wise*, ed Thurman L. Hood, 1933.
*New Letters of Robert Browning*, ed W. C. DeVane and K. L. Knickerbocker, New Haven 1950.
*Dearest Isa: Robert Browning's Letters to Isabella Blagden*, ed Edward C. McAleer, Austin, Texas 1951.
*Letters of the Brownings to George Barrett*, ed Paul Landis and R. E. Freeman, Urbana, Illinois 1958.
*Browning to His American Friends: Letters Between the Brownings, the Storys, and James Russell Lowell (1841–1890)*, ed Gertrude Reese Hudson, 1965.
*Learned Lady: Letters from Robert Browning to Mrs Thomas Fitzgerald 1876–1889*, ed Edward C. McAleer, Cambridge, Mass., 1966.


4. GENERAL STUDIES
Altick, Richard D., 'Memo to the Next Annotator of Browning', *VP* I, 1963.
Armstrong, Isobel (ed), *The Major Victorian Poets: Reconsiderations*, 1969.
—— 'Browning and the "Grotesque" Style.' [A]

Badger, Kingsbury, 'See the Christ Stand!: Browning's Religion', *Boston University Studies in English* I, 1955–6. [D]

Blackburn, Thomas, *Robert Browning: A Study of his Poetry*, 1967.

Bonnell, J. K., 'Touch Images in the Poetry of Browning' *PMLA* XXXVII, 1922.

Boulton, J. A., 'Browning: A Potential Revolutionary' *EC* III, 1953.

Brooke, Stopford A., *The Poetry of Robert Browning*, 1902.

Burrows, Leonard, *Browning the Poet: An Introductory Study*, University of Western Australia 1969.

Cadbury, William, 'Lyric and Anti-Lyric Forms: A Method for Judging Browning', *UTQ* XXXIV, 1964. [T]

Carter, John, and Graham Pollard, *An Enquiry into the Nature of Certain Nineteenth Century Pamphlets*, 1934.

Charlton, H. B., 'Browning: The Poet's Aim', *BJRL* XXII, 1938.

— 'Browning as Dramatist', *BJRL* XXIII, 1939.

— 'Browning's Ethical Poetry', *BJRL* XXVII, 1942.

— 'Browning as Poet of Religion', *BJRL* XXVII, 1943.

— 'Browning: The Making of the Dramatic Lyric', *BJRL* XXXV, 1953.

Chesterton, G. K., *Robert Browning*, 1903.

Cohen, J. M., *Robert Browning*, 1952.

Collins, Thomas J., *Robert Browning's Moral-Aesthetic Theory 1833–1855*, Lincoln, Nebraska 1967.

— 'Browning's Essay on Shelley: In Context'. *VP* II, 1964.

Cramer, M. B., 'Browning's Friendships and Fame before Marriage, 1833–46', *PMLA* LV, 1940.

— 'What Browning's Literary Reputation Owed to the Pre-Raphaelites, 1847–56', *Journal of English Literary History*, VIII 1941.

— 'Browning's Literary Reputation and Oxford, 1855–59', *PMLA* LVII, 1942.

Crowell, Norton B., *The Convex Glass: The Mind of Robert Browning*, Albuquerque 1968.

— The Triple Soul: Browning's Theory of Knowledge, Albuquerque 1963.

Davies, Hugh Sykes, *Browning and the Modern Novel*, Hull, 1962.

Dowden, Edward, *The Life of Robert Browning*, 1904.

Drew, Philip, 'Henry Jones on Browning's Optimism', *VP* II, 1964.

— *The Poetry of Browning: A Critical Introduction*, 1970.

—(ed) *Robert Browning: A Collection of Critical Essays*, 1966.

Dubois, A. E., 'Robert Browning, Dramatist', *SP* XXXIII, 1936.

Duckworth, F. R. G., *Browning: Background and Conflict*, 1931.

Duffin, H. C., *Amphibian: A Reconsideration of Browning*, 1956.

Duncan, Joseph E., 'The Intellectual Kinship of John Donne and Robert Browning', *SP* L, 1953.

Fairchild, Hoxie Neale, 'Browning the Simple-Heart Casuist', *UTQ* XVIII, 1949. [LK]

— *Religious Trends in English Poetry*, vol. IV, *1830–1880 Christianity and Romanticism in the Victorian Period*, New York 1957.

Gransden, K. W., 'The Uses of Personae.' [T]

Greene, H. E., 'Browning's Knowledge of Music', *PMLA* LXII, 1947.

Greer, Louise, *Browning and America*, Chapel Hill 1952.

Gridley, Roy E., 'Browning and His Reader, 1855–1869', *The Nineteenth-Century Writer and his Audience*, ed Harold Orel and George J. Worth, University of Kansas Humanistic Studies 1969.

Groom, Bernard, *On the Diction of Tennyson, Browning, and Arnold*, 1939.

Harrison, Thomas P., 'Birds in the Poetry of Browning', *RES* n.s. VII, 1956.

Hatcher, H. H., *The Versification of Robert Browning*, Columbus, Ohio 1928.

Herford, C. H., *Robert Browning*, 1905.

Hitner, John M., 'Browning's Grotesque Period', *VP* IV, 1966.

Holmes, S. W., 'Browning: Semantic Stutterer', *PMLA* XL, 1945.

Honan, Park, *Browning's Characters: A Study in Poetic Technique*, New Haven 1961.

Jack, Ian, 'Robert Browning', *Proceedings of the British Academy*, LIII, 1968.

James, Henry, 'Browning in Westminster Abbey', *The Speaker* 4 Jan 1891, and *English Hours*, 1905. [D]

Johnson, E. D. H., *The Alien Vision of Victorian Poetry*, Princeton 1952.

Jones, A. R., 'Robert Browning and the Dramatic Monologue', *Critical Quarterly*, IX, 1967.

Jones, Sir Henry, *Browning as a Philosophical and Religious Teacher*, 1891.

King, Roma A. Jr., *The Bow and the Lyre: The Art of Robert Browning*, Ann Arbor, Michigan 1957.

— *The Focusing Artifice: The Poetry of Robert Browning*, ` ` ens, Ohio 1968.

Langbaum, Robert, *The Poetry of Experience: The Dramatic Monologue in Modern Literary Tradition*, 1957.

— 'Browning and the Question of Myth', *PMLA* LXXXI, 1961, and *The Modern Spirit*, 1970.

Litzinger, Boyd, *Time's Revenges: Browning's Reputation as a Thinker 1889–1962*, Knoxville, Tennessee 1964.

— and K. L. Knickerbocker (eds), *The Browning Critics*, Kentucky 1965.

— and Donald Smalley (eds) *Browning: The Critical Heritage*, 1970.

Lounsbury, T. R., *The Early Literary Career of Robert Browning*, New York 1911.

MacCallum, M. W., 'The Dramatic Monologue in the Victorian Period', *Proceedings of the British Academy* XI, 1925.

McCormick, James Patton, 'Robert Browning and the Experimental Drama', *PMLA* LXVIII, 1953.

Melchiori, Barbara, *Browning's Poetry of Reticence*, 1968.

Miller, J. Hillis, *The Disappearance of God*, Cambridge, Mass., 1963.

Partington, Wilfred, *Thomas J. Wise in the Original Cloth*, 1946. First published as *Forging Ahead*, New York 1939.

Peterson, William S., *Interrogating the Oracle: A History of the London Browning Society*, Athens, Ohio 1970.

Phelps, W. L., *Robert Browning: How to Know Him*, Indianapolis, 1915: rev. ed. 1932.

Pottle, Frederick A., *Shelley and Browning: A Myth and Some Facts*, Chicago, 1923.

Preyer, Robert, 'Robert Browning: A Reading of the Early Narratives', *Journal of English Literary History* XXVI, 1959. [D]

— 'Two Styles in the Verse of Robert Browning', *Journal of English Literary History* XXXII, 1965.

Raymond, W. O., *The Infinite Moment and Other Essays in Robert Browning*, Toronto, 1950: rev. ed. 1965.

Ridenour, George M., 'Browning's Music Poems: Fancy and Fact', *PMLA* LXXVIII, 1963. [T]

Ryan, W. M., 'The Classifications of Browning's "Difficult Vocabulary"', *SP* LX, 1963.

Santayana, George, 'The Poetry of Barbarism', *Interpretations of Poetry and Religion*, 1900. [D] [LK]

Sessions, Ina Beth, 'The Dramatic Monologue', *PMLA* LXII, 1947.

Sharp, William, *Life of Robert Browning*, 1890.

Shaw, W. David, *The Dialectical Temper: The Rhetorical Art of Robert Browning*, Ithaca, New York 1968.

Smalley, Donald, *Browning's Essay on Chatterton*, Cambridge, Mass., 1948.

Smith, C. Willard, *Browning's Star-Imagery*, Princeton, 1941.

Stange, G. Robert, 'Browning and Modern Poetry', *The Pacific Spectator* VIII, 1954. [T]

Stevenson, Lionel, 'The Pertinacious Victorian Poets', *UTQ* XXI, 1952.

Symons, Arthur, *An Introduction to the Study of Browning*, 1886, rev. ed. 1906.

Tracy, C. R., 'Browning's Heresies', *SP* XXXIII, 1936.

—— (ed) *Browning's Mind and Art*, 1968.

Trickett, Rachel, 'Browning's Lyricism', *Proceedings of the British Academy*, LVII, 1971.

Watkins, Charlotte C., 'Browning's "Fame Within These Four Years"', *MLR* LIII, 1958.

—— 'Browning's *Men and Women* and the Spasmodic School', *JEGP* LVII, 1958.

Whitla, William, *The Central Truth: The Incarnation in Browning's Poetry*, Toronto 1963.

5. STUDIES OF SPECIFIC POEMS AND PLAYS

Items listed under 'General Studies' which contain detailed discussions of specific poems or plays, or which deal generally with one particular period of Browning's work, are not in the main re-listed in this section.

(a) *Early*:

Ariail, I. M., 'Is *Pippa Passes* a Dramatic Failure?' *SP* XXXVII, 1940.

Clarke, G. H., 'Browning's *A Blot in the 'Scutcheon*: A Defence', *Sewanee Review* XXVIII, 1920.

Collins, Thomas J., 'Shelley and God in Browning's *Pauline*: Unresolved Problems', *VP* III, 1965.

Columbus, Robert R. and Claudette Kemper, 'Sordello and the Speaker: A Problem in Identity', *VP* II, 1964.

DeVane, William C., 'Sordello's Story Retold', *SP* XXVII, 1930.

Eggenschwiler, David, 'Psychological Complexity in "Porphyria's Lover"', *VP* VIII, 1970.

Glen, Margaret E., 'The Meaning and Structure of *Pippa Passes*', *UTQ* XXIV, 1955.

Hill, Archibald A., 'Pippa's Song: Two Attempts at Structural Criticism', *University of Texas Studies in English*, XXXV, 1956. [T]

Holloway, Sister Marcella M., 'A Further Reading of "Count Grismond"', *SP* LX, 1963.

Holmes, S. W., 'Browning's *Sordello* and Jung: Browning's *Sordello* in the Light of Jung's Theory of Types', *PMLA* LVI, 1941.

— 'The Sources of Browning's *Sordello*' *SP* XXXIV, 1937.

Jerman, B. R., 'Browning's Witless Duke', *PMLA* LXXII, 1957. [LK]

Korg, Jacob, 'A Reading of *Pippa Passes*', *VP* VI, 1968.

Kramer, Dale, 'Character and Theme in *Pippa Passes*', *VP* II, 1964.

Mason, Michael, 'The Importance of *Sordello*.' [A]

McNally, James, 'Suiting Sight and Sound to Sense in "Meeting at Night" and "Parting at Morning"', *VP* V, 1967.

Melchiori, Barbara, 'Where the Bishop Ordered His Tomb', *A Review of English Literature*, V, 1964.

Miyoshi, Masao, 'Mill and *Pauline*: The Myth and Some Facts', *VS* IX, 1965.

Orel, Harold, 'Browning's Use of Historical Sources in *Strafford*', *Six Studies in Nineteenth Century English Literature and Thought*, ed H. Orel and George J. Worth, Lawrence, Kansas 1962.

Perrine, Laurence, 'Browning's Shrewd Duke', *PMLA* LXXII, 1957. [LK]

Priestley, F. E. L., 'The Ironic Pattern of Browning's *Paracelsus*', *UTQ* XXXIV, 1964.

Purcell, J. M., 'The Dramatic Failure of *Pippa Passes*', *SP* XXXIII, 1939.

Raymond, W. O., 'Browning's Conception of Love as Represented in *Paracelsus*', *The Infinite Moment*, 1965.

Starkman, Miriam K., 'The Manichee in the Cloister: A Reading of Browning's "Soliloquy of the Spanish Cloister"', *MLN* LXXV, 1960.

Stempel, Daniel, 'Browning's *Sordello*: The Art of the Makers-See', *PMLA* LXXX, 1965.

Tilton, J. W. and R. D. Tuttle, 'A New Reading of Count Grismond', *SP* LIX, 1962.

(b) *Middle*:

Altick, Richard D., 'Browning's "Transcendentalism"', *JEGP* LVIII, 1959.

— '"A Grammarian's Funeral": Browning's Praise of Folly?' *Studies in English Literature* III, 1963. [D]

— 'The Symbolism of Browning's "Master Hugues of Saxe-Gotha', *VP* III, 1965.

— '"Andrea Del Sarto": The Kingdom of Hell is Within.' [T]

Armstrong, Isobel, 'Browning's "Mr. Sludge, The Medium"', *VP* II, 1964. [D]

Brown, E. K., 'The First Person in "Caliban upon Setebos"', *MLN* LXVI, 1951.

Clarke, C. C., 'Humour and Wit in "Childe Roland"' *MLQ* XXIII, 1962.

DeVane, William C., 'The Landscape of Browning's "Childe Roland"', *PMLA* XL, 1925.

Erdman, David V., 'Browning's Industrial Nightmare' (on 'Childe Roland'), *PQ* XXXVI, 1957.

Golder, Harold, 'Browning's "Childe Roland"', *PMLA* XXXIX, 1924.

Greenberg, Robert A., 'Ruskin, Pugin, and the Contemporary Context of "The Bishop Orders His Tomb"', *PMLA* LXXXIV, 1969.

Guskin, Phyllis J., 'Ambiguities in the Structure and Meaning of Browning's *Christmas Eve*', *VP* IV, 1966.

Honan, Park, 'Belial upon Setebos', *Tennessee Studies in Literature* IX, 1964.

Howard, John, 'Caliban's Mind', *VP* I, 1963. [D]

Kelley, Robert L., 'Dactyls and Curlews: Satire in "A Grammarian's Funeral"', *VP* V, 1967.

King, Roma A. Jr., 'Browning "Mage" and "Maker"—a Study in Poetic Purpose and Method' (on 'Cleon'), *Victorian Newsletter*, No. 20, 1961. [D]

Kintgen, Eugene R., 'Childe Roland and the Perversity of the Mind', *VP* IV, 1966.

Kirkconnell, Watson, 'The Epilogue to Dramatis Personae', *MLN* XLI, 1926. [D]

Lee, Young, G., 'The Human Condition: Browning's "Cleon"', *VP* VII, 1969.

Melchiori, Barbara, 'Browning and the Bible: An Examination of "Holy Cross Day"', *A Review of English Literature* VII, 1966.

Monteiro, George, 'The Apostasy and Death of St. Praxed's Bishop', *VP* VIII, 1970.

Mudford, P. G., 'The Artistic Consistency of Browning's "In a Balcony"', *VP* VII, 1969.

Omans, Glen, 'Browning's "Fra Lippo Lippi", A Transcendentalist Monk', *VP* VII, 1969.

Palmer, Rupert E. Jr., 'The Uses of Character in "Bishop Blougram's Apology"', *MP* LVIII, 1960.

Perrine, Laurence, 'Browning's "Caliban upon Setebos": A Reply', *VP* II, 1964.

— 'Browning's "Too Late": A Re-interpretation', *VP* VII, 1969.

Phipps, Charles T., 'The Bishop as Bishop: Clerical Motif and Meaning in "The Bishop Orders His Tomb at St. Praxed's Church"', *VP* VIII, 1970.

Priestley, F. E. L., 'Blougram's Apologetics', *UTQ* XV, 1946. [LK]

Raymond, W. O., 'The Statue and the Bust', *UTQ* XXVIII, 1959, and *The Infinite Moment*.

Svaglic, Martin, 'Browning's Grammarian: Apparent Failure or Real?' *VP* V, 1967.

Shaw, W. David, 'The Analogical Argument of Browning's "Saul"', *VP* II, 1964.

Tracy, C. R., 'Caliban upon Setebos', *SP* XXXV, 1938.

Willoughby, John W., 'Browning's "Childe Roland to the Dark Tower Came"', *VP* I, 1963.


(c) *The Ring and the Book*:

Altick, Richard D. and James F. Loucks, II, *Browning's Roman Murder Story: A Reading of "The Ring and the Book"*, Chicago 1968.

Armstrong, Isobel, '*The Ring and the Book*: The Uses of Prolixity.' [A]

Charlton, H. B., 'Poetry and Truth: An Aspect of Browning's *The Ring and the Book*', *BJRL* XXVIII, 1944.

Cook, A. K., *A Commentary upon Browning's "The Ring and the Book"*, 1920.

Corrigan, Beatrice, *Curious Annals: New Documents Relating to Browning's Roman Murder Story*, Toronto 1956.

Coyle, William, 'Molinos: "The Subject of the Day" in *The Ring and the*

Book', *PMLA* LXVII, 1952.

Gest, Judge J. M., *The Old Yellow Book . . . A New Translation*, Boston 1925.

Hodell, C. W. *tr The Old Yellow Book*, Washington 1908; Everyman's Library 1911.

James, Henry, 'The Novel in *The Ring and the Book*', *Notes on Novelists*, 1914.

Johnson, E. D. H., 'Browning's Pluralistic Universe: A Reading of *The Ring and the Book*', *UTQ* XXXI, 1961.

Killham, John, 'Browning's "Modernity": *The Ring and the Book*, and Relativism'. [A]

Langbaum, Robert, '*The Ring and the Book*: A Relativist Poem', *PMLA* LXXI, 1956, and *The Poetry of Experience*. [LK]

Raymond, W. O., 'New Light on the Genesis of *The Ring and the Book*', *The Infinite Moment*.

Smalley, Donald, 'Browning's View of Fact in *The Ring and the Book*', *Victorian Newsletter*, No. 20, 1960.

Sullivan, Mary Rose, *Browning's Voices in "The Ring and the Book": A Study of Method and Meaning*, Toronto 1969.

Treves, Sir Frederick, *The Country of The Ring and the Book*, 1913.

*Victorian Poetry* VI (1968), Centennial Issue ed Roma A. King. Contains the following articles: Park Honan, 'The Murder Poem for Elizabeth'; Mary Rose Sullivan, 'The Function of Book I in *The Ring and the Book*'; Morse Peckham, 'Historiography and *The Ring and the Book*'; L. J. Swingle, 'Truth and *The Ring and the Book*: A Negative View'; Isobel Armstrong, 'A Note on the Conversion of Caponsacchi'; Roy E. Gridley, 'Browning's Caponsacchi: "How the Priest Caponsacchi said his say."'; Philip Drew, 'A Note on the Lawyers'; Jerome L. Wyant, 'The Legal Episodes in *The Ring and the Book*'; W. O. Raymond, 'The Pope in *The Ring and the Book*'; Helen M. Loschky, 'Free Will Versus Determinism in *The Ring and the Book*'; Henri A. Talon, '*The Ring and the Book*: Truth and Fiction in Character-painting'; John F. Stasny, 'Selected Bibliography'.

Wasserman, George R., 'The Meaning of Browning's Ring-Figure' *MLN* LXXVI, 1961.

(d) *Late*:

DeVane, William C., *Browning's Parleyings: The Autobiography of a Mind*,

New Haven 1927.

Drew, Philip, 'Another View of *Fifine at the Fair*', *EC* XVII, 1967.

Fairchild, Hoxie N., *'La Saisiaz* and *The Nineteenth Century'*, *MP* XLVIII, 1950.

Friend, Joseph H., 'Euripides Browningized: The Meaning of *Balaustion's Adventure'*, *VP* II, 1964.

Hitner, John Meigs, *Browning's Analysis of a Murder: A Case for "The Inn Album"*, Marquette, Michigan 1969.

Knickerbocker, K. L., 'An Echo from Browning's Second Courtship' (on 'St. Martin's Summer'), *SP* XXXII, 1935.

Melchiori, Barbara, 'Browning's Don Juan' *EC* XVI, 1966, and *Browning's Poetry of Reticence*.

Priestley, F. E. L., 'A Reading of *La Saisiaz'*, *UTQ* XXV, 1955. [D]

Raymond, W. O., 'Browning's Dark Mood: A Study of *Fifine at the Fair'*, *The Infinite Moment*.

Ryals, Clyde de L., 'Browning's Amphibian: Don Juan at Home', *EC* XIX, 1968.

— 'Browning's *Fifine at the Fair*: Some Further Sources and Influences', *English Language Notes*, VII, 1969.

Szladits, Lola L., 'Browning's French Night-Cap', *Bulletin of the New York Public Library*, LXI, 1957.

Tracy, C. R., 'The Source and Meaning of Browning's "Tray"', *PLMA* LV, 1940.

Watkins, Charlotte C., 'The "Abstruser Themes" of Browning's *Fifine at the Fair'*, *PMLA* LXXIV, 1959.

— 'Browning's *Red Cotton Night-Cap Country* and Carlyle', *VS* VII, 1964.

# Index

Prepared by Mrs Brenda Hall M A